BEYOND THE ESTABLISHED LEGAL ORDERS

A lively debate on the constitutionalisation of the international legal order has emerged in recent years. A similar debate has also taken place within the European Union. This book complements that debate, exploring the underlying realities that the moves towards constitutionalism seek to address. It does this by focusing on the substantive interconnections that the EU has developed over the years with the rest of the world, and assesses the practical impact these have both in the development of its legal order as well as in the international community.

Based on papers delivered at the bi-annual EU/International Law Forum organised by the University of Bristol in March 2009, this collection of essays examines policy areas of economic governance (trade, financial services, migration, environment), political governance (human rights, criminal law, responses to financing terrorism), security governance (counter-terrorism, use of force, non-proliferation), and the issue of the emergence of European and global values. How are these areas shaped by the interaction between EU law and other legal orders and polities? In what ways does the EU impact on other transnational legal systems? And how are its own rules and principles shaped by such systems? These questions are addressed in the light of the specific legal and political context within which the EU pursues its policies by interacting with the rest of the world.

Beyond the Established Legal Orders

Policy Interconnections between the EU and the Rest of the World

Malcolm Evans and Panos Koutrakos

• HART •
PUBLISHING
OXFORD AND PORTLAND, OREGON
2011

Published in the United Kingdom by Hart Publishing Ltd
16C Worcester Place, Oxford, OX1 2JW
Telephone: +44 (0)1865 517530
Fax: +44 (0)1865 510710
E-mail: mail@hartpub.co.uk
Website: http://www.hartpub.co.uk

Published in North America (US and Canada) by
Hart Publishing
c/o International Specialized Book Services
920 NE 58th Avenue, Suite 300
Portland, OR 97213-3786
USA
Tel: +1 503 287 3093 or toll-free: (1) 800 944 6190
Fax: +1 503 280 8832
E-mail: orders@isbs.com
Website: http://www.isbs.com

British Library Cataloguing in Publication Data
Data Available

ISBN: 978-1-84946-148-1

Typeset by Compuscript Ltd, Shannon
Printed and bound in Great Britain by
CPI Antony Rowe, Chippenham, Wiltshire

Summary Contents

Contents

List of Contributors

Per Cramér, Professor of European Law at the School of Business, Economics and Law, Department of Law of the University of Gothenburg.

Marise Cremona, Professor of European Law and Head of the Department of Law at the European University Institute, Florence.

Malcolm Evans OBE, Professor of Public International Law at the University of Bristol.

Eilis Ferran, Professor of Company and Securities Law at the University of Cambridge.

Elspeth Guild, Jean Monnet Professor *ad personam* at Radboud University, Nijmegen, also works for Kingsley Napley, London.

Joris Larik, a Researcher at the European University Institute, Florence.

Jan Klabbers, Professor of International Organisations Law at the University of Helsinki, and Director of the Academy of Finland Centre of Excellence in Global Governance Research.

Panos Koutrakos, Professor of European Union Law and Jean Monnet Professor of European Law at the University of Bristol.

Valsamis Mitsilegas, Professor of European Criminal Law at Queen Mary, University of London.

Joost Pauwelyn, Professor of International Law at the Graduate Institute of International and Development Studies, Geneva, Co-Director of the Centre for Trade and Economic Integration.

George Pavlakos, Research Professor of Globalisation and Legal Theory at the Faculty of Laws, University of Antwerp, Sometime Professor at the School of Law, University of Glasgow.

Takis Tridimas, Sir John Lubbock Professor of Banking Law at Queen Mary, University of London, Nancy A Patterson Distinguished Faculty Scholar at the Dickinson School of Law, Penn State University.

Hans Vedder, Professor of Economic Law at the University of Groningen.

Bruno De Witte, Professor of European Law at the University of Maastricht.

Introduction

THIS VOLUME IS the product of the Ninth EU/International Law Forum hosted by the School of Law at Bristol University in 2009. The origins of the Forum Series lie in the recognition of a need to ensure that scholarship in European Law and scholarship in International Law remain in contact with each other, and a need to explore and reflect upon developments of common interest together. Fulfilling these ambitions has, however, become both more urgent and more difficult in recent times.

It has become more urgent because of the manner in which the European Union has developed both spatially and conceptually, as a result of which it has evolved from being a key organ of regional economic and political organisation to a key participant on the global stage. At the same time, the rules of choreography upon that stage—those of the international legal order—have themselves undergone profound change, acquiring both greater focus and penetration, whilst also being asked to shoulder a greater burden in terms of value-bearing than had been the case in recent times.

In the most general of terms, one might suggest that European Law, as the Law of the European Community and Union, has seen a shift from being the bearer of a 'vision' of Europe for its Member States into being the medium though which the ordering of that Union, its affairs and those of its Members is increasingly mediated. This has come about through, amongst other things, the gradual development not only of the ambition of the Union to enhance its role on the international scene, but also of the notion of responsibility which it has been articulating with increasing regularity and which accompanies this ambition. In the Laeken Declaration, which set in motion in December 2001 the process which led to the adoption of the Lisbon Treaty, the European Council raises the following revealing question:

> [d]oes Europe not, now that it is finally unified, have a leading role to play in a new world order, that of a stabilising role worldwide and to point the way ahead for many countries and peoples?[1]

And its understanding of this role is spelled out equally clearly:

> [n]ow that the Cold War is over and we are living in a globalised, yet also highly fragmented world, Europe needs to shoulder its responsibilities in the governance of globalisation.[2]

[1] Laeken Declaration, 14–15 December 2001, at 2.
[2] *Ibid.*

This notion of responsibility is also articulated in the European Security Strategy, which states that 'Europe should be ready to share in the responsibility for global security and in building a better world'.[3]

This combination of ambition and responsibility shaped the long and painful process which the Union and its Member States underwent in order to amend the Treaty of Nice: the drafting, negotiation and ratification of the Treaty Establishing a Constitution for Europe—and after its demise, the Treaty of Lisbon—were focused, amongst other things, on the international role of the Union. On the day of the signing of the Constitutional Treaty, the then President of the European Commission, Romano Prodi, stated that

> today, Europe is reaffirming the unique nature of its political organization in order to respond to the challenges of globalisation, and to promote its values and play its rightful role on the international scene.[4]

The Lisbon Treaty, which drew upon the Constitutional Treaty and entered into force on 1 December 2009, maintained this focus.[5] Therefore, the ambition of the Union to engage with the international community in proactive ways and the sense of responsibility which accompanies it became central points of reference in the Union's recent quest as to how best to organise and manage its idiosyncratic legal order.

At the same time, International Law has moved in the opposite direction, becoming rather less focused on facilitating the interaction of the international community and more intent on providing a means of articulating and furthering visions of what that international community should be or might become. Such developments bring both European law and International Law closer to the traditional orbit of the other and, as cases such as *Kadi* and the issues surrounding the MOX Plant litigation illustrate, the resulting conjunctions pose challenging legal and policy questions which have to be addressed rather than circumvented.

There are different reasons why it has become more difficult to realise the ambitions of the Forum Series. The increasingly specialist nature of both European Law and International Law poses challenges for those seeking to engage in such dialogue—not because it is particularly difficult to find subject specialists able and willing to do so, but because those specialisms are becoming increasingly isolated within the broader discipline of which they form a part (if indeed they continue to do so!). This is possibly more of a difficulty for the international

[3] *A Secure Europe in a Better World—European Security Strategy* (Brussels, 12 December 2003), 1.

[4] Speech delivered in Rome at the ceremony on the signing of the Constitutional Treaty, available at <*http://www.europa.eu.int/constitution/speaches en.htm*>.

[5] See IGC 2007 Mandate, Council SG/11218/07, POLGEN74, para 1. The 2008 Report on the Implementation of the European Security Strategy states that '[t]he provisions of the Lisbon Treaty provide a framework to achieve [the coherence of the EU's action through better institutional co-ordination and more strategic decision-making]' (Report on the Implementation of the European Security Strategy - Providing Security in a Changing World, Brussels, 11 December 2008, at 9).

lawyer, whose discipline is increasingly fragmented into 'general principles' and 'fields of application', with issues such as those pertaining to the sources of law, to questions of personality, of jurisdiction and of responsibility falling into the former, whilst international economic, environmental, human rights and criminal law fall into the latter. As this happens, approaches within each area of application emerge which challenge—or just simply contradict—the approach taken within another. Whilst this may enrich discussion between international lawyers, it makes for difficulties when crafting wider debates. Put simply, a conversation between EU scholars on the one hand and with international lawyers on the other tends to look and sound very different depending upon whether it is, for example, being conducted with general international lawyers or with WTO or international human rights lawyers.

As a result, it is increasingly difficult to conduct a thorough-going discussion of a major and overarching issue in a single gathering, since the sheer number of perspectives which need to be canvassed in order to make for a satisfying whole has become daunting. In consequence, it is becoming increasingly necessary to view sessions of the EU/IL Forum as something of a continuing conversation. Whilst each individual gathering can and should produce an outcome of worth, the worth of those outcomes is increased by their being taken up, complemented and challenged by those gatherings which surround and contextualise them, each forming a part of a greater whole. The Ninth Forum, and this collection, was conceived in this spirit, and so it is necessary backtrack a little in order to explain its rationale and purpose.

The Seventh Forum, held in 2005, addressed the issue of constitutionalism, concerning itself with international and European perspectives regarding the tendency within both legal orders to conceive of themselves in constitutional terms. Rather than explore the allegedly constitutional nature of particular treaties or regimes, or examine the processes by and through which the 'constitutionalisation' of the particular legal orders was, allegedly, occurring, the Forum—and the volume which resulted from it[6]—chose to focus on the broader issues which underpinned the impulse towards constitutionalism within them, though it did, of course, also touch on the outworking of these impulses in a variety of contexts. The aforementioned volume forms part of an ever-expanding literature on constitutionalism in the international arena. Whilst it is well beyond the scope of this introduction to review and engage with that literature, some general reflections upon it should help to illustrate how this current collection is intended to complement that earlier volume within the Forum Series.

Those general reflections might usefully be made, by way of example, with reference to one of the more recent contributions to that literature, *Ruling the World*,

[6] N Tsagourias (ed), *Transnational Constitutionalism: International and European Perspectives* (Cambridge, Cambridge University Press, 2007).

edited by Professors Dunoff and Trachtman.[7] This fine collection of informative and stimulating essays addresses international constitutionalism from a variety of perspectives, but it is that very variety which can induce the feeling that what it really happening in the more general debate of which it forms a part is not so much an exploration of a phenomenon as an assertion of a phenomenon, and a contestation as to how various elements of the international regime either reflect or can claim ownership of it.

This finds its most familiar reflection in the longstanding claim that the Charter of the United Nations stands as a constitution for the international community. Yet when analysed as a 'constituting' document, the Charter falls far short of what is necessary to substantiate that claim—or it would do if the points of reference for what amounts to the constituting instrument of the 'international community' were to be those which fulfil that function in the domestic arena. But as is so often pointed out, these provide an inappropriate point of reference, since the subjects of the international community, and the aims of its constituting, are very different from those of States themselves. The solution, is it claimed, lies in re-conceiving the hallmarks of constitutionalism for the international community in order that they better reflect their subjects, their values, their aims and their purposes. And yet, no matter how convincing the exercise may appear, it remains somewhat self-referential. Assuming that one accepts that a constitutional instrument in an international context will be of a different nature from that found within the State context—and why would one not?—this does little more than remove from the discussion particular points of reference that might otherwise be used to assist in evaluating whether a particular instrument, or set of principles, does in fact exhibit the 'necessary' characteristics to achieve such a status: it does not assist in determining what those characteristics are. Nevertheless, having 'created the space' by dismissing the relevance of more generally recognised constitutional features, it becomes relatively easy to fill that space with those features which are the hallmarks of the particular 'constitutional candidate' in question—should one wish to do so. For those who see the need for greater 'order' in the 'international order', the impulse towards constitutionalism offers both an agenda and an opportunity.[8]

But whose agenda, and whose opportunity? Here lies the conundrum, for it is clear that the various 'candidates' offer very different visions of what international constitutionalism is about. Turning once again to the example of the

[7] J Dunoff and J Trachtman (eds) *Ruling the World: Constitutionalism, International Law and Global Governance* (Cambridge, Cambridge University Press, 2009).

[8] See, eg, B Fassbender, 'Rediscovering a Forgotten Constitution: Notes of the Place of the UN Charter in the International Legal Order' in Dunoff and Trachtman, above n 7, at 133. It may be that this is less of a rediscovery than a reinvention (see, eg, works such as M Mazower, *No Enchanted Palace: The End of Empire and the Ideological Origins of the United Nations* (Princeton, Princeton University Press, 2009) for less sanguine appraisals of the motivations of the UN's founders), but this does not matter: if the Charter has acquired a constitutional character as a result of an evolution of its place in international society—then it has. The relevant question, as discussed by Fassbender and others is, 'has it'?

UN Charter, the strength of the arguments in favour of its being understood as 'constitutional' depend on what one considers this to mean. It is a trite observation that the founding instrument of any organisation, like that of any association, is 'constitutional' in the sense that it has the formal effect of 'constituting' the body in question, but this can hardly be what we are concerned with: constitutionalism within the international arena is not to be realised through the reification of international institutional law. Constitutionalism is an approach to the crafting of a particular form of relationship—the constitution being its practical crystallisation. Moreover, some constitutions are produced whilst others emerge. For instance, the constitutional function of the primary rules of the then Community legal order became apparent over the years in the light of the case law of the European Court of Justice: having interpreted the international Treaty which governs the Community legal order in a distinctly constitutional manner, the Court has been referring to it as 'the basic constitutional charter' of the Community.[9] And the backlash from the reception of the Constitutional Treaty, and the subsequent statement in the mandate for the 2007 Intergovernmental Conference that '[t]he constitutional concept ... is abandoned', does not remove this constitutional dimension.

Therefore, an alternative approach is to identify those elements of the international order which can be understood as constitutional in nature if not in design, and through them discern the contours of a process which incrementally lends a 'constitutional shape' to the ordering of the community—a process-orientated approach which may be termed 'constitutionalisation'.[10]

Thus we can have a mindset (constitutionalism), a process (constitutionalisation) and a product (a constitution). The process links the mindset to the product and can be seen as the channel through which that mindset directs itself towards the realisation of its goal. One might be able to identify a process of constitutionalisation, but in order to critique it, one must understand what drives it: put simply, if you do not know where you are going, how can you tell if you are *en route* or, indeed, whether you have already arrived? Or, to put it another way, what is constitutionalism *for*? If it is simply to lend descriptive coherence to an existing pattern of interrelationships then there is little more that need be said about it, since the discussion would have little substantive impact. But of course this is rarely the case. Those who analyse from a constitutionalist perspective tend to seek to shape our understanding of the order which is being addressed by infusing it with the values which underpin their particular conceptions of constitutionalism, such as the rule of law, democracy, legitimacy, fairness, equality. Other values might also be brought into play—such as cosmopolitanism, human rights, autonomy, self-determination and more

[9] See Case 294/83 *Parti Ecologiste 'Les Verts' v European Parliament* [1986] ECR 1339 at para 23. See also *Opinion 1/91 (re: Draft EEA Agreement)* [1991] ECR I-6079 and, more recently, Joined Cases C-402/05P and C-415/05 P *Kadi and Al-Barakaat* [2008] ECR I-6351.

[10] For an excellent example of this approach, see J Klabbers, A Peters and G Ulfstien, *The Constitutionalization of International Law* (Oxford, Oxford University Press, 2009).

besides. As Samantha Besson has pointed out,[11] much writing on international constitutionalism consciously distances itself from statist premises which it implicitly rejects, but having done so fails to justify its own. It is difficult, then, to avoid the suspicion that the reinvigoration in constitutionalist thinking is as much about reconstituting conceptions of the international community as it is about constitutionalising an existing legal order. In other words, the debate may not necessarily be what it seems. Underneath the veneer of constitutional discourse lies a instrumental purpose—at best unarticulated, potentially unrecognised and, at worst, unknown.

If this is the dilemma latent within international constitutionalist discourse, the same can hardly be said with regard to the European Union, where the implications of the 'constitutional turn' were plain from the outset. The idea of European constitutionalism was indeed both instrumental and constitutive—to bring into being a new conception of European inter-connection which would not only bring greater functionality to the Union, but which would also invest it with additional capacities reflecting the enhanced legitimacy that its constitutionalisation is perceived to bestow. For instance, the broad construction of the four freedoms by the Court of Justice and the instrumentalisation of national mechanisms for the enforcement of harmonisation both broaden the arena where traders and consumers (ultimately citizens) act in order to protect their interests. In so doing, a reconstituted market emerges, which is so broad in its scope and far-reaching in the implications of its management that it reconstitutes the Union as a locus of democratic legitimation.[12] This is not the place to explore the fate of this enterprise. Nevertheless, it is important to recall it, since the experience is critical to the conception behind this volume.

Shorn of all subtlety, this volume seeks to offer an alternative—or more properly, a complementary—approach to what might be called the 'top down' approach adopted by much of the literature addressing the emergent ordering of international communities. Some who have written on the subject of international constitutionalism have expressed their unease at the idea of bringing constitutionalist thinking to bear *at all*, concerned that this already pre-determines the nature of the discussions and begs the question of why one should be doing so in the first place. As David Kennedy puts it, 'the current appeal of constitutionalism among those who concern themselves with global governance is a puzzle', these being the opening words of a section in an essay entitled 'The Mystery of Global Governance', the heading of which comprises the assertion that 'Constitution

[11] S Besson, 'Whose Constitution(s)? International Law, Constitutionalism and Democracy' in Dunoff and Trachtman, above n 7, at 381.

[12] See A Menon and S Weatherill, 'Legitimacy, Accountability and Delegation in the European Union' in A Arnull and D Wincott (eds), *Accountability and Legitimacy in the European Union* (Oxford, Oxford University Press, 2002) 113, and S Weatherill, 'Preemption, Harmonisation and the Distribution of Competence to Regulate the Internal Market' in C Barnard and J Scott (eds), *The Law of the Single European Market—Unpacking the Premises* (Oxford, Hart Publishing, 2002) 41.

or Not, Global Governance Will Be Transformed'.[13] This assertion seems to be beyond contradiction, if only because, as Kennedy notes, simply but pertinently, 'things like Governance do change'.[14] The focus, inevitably, then switches from the 'whether' to the 'why' and the 'how'. Kennedy himself has stressed the need to explore the role of 'experts' in effecting transformations in counterpoint to the more theoretically-driven approaches of others.

This volume sets aside the task of identifying potential agents of change and of exploring their agendas. Rather, it seeks to proceed from an entirely different entry point. Taking as a given the idea that 'things do change', it seeks to provide material which enables the reader to reflect on what such change as is occurring might mean for ideas of governance in what are perceived as key areas of EU institutional activity. The reason for the focus on EU institutional activity follows not only, naturally enough, from this exercise being conducted in the context of the EU/IL Forum, but also from the role of the Union as a point of reference in the wider constitutionalisation debate. This is illustrated by the discussion about the constitutionalisation of the international economic order in general and the World Trade Organisation in particular which has drawn upon the incrementally developed constitutional identity of the European Union.[15] This rather implies that a similar exercise might be conducted from the perspective of general international law in due course. It also suggests that there may be a need to consider holding a further exercise which places these twin explorations alongside that conducted in the earlier Forum in this series exploring transnational constitutionalism.[16] There is, then, an academic agenda here which transcends the boundaries of each component to make, in time, a more elaborate—but one hopes more satisfying—whole.

Inevitably, some choices have to be made concerning the broad areas within which issues of governance are to be addressed, and we have opted for what we consider to be the most significant and the most general, these being Economic, Political and Security Governance. However, it would defeat the object of the exercise if within these general headings authors were to consider issues of governance *per se*: indeed, the entire exercise is premised on the belief that it is helpful to build up an idea of emerging issues of governance from a 'bottom up' rather than a 'top down' approach, and this would be lost if the building blocks through which this exercise is to be constructed were focusing on governance issues *per se*. At the

[13] See D Kennedy, 'The Mystery of Global Governance' in Dunoff and Trachtman, above n 7, 37 at 65.

[14] *Ibid*. The truth of this is vividly illustrated by the outcome of the 2010 UK General Election, which is unfolding as this Introduction is being written.

[15] See E-U Petersmann, 'European and Constitutional Law: Time for Promoting "Cosmopolitan Democracy" in the WTO' in G de Búrca and J Scott (eds), *The EU and the WTO—Legal and Constitutional Issues* (Oxford, Hart Publishing, 2001) 81. For the debate on the constitutionalisation of the WTO, see D Cass, *The Constitutionalization of the World Trade Organization* (Oxford, Oxford University Press, 2005).

[16] See above n 6.

same time, in bearing in mind that the object of the Forum Series is to explore the inter-connections between the EU and international legal orders, the contributions do nevertheless aim, where possible, to look outwards from the EU and consider its interconnectedness with the rest of the world—hence the title of this volume. We hope that this will not only shed light on the trajectory of EU policy, but also contribute to the broader aim of furthering an understanding of the emerging patterns of global governance, not by imposing 'visions of order' from above, but by building up a picture of how the policy interconnections between the EU and the rest of the world are developing, and what they may reveal.

There is another reason which makes this exercise timely. On the one hand, in the wake of the international financial crisis, Member States have been tempted to return to a kind of protectionism which threatened not to leave the functioning of the internal market unscathed. On the other hand, the European Union has been going through its very own economic crisis, in the context of which the very real possibility of sovereign default has undermined the strength of the common currency, has alarmed national governments and has led to extraordinary measures aiming to sustain the economic position of the Union. These developments have added an existential dimension in the debates about the governance of the Union: the German Chancellor, Angela Merkel, convinced the *Bundestag* to approve of the German aid to Greece, arguing that that was necessary for the future of Europe,[17] the same argument used by the Portuguese Prime Minister, José Sócrates, to justify the introduction of austerity measures by his government.[18] Given that the starting point for the Union's ambitious role in the world is the success of its internal policies,[19] its current existential crisis is bound to have implications for the ways in which it relates to the rest of the world. It is, therefore, useful at this juncture to take stock of the range and intensity of the policy interconnections on the international scene.

Of course, although this volume forms a part of a larger whole (and which is work in progress), this does not mean it need not be a coherent whole in itself, and so it not only offers a selection of essays pertinent to the selected areas of governance, but concludes with a pair of overarching reflections which seek to identify emergent values relevant to the processes of European and of global integration (Pavlakos and Pauwelyn, and Cremona). The sub-themes within each Part are inevitably selective rather than comprehensive. However, we hope to have focused on issues which are topical and of intrinsic interest, as well as being useful to the enterprise as a whole. In sum, then, this collection aims to offer a series of reflections on policy interconnections between the EU and the rest of the world. As regards economic governance, these concern trade (Larik), financial services (Ferran), migration (Guild) and the environment (Vedder)

[17] *Financial Times,* 14 May 2010, 9.
[18] *Financial Times,* 13 May 2010, 8.
[19] The very first sentence of the European Security Strategy reads as follows: 'Europe has never been so prosperous, so secure nor so free' (n 3 above).

(which, through the EU lens, takes on, we perceive, a economic dimension). As regards political governance, these concern human rights (de Witte), criminal law (Mitsilegas) and, of course, the relationship between the EU and international legal order itself (Tridimas). As regards security governance, these concern counter-terrorism (Klabbers), the European Security and Defence Policy (Cramer) and non-proliferation (Koutrakos). We hope that just as each chapter says something of value as regards the topic it addresses, each section will reveal something of the emergent approaches to governance within that thematic area. Likewise, we hope that in combination they will offer some insights into trends in governance from an operational perspective which, when combined with the concluding reflections on emergent values, will offer both a coherent whole and a contribution to the broader exploration of which this forms a part. No attempt is made to draw these threads together since this would be premature, though we trust that readers will be able to draw their own interim conclusions regarding the lessons to be learnt from this means of exploring the issues concerning the changing modes of interconnectedness which affect us all.

Malcolm Evans and Panos Koutrakos
Bristol, December 2010

Part One

Economic Governance

1

Much More Than Trade: The Common Commercial Policy in a Global Context

JORIS LARIK[1]

I. INTRODUCTION

IN ASSESSING THE law and policy interconnections between the European Union (EU) and the rest of the world, trade appears as an appropriate point of departure. As the European Commission's Directorate-General for Trade (DG Trade) boldly puts it in one of their brochures, 'Europe's single most important contact with the world beyond its borders is through trade.'[2] Being the world's largest exporter of goods and services, and being the largest export market for over a hundred countries, DG Trade stresses that trade is 'at the centre of Europe's place in the world'.[3] This is not simply a case of institutional self-assertion but an observation echoed in the academic community. For Cartou and others, for a long time the Union's Common Commercial Policy (CCP) constituted 'l'essentiel'[4] of the EU's external relations. For Eeckhout, the CCP still 'remains the centrepiece of the EU's external policies'.[5] Similarly, Cremona underlines that it is 'as an active player in the global market that the Union has played its first and still most-high profile role'.[6] For Meunier and Nicolaïdis, trade is nothing less than 'the EU's *raison d'être*'.[7] But they also stress that the Union is not simply 'a formidable power *in*

[1] The author expresses his gratitude to Marise Cremona, Panos Koutrakos, Malcolm Evans and David Kleimann for their valuable comments on earlier drafts, as well as to the various officials of the European Commission's Directorate-General for Trade and the Trade Team of the Commission Legal Service, who kindly provided extensive information in the course of writing this chapter. Of course, any shortcomings remain the author's alone.

[2] European Commission, DG Trade, *What is Europe's Trade Policy?*, April 2009, at 2.

[3] *Ibid.*

[4] L Cartou, J-L Clergerie, A Gruber and P Rambaud, *L'Union européenne*, 4th edn (Paris, Dalloz, 2002), at 684.

[5] P Eeckhout, *External Relations of the European Union: Legal and Constitutional Foundations* (Oxford, Oxford University Press, 2004), at 347.

[6] M Cremona, 'The Union as a Global Actor: Roles Models and Identity' (2004) 41 *CML Rev* 553, at 555.

[7] S Meunier and K Nicolaïdis, 'The European Union as a Trade Power' in C Hill and M Smith (eds), *International Relations and the European Union* (Oxford, Oxford University Press, 2005), at 248.

trade'[8] but also 'a power *through* trade'.[9] It is not only a 'laboratory' and 'dynamic experiment' for itself, but also a 'magnet' for those surrounding it and 'a model' for other regions as well as for the system as a whole,[10] turning the mere power of attraction into actual rapprochement or transformation.

The latest leap in this dynamic experiment is the entry into force of the Lisbon Treaty on 1 December 2009,[11] bringing to a close the reform effort started with the—eventually unsuccessful—Constitutional Treaty project launched at the Laeken Council in 2001.[12] As from that day, the Maastricht pillar structure has legally vanished. So has the European Community, having been absorbed by the single legal personality of the European Union.[13]

The new institutional structure also brought important changes in the area of trade.[14] Most significantly, the entire CCP it is now an area of exclusive Union competence.[15] This is the way it started out in the Treaty of Rome and was confirmed by the European Court of Justice (ECJ) in *Opinion 1/75* when this concerned only trade in goods.[16] But with the emergence of a deeper trade agenda involving services and intellectual property rights in the Uruguay Round, the ECJ ruled that in the latter two areas, competence was partly shared with the Member States.[17] This was then recognised in the Amsterdam Treaty by convoluted provisions aimed at carving out reservoirs of shared competence, which were later in part rolled back in the Nice Treaty.[18] Under Lisbon, these have been removed, while unanimity in the Council has been retained for the conclusion of agreements in certain sensitive areas such as cultural, education and health services.[19]

[8] *Ibid*, at 265.

[9] *Ibid*, at 266.

[10] Cremona, above n 6, at 553–55.

[11] Reference will be made throughout this chapter to the Treaties as amended by the Lisbon Treaty, ie to the Treaty on European Union (TEU) and the Treaty on the Functioning of the European Union (TFEU) as they are in force as of 1 December 2009.

[12] For a discussion of this see, eg, G de Búrca, 'The EU on the Road from the Constitutional Treaty to the Lisbon Treaty', *Jean Monnet Working Paper 03/08* (New York, New York University School of Law, 2008).

[13] Arts 1(3) and 47 TEU.

[14] See E Pache, 'Organgefüge und Handlungsträger der EU nach Lissabon' in E Pache and F Schorkopf (eds), *Die Europäische Union nach Lissabon: Beiträge zu Organisation, Außenbeziehungen und Stellung im Welthandelsrecht*, Kolloquium aus Anlass des 70. Geburtstages von Professor Dr Meinhard Hilf (Baden-Baden, Nomos, 2009); P-C Müller-Graff, 'The common commercial policy enhanced by the Reform Treaty of Lisbon' in A Dashwood and M Maresceau (eds), *Law and Practice of EU External Relations: Salient Features of a Changing Landscape* (Cambridge, Cambridge University Press, 2008).

[15] Art 3(1)(e) TEU.

[16] *Opinion 1/75* [1975] ECR 01355.

[17] *Opinion 1/94* [1995] ECR I-05267.

[18] Ex Art 133 Treaty on establishing the European Community (TEC); for the changing scope of (then) Community competence, see *Opinion 1/08* of 30 November 2009, *nyr*, paras 117–74. See also Eeckhout, above n 5, at 9–53; A Cebada Romero, *La Organización Mundial del Comercio y la Unión Europea* (Madrid, La Ley, 2002), at 253–65; and I Blázquez Navarro, *Integración europea y diferencias comerciales en la OMC* (Madrid, Marcial Pons, 2007), at 153–202.

[19] Art 207(4) TFEU; for a detailed account of trade in the area of culture, see B de Witte, 'Trade in Culture: International Legal Regimes and EU Constitutional Values' in G de Búrca and J Scott (eds), *The EU and the WTO: Legal and Constitutional Issues* (Oxford, Hart Publishing, 2001).

Also, the CCP is now under the general umbrella of the Union's external action, which is to be guided by the principles set out in the Treaty on European Union (TEU):

> In its relations with the wider world, the Union shall uphold and promote its values and interests and contribute to the protection of its citizens. It shall contribute to peace, security, the sustainable development of the Earth, solidarity and mutual respect among peoples, free and fair trade, eradication of poverty and the protection of human rights, in particular the rights of the child, as well as to the strict observance and the development of international law, including respect for the principles of the United Nations Charter.[20]

Within the Treaty on the Functioning of the European Union (TFEU), the CCP is situated as the first specified area of EU external action (Part V, Title II). According to Article 206 TFEU:

> By establishing a customs union in accordance with Articles 28 to 32, the Union shall contribute, in the common interest, to the harmonious development of world trade, the progressive abolition of restrictions on international trade and on foreign direct investment, and the lowering of customs and other barriers.[21]

Further, Article 207 TFEU expands the 'uniform principles' of the CCP to the entirety of trade in services, commercial aspects of intellectual property and foreign direct investment, and reiterates that the CCP is to 'be conducted in the context of the principles and objectives of the Union's external action.'[22] Also, the consent of the European Parliament will henceforth be required for the conclusion of trade agreements with third countries.[23]

The wider implications of the trade relations of the European Union have always enjoyed vivid attention from the academic community in various regards. These include such 'classics', if you will, as the relationship between the law of the World Trade Organisation (WTO) and EU law (and particularly the effect of the former in the latter order),[24] the coherence debate between trade and development, human rights, environment, etc[25] and, related to that, the desirability

[20] Art 3(5) TEU.

[21] Art 206 TFEU. Compare also the stronger language and shift in perspective ('... the Union shall contribute ...') with the weaker wording before Lisbon: 'By establishing a customs union between themselves Member States aim to contribute ...' (ex Art 131 TEC).

[22] Art 207 TFEU.

[23] Art 218(6)(v) *juncto* Art 207(2) and (3).

[24] See eg P Hilpold, *Die EU im GATT/WTO-System*, 3rd edn (Baden-Baden, Nomos, 2009); Cebada Romero, above n 18, at 407–92; P Koutrakos, *EU International Relations Law* (Oxford, Hart Publishing, 2006), at 251–99; PJ Kuijper, 'From initiating proceedings to ensuring implementation: the links with the Community legal order' in G Sacerdotti, A Yanovich, J Bohanes (eds), *The WTO at Ten: The Contribution of the Dispute Settlement System* (Cambridge, Cambridge University Press, 2006); A von Bogdandy and T Makatsch, 'Collision, Co-existence or Co-operation? Prospects for the Relationship between WTO Law and European Union Law' in de Búrca and Scott (eds), above n 19.

[25] See eg E Vranes, *Trade and the Environment: Fundamental Issues in International Law, WTO Law, and Legal Theory* (Oxford, Oxford University Press, 2009); N Schrijver, 'The EU's Common Development

of conditionality,[26] as well as the more recent discussion on rethinking the global order, and in particular the WTO, in 'constitutional' terms (ie the 'constitutionalisation' debate) and the EU's role therein.[27]

Given the extensive literature already available in all these areas, the objective of this chapter is not to revisit all these debates in detail. What it does endeavour to do is to take a step back, now that the dust of the EU's own reform processes has begun to settle after entry into force of the Lisbon Treaty, and to provide an overview of the different ways in which trade serves as a channel for interaction between the EU and the rest of the world, by way of selective, but pertinent, examples.

This will be done in the following three steps, which are not necessarily chronological but rather organised by the level of ambition the EU shows to influence the outside world. As a first step, section II. will discuss the EU's trade policy as a necessary corollary for the maintenance of its internal market. Here, European integration itself was launched in the shadow of the pre-existing General Agreement on Tariffs and Trade (GATT), and continues to be shaped within the more comprehensive WTO framework. Subsequently, section III. will address the role of trade policy as a vehicle for various other external policies of the EU. Here, the EU uses trade to export its own values and model of integration to other countries and regions. Lastly, section IV. will assess the role of the EU's trade policy in constituting and 'constitutionalising' the entire system of global economic governance.

Cooperation Policy' in M Telò (ed), *The European Union and Global Governance* (Abingdon, Routledge, 2009); L Bartels, 'The Trade and Development Policy of the European Union' in M Cremona (ed), *Developments in EU External Relations Law* (Oxford, Oxford University Press, 2008); M Carbone, *The European Union and International Develoment: The Politics of Foreign Aid* (London, Routledge, 2007), at 30–59; J Harrison, *The Human Rights Impact of the World Trade Organisation* (Oxford, Hart Publishing, 2007); H Hestermeyer, *Human Rights and the WTO: The Case of Patents and Access to Medicines* (Oxford, Oxford University Press, 2007); generally S Nuttall, 'Coherence and Consistency' in C Hill and M Smith (eds), *International Relations and the European Union* (Oxford, Oxford University Press, 2005).

[26] See eg A Bigsten, 'Development policy: coordination, conditionality and coherence' in A Sapir (ed), *Fragmented Power: Europe and the Global Economy* (Brussels, Bruegel Books, 2007); L Bartels, *Human rights conditionality in the EU's international agreements* (New York, Oxford University Press, 2005).

[27] See eg N Walker, 'The Politics of International Constitutions' in J Dunoff and J Trachtman (eds), *Ruling the World? Constitutionalism, International Law, and Global Governance* (Cambridge, Cambridge University Press, 2009); E-U Petersmann, 'Multilevel Trade Governance in the WTO Requires Multilevel Constitutionalism' in C Joerges and EU Petersmann (eds), *Constitutionalism, Multilevel Trade Governance and Social Regulation* (Oxford, Hart Publishing, 2006); J Trachtman, 'The Constitutions of the WTO' (2006) 17 *European Journal of International Law* 623; J Dunhoff, 'Constitutional Conceits: The WTO's "Constitution" and the Discipline of International Law' (2006) 17 *European Journal of International Law* 647; D Cass, *The Constitutionalization of the World Trade Organization: Legitimacy, Democracy, and Community in the International Trading System* (Oxford, Oxford University Press, 2005); N Walker, 'The EU and the WTO: Constitutionalism in a New Key' in de Búrca and Scott (eds), above n 19; R Howse and K Nicolaïdis, 'Legitimacy and Global Governance: Why Constitutionalizing the WTO is a Step Too Far' in R Porter, P Sauvé, A Subramanian and A Beviglia Zampetti (eds), *Efficiency, Equity, and Legitimacy: The Multilateral Trading System at the Millenium* (Washington, DC, Brookings Institution Press, 2001).

II. THE CCP AS A COROLLARY OF THE INTERNAL MARKET

As a first step in appraising the interconnections between the EU and the world in terms of trade, we have to go back to the beginning of European integration itself. It started as an economic project, and retained a stark economic character, with the internal market at its core. As the Court noted in *Opinion 1/75* when introducing the concept of exclusive competence in trade policy, 'a commercial policy is in fact made up by the combination and interaction of internal and external measures'.[28] Thus, as Nugent notes, without a unified CCP 'the unified internal market would not be possible'.[29] Consequently, the issues of the compatibility of the European project with the GATT, measures to defend the internal market and, lastly, its (partial) extension will be addressed.

A. The GATT Compatibility of the Internal Market

When the Treaty of Rome was signed in 1957, the (pre-WTO) GATT, as a proto-international organisation, had already been in place for 10 years.[30] The EU did thus not found the GATT, it only succeeded, as confirmed by the ECJ in *International Fruit*,[31] into the position of the Member States, as it had come to exercise their competence in trade through the CCP.

Therefore, the EU itself had to comply with the pre-existing international rules. The London Conference draft of 1946 already contained a provision on customs unions, which was later extended to free trade areas (FTAs) at the Havana Conference. Ultimately, this would become Article XXIV GATT,[32] which constitutes an exception to the general trade rules of most-favoured nation treatment (MFN)[33] and non-discrimination.[34] It should be recalled that earlier attempts to diverge from MFN rules and set up a structure of pan-European preferences in the period between the World Wars had failed, also due to resistance from the United States.[35] According to Chase's historic account, it was therefore not with the

[28] *Opinion 1/75* [1975] ECR 01355, at 1363.

[29] N Nugent, *The Government and Politics of the European Union* (Houndmills, Palgrave Macmillan, 2006), at 483.

[30] For an extensive historical account, see D Irwin, P Mavroidis and A Sykes, *The Genesis of the GATT* (Cambridge, Cambridge University Press, 2008); also I Neugärtner, 'GATT 1947' in M Hilf and S Oeter (eds), *WTO-Recht: Rechtsordnung des Welthandels* (Baden-Baden, Nomos, 2005).

[31] Joined Cases 21 to 24-72 *International Fruit* [1972] ECR-01219, para 18.

[32] See also Art V of the General Agreement on Trade in Services (hereafter 'GATS').

[33] Art I GATT; Art II GATS.

[34] Art III GATT; Art XVII GATS; See in detail G Marceau and C Reiman, 'When and How is a Regional Trade Agreement Compatible with the WTO?' (2001) 28 *Legal Issues of Economic Integration* 297.

[35] This concerned the wheat sector. See FG von Graevenitz, 'From kaleidoscope to architecture: Interdependence and integration in wheat politics, 1927–1957' in K Patel (ed), *Fertile Ground for Europe? The History of European Integration and the Common Agricultural Policy Since 1945* (Baden-Baden, Nomos, 2009), at 33–36. Of course, this was in the framework of the League of Nations and in the absence of a general, multilateral MFN rule.

Schuman Plan in mind that this exception was introduced, but due to an envisaged (but never ratified) FTA between the United States and Canada.[36] This would reinforce Howse's and Nicolaïdis' claim that originally the post-war multilateral trading system was 'a product, mostly, of the Anglo-Saxon mind'.[37]

In any event, as de Búrca and Scott point out, 'the EEC's common market was modelled partly on the GATT, and many of the EC Treaty provisions clearly reflect this',[38] making it a sort of regional mini-GATT. When European integration then reached the stage of customs union, the issue of compliance with Article XXIV GATT arose. Under this provision substantially all the trade has to be liberalised among the members of the customs union, and the level of duties with the other trading partners not part of it should on the whole not be increased.[39] The most critical point in this respect concerns the EU's Common Agricultural Policy (CAP), which exempts the Union's agricultural sector from the general liberalisation of the internal market and provides it with wide-ranging protection. For Carpenter, this suffices to conclude that '[t]he Treaty of Rome clearly did not comply with the spirit of Article XXIV'.[40] The CAP (especially with regard to agricultural subsidies to keep EU producers competitive) has remained a highly contentious issue to the present day,[41] despite significant reform and liberalisation efforts by the EU. As Roederer-Rynning puts its, today the 'walls are still there—but they are lower'.[42] However, the Article XXIV compatibility of the EU itself has never been scrutinised, neither through dispute settlement nor through the Committee on Regional Trade Agreements (CRTA).[43] Given the rather soft

[36] K Chase, 'Multilateralism Compromised: The Mysterious Origins of GATT Article XXIV' (2006) 5 *World Trade Review* 1; see also Irwin *et al*, above n 30, at 167–68.

[37] K Nicolaïdis and R Howse, '"This is my EUtopia ...": Narrative as Power' (2002) 40 *Journal of Common Market Studies* 767, at 775. International trade and economic cooperation were also already part of the US-UK Atlantic Charter of 1941.

[38] G de Búrca and J Scott, 'The Impact of the WTO on EU Decision-making' in de Búrca and Scott (eds), above n 19, at 2; also JHH Weiler, 'The Constitution of the Common Market Place: Text and Context in the Evolution of the Free Movement of Goods' in P Craig and G de Búrca, *The Evolution of EU Law* (Oxford, Oxford University Press, 1999); and Eeckhout, above n 5, at 9–11.

[39] Art XXIV GATT. Of course, in doing so the customs union also has to comply with the general trade rules such as MFN and national treatment. In detail see Hilpold, above n 24, at 19–85.

[40] T Carpenter, 'A historical perspective on regionalism' in R Baldwin and P Low (eds), *Multilateralizing Regionalism: Challenges for the Global Trading System* (Cambridge, Cambridge University Press, 2009), at 17.

[41] For an extensive account, see C Daugbjerg and A Swinbank, *Ideas, Institutions, and Trade: The WTO and the Curious role of EU Farm Policy in Trade Liberalization* (Oxford, Oxford University Press, 2009); and H Jessen, 'Landwirtschaft' in Hilf and Oeter (eds), above n 30.

[42] C Roederer-Rynning, 'The Common Agricultural Policy: The Fortress Challenged' in H Wallace, M Pollack and A Young (eds), *Policy-Making in the European Union* (Oxford, Oxford University Press, 2010), at 203.

[43] For the latest report of the Committee, see *Report (2009) of the Committee on Regional Trade Agreements to the General Council*, WT/REG/20 of 16 October 2009. It simply states that the 'factual examination' of the Treaty of Rome has been completed (at 5). See also P Mavroidis, 'Do not Ask Too Many Questions: The Institutional Arrangements for Accommodating Regional Integration within the WTO' in E Kwan Choi and JC Hartigan (eds), *Handbook of International Trade* (Oxford, Blackwell, 2005); and T Bender, 'GATT 1994' in Hilf and Oeter (eds), above n 30, at 180–84; on this, as well

language of ex Article 131 TEC that the EU Member States would merely 'aim to contribute, in the common interest, to … the progressive abolition of restrictions on international trade and the lowering of customs barriers', this can be considered as avoiding any strict commitment by the EU itself to comply with the GATT rules on customs unions.[44] The stronger wording of Article 206 TFEU could thus be seen an indication of stricter adherence to GATT/WTO rules.

This does not mean, however, that the issue remains without relevance. In terms of WTO compatibility of the internal market, we also have to consider the significant enlargement of the EU from six founding members to presently 27 members. It has been widely held that enlargement has been the area in which the EU has most clearly had an impact on domestic policy abroad. Through the leverage of attraction to the prosperous internal market, it prompted candidate countries to carry out wide-ranging reforms and to absorb the entire *acquis communautaire*.[45] By doing so, it also transcends the traditional divide between internal and external policies. This has an important trade dimension, evidenced through pre-accession agreements with the candidates with trade preferences,[46] and the final integration into the EU (and its CCP) with the ensuing trade creation, as well as diversion,[47] which have to conform with WTO disciplines.

B. Defending the Internal Market

Another instance where the CCP enters the picture as a necessary corollary to the internal market is where it is used to defend it from external influences considered harmful to it. This concerns first of all the classic trade defence instruments, such as antidumping and countervailing measures.[48] These can be seen as the external

as on the WTO's Transparency Mechanism for Regional Trade agreements established in 2006, see Y Devuyst and A Serdarevic, 'The World Trade Organization and Regional Trade Agreements: Bridging the Constitutional Credibility Gap' (2007) 18 *Duke Journal of Comparative & International Law* 1.

[44] M Cremona, 'Neutrality or Discrimination? The WTO, the EU and External Trade' in de Búrca and Scott (eds), above n 19, at 152.

[45] R Epstein and U Sedelmeier, 'Beyond Conditionality: International Institutions in Postcommunist Europe after Enlargement' in R Epstein and U Sedelmeier (eds), *International Influence Beyond Conditionality: Postcommunist Europe after EU Enlargement* (London, Routledge, 2009); F Schimmelfennig, 'EU political accession conditionality after enlargement: consistency and effectiveness' (2008) 15 *Journal of European Public Policy* 918; generally A Tatham, *Enlargement of the European Union* (Alphen aan den Rijn, Kluwer, 2009).

[46] Eg the former Europe Agreements with the Central European countries that acceded in 2004 and 2007, and the current Stabilisation and Association Agreements with the Western Balkans. As Meunier and Nicolaïdis note, 'on the eve of the [2004] enlargement, over 95% of the trade of the EU-15 with the new entrants was already free' (Meunier and Nicolaïdis, above n 7, at 258).

[47] For an account of third countries' anxiety about EU enlargement and the lack of compensatory negotiations, see Hilpold, above n 24, at 260–76; for a study on trade diversion, *inter alia* in the context of EU enlargement, see C Freund and J McLaren, 'On the Dynamics of Trade Diversion: Evidence from Four Trade Blocs', *International Finance Working Paper No 637*, June 1999.

[48] European Commission, *Europe's trade defence instruments in a changing global economy: A Green Paper for public consultation*, COM(2006) 763 final, Brussels, 6 December 2006, at 2.

complement to the competition and State aid policy of the Union. While the latter is aimed at guaranteeing a fair and level playing field within the EU, the former combats any outside interference with, or abuse of, this playing field.[49]

Regarding subsidies, on the other hand, the WTO Agreement on Subsidies and Countervailing Measures defines specific categories that are either prohibited or can be challenged through dispute settlement or coutervailing measures, especially when the subsidies are used to protect one's market and adversely affect trading partners. Such a question of subsidisation concerned the disputes between the US and EU on *Large Civil Aircraft*, with both sides accusing the other of subsidising their respective civil aviation champions.[50] Given that both Boeing and Airbus (as part of EADS) are also military producers, and that large defence equipment projects are also alleged to serve as masked subsidies, this matter is all but exclusively civil, and relates to the EU's efforts for armaments cooperation.[51]

More generally, this reveals that where the internal market is not fully developed, a common trade approach is also lacking.[52] The absence of a truly common European defence equipment market due to an overbroad interpretation by the Member States of Article 346 TFEU[53] therefore also leads to a weaker policy in terms of arms exports, which is currently not addressed in terms of the internal market (or what used to be the first pillar) but through Common Foreign and Security Policy (CFSP) measures (the former second pillar),[54] which is governed by 'specific rules and procedures' and excluded from ECJ jurisdiction.[55]

Also, restrictions on trade based on health concerns, which is multilaterally addressed by the Agreement on Sanitary and Phytosanitary Measures (SPS),

[49] For a comprehensive account, see I van Bael and J-F Bellis, *Anti-dumping and Other Trade Protection Laws of the EC*, 5th edn (The Hague, Kluwer Law International, 2009); for an overview of the debate surrounding antidumping as hampering competition and developing countries' perspectives on the issue see R Raslan, *Antidumping: A Developing Country Perspective* (The Hague, Kluwer Law International, 2009).

[50] *United States—Measures Affecting Trade in Large Civil Aircraft*, Request for consultations by the European Communities of 12 October 2004, WT/DS317/1; *European Communities and Certain Member States—Measures Affecting Trade in Large Civil Aircraft*, Request for Consultations by the United States of 12 October 2004, WT/DS316/1. These disputes are still pending due to the complexity of the issues and the volume of materials involved.

[51] This matter is further complicated through transatlantic armaments co-operation, considering, eg, the controversial cancellation in late 2008 of European refuelling aircraft previously ordered by the Pentagon, and the subsequent dropping-out of Airbus from the follow-up tender.

[52] M Cremona, 'The External Dimension of the Single Market: Building (on) the Foundations' in C Barnard and J Scott (eds), *The Law of the Single European Market: Unpacking the Premises* (Oxford, Hart Publishing, 2002).

[53] Ex Art 296 TEC. Note also the close resemblance of Art 346 TFEU to Art XXI GATT.

[54] Council Common Position 2008/944/CFSP of 8 December 2008 defining common rules governing control of exports of military technology and equipment [2008] OJ L335/99; Council Joint Action 2008/230/CFSP of 17 March 2008 on support for EU activities in order to promote the control of arms exports and the principles and criteria of the EU Code of Conduct on Arms Exports among third countries [2008] OJ L75/81. This also includes the cases of arms embargoes (see section III.B.). Nonetheless, the adoption of such legally binding instruments is progress in comparison to the previous regime, which existed only in the form of a code of conduct.

[55] Art 24(1), 2nd indent TEU.

demonstrate that maintaining a customs union and an internal market is not simply a matter of technical, uncontroversial 'low politics'[56] but can become a highly politicised matter. This was illustrated by the well-known cases concerning *Beef Hormones*[57] and genetically modified organisms, *GMOs*.[58] These raised fundamental questions about the scope of the precautionary principle in terms of health protection and the 'justiciability' of scientific evidence by the Appellate Body.[59] However, the status of the EU as bulwark, or 'incidental fortress',[60] against genetically modified foodstuffs has decreased following the expiry of the six-year GMO moratorium in 2004. A recent example is the decision to allow the large-scale cultivation of the genetically modified 'Amflora' potato,[61] which is only the latest addition to an already large number of GMOs permitted by the Commission.[62]

C. Extending (parts of) the Internal Market

The impact of the internal market exceeds the dimension of EU enlargement, and thus produces additional trade implications. Where accession is excluded or not politically desired (for the time being), the EU has already largely extended its internal market to the countries of the European Economic Area (EEA), Switzerland and Turkey. It also promised its post-enlargement neighbourhood a so-called 'stake in the EU's Internal Market'[63] or, as former European

[56] As coined by Stanley Hoffmann; S Hoffmann, *The European Sisyphus: Essays on Europe, 1964–1994* (Boulder, Col, Westview Press, 1994).

[57] *European Communities—Measures Concerning Meat and Meat Products (Hormones)*, Appellate Body Report (adopted 13 February 1998) WT/DS26/AB/R, WT/DS48/AB/R.

[58] *European Communities—Measures Affecting the Approval and Marketing of Biotech Products*, Panel Reports (adopted 21 November 2006) WT/DS291/R, WT/DS292/R, WT/DS293/R.

[59] For discussion see W Davey, 'Reflections on the Appellate Body Decision in the *Hormones* Case and the Meaning of the SPS Agreement' in G Bermann and P Mavroidis (eds), *Trade and Human Health and Safety* (Cambridge, Cambridge University Press, 2006); A Sykes, 'Domestic Regulation, Sovereignty and Scientific Evidence Requirements', *ibid.*

[60] A Young, 'The Incidental Fortress: The Single European Market and World Trade' (2004) 42 *Journal of Common Market Studies* 393.

[61] Commission Decision 2010/135 of 2 March 2010 concerning the placing on the market, in accordance with Directive 2001/18/EC of the European Parliament and of the Council, of a potato product (Solanum tuberosum L. line EH92-527-1) genetically modified for enhanced content of the amylopectin component of starch [2010] OJ L53/11; Commission Decision 2010/136 of 2 March 2010 authorising the placing on the market of feed produced from the genetically modified potato EH92-527-1 (BPS-25271-9) and the adventitious or technically unavoidable presence of the potato in food and other feed products under Regulation (EC) No 1829/2003 of the European Parliament and of the Council [2010] OJ L53/15.

[62] In detail MA Pollack and GS Schaffer, *When Cooperation Fails: The International Law and Politics of Genetically Modified Organisms* (Oxford, Oxford University Press, 2009), at 245–78.

[63] European Commission, *European Neighbourhood Policy Strategy Paper*, COM(2004) 373 final, Brussels, 12 May 2004, at 3; see also S Gstöhl, 'Blurring Economic Boundaries: Trade and Aid in the EU's Near Abroad' in D Mahncke and S Gstöhl (eds), *Europe's Near Abroad: Promises and Prospects of the EU's Neighbourhood Policy* (Brussels, Peter Lang, 2008); and M Cremona, 'The European

Commission President Prodi put it, 'sharing everything with the Union but institutions'.[64]

This has been continued in the latest recasting of the EU's relations with its close surroundings. To the East, the Joint Declaration of the Prague Eastern Partnership Summit of May 2009 called for 'New Association Agreements' to

> provide for the establishment or the objective of establishing deep and comprehensive free trade areas, where the positive effects of trade and investment liberalization will be strengthened by regulatory approximation leading to convergence with EU laws and standards.[65]

Of special importance is also the bilateral treaty framework with Russia, in particular as long as the country remains outside of the legal framework of the WTO. Currently, this relationship is still governed by the 1997 Partnership and Cooperation Agreement (PCA),[66] while negotiations for a successor agreement continue. As established at the 2005 EU–Russia Summit, this is ultimately to lead to a Common Economic Space between the two.[67]

Similarly, to the South, the Union for the Mediterranean, founded in July 2008, is mandated with the establishment of an FTA by 2010.[68] Before this will be achieved, the EU has put in place a number of FTAs with individual countries. Most recently, the FTAs between the EU and Israel and the Palestinian National Authority respectively received widespread attention through the *Brita* case. The Court had to rule on the question whether the origin of drink-makers for sparkling water produced in the West Bank had to be considered as produce of Israel, which it declined.[69] This also reveals the political sensitivities that can underlie such seemingly 'low-politics' agreements, as well as the wider announcement effect of the ECJ's rulings.

While the EU as such has been spared scrutiny by the WTO, extensions of the internal market have not. In the 1999 *Turkey—Textiles* case, the Appellate Body confirmed that certain quantitative restrictions on textiles could not be justified

Neighbourhood Policy: More than a Partnership?' in M Cremona (ed), *Developments in EU External Relations Law* (Oxford, Oxford University Press, 2008).

[64] R Prodi, *A Wider Europe—A Proximity Policy as the Key to Stability*, Sixth ECSA World Conference, Speech/02/619 (2002), Brussels, 5–6 December 2002, at 6.

[65] Council of the European Union, *Joint Declaration of the Prague Eastern Partnership Summit*, 8435/09 (Presse 78), Prague, 7 May 2009, at 7.

[66] Agreement on partnership and cooperation establishing a partnership between the European Communities and their Member States, of one part, and the Russian Federation, of the other part—Protocol 1 on the establishment of a coal and steel contact group—Protocol 2 on mutual administrative assistance for the correct application of customs legislation—Final Act—Exchanges of letters—Minutes of signing [1997] OJ L327/1.

[67] See in detail, C Filis and M Papadakou, 'Assessment of the common economic space' in K Nikolov (ed), *Assessing the Common Spaces between the European Union and Russia* (Sofia, BECSA, 2009).

[68] European Commission, *Barcelona Process: Union for the Mediterranean*, COM(2008) 319 final, Brussels, 20 May 2008, para 10; also M Montanari, 'The Barcelona Process and the Political Economy of Euro-Mediterranean Trade Integration' (2007) 45 *Journal of Common Market Studies* 1011.

[69] Case C-386/08 *Brita GmbH v Hauptzollamt Hamburg-Hafen*, judgment of 25 February 2010, *nyr*.

through the customs union between the EU and Turkey.[70] The Appellate Body ruled that Article XXIV GATT only serves as an exceptional defence, where

> the party claiming the benefit of this defence must demonstrate that the measure at issue is introduced upon the formation of a customs union that fully meets the requirements of sub-paragraphs 8(a) and 5(a) of Article XXIV.[71]

and that 'that party must demonstrate that the formation of that customs union would be prevented if it were not allowed to introduce the measure at issue.'[72] The Appellate Body thus shows that such questions of WTO-conformity of extensions of the internal market are indeed fully justiciable, and that it is for the Appellate Body to define further the necessary benchmarks for such compatibility,[73] notwithstanding any political assessment by the CRTA.[74]

In sum, as to the CCP as a corollary of the internal market, we can see that the Union was shaped right from the beginning, and still is being shaped, by the GATT/WTO. While the GATT/WTO conformity of the Union itself, and its enlargement, have not been scrutinised, the Appellate Body certainly exercised its review powers for non-membership extension of the internal market, as well as a number of measures pertaining to internal policies. Moreover, it becomes clear that maintaining an internal market cannot be kept separate from other policy areas. Whereas enlargement serves to as an example where the internal/external policy division is successfully transcended, other areas, such as armaments trade and agriculture, show that internal deficiencies also lead to external difficulties.

III. THE CCP AS A VEHICLE FOR FOREIGN POLICY

In the European Commission's 2006 Global Europe Strategy it is stated that '[t]hrough our trade policies, we also seek to contribute to a range of the Union's external goals, in particular development and neighbourhood objectives.'[75] While the latter concerns a stake in the internal market discussed in the previous section within the framework of the EU's neighbourhood policy, let us now turn to the external aspects of trade policy proper. It is here that that the EU makes sure that its own advantages and benefits are not hampered by its trading partners. But the CCP also goes a lot further. Just as the internal market is used as the carrot in matters of enlargement and neighbourhood policy, for countries to which membership or a

[70] See, for the customs union, EC–Turkey Association Council, Decision No 1/95 of 22 December 1995 on implementing the final phase of the Customs Union [1996] OJ L35/1.

[71] *Turkey—Restrictions on Imports of Textile and Clothing Products (Turkey—Textiles)*, Appellate Body Report (adopted 19 November 1999) WT/DS34/AB/R, para 58.

[72] *Ibid.*

[73] *Ibid.* Note, eg, that the complete alignment of quantitative restrictions is not required to form a customs union (para 62).

[74] See also Bender, above n 43, at 182–83.

[75] European Commission, *Global Europe: Competing in the World. A Contribution to the EU's Growth and Jobs Strategy*, COM(2006) 567 final, Brussels, 4 October 2006, at 2.

'stake' in the market cannot be provided, preferential treatment and market access are used as a means of conditionality to shape the domestic policies of the EU's trading partners. More recently, the EU has also put an emphasis on exporting its very model of regional integration to other parts of the world.

A. Ensuring the EU's Trade Benefits Abroad

The EU has developed specific instruments to make sure its own trade benefits are not impaired by its trading partners. Thus, while antidumping and countervailing measures prevent unfair competition distorting the internal market, EU measures are also utilised to ensure fair trading conditions abroad. The most prominent of these instruments is the Trade Barriers Regulation of 1994,[76] which gives businesses and trade associations a right to lodge complaints with the European Commission where they feel they have fallen victim to non-compliance with WTO rules in third countries. This is of importance, since WTO Dispute Settlement itself is open only to WTO Member States and not to the economic operators actually concerned. Consequently, those operators have to lobby their respective governments to launch a dispute at the WTO. The Trade Barriers Regulation thus provides a formal avenue for private parties to prompt the Commission to act multilaterally. This does not extend, however, 'to a near automatic right to have one's complaint turned into a WTO dispute settlement case if it turns out to be well founded',[77] as there also needs to be a Union interest involved for the Commission to be obliged to act.[78]

Furthermore, the Commission is pursuing an active strategy of promoting market access and the removal of non-tariff barriers in third countries. In 2007, it integrated a reinforced Market Access Strategy into its Global Europe Strategy.[79] As part of a wider dialogue between the EU, business and third countries, it has set up so-called Market Access Teams, ie networks of relevant stakeholders, which actively engage foreign authorities to remove non-tariff barriers before an actual multilateral dispute arises.[80] For easy public access, it also introduced an online Market Access Database listing the trade barriers identified by the teams.[81]

[76] Council Regulation (EC) No 3286/94 of 22 December 1994 laying down Community procedures in the field of the common commercial policy in order to ensure the exercise of the Community's rights under international trade rules, in particular those established under the auspices of the World Trade Organization [1994] OJ L349/71.

[77] Kuijper, above n 24, at 273, who compares this situation with the US, where § 301 of the US Trade Act in fact grants such a right; see generally M Bronckers and N McNelis, 'The EU Trade Barriers Regulation Comes of Age' (2001) 35 *Journal of World Trade* 427.

[78] Council Regulation (EC) No 3286/94, Arts 8(1), 11(1) and 12(1).

[79] European Commission, *Global Europe: A Stronger Partnership to Deliver Market Access for European Exporters (Market Access Strategy)*, COM(2007) 183, Brussels, 18 April 2007.

[80] For an assessment of these teams, see A Tiedemann, 'EU Market Access Teams: New Instruments to Tackle Non-tariff Barriers to Trade', *College of Europe EU Diplomacy Paper 9/2009*, December 2009.

[81] See <madb.europa.eu/mkaccdb2/indexPubli.htm>.

B. Shaping of Foreign Governance through Trade

The CCP, however, goes far beyond ensuring the reciprocal enjoyment of trade benefits, and has a long history of serving as a vehicle for other policy areas. With regard to developing countries it is used not only as a means of development, but also as a means of shaping governance within these countries in areas such as human rights or environmental standards. In extreme cases, the EU will even use restrictive trade measures, ie sanctions, to this end.

As stated in the 2005 European Consensus on Development, the EU is 'the most important economic and trade partner for developing countries, offering specific trading benefits to developing countries, mainly to the LDCs [least developed countries] among them'.[82] This development dimension of trade now also features in primary law, as the new Article 3(5) TEU mandates the EU to contribute, in its external action, to the 'free and fair trade [and the] eradication of poverty', setting out the 'context' in which also the CCP itself is to be conducted under Article 207 TFEU.

This flows from a long historical relationship between the Union's trade and development policies. As Bartels argues, development objectives were inherent in the CCP from the outset, being carried over from the ties of the Member States with their former colonies.[83] This also explains the EU's categorisation of the outside (non-developed) world into African, Caribbean and Pacific (ACP) countries and everyone else. However, a special reference to the ACP-relationship in the treaties has been removed by Lisbon.[84] In the GATT, a chapter on 'Trade and Development'[85] was added only in 1966 under the pressure of the United Nations Conference on Trade and Development (UNCTAD), which had been created as an alternative forum in the framework of calls for a new international economic order.[86] A renewed emphasis on development has been put on the current round of trade negotiations, the Doha Development Round.

This special association relationship between the EU and the ACP countries was anchored in a series of international conventions, starting with Yaoundé I in 1963 and II in 1969, the four Lomé Conventions spanning the time from 1975 until 2000, and finally the Cotonou Agreement of 2000, the trade provisions of which expired in 2007. Also these agreements, by granting preferential treatment and thus derogating from WTO rules of MFN treatment and non-discrimination, raised the issue of WTO conformity.

[82] Joint statement by the Council and the representatives of the governments of the Member States meeting within the Council, the European Parliament and the Commission on European Union Development Policy: The European Consensus [2006] OJ C46/1, para 2.

[83] Bartels, above n 25, at 128–32.

[84] Ex Art 179(3) TEC. The differentiation remains, though, institutionally. While external relations are now generally handled by the European External Action Service, there remains a Directorate-General for Development, which handles relations with the ACP countries.

[85] Arts XXXIV to XXXVIII GATT.

[86] In detail see M Michaelis and H Jessen, 'WTO und Entwicklung' in Hilf and Oeter (eds), above n 30.

It is in this context that the *Bananas* dispute arose, which would become the EU's longest-lasting trade dispute. The United States and several Latin American countries challenged the EU's regime for the import, sale and distribution of bananas favouring ACP countries. The Appellate Body repeatedly found that the EU's preferential treatment, even after several reconfigurations, violated WTO rules.[87] The EU had exceeded the derogations introduced in the GATT/WTO system favouring developing countries, as well as the special waiver granted to the EU in 1994 for the Lomé Agreement.[88] Recently, the EU agreed to reduce the overall import tariffs for bananas in exchange for a no-litigation commitment from the Latin American countries. Consequently, an eroded preferential banana market organisation for the ACP countries will remain, but in order to adjust to the stiffer competition the EU decided to pay additional financial aid to the ACP countries.[89] While this is arguably a positive move in terms of WTO compliance, it also appears as an implicit acknowledgement of the failure of this particular example of development through trade. More generally, the EU has abandoned its ACP-wide approach for granting trade preferences, and has moved to negotiate WTO-compatible bi-regional agreements.

Apart from this ACP-centred approach, the EU also provides for general, non-reciprocal benefits to developing countries through the WTO's 1979 'enabling clause'.[90] On this basis the EU, like most other developed economies, maintains a so-called Generalised System of Preferences (GSP), providing preferential access to its market for developing countries.[91] The EU added to this standard GSP two other schemes: the 'Special incentive arrangement for sustainable development and good governance' (better known as GSP+), and the 'Special arrangement for the least-developed countries' (better known as 'Everything but Arms' (EBA)). In order to qualify for the additional benefits provided by GSP+, eligible developing countries, as well as being 'vulnerable economies',[92] must have 'ratified and effectively implemented all the conventions listed in Annex III', ie 27 international conventions concerning labour standards, human rights, sustainable development and good governance.[93] Further, each country wishing to benefit from GSP+ has to give an undertaking that it will allow the Commission to monitor the implementation

[87] *European Communities—Regime for the Importation, Sale and Distribution of Bananas*, Appellate Body Report (adopted 25 September 1997) WT/DS27/AB/R; see J Cascante and G Sander, *Der Streit um die EG-Bananenmarktordnung* (Berlin, Duncker & Humblot, 1999).

[88] GATT, *The Fourth ACP–EEC Convention of Lomé*, Decision of 9 December 1994, L/7604.

[89] European Union, *Ending the longest trade dispute in history: EU initials deal on bananas with Latin American countries*, Press release P/09/1938, Brussels, 15 December 2009, available at <http://www.europa.eu/rapid/pressReleasesAction.do?reference=IP/09/1938>.

[90] GATT, *Decision on Differential and More Favourable Treatment, Reciprocity and Fuller Participation of Developing Countries*, Decision of 28 November 1979, L/4903.

[91] For the current legislation in force, see Council Regulation (EC) No 732/2008 of 22 July 2008 applying a scheme of generalised tariff preferences for the period from 1 January 2009 to 31 December 2011 [2008] OJ L211/1.

[92] *Ibid*, Art 8(1)(c) *juncto* Art 8(2). This comprises countries that are not high-income (as classified by the World Bank), of which exports are not diversified and of which the imports into the Union covered by the scheme amount to less than 1% in value of the total GSP-covered imports into the Union.

[93] *Ibid*, Art 8(1)(a).

of the conventions.[94] Under EBA, least-developed countries[95] are granted duty-free and quota-free access to the EU for all products, except arms and ammunitions.[96] Therefore, applying for GSP+ is of little interest for the least-developed countries, while they are likely to be the ones most in need of the governance reforms that GSP+ membership would entail. The EBA arrangement therefore resembles rather a form of humanitarian assistance, which is also normally unconditional.

In terms of enforcement, the benefits under GSP+ can be withdrawn temporarily in cases where incorporation into domestic law and/or implementation of the 27 conventions on the part of the beneficiary country is lacking.[97] Similarly, the benefits under all three schemes can be withdrawn temporarily, eg due to 'the serious and systematic violation' of the principles set out in the core human and labour rights conventions as established by the relevant monitoring bodies (normally the Commission).[98] This also concerns those countries not benefitting from GSP+ and that are thus not actually obliged to ratify these conventions. Another ground for suspension comprises 'serious and systematic unfair trading practices which have an adverse effect on the [Union's] industry', which, importantly, have to be 'based on a previous determination to that effect by the competent WTO body'[99] and not on an assessment by the Commission. This way, the Union ensures that these countries comply with this collection of international obligations, representing norms and values on which the EU itself is founded and promotes worldwide.[100] Recently, it has withdrawn GSP+ benefits from Sri Lanka, having determined a lack of implementation of three relevant human rights conventions.[101]

Presently, while 176 developing countries fall under GSP and 49 under EBA, only 16 countries have qualified for GSP+. Also, the economic benefits given by the schemes may seem greater than they actually are. As Bartels points out, the GSP covers only 9 per cent of all imports into the EU, half of which is actually utilised.[102] This is partly due to the complexity and restrictiveness of the rules of origin determining which products actually qualify as coming from a country covered by the scheme.[103]

[94] *Ibid*, Art 8(1)(b).

[95] Those are the least-developed countries according to the United Nations (*ibid*, Art 11(8)). Note that for the notion of 'developing country', the ECJ maintains an autonomous EU law definition, Case C-155/07, *Parliament v Council* [2008] ECR I-08103, para 52.

[96] Council Regulation (EC) No 732/2008, above n 91, Art 11. The transitional periods for bananas and rice have already expired. The one exempting sugar will expire on 30 September 2012.

[97] *Ibid*, Art 15(2).

[98] *Ibid*, Art 15(1)(a), referring to 'principles laid down in the conventions listed in Part A of Annex III', thus excluding Part B containing the environmental and good governance-related conventions.

[99] *Ibid*, Art 15(1)(d).

[100] See also the contributions by B de Witte, M Cremona, and G Pavlakos and J Pauwelyn in this volume.

[101] Implementing Regulation (EU) No 143/2010 of the Council of 15 February 2010 temporarily withdrawing the special incentive arrangement for sustainable development and good governance provided for under Regulation (EC) No 732/2008 with respect to the Democratic Socialist Republic of Sri Lanka [2010] OJ L 45/1.

[102] Bartels, above n 25, at 155–56.

[103] In detail *ibid*, at 154–65.

In addition, there is a distinction between 'non-sensitive' and 'sensitive' products, the latter comprising mainly agricultural products of interest for the developing countries concerned that merely receive a reduction in tariffs (EBA apart).

The GSP scheme is not beyond judicial control by the WTO, as evidenced by the *EC—Tariff Preferences* dispute, in which the Appellate Body confirmed that certain forms of its conditionality were not covered by the enabling clause.[104] This concerned a special 'drug regime' which granted tariff preferences as a form of assistance to the anti-drug efforts of third countries.

Next to development, the issue of environmental protection has received more heightened attention in view of the emerging threat of climate change. Both are linked through the notion of sustainable development, which features both in the EU Treaties[105] and in the Preambles to the Marrakech Agreement and the Doha Ministerial Declaration.[106] However, as WTO Director General Lamy pointed out,

> until a truly global consensus emerges on how best to tackle the issue of climate change, WTO Members will continue to hold different views on what the multilateral trading system can and must do.[107]

What role WTO Dispute settlement can play here is also uncertain, but in view of the Appellate Body Report in *Shrimp Turtle*,[108] there is a scope to consider products being made in an environmentally unfriendly way to be 'unlike' similar products using more environmentally friendly production methods.[109]

On the EU side, noteworthy trade-related environmental protection measures include the regulation on waste shipment,[110] which transposes into EU Law the Basel Convention on the Control of Transboundary Movements of Hazardous Wastes and their Disposal, and the adherence of the Union to the Rotterdam

[104] *European Communities—Conditions for the Granting of Tariff Preferences to Developing Countries*, Appellate Body Report (adopted 20 April 2004) WT/DS246/AB/R; see also R Howse and S Esserman, 'The Appellate Body, the WTO dispute settlement system, and the politics of multilateralism' in G Sacerdoti, A Yanovich and J Bohanes (eds), *The WTO at Ten: The Contribution of the Dispute Settlement System* (Cambridge, Cambridge University Press, 2006), at 69–74.

[105] More prominently after Lisbon: Art 3(3) TEU on 'sustainable development of Europe'; Art 3(5) TEU on 'sustainable development of the Earth'; and Art 21(2)(d) TEU on 'sustainable economic, social and environmental development of developing countries'. See also the contribution by H Vedder in this volume.

[106] WTO, *Ministerial Declaration*, adopted on 14 November 2001, WT/MIN(01)/DEC/1, point 6; see also points 31–33; for an extensive account, see S Maljean-Dubois, *Droit de l'Organisation mondiale du commerce et protection de l'environnement* (Bruxelles, Bruylant, 2003).

[107] Pascal Lamy, speech to a European Parliament panel on 29 May 2008, Brussels, available at <http://www.wto.org/english/news_e/sppl_e/sppl91_e.htm>.

[108] *United States—Import Prohibition of Certain Shrimp and Shrimp Products*, Appellate Body Report (adopted 6 November 1998), WT/DS58/AB/R; see also R Howse, 'The Appellate Body Rulings in the Shrimp/Turtle Case: A New Legal Baseline for the Trade and Environment Debate' (2002) 27 *Columbia Journal of Environmental Law* 491.

[109] For an extensive account of the 'like products' debate, see W-M Choi, *'Like products' in international trade law: towards a consistent GATT/WTO jurisprudence* (Oxford, Oxford University Press, 2003).

[110] Regulation (EC) No 1013/2006 of the European Parliament and of the Council of 14 June 2006 on shipments of waste [2006] OJ L190/1.

Convention on the Prior Informed Consent Procedure for Certain Hazardous Chemicals and Pesticides in International Trade.[111] These have, however, also been the site of inter-institutional turf wars between the Commission and the Council and Parliament.[112] Another area where the EU has combined trade with environmental protection is through the establishment of a regional emissions trading scheme, linked on the global level to the Kyoto Protocol.[113] At the WTO level, however, the *Swordfish* dispute shows that the EU has also not hesitated to launch a complaint against Chile for adopting conservation measures for alleged adverse effects on its trade benefits.[114]

Environmental conventions also figure among the conventions to be ratified in order to qualify for GSP+.[115] However, while the benefits under GSP+ can be withdrawn when a country no longer effectively implements these conventions,[116] the 'serious and systematic violation' of the principles of these conventions by non-GSP+ countries would not trigger suspension of GSP benefits, as they are excluded from this provision.[117] These different degrees of strictness in terms of enforcement could be seen as a hint as regards a certain hierarchy between these norms in terms of importance.

Lastly, there is also the intricate relation between the CCP and the CFSP. This concerns the question of economic sanctions as the negative counterpart to trade benefits, used in order to induce compliance with international norms the Union supports. According to Article 215 TFEU,[118] where a decision adopted under the 'specific rules and procedures' of the CFSP 'provides for the interruption or reduction, in part or completely, of economic and financial relations with one or more

[111] Council Decision 2006/730/EC of 25 September 2006 on the conclusion, on behalf of the European Community, of the Rotterdam Convention on the Prior Informed Consent Procedure for certain hazardous chemicals and pesticides in international trade [2006] OJ L299/23.

[112] While the ECJ ruled that the Rotterdam Convention fell simultaneously under the scope of the CCP and the Union's environmental policy (Case C-94/03 *Commission v Council* [2006] ECR I-00001), it ruled that the Waste Shipment Regulation falls outside the scope of the CCP in terms of legal basis (Case C-411/06 *Commission v Parliament and Council*, judgment of 8 September 2009, *nyr*).

[113] See J Lefevere, 'Linking Emission Trading Schemes: The EU ETS and the "Linking Directive"' in D Freestone and C Streck (eds), *Legal Aspects of Implementing the Kyoto Protocol Mechanisms* (Oxford, Oxford University Press, 2005).

[114] *Chile—Measures Affecting the Transit and Importation of Swordfish*, Request for consultations by the European Communities of 19 April 2000, WT/DS193/1. Chile had also brought proceedings against the EU at the International Tribunal of the Law of the Sea (ITLOS). While the ITLOS case has been discontinued, the WTO proceedings have been suspended due to a provisional arrangement between the two parties.

[115] Council Regulation (EC) No 732/2008, above n 91, Annex III, Part B. These include the Montreal Protocol on Substances that Deplete the Ozone Layer, Basel Convention on the Control of Transboundary Movements of Hazardous Wastes and Their Disposal, Stockholm Convention on Persistent Organic Pollutants, Convention on International Trade in Endangered Species of Wild Fauna and Flora, Convention on Biological Diversity, Cartagena Protocol on Biosafety, Kyoto Protocol to the United Nations Framework Convention on Climate Change.

[116] Council Regulation (EC) No 732/2008, above n 91, Art 15(2).

[117] *Ibid*, Art 15(1)(a), which merely refers to 'conventions listed in Part A of Annex III', while the environmental conventions are all in Part B.

[118] Ex Art 301 TEC.

third countries', or for restrictive measures against natural or legal persons, the Council shall adopt such sanctions. Today, these usually include an arms ban and targeted ('smart') sanctions against leading persons in the third country,[119] instead of overall trade restrictions with potentially damaging effects on the population. Here too, the Lisbon Treaty clarifies a previously rather ambiguous legal framework. Originally, economic sanctions were considered an act of foreign policy falling outside of the scope of Union (then Community) competence.[120] In terms of effectiveness and to avoid disturbances of the internal market, they were later nonetheless 'communitarised' under the CCP, but with references to their political origin in what was known as European Political Cooperation (EPC).[121] With the creation of the CFSP in Maastricht, sanctions were turned into a so-called 'inter-pillar' exercise with a dual-legal basis.[122] Notwithstanding this dual character of sanctions, the ECJ had ruled that given the CCP, competence of Member States in the area of foreign policy did not exempt them from their EU law obligations, even when they exercised it in order to implement UN Security Council Resolutions.[123] Instead, the Court pointed out that the application of sanctions requires uniform and effective interpretation and application by the Union as a whole.[124]

Common Security and Defence Policy (CSDP) missions can also be used to protect the Union's trade interests. This has been recently illustrated by the launching of the EU's first naval operation, Operation EUNAVFOR Somalia ('Atalanta'), in December 2008 to fight piracy in the Gulf of Aden, a maritime chokepoint through which a large part of trade between the EU and Asia passes.[125] The mandate of this operation explicitly includes the protection of merchant vessels.[126]

C. Reproducing the EU's Own Model through Trade

While the preceding section concerned the defence of specific interests and the promotion of specific norms, it can also be observed that more recently the Union

[119] Eg Council Common Position 2002/145/CFSP of 18 February 2002 concerning restrictive measures against Zimbabwe [2002] OJ L50/1.

[120] Covered by ex Art 297 TEC.

[121] On this development over time, see in detail P Koutrakos, *Trade, Foreign Policy & Defence in EU Constitutional Law: The Legal Regulation of Sanctions, Exports of Dual-use Goods and Armaments* (Oxford, Hart Publishing, 2001), at 49–91.

[122] P Koutrakos, 'Inter-Pillar Approaches to the European Security and Defence Policy—the Economic Aspects of Security' in V Kronenberger (ed), *The European Union and the International Legal Order: Discord or Harmony?* (The Hague, TMC Asser Press, 2001).

[123] Case C-70/94 *Fritz Werner Industrie-Ausrüstungen GmbH* [1995] ECR I-03189; Case C-83/94 *Criminal proceedings against Peter Leifer et al* [1995] ECR I-03231; Case C-124/95 *Centro-Com* [1997] ECR I-00081.

[124] Case C-84/95 *Bosphorus* [1996] ECR I-03953; Case C-177/95 *Ebony Maritime* [1997] ECR I-01111; for extensive accounts, see Eeckhout, above n 5, at 424–36; and Koutrakos, above n 24, at 416–52.

[125] Council Joint Action 2008/851/CFSP of 10 November 2008 on a European Union military operation to contribute to the deterrence, prevention and repression of acts of piracy and armed robbery off the Somali coast [2009] OJ L301/33. See also the contribution by P Cramér in this volume.

[126] Council Joint Action, above n 125, Art 2(b).

has put a special emphasis on regional integration through trade beyond Europe. Even though the promotion of regional integration is not explicitly mentioned as one of the guiding principles of the EU's external action, it seems to be implied in the promotion of its overall interests and values. With its image of, in the words of Söderbaum, '"world champion" of regional integration' and '"natural" point of reference for regional initiatives',[127] the EU aims at (partly) reproducing its own model in various other parts of the world.

Concluding FTAs serves here as a preliminary step towards such integration. Aware also of the risks of regionalism as a means of undermining the multilateral framework, the 2006 Global Europe Strategy stresses that such FTAs

> if approached with care, can build on WTO and other international rules by going further and faster in promoting openness and integration, by tackling issues which are not ready for multilateral discussion and by preparing the ground for the next level of multilateral liberalisation.[128]

This way, it also hints at the deadlock of the Doha Round and the need for alternative, ie non-multilateral, ways to move forward. Moreover, it underlines that

> Many key issues, including investment, public procurement, competition, other regulatory issues and IPR [intellectual property rights] enforcement, which remain outside the WTO at this time can be addressed through FTAs.[129]

Hence, FTAs are to 'serve as a stepping stone, not a stumbling block for multilateral liberalisation'.[130]

Taking the step from a mere FTA to regional integration is then made with a view to development. According to the 2005 European Consensus on Development, by

> [d]rawing on its own experiences, and exclusive competence in trade, the Community [now Union] has a comparative advantage in providing support to partner countries to integrate trade into national development strategies and to support regional cooperation whenever possible.[131]

Such regional cooperation is seen in the first place as a means to reduce trade barriers between developing countries, but also to make these countries ready for cooperation with the EU. With regard to this second aspect, the internal market re-enters the picture, as the Consensus stresses that for 'many countries, but especially those for which the EU is the largest trading and investment partner, approximation of the EU single market regulations is beneficial'.[132] 'Trade and

[127] F Söderbaum, 'African Regionalism and EU-African Interregionalism' in M Telò (ed), *European Union and New Regionalism: Regional Actors and Global Governance in a Post-Hegemonic Era*, 2nd edn (Aldershot, Ashgate, 2007), at 197.

[128] European Commission, above n 75, at 8.

[129] *Ibid.*

[130] *Ibid.*

[131] The European Consensus, above n 82, para 49.

[132] *Ibid*, para 74.

Regional Integration' was also designated one of the eight strategic partnerships between the EU and Africa in 2007.[133]

Putting this commitment to regionalism into practice, the Union, upon expiry of the Cotonou Agreement and the waivers covering it (see section III.B.), went on to subdivide the ACP group into eight regional groups. With each of these, the EU is aiming to conclude so-called Economic Partnership Agreements (EPAs). The objective, according to the Commission, is

> to establish new WTO-compatible trade arrangements … and to support ACP regional integration and foster the smooth and gradual integration of the ACP States into the world economy, particularly by helping create larger ACP regional markets, thereby contributing to sustainable development and poverty reduction.[134]

In short, the EPAs are advertised as 'trade and cooperation agreements at the service of development'.[135] Thus far, the EU has concluded an EPA with the CARIFORUM States (but not CARIFORUM itself),[136] and has put in place several other interim and so-called 'stepping-stone' agreements with individual countries while negotiations continue. However, in terms of the effectiveness of this effort to reproduce the EU's successful model elsewhere and bolster its partners' integration through trade, it is bewildering that the regional groups with which the EU is negotiating hardly match the regional arrangements already in place.[137] While this may be partly due to overlaps and competing arrangements in these regions, there is a danger that by 'the splitting of existing regional arrangements into different EPA negotiating groups' the EU might actually contribute towards undermining integration processes already underway.[138]

Apart from this historical and development-orientated track of inter-regionalism, the EU is also engaged in inter-regional cooperation with other parts of the world, usually with the goal of creating comprehensive inter-regional FTAs.[139] Of particular importance here is the envisaged EU–MERCOSUR FTA, which has been

[133] Council of the European Union, *The Africa-EU Strategic Partnership: A Joint Africa-EU Strategy*, Lisbon, 9 December 2007, 16344/07 (Presse 291), at 10–12.

[134] European Commission, *Economic Partnership Agreements*, COM(2007) 635 final, Brussels, 23 October 2007, at 2.

[135] Report from the Commission to the Council and the European Parliament, Annual Report 2009 on the European Community's Development and External Assistance Policies and their Implementation in 2008, SEC(2009) 831 final, Brussels, 30 June 2009, at 16.

[136] Economic Partnership Agreement between the CARIFORUM States, of the one part, and the European Community and its Member States, of the other part [2008] OJ L289/3. CARIFORUM is an umbrella organisation comprising the Caribbean Community (CARICOM, a single market with 15 Member States) and the Dominican Republic.

[137] In detail Bartels, above n 25, at 166–69.

[138] *Ibid*, at 167; see also Söderbaum, above n 127, at 199, stressing the asymmetric nature of these relationships (in Africa) and calling the EU's approach even 'soft imperialism'; also critical are P Draper and M Qobo, 'Multilateralizing regionalism: case study of African regionalism' in R Baldwin and P Low (eds), *Multilateralizing Regionalism: Challenges for the Global Trading System* (Cambridge, Cambridge University Press, 2009).

[139] See F Söderbaum and L van Langenhove, 'Introduction: The EU as a Global Actor and the Role of Interregionalism' (2009) 27 *Journal of European Integration* 249; and N Alecu de Flers and

negotiated for a decade now, and which would, when concluded, constitute the first inter-regional FTA (ie MERCOSUR itself would be a member).[140] Another example is an envisaged FTA between the EU and ASEAN that the Commission has been negotiating since April 2007.[141] With negotiations paused, however, the Union has begun to negotiate bilateral agreements with individual countries, which, according to Trade Commissioner De Gucht, are to serve as 'an important stepping-stone in the EU's engagement with the ASEAN region'.[142]

This adherence to regional integration does not, however, stop the Union from 'cracking open' other trade arrangements in a dispute settlement procedure where its own commercial interests are impaired, as can be seen in the *Brazilian Tyres* dispute. There, the EU succeeded with a WTO complaint against Brazil for imposing an import ban on retreaded tyres, *inter alia* based on health grounds. Given that the import ban did not apply to Brazil's fellow MERCOSUR members following a MERSOCUR dispute settlement procedure, the Appellate Body ruled that this constituted discriminatory treatment *vis-à-vis* non-MERCOSUR countries.[143] This can be contrasted with attempts by other WTO members to attack individual EU Member States, eg in the *Asbestos* dispute, which failed as it was always the Union as a whole that responded to complaints.[144]

In sum, regarding the CCP as a vehicle for foreign policy, it might be observed that the Union interacts in various ways through trade with the other parts of the world. In addition to merely ensuring compliance in respect of its own trade benefits, it has also created elaborate schemes and arrangements, and linked different policy areas, in order to promote its interests and values. However, the interest of

E Regelsberger, 'The EU and Inter-regional Cooperation' in C Hill and M Smith (eds), *International Relations and the European Union* (Oxford, Oxford University Press, 2005).

[140] MERCOSUR (Mercado Común del Sur) is a regional trade agreement with four Latin American member countries. The arrangement already in place is the Interregional Framework Cooperation Agreement between the European Community and its Member States, of the one part, and the Southern Common Market and its Party States, of the other part [1996] OJ L69/4. See also A Vasconcelos, 'European Union and MERCOSUR' in Telò (ed), above n 127. Negotiations on a trade agreement with the Andean countries, on the other hand, have thus far not envisaged the Andean Community of Nations as a party.

[141] In detail see A Petchsiri, 'ASEAN to AFTA: from peace and security zone to free trade area and beyond?' in A Ott and E Vos (eds), *Fifty Years of European Integration: Foundations and Perspectives* (The Hague, TMC Asser Press, 2009).

[142] European Commission, DG Trade, *EU to start bilateral trade negotiations with Singapore*, press release, available at <http://www.trade.ec.europa.eu/doclib/press/index.cfm?id=519&serie=320&langId=en>. A similar FTA is also being negotiated with the Gulf Cooperation Council countries.

[143] *Brazil—Measures Affecting Imports of Retreaded Tyres*, Appellate Body Report (adopted 17 December 2007) WT/DS332/AB/R, paras 226–39. Note also that on appeal '[t]he European Communities [now EU] further criticize[d] the Panel for not verifying whether MERCOSUR is a customs union that complies with the requirements of Article XXIV of the GATT 1994' (para 32).

[144] *EC—Measures Affecting Asbestos and Asbestos-Containing Products*, Appellate Body Report (adopted 5 April 2001) WT/DS135/AB/R. See also J Heliskoski, *Mixed Agreements as a Technique for Organizing the International Relations of the European Community and Its Member States* (The Hague, Kluwer Law International, 2001), at 178–93. Of course, MERCOSUR itself is not a WTO member against which a complaint could be launched.

the addressees in being thus shaped turns out to be rather limited, and is met with hostility by others who feel discriminated against. What is remarkable about the renewed emphasis on regionalism is the shift from advertising (inter-) regional FTAs as stepping-stones to truly multilateral free and fair trade, to promoting bilateral FTAs (ie EU with a single third country) as stepping-stones to regional or inter-regional FTAs (ie EU with several third countries from another region, or even another regional organisation). Consequently, while awaiting such true inter-regionalism (and further down the road, true multilateralism), the EU is engaged in rather asymmetrical relationships by negotiating with individual third countries. Later, after the conclusion of such bilateral FTAs, the added value to the EU in pursuing further the conclusion of regional FTAs is questionable, especially in terms of conditionality leverage. Moreover, offering FTAs to a wider range of countries also puts in question the 'special' nature of the relationship of the Union with its neighbourhood, since ultimately a 'stake in the internal market', in terms of deep integration going beyond trade in goods, can be offered regardless of geographic location.

IV. THE CCP AS CONTRIBUTOR TO CONSTITUTIONALISATION

Having discussed the ways in which trade influences the EU's own order, as well as the ways in which the EU influences other countries and regions through trade, we now turn to the relationship between the EU and the system as a whole. This concerns primarily the relationship between the EU and the WTO as the global institutional framework for trade. We shall look in turn at the role of the EU within the WTO, at the present relationship between these two legal orders and at how this relationship relates to the debate on the 'constitutionalisation' of the international system.

A. The EU and the Uruguay Round

Whereas, as we saw above, European economic integration itself can be seen 'as a child of the GATT',[145] the EU, alongside its Member States, served as one of the founding fathers of the WTO, providing considerable input for its establishment in 1995 at the conclusion of the Uruguay Round.[146] The EU's status as

[145] Cremona, above n 44, at 151–52.

[146] This despite various internal competence disputes and institutional turf wars: see P van den Bossche, 'The European Community and the Uruguay Round Agreements' in J Jackson and A Sykes (eds), *Implementing the Uruguay-Round* (Oxford, Clarendon Press, 1997); F Behrens, 'Uruguay-Runde und Gründung der WTO' in Hilf and Oeter (eds), above n 30; and M Beise, *Die Welthandelsorganisation (WTO): Funktion, Status, Organisation* (Baden-Baden, Nomos 2001), at 73–75.

an original member of the WTO is recognised in the Marrakech Agreement.[147] In terms of decision-making, it is specifically acknowledged that whenever 'the European Communities exercise their right to vote, they shall have a number of votes equal to the number of their member States'.[148] This is remarkable, given that the EU often experiences problems in joining international organisations and UN agencies due to their 'States only' membership, and thus is often allowed to participate only as an observer.[149] This is both a reflection of the existing GATT practice of the EU succeeding into the Member States' exercise of competence, as well as of the more flexible membership of the WTO which is open to any 'State or separate customs territory possessing full autonomy in the conduct of its external commercial relations'.[150] This also allows non-countries, such as Hong Kong and Macao, to be members. However, the EU did not embrace its new creation too closely, as the Council Decision for the conclusion of the Uruguay Round Agreements already stipulated in the Preamble that 'by its nature, the Agreement establishing the World Trade Organization, including the Annexes thereto, is not susceptible to being directly invoked in Community or Member State courts'.[151] The issue of (lack of) direct effect of WTO law would become a defining feature of the relationship between these two legal orders (see section IV.B.).

Given the changes introduced by the Lisbon Treaty, above all the absorption of the Community by the Union and the now exclusive Union competence for the entire CCP, not only the name had to be changed to 'European Union' as a WTO member, but also the parallel membership of the Member States appears increasingly superfluous given their lack of competence.[152] Thus far the EU remains the only supranational member and actor within the WTO.

As far as the setting-up of the WTO itself is concerned, it may be described as a watershed in the sophistication of international governance. First, the scope of international trade issues under its institutionalised umbrella expanded from

[147] Marrakech Agreement Establishing the WTO, Art XI(1), listing as the 'Original Membership' the 'contracting parties to GATT 1947 ... and the European Communities'.

[148] *Ibid*, Art IX(1).

[149] F Hoffmeister and PJ Kuijper, 'The Status of the European Union at the United Nations: Institutional Ambiguities and Political Realities' in J Wouters, F Hoffmeister and T Ruys (eds), *The United Nations and the European Union: An Ever Stronger Partnership* (The Hague, TMC Asser Press, 2006), 9–34; I Govaere, J Capiau and A Vermeersch, 'In-Between Seats: the Participation of the European Union in International Organizations' (2004) 9 *European Foreign Affairs Review* 155; also Eeckhout, above n 5, at 199–206.

[150] Marrakech Agreement Establishing the WTO, Art XII(1).

[151] Council Decision 94/800/EC of 22 December 1994 concerning the conclusion on behalf of the European Community, as regards matters within its competence, of the agreements reached in the Uruguay Round multilateral negotiations (1986–1994) [1994] OJ L336/1.

[152] The WTO Agreements have now become what Schermers dubbed 'false' mixed agreements; see HG Schermers, 'A Typology of Mixed Agreements' in D O'Keeffe and HG Schermers (eds), *Mixed Agreements* (Deventer, Kluwer Law and Taxation, 1983), at 27.

goods to services (GATS)[153] and intellectual property rights (TRIPS).[154] Secondly, the institutional structure was changed from an almost entirely member-driven negotiating forum to a more rule-based system. A Trade Policy Review Mechanism was established, periodically monitoring the WTO members' performance.[155]

Arguably the most important institutional change was the judicialisation of dispute settlement. According to former WTO Director General Ruggerio, this represents 'the heart of the WTO system'.[156] Under the old GATT, panel reports could easily be turned down because of the consensus required among the Contracting Parties for their adoption, and the enforcement mechanism was only rudimentary. Under the new Understanding on Rules and Procedures Governing the Settlement of Disputes (DSU),[157] on the contrary, reports by panels and the newly-established permanent Appellate Body are adopted within a strict timeframe and on the basis of so-called 'reverse consensus', ie unless there is consensus among the members gathered as the Dispute Settlement Body (DSB) not to adopt the reports, they shall be adopted.[158] In case of non-compliance with WTO obligations, the member whose measures have been deemed WTO-inconsistent can be ordered to pay compensation by the DSB, or the DSB can authorise suspension of concessions by the complaining member, which can also be cross-sector.[159]

This distinguishes the WTO dispute settlement mechanism from the procedures before the International Court of Justice, which requires the consent of all the parties to a dispute in order to have jurisdiction and which cannot rely on an organised enforcement mechanism.[160] But given that only WTO members, and not individuals, have access to WTO dispute settlement, its jurisdiction is more

[153] See eg P Eeckhout, 'Constitutional Concepts for Free Trade in Services' in de Búrca and Scott (eds), above n 19.

[154] For an extensive account of this agreement and its role in the EU legal order, see C Hermes, *TRIPS im Gemeinschaftsrecht: Zu den innergemeinschaftlichen Wirkungen von WTO-Übereinkünften* (Berlin, Duncker & Humblot, 2002). The WTO also covers several other multilateral and so-called plurilateral agreements (ie not binding all WTO members).

[155] Annex 3 to the Marrakech Agreement Establishing the WTO; see also M Gehring, 'Mechanismus zur Überprüfung der Handelspolitik (TPRM)' in Hilf and Oeter (eds), above n 30.

[156] Cited in M Hilf, 'Das Streitbeilegunssystem der WTO' in Hilf and Oeter (eds), above n 30, at 506; see also eg T Cottier, 'Dispute Settlement in the World Trade Organization: Characteristics and Structural Implications for the European Union' (1998) 35 *CML Rev* 325; J Jackson, 'The WTO dispute settlement system after ten years: the first decade's promises and challenges' in Y Tanigushi, A Yanovich and J Bohanes (eds), *The WTO in the Twenty-first Century: Dispute Settlement Negotiations, and Regionalism in Asia* (Cambridge, Cambridge University Press, 2007); and EU Petersmann, 'WTO dispute settlement practice 1995–2005: Lessons from the past and future challenges' in Tanigushi *et al* (eds), *ibid*.

[157] Annex 2 to the Marrakech Agreement Establishing the WTO.

[158] Arts 16(4) and 17(4) DSU; see P van den Bossche, 'From afterthought to centrepiece: the WTO Appellate Body and its rise to prominence in the world trading system' in G Sacerdotti, A Yanovich, J Bohanes (eds), *The WTO at Ten: The Contribution of the Dispute Settlement System* (Cambridge, Cambridge University Press, 2006).

[159] Art 22 DSU.

[160] Statute of the International Court of Justice, Art 36, and UN Charter, Art 94.

limited than that of of the ECJ[161] or the European Court of Human Rights.[162] Private parties are allowed to submit *amicus curiae* briefs only in certain circumstances, as the Appellate Body decided in *Asbestos*.[163] This was widely seen by the WTO members as an act exceeding the Appellate Body's competence, and initially did not receive support from the EU.[164]

Thus far, the EU itself has made ample use of the WTO's dispute settlement mechanism. It has acted as complainant in 81 cases and was respondent in 67 cases, making it the second most active member after the US with 94 cases as complainant, and 109 as respondent. The EU and US have faced each other in 50 disputes.[165] Even though the EU has suffered suspension of concessions itself (for instance in the course of the *Bananas* disputes, see section III.B.), it has also achieved some remarkable successes through dispute settlement. One prominent example would be the withdrawal of steel tariffs by the US in late 2003.[166]

B. WTO Law Obligations and the Union Legal Order

With the EU having contributed to the establishment of the WTO, with as its hallmark the judicialisation of the system, we now turn to the effects of this on the Union legal order. Generally, just as under Nice, also under Lisbon, '[a]greements concluded by the Union are binding upon the institutions of the Union and on its Member States'.[167] As to their place in the hierarchy of norms, the ECJ established that international agreements are superior to national law and secondary Union law.[168] The agreements in the WTO framework are no exception in these respects.

However, the ECJ has always accorded a special place to the WTO agreements in terms of enforceability. For the pre-WTO GATT, the Court pointed to its

161 Art 263(4) TFEU (ex Art 230 TEC).

162 European Convention on Human Rights, Art 34. This would of course presuppose that WTO law is intended to confer individual rights, which is a contentious issue related to the wider question of 'constitutionalisation' (see section IV.C.).

163 *European Communities—Measures Affecting Asbestos and Asbestos-Containing Products*, Communication from the Appellate Body of 8 November 2000, WT/DS135/9.

164 Nicolaïdis and Howse, above n 37, at 786; and J Wouters and B De Meester, *The World Trade Organization: A Legal and Institutional Analysis* (Antwerp, Intersentia, 2007), at 251–53.

165 WTO, *Disputes by country*, available at <http://www.wto.org/english/tratop_e/dispu_e/dispu_by_country_e.htm>. On transatlantic trade disputes in detail, see E-U Petersmann, 'Prevention and Settlement of Transatlantic Economic Disputes: Legal Strategies for EU/US Leadership' in EU Petersmann and MA Pollack (eds), *Transatlantic Economic Disputes: The EU, the US and the WTO* (Oxford, Oxford University Press, 2003).

166 *United States—Definitive Safeguard Measures on Imports of Certain Steel Products (EC)*, Appellate Body Report (adopted 10 December 2003) WT/DS248/AB/R.

167 Art 216(2) TFEU (ex Art 300(7) TEC).

168 Case C-61/94 *Commission v Germany* [1996] ECR I-03989.

> settled law that GATT, which according to its preamble is based on the principle of negotiations undertaken on the basis of 'reciprocal and mutually advantageous arrangements', is characterised by the great flexibility of its provisions, in particular those conferring the possibility of derogation, the measures to be taken when confronted with exceptional difficulties and the settlement of conflicts between the contracting parties.[169]

This in turn prevented both individuals and Member States from relying on GATT in order to have acts of the Union reviewed,[170] or directly applying GATT rules in the domestic legal systems of the Member States.[171] The Court carved out two exceptions to this rule: first, as established in *Fediol*, for legislation through which the Union intended to implement a particular obligation under GATT;[172] and, secondly, as established in *Nakajima*, where Union legislation specifically refers to GATT provisions (so far only the case for anti-dumping).[173]

The advent of the WTO did not substantially change that position for the Court. Even though it acknowledged that the new

> WTO agreements ... differ significantly from the provisions of GATT 1947, in particular by reason of the strengthening of the system of safeguards and the mechanism for resolving disputes, the system resulting from those agreements nevertheless accords considerable importance to negotiation between the parties.[174]

Hence, given that the DSU provided for interim alternative measures to immediate compliance in the form of compensation payments,[175] the Court reasoned that granting direct effect to WTO law would limit the Union's negotiating capacity.[176] The Court referred, in addition, to a lack of reciprocity should direct effect be accorded, given that other WTO members, including the EU's 'most important commercial partners', did not make WTO rules directly applicable in their domestic legal systems either.[177]

[169] Case C-280/93 *Germany v Council* [1994] ECR I-04973, para 106; Joined Cases 21 to 24-72 *International Fruit* [1972] ECR-01219; see also M Bronckers and PJ Kuijper, 'WTO Law in the European Court of Justice' (2005) 42 *CML Rev* 1313.

[170] Case C-280/93 *Germany v Council* [1994] ECR I-04973, para 109.

[171] *Ibid*, para 110; also Case C-377/02 *Van Parys v Belgisch Interventie- en Restitutiebureau* [2005] ECR I-01465.

[172] Case 70/87 *Fediol v Commission* [1989] ECR 1781. This case concerned the predecessor to the current Trade Barriers Regulation.

[173] Case C-69/89 *Nakajima v Council* [1991] ECR I-2069. These appear to be the only two exceptions recognised by the Court, see Case C-377/02 *Van Parys v Belgisch Interventie- en Restitutiebureau* [2005] ECR I-01465, paras 39–40.

[174] Case 149/96 *Portugal v Council* [1999] ECR I-8395, para 36.

[175] Art 22(1) DSU. Note also that the 'preferred' mode of settlement of the DSU is the parties reaching a mutually agreed solution, 'consistent with the covered agreements' (Art 3(7) DSU).

[176] Case 149/96 *Portugal v Council* [1999] ECR I-8395, paras 37–42.

[177] *Ibid*, para 43.

This reasoning has attracted severe criticism as being politically motivated.[178] As Advocate General Colomer put it in his Opinion in the *Merck* case, 'the Court of Justice has transformed the implementation in the Community of the *ius gentium*, and of the WTO agreements, into a means of evading its obligations.'[179] His reference also to international law more generally is quite appropriate, given that in a string of recent judgments, it appears that the former exception of the non-enforceability of WTO agreements is becoming the rule for international law in general, extending, for instance, to the United Nations Convention on the Law of the Sea (*Intertanko*)[180] as well as, albeit under somewhat different circumstances, the United Nations Charter (*Kadi and Al Barakaat*).[181] Moreover, in the *FIAMM & Fedon* case, the Court denied non-contractual liability of the Union in cases where individuals had suffered damages from suspensions of concessions authorised by the DSB following non-compliance with WTO obligations by the Union.[182]

However, short of granting direct effect, the ECJ has developed the concept of harmonious interpretation with WTO law. In *Schieving Nijstad*[183] and *Dior*,[184] the Court gave detailed guidance to national courts on how to conduct national procedures in conformity with the TRIPS agreement.[185] Also, according to Bronckers, the Court may be tacitly pushing for compliance with WTO obligations through what he calls a 'muted dialogue' between the Court and the Appellate Body.[186] He

[178] See eg E-U Petersmann, 'Darf die EG das Völkerrecht ignorieren?' (1997) 8 *Europäische Zeitschrift für Wirtschaftsrecht* 325; see generally on this extensively covered area P Craig and G de Búrca, *EU Law: Text, Cases and Materials*, 4th edn (Oxford, Oxford University Press, 2008), at 206–13; Cebada Romero, above n 18, at 436–90; and M Herdegen, *Europarecht*, 6th edn (Munich, CH Beck, 2004), at 389–96.

[179] Case C-431/05 *Merck*, Opinion of AG Ruiz-Jarabo Colomer, delivered on 23 January 2007, [2007] ECR I-07001, para 78; referring to P Pescatore, 'Free World Trade and the European Union' in A Pérez van Kappel and W Heusel (eds), *Free World Trade and the European Union—The reconciliation of Interest and the Review of the Understanding on Dispute Settlement in the Framework of the World Trade Organisation* (Cologne, Bundesanzeiger, 2000), at 12.

[180] Case C-308/06 *Intertanko* [2008] ECR I-04057.

[181] Joined Cases C-402/05 P and C-415/05 P *Kadi and Al Barakaat* [2008] ECR I-06351. Of course, the EU is not a member of the UN, and the ECJ did indeed stress the special importance of the UN Charter (paras 293–98) and showed awareness of the specificities of the UN sanctions regime in its decision (paras 361–65); for discussion, see G de Búrca, 'The European Courts and the Security Council: Between Dédoublement Fonctionnel and Balancing of Values: Three Replies to Pasquale De Sena and Maria Chiara Vitucci' (2009) 20 *European Journal of International Law* 853; and G de Búrca, 'The ECJ and the International Legal Order after Kadi' (2010) 51 *Harvard International Law Journal* 1. See also the contribution by Tridimas in this volume.

[182] Joined Cases C-120/06 P and C-121/06 P *FIAMM & Fedon* [2008] ECR I-06513. The non-compliance concerned, once again, the EU–ACP preferential scheme on bananas.

[183] Case C-89/99 *Schieving Nijstad* [2001] ECR I-5851.

[184] Joined Cases C-300/98 and C-392/98 *Parfums Christian Dior* [2000] ECR I-11307.

[185] See also Kuijper, above n 24, at 270–71.

[186] M Bronckers, 'From "Direct Effect" to "Muted Dialogue"' (2008) 11 *Journal of International Economic Law* 885.

observes that the ECJ in the *Ikea*[187] and *FTS International*[188] cases found measures to be inconsistent with Union law due to use of the zeroing methodology in calculating dumping margins, but without referring to prior findings of the WTO Appellate Body establishing a similar inconsistency in terms of WTO law. Taking into account that in *Kadi and Al-Barakaat* too, the Court managed to avoid (for the time being) putting both the EU and the Member States in a state of non-compliance with UN Security Council resolutions by temporarily extending the application of the annulled measures,[189] this can be seen as part of a more general pattern. These rather subtle ways of compliance with international obligations might ultimately refute Colomer's claim that the Court is actively trying to evade the EU's international obligations or, as de Búrca argues, 'has adopted a largely instrumentalist and self-serving approach'[190] not so 'different from the US in its hard-headed, pick-and-choose attitude to international obligations.'[191] Picking up on the zeroing example, compliance by the US is still wanting, despite numerous Appellate Body rulings and compliance proceedings.[192]

C. The EU, the WTO and the Multiplicity of 'Constitutional' Claims

Having looked at how the EU constituted the WTO, and how the two legal orders relate to each other, we can now turn to the question of the actual 'constitutionalisation' of the WTO and the role of the EU therein. This has been a hotly debated topic during recent years, but for both those opposed and those in favour, the EU has served as a point of reference or benchmark in discussing the degree

[187] Case C-351/04 *Ikea v Commissioners of Customs & Excise* [2007] ECR I-7723; the corresponding Appellate Body report is *European Communities—Anti-Dumping Duties on Imports of Cotton-Type Bed Linen from India*, Appellate Body Report (adopted 12 March 2001) WT/DS141/AB/R.

[188] Case C-310/06 *FTS International v Belastingdienst—Douane West* [2007] ECR I-6749; the corresponding Appellate Body report is *European Communities—Customs Classification of Frozen Boneless Chicken Cuts*, Appellate Body Report (adopted 27 September 2005) WT/DS269/AB/R, WT/DS286/AB/R.

[189] Joined Cases C-402/05 P and C-415/05 P *Kadi and Al Barakaat* [2008] ECR I-06351, paras 373–76; see J Larik, 'Two Ships in the Night or in the Same Boat Together: Why the European Court of Justice Made the Right Choice in the Kadi Case', *College of Europe EU Diplomacy Paper 3/2009*, June 2009, at 18–20.

[190] de Búrca, 'The European Courts and the Security Council', above n 181, at 853.

[191] *Ibid*, at 854; generally on the EU's compliance with WTO law, see A Tancredi, 'EC Practice in the WTO: How Wide is the "Scope for Manoeuvre"?' (2004) 15 *European Journal of International Law* 933.

[192] Eg *United States—Measures Relating to Zeroing and Sunset Reviews*, Appellate Body Report (adopted 23 January 2007) WT/DS322/AB/R; *United States—Laws, Regulations and Methodology for Calculating Dumping Margins (zeroing)*, Appellate Body Report (adopted 9 May 2006) WT/DS294/AB/R; see for the relevant US case at the United States Court of Appeal for the Federal Circuit, *Corus Staal BV v Dep't of Commerce*, 395 F.3d 1343 (Fed Cir 2005); for discussion see J Greenwald, 'After Corus Staal—Is There Any Role, and Should There Be—For WTO Jurisprudence in the Review of US Trade Measures by US Courts?' (2007) 39 *Georgetown Journal of International Law* 199. In late January 2010, the EU requested the DSB to authorise suspension of concessions.

of the WTO's 'constitutionalisation' or its desirability.[193] Instead of reopening this debate, this section aims at putting the EU–WTO dichotomy in the wider context of multiple 'constitutional' claims in today's multilevel and multisector governance.

As appropriately summarised by Oeter, the 'constitutionalisation' of international law means the transformation of that legal order into a '*Wertordnung*' (normative order) based on common principles and a shared understanding of public goods ultimately detached from the *ad hoc* consensus of States.[194] In the WTO context, the process towards 'constitutionalisation' would then be captured by the shift from a 'member-driven' to a 'rule-based system'. Such a detachment from (short-term) State interests is primarily carried by the WTO's dispute settlement mechanism and its quasi-compulsory jurisdiction, while democratic legitimacy as well as regulatory powers are deficient due to the continuing paramount importance of the States' executive branches as trade negotiators,[195] ie the organisation has remained 'member-driven' to a large extent. As only States can be the parties in WTO dispute settlement procedures, so the effectiveness of its capacity to protect individual rights (at least for those considering such rights part of the *Wertordnung*)[196] is also limited.

Notwithstanding individual rights and democratic legitimacy, it is also important to consider the expansion of the WTO's agenda to development and the environment. Such an expanded agenda is indeed called for, given that otherwise the 'constitutionalisation' of WTO law would go hand in hand with the 'fragmentation' of international law.[197] This is to recall that just as trade policy is linked in its operation to various other policy areas, different legal orders (or sub-orders) are also linked. Hence, we are today faced with several competing 'constitutional' claims from entities beyond the State. This refers, next to the EU of course, also to the United Nations and the European Convention on Human Rights (ECHR). Without being ignorant of one another, but also not showing unlimited

[193] See Nicolaïdis and Howse, above n 37; and references under n 27.

[194] S Oeter, 'Welthandelsordnung im Spannungsfeld von Wirtschaft, Recht und Politik' in Hilf and Oeter (eds), above n 30, at 17–18; for an in-depth discussion of the concepts of 'constitution' and 'constitutionalism', see A Stone Sweet, 'Constitutionalism, Legal Pluralism, and International Regimes' (2009) 16 *Indiana Journal of Global Legal Studies* 621, at 623–31.

[195] Oeter, above n 194, at 16–19.

[196] E-U Petersmann, 'Time for a United Nations "Global Compact" for Integrating Human Rights into the Law of Worldwide Organizations: Lessons from European Integration' (2002) 13 *European Journal of International Law* 621; S Peers, 'Fundamental Rights or Political Whim? WTO Law and the European Court of Justice' in de Búrca and Scott (eds), above n 19; for a critique, see P Alston, 'Resisting the Merger and Acquisition of Human Rights by Trade Law: A Reply to Petersmann' (2002) 13 *European Journal of International Law* 815; for an overview, see S Hörmann, 'WTO und Menschenrechte' in Hilf and Oeter (eds), above n 30.

[197] See *Fragmentation of International Law: Difficulties Arising From the Diversification and Expansion of International Law*, Report of the Study Group of the International Law Commission Finalized by Martti Koskenniemi, A/CN.4/L.682, 13 April 2006. In the report, the EU, the WTO and human rights regimes had received particular attention as possible 'self-contained regimes'.

deference, a complicated interplay between these orders, as well as with the established national constitutional orders, unfolds.

For the UN, despite the wealth of academic literature proclaiming the UN Charter as a world constitution,[198] it is evident that unlike the three other cases there is no compulsory judicial review, not even for States or for the UN's own institutions.[199] In relation to the WTO, a clear rule of conflict is set out in Article XXI(c) GATT on 'security exceptions', allowing a WTO member 'any action in pursuance of its obligations under the United Nations Charter for the maintenance of international peace and security'. This indicates that WTO law obligations (and arguably any implied human rights obligations in WTO law) could not be used as justification for failure to comply with UN Charter obligations.

For the EU, things are quite different, setting it far apart from the WTO. First, the 'constitutional' character of the Union legal order is not just something discussed academically, even though there it has been with great rigour.[200] The 'constitutional' quality of EU primary law and its general principles (including fundamental rights) has been proclaimed by the ECJ itself, in a process starting from recognising the EU as 'a new legal order of international law',[201] to a 'community based on the rule of law' with the Treaties as its 'constitutional charter'.[202] Given the hierarchy within EU law (see section IV.B.), the Court made it clear in *Kadi and Al-Barakaat* that

> the obligations imposed by an international agreement cannot have the effect of prejudicing the constitutional principles of the EC Treaty, which include the principle that all Community acts must respect fundamental rights, that respect constituting a condition of their lawfulness which it is for the Court to review in the framework of the complete system of legal remedies established by the Treaty.[203]

[198] See eg B Fassbender, 'Rediscovering a Forgotten Constitution: Notes on the Place of the UN Charter in the International Legal Order' in J Dunhoff and J Trachtman (eds), *Ruling the World? Constitutionalism, International Law, and Global Governance* (Cambridge, Cambridge University Press, 2009); S Kadelbach and T Kleinlein, 'Überstaatliches Verfassungsrecht: Zur Konstiutionalisierung im Völkerrecht' (2006) 44 *Archiv des Völkerrechts* 236; T Franck, 'Is the UN Charter a Constitution?' in Jochen Frowein *et al* (eds), *Verhandeln für den Frieden/Negotiating for Peace: Liber Amicorum Tono Eitel* (Berlin, Springer, 2003); and P-M Dupuy, 'The Constitutional Dimension of the Charter of the United Nations Revisited' (1997) 1 *Max Planck Yearbook of United Nations Law* 1.

[199] For the relevant ICJ case, see *Questions of Interpretation and Application of the 1971 Montreal Convention arising from the Aerial Incident at Lockerbie (Libyan Arab Jamahiriya v United States of America)*, Request for the indication of Provisional Measures, Order of 14 April 1992, [1992] *ICJ Rep* 114, paras 43–45; see also K Roberts, 'Second-Guessing the Security Council: The International Court of Justice and Its Powers of Judicial Review' (1995) 7 *Pace International Law Review* 281.

[200] See eg N Walker, 'Reframing EU Constitutionalism' in J Dunhoff and J Trachtman (eds), *Ruling the World? Constitutionalism, International Law, and Global Governance* (Cambridge, Cambridge University Press, 2009); JHH Weiler, *The Constitution of Europe: Do the New Clothes Have an Emperor? and Other Essays on European Integration* (Cambridge, Cambridge University Press, 1999); M Poiares Maduro, *We the Court: The European Court of Justice and the European Economic Constitution: A Critical Reading of Article 30 of the EC Treaty* (Oxford, Hart Publishing, 1998).

[201] Case 26/62 *Van Gend en Loos* [1962] ECR (English special edition) 00001, para 9.

[202] Case 294/83 *Les Verts* [1986] ECR 01339, para 23.

[203] Joined Cases C-402/05 P and C-415/05 P *Kadi and Al Barakaat* [2008] ECR I-06351, para 285.

Obligations under the UN Charter were no exception for the ECJ. This is now also more clearly reflected after Lisbon, where provisions have been added ensuring that 'necessary provisions on legal safeguards'[204] are to be included in economic sanctions, against both States and natural or legal persons. One should not forget, however, that such a bold stance *vis-à-vis* the outside world and in favour of fundamental rights is also required due to 'constitutional' pressure 'from below', ie from national constitutional courts that accept EU law's supremacy (and therefore 'constitutionality') only as long as it guarantees these rights to a degree equivalent to the national constitution.[205] The most recent expression of this pressure can be seen in the German Constitutional Court's *Lisbon* judgment, stressing that the EU could not be qualified as a 'real', ie nation-state-like constitutional order due to its democratic deficit.[206]

Somewhat paradoxically, however, the EU Treaties explicitly acknowledge the special role of the UN but are silent on the WTO. As stipulated in Article 3(5) TEU, the Union's external action is committed to, *inter alia*, 'free and fair trade' and 'the strict observance and the development of international law, including respect for the principles of the United Nations Charter'. It should be recalled that the EU is a founding member of the WTO with exclusive competence in its matters, and not a member of the UN and with only limited competence in international security matters. Why not say, then, 'free and fair trade in accordance with the principles of the WTO'?[207] It must be assumed that the WTO is just another international organisation for the EU and the obligations under WTO just part of general international law.

Similarly, the European Court of Human Rights has defined the ECHR as a 'constitutional instrument of European public order'.[208] In the *Bosphorus* case, it pointed to the limits of deference to the European Union. In cases where the protection of the rights enshrined by the Convention was 'manifestly deficient', 'the interest of international cooperation would be outweighed by the Convention's role as a "constitutional instrument of European public order" in the field of human rights'.[209] In more recent cases, however, it showed a wide notion of deference to the United Nations.[210]

[204] Art 215(3) TFEU.

[205] *Bundesverfassungsgericht* (German Constitutional Court), 2 BvR 197/83 vom 22.10.1986, BVerfGE 73, 339 ff.

[206] *Bundesverfassungsgericht* (German Constitutional Court), 2 BvE 2/08 vom 30.6.2009, BVerfGE 123, 267 ff.

[207] The same is true for Art 21(1) TEU on the general provisions of the Union's external action, which also includes a special reference to 'respect for the principles of the United Nations Charter and international law' and mandates the Union to 'promote multilateral solutions to common problems, in particular in the framework of the United Nations'. Note, however, that the 1957 Treaty of Rome contained a reference to the GATT in Art 229, which was later omitted by the Amsterdam Treaty.

[208] *Loizidou v Turkey* (preliminary objections), Series A no 310 (1995) 20 EHRR 99, para 75.

[209] *Bosphorus v Ireland* (2005-VI) 42 EHRR 1, para 156.

[210] *Behrami and Behrami v France* and *Saramati v France, Germany and Norway* (decision) (2007) 45 EHRR SE10.

What does this mean for the WTO? Trying to fit these different and closely-linked orders into a hierarchical relationship (akin to one found in national constitutional orders) seems impossible. Rather we are faced with what Klabbers calls 'Escherian images', ie legal relationships intertwined like a convoluted web of staircases, where you never know whether you will end up on top or at the bottom.[211] But this need not be a reason to despair. Arguably, one does not need constitutional hierarchy (or 'top down' or 'hard constitutionalism') in order to have a constitution. Again, the EU serves as a case in point, with its successful structure of 'constitutional pluralism'[212] which, if extended to the international sphere, would coincide with the calls for a 'soft' notion of constitutionalism.[213] Nonetheless, the European experience also shows the limits of any attempt at 'partial constitutionalisation', ie economic integration without any political integration or human rights guarantees, or for having a consolidated internal market without an effective common commercial policy, an environmental policy, a development policy, etc. This also reminds us of the legal importance of coherence between different policy areas, as lack of such puts the 'constitutional' quality of the whole in question. The Lisbon Treaty, with its manifold references to coherence, confirms this.[214] Therefore, just like the EU and its Member States, the WTO is also to be put, to use the words of the newly-appointed President of the German Constitutional Court, Voßkuhle, into a global '*Ergänzungsverhältnis*'[215] (a relationship of complementarity) with the other established and aspiring sources of 'constitutional' authority that affect its widening area of operation. In view of the recent case law (see section IV.B.), it appears that the ECJ in fact displays efforts to avoid discord between the EU and WTO legal orders, and therefore actively contributes to such a relationship of complementarity.

In sum, in terms of the CCP as a contributor to the constitutionalisation of the international trading order, we could behold the emergence of the EU as an important international actor, from being founded in the shadow of the GATT to becoming a founding member of the WTO. Ever since, the EU has been an active participant on that stage, and the WTO arguably remains the place where the EU appears most like a unitary, State-like actor. It is thus first and foremost the EU that it 'constitutionalised' further through its WTO membership (which could be called 'reverse constitutionalisation'). This 'actorness' and its legal autonomy

[211] J Klabbers, *Treaty Conflict and the European Union* (Cambridge, Cambridge University Press, 2009), at 173, used in the context of ECJ case law on the UN and the ECHR.

[212] See Stone Sweet, above n 194, at 631–39; M Poiares Maduro, 'Contrapunctual Law: Europe's Constitutional Pluralism in Action' in N Walker (ed), *Sovereignty in Transition* (Oxford, Hart Publishing, 2003); and N Walker, 'The Idea of Constitutional Pluralism' (2002) 65 *Modern Law Review* 317.

[213] de Búrca, 'The European Court of Justice and the International Legal Order after Kadi', above n 181, at 39–40.

[214] Art 13(1) TEU; Art 16(6), 2nd indent TEU; Art 18(4) TEU; Art 21(3), 2nd indent TEU; Art 26(2) TEU; Art 7 TFEU; Art 334 TFEU.

[215] Cited in M Reissenberger, 'Ein unabhängiger Denker mit europäischer Vision', *Tagesschau*, available at <http://www.tagesschau.de/inland/vosskuhle100.html>.

also define the way in which it contributes to the 'constitutionalisation' of the WTO. Despite the achievement of establishing a quasi-judicial dispute settlement mechanism with compulsory jurisdiction, the WTO remains to a large extent 'member-driven'. As a result, the EU's courts continue to deny direct effect to WTO law in order to guarantee its trade negotiators the necessary leeway, at times as the expense of prompt compliance with WTO rules as interpreted by the Appellate Body. However, in other instances, the ECJ has shown more subtle ways of ensuring compliance with WTO law at least indicating a relationship of complementarity between the two legal orders and their judicial bodies. In order to develop this relationship further, especially in view of the wider context of the process of 'constitutionalisation', ie in both a vertical (multilevel) and a horizontal (sectoral: trade, security, human rights, environment, etc) way, the EU's internal model of 'constitutional pluralism' and emphasis on coherence continue to serve as a model.

V. CONCLUSION

Following this discussion of the trade policy of the EU as an expression of the interconnections between different policies as well as legal orders, the following three basic tenets emerge: First, where there is a common market, there needs to be a common trade policy. Secondly, where there is a common trade policy, foreign policy is right around the corner. Thirdly, the more complicated and intertwined international trade and the connected foreign policy questions become, the greater the need for a framework in which a fair balance between the different goals pursued can be struck and that consequently lends legitimacy to the decision-making process, ie greater need for institutions based on a *Wertordnung* or, put in legal terms, a 'constitution'.

We could see that the internal market was from the start—and it still is—being shaped by the rules of international trade. Moreover, maintaining an internal market cannot be kept separate from other policy areas, and in many areas the EU has gradually accommodated international requirements, both by changing certain policies and by interpreting its own law in greater harmony with WTO law. But the external trade policy proper cannot be viewed in isolation, as trade also serves as a vehicle for development, which needs to be widely defined in order to be sustainable. That means it needs to respect human rights, good governance as well as environmental norms. In order to attain all these different aims, the EU has put an emphasis on reproducing not only specific norms, but also its entire model of regional integration in other parts of the world. To what degree this will be successful and to what degree this indeed serves as a 'stepping-stone' to multilateralism is still an open question. The 'stepping-stone' metaphor also relates to the 'constitutionalisation' debate, and the argument to what extent the EU can or should be reproduced on a global scale. It is argued here that such a reproduction cannot be properly conceptualised by sticking to the EU–WTO dichotomy.

Just as the 'constitutionalisation' of the EU cannot be imagined without the ECHR and constitutional traditions of the Member States in mind, so any constitutional claims of the WTO have to be viewed in the wider context. In other words, the WTO system can surely be viewed as an incipient global 'economic constitution', but which would by itself also remain only a partial constitution. In order to capture a more complete picture of an emerging global constitutional order, other constitutional claims have to be taken into account too. The notion of 'constitutional pluralism' allows for such a broadened understanding, making it possible to complete the picture without having to water down or abandon concurrent claims of constitutionality.

In any event, the EU also shows that one need not wait for a 'constitutional moment' to occur in order to discuss the WTO in constitutional terms. Looking to the future, optimism in that respect can be drawn from the fact that both the EU and WTO share strong institutional resilience. The GATT came about and functioned despite the more ambitious International Trade Organisation never seeing the light. European integration proceeded despite failures such as the European Political and Defences Communities. To this one would now have to add the failure of the EU's Constitutional Treaty. This observation is particularly important in terms of 'constitutionalisation', as it shows that one does not need a document called a 'constitution' in order to find oneself in a 'constitutional' system. It is the area of trade in particular that underlines this insight. Instead of ceremonial 'constitutional moments', the background of many 'constitutionalising' moments was much more humble, and related to trade. Just as the direct effect of EU law came forth in a case concerning duties for the importation of urea-formaldehyde by the *Van Gend & Loos* company, the Boston Tea Party was an act of resistance against taxes on tea imposed by the British Government. Therefore, to roughly paraphrase Bismarck in a 21st-century way,[216] the great questions of the constitution of international trade will not be decided through speeches and lofty 'constitutional moments' but will continue to be decided by such seemingly mundane things as bananas, potatoes, steel plates and shrimps.

[216] The original quote was rather bellicose: 'Nicht durch Reden oder Majoritätsbeschlüsse werden die großen Fragen der Zeit entschieden …, sondern durch Eisen und Blut' ('Not through speeches and majority decisions will the great questions of our times be decided ... but through iron and blood', tr by author) Cited in W Schüßler, 'Otto von Bismarck, Reden, 1847–1869' in H von Petersdorff (ed), *Bismarck: Die gesammelten Werke, Band 10* (Berlin, Otto Stolberg, 1924), at 139–40.

2

Capital Market Openness After Financial Turmoil[*]

EILIS FERRAN

I. INTRODUCTION

REALIST SCHOLARS OF political science contend that global regulation reflects the preferences of the dominant sovereign powers.[1] The history of international financial market regulation for most of the second half of the 20th century provides compelling evidence to support this viewpoint. The post-World War II global financial system differed from other areas of international activity in the extent to which it was dominated by one country, the United States. This made it possible to understand the mechanisms of harmonisation in the international capital markets as a system that had regulatory innovation by the dominant financial centre, the United States, at its heart.[2]

Toward the end of the 20th century, however, there were signs that the European Union was mounting an increasingly serious challenge to the US's position as global economic powerhouse, and that this realignment of financial might was having spill-over effects in the regulatory sphere. The intensive period of regulatory reform that was triggered by the Financial Services Action Plan (1999) included within its goals the aim of

> The EU ... [assuming] a key role in ensuring that its voice is clearly heard in international financial regulatory fora to ensure that sound and coherent regulations are promulgated that guarantee level-playing fields.[3]

[*] In working on this chapter I have benefitted from opportunities to present early versions at the Bristol EC-International Law Forum (March 2009) and to the LLM Corporate Finance Class at University London (March 2009). I am also grateful for comments from Professor Niamh Moloney (LSE). This chapter takes account of events up to September 2009, but it has been possible to mention a few later developments briefly.

[1] DW Drezner, 'The Realist Tradition in American Public Opinion' (2008) 6 *Perspectives on Politics* 51.

[2] B Simmons, 'The International Politics of Harmonization: the Case of Capital Market Regulation' (2001) 55 *International Organization* 589–620.

[3] COM(1999)232, p 13.

In pursuit of this goal, numerous strategies were employed, including vocal promotion of the suitability of European regulatory innovations as models for the rest of the world ('leading by example'); support for the work of international standard-setters, thereby demonstrating a commitment to multilateralism, but also leaving no one in any doubt that the 'price' of such support was an expectation that the European viewpoint would carry increasing weight in international-level deliberations; and bilateral alignments with other leading economic powers (especially the United States) aimed not only at removing regulatory frictions and tackling common problems in their respective jurisdictions, but also at propelling voluntary regulatory adaptation by other countries to the preferences of the dominant powers.

In the immediate aftermath of the turmoil in the financial markets between 2007 and 2009, it is possible to see a new economic order emerging, with China moving to the centre and the other rapidly developing economies (especially Brazil and India) becoming increasingly powerful. The serious challenge that China and others are posing to Euro-American dominance of the world economic system is likely, over time, to influence the shape of international financial regulation.[4] Already the membership of international standard-setting and oversight bodies is being expanded to bring more countries on board.[5] However, for now at least, the EU remains a key economic player[6] and its institutions remain committed to using that power within a global setting both to complement the work of international bodies and in order to promote the EU's regulatory framework.[7]

This chapter aims to take stock of the EU's relations with the rest of the world at this critical point in the development of financial regulation, focusing in particular on capital market regulation. In section II. it provides a brief overview of the strengthening of the EU's voice in key areas of capital market regulation in the period immediately before the financial crisis. Section III. considers the impact of the financial crisis. It makes the point that after a brief hiatus while the crisis was at its height, policy analysis in the area of capital market regulation returned to the idea that openness of markets through alleviating complexities, costs and burdens imposed by different national rules was an objective that needed to be pursued vigorously. Sections IV. and V. look at regulatory strategies for opening up capital markets and the mechanisms for putting

[4] This has been acknowledged by the European Commission, *Financial Integration Report 2009* (SEC(2009) 1702), §§ 5.4–5.6.

[5] Eg, the Financial Stability Board, which broadened its membership in March 2009 by adding Argentina, Brazil, China, India, Indonesia, Korea, Mexico, Russia, Saudi Arabia, South Africa, Turkey, Spain and the European Commission.

[6] On a number of measures (bank assets, insurance premiums, debt securities) the EU made the biggest contribution to world economic activity during 2008–09 and was second only to the US on another (stock market capitalisation) (the US had the same share of debt securities as the EU): European Commission, above n 4, chart 5.1.

[7] *Ibid*, § 5.4.

those strategies into effect. Section VI. examines in some detail the development of global accounting standards. This is an area that merits close study because it is a field in which the development of a truly international detailed regulatory framework is particularly mature and which therefore provides an especially good illustration of the way in which the EU both interacts with an international standard-setter (the International Accounting Standards Board or IASB) and also engages bilaterally with the US in order to promote international regulatory convergence. It also usefully demonstrates the complexity of these processes and the tensions that can arise when the EU's own interests are imperfectly aligned with those of other key players. Section VII. considers international mutual recognition, an area in which the EU might be expected to lead the way and which it is continuing to promote, notwithstanding a loss of momentum caused, in part, by a reorientation of policy priorities engendered by the financial turmoil. Section VIII. concludes the chapter.

II. BACKGROUND: WHERE WE WERE

It is a truism in capital market scholarship that 'the regulatory framework consisting of generally independent national regulatory systems no longer matches the reality of global capital flows'.[8] Yet, and in distinct contrast to the dynamic pace in the markets themselves, the international regulatory system governing capital markets, which historically has been dominated by the US regulatory viewpoint, has been slow to change. While the ineffectiveness of national boundaries as a mechanism for the containment of financial crime and destabilising activity compels governments and regulators to cooperate in surveillance and enforcement, working together to simplify international regulation to enable cross-border business to operate more efficiently can appear to be a less urgent matter. Market-opening initiatives that involve the prospect of modifying domestic regulatory requirements to accommodate foreign players can encounter powerful opposition based on concerns about compromising 'gold standards' of national regulation.

The consequence of limited progress in capital market opening is that those engaging in international investment activity have had to make do with only limited regulatory concessions aimed at facilitating their operations, and have had to build their business by navigating carefully around numerous sets of different national regulatory requirements. They have certainly succeeded in overcoming many difficulties: the huge amounts of capital that investors have channelled

[8] ME Tahyar, J Willeumier, EJ Pan, HE Jackson and E Ferran, *Report of the Securities Law Subcommittee of the Task Force on Extraterritorial Jurisdiction of the International Bar Association* (July 2008, SSRN abstract=1109061).

into foreign investments[9] and the vast business empires that financial firms have established outside their home countries[10] demonstrate that regulatory obstacles have not been insuperable. Nevertheless, to many the situation has long seemed unsatisfactory, and there have been numerous calls for more coordinated efforts to dismantle regulatory barriers to global investment activity.

In 2006–07 the US Securities and Exchange Commission (SEC) threw its weight behind some quite radical reform initiatives in relation to the regulation of cross-border activity. A particularly significant breakthrough was its relaxation of financial reporting requirements for foreign issuers. Other potentially major changes appeared to be in the pipeline. It seemed that the SEC was finally prepared to make bold inroads into the principle of adherence to US domestic regulatory standards as a precondition to entry to US markets by foreign actors. Commentators began to write about the SEC being engulfed by a 'tsunami of globalization'[11] and reacting to it by showing greater willingness to make the concept of mutual recognition of foreign standards a significant practical reality in the US response to market interdependency.[12] These changes in the SEC's attitude occurred against a background of intense debate in the United States about whether the US capital markets, long accustomed to being the destination of choice for internationally-mobile issuers because of the depth of the pools of capital available and other benefits associated with being listed on a US trading platform, were losing their competitive edge, and if, or to the extent that, they were, whether this was the fault of a sub-optimal regulatory structure. These concerns attracted attention at the highest political level.[13]

On the other side of the Atlantic the mood at that time was buoyant. With 26 per cent of global stock market capitalisation in 2007 located in EU-15, compared to 39 per cent in the US, the EU could credibly claim to be leading the challenge to the United States in the capital markets.[14] In addition, it

[9] Eg, market value of foreign holdings of US securities as of 30 June 2008 was $10,322 bn; market value of US holdings of foreign securities as of 31 December 2007 was $7,212 bn: Department of the Treasury, Federal Reserve Bank of New York and Board of Governors of the Federal Reserve System, *Report on Foreign Portfolio Holdings of US Securities as of June 30, 2008* (April 2009); Department of the Treasury, Federal Reserve Bank of New York and Board of Governors of the Federal Reserve System, *Report on US Portfolio Holdings of Foreign Securities as of December 31, 2007* (October 2008). International data on cross-border holdings of securities are compiled and maintained by the IMF via its annual Coordinated Portfolio Investment Survey (CPIS). See <http://www.imf.org/external/np/sta/pi/datarsl.htm>.

[10] Eg, in 2005, 27 US banking organisations were operating in EU, with aggregate EU assets of over $650 bn; there were 66 EU-based banking organisations with total US assets of over $1.7 trillion conducting commercial banking and other financial services in the US: Deutsche Bank Research, *Transatlantic Financial Market Integration: Ambition Needed* (EU Monitor No 29, November 2005).

[11] JD Cox, 'Coping in a Global Marketplace: Survival Strategies for a 75-Year-Old SEC' (2009) 95 *Virginia Law Review* 941, 942.

[12] *Ibid*. See also R Karmel, 'The SEC Embraces Mutual Recognition' in M Tison, H de Wulf, C van der Elst and R Steennot (eds), *Perspectives in Company Law and Financial Regulation* (Cambridge, Cambridge University Press, 2009); DC Langevoort, 'Steps Towards the Europeanization of US Securities Regulation', *ibid*.

[13] Department of the Treasury, *Blueprint for a Modernized Financial Regulatory Structure* (March 2008), 25.

[14] *European Financial Integration Report* (SEC(2007) 1696), 5–6.

could point to its dominant position in world foreign exchange markets (60 per cent) and its holding of the majority of global banking assets (52 per cent).[15] In a speech reflecting on the need for close cooperation between the US and the EU in relation to the regulation of capital markets, the then European Commission's Internal Market Commissioner, Charles McCreevy, described Europe's rise in these terms:

> Five years ago, my predecessor would have either been shouted down or laughed at had he dared to come to New York and give a lecture on building a transatlantic marketplace. Had he gone on to suggest that New York would have been looking over its shoulder nervously at competition from London, Paris and Frankfurt, the hoots of derision would have been louder still. Yet here we are in 2007, witnessing the first transatlantic securities exchange merger. Witnessing unprecedented talk of global alliances. Witnessing a debate in the US about whether current regulations and regulatory structures are up to the task or need to learn from Europe.[16]

As is common in statements by European Commission officials, this passage links market development to regulatory design in a manner that glosses over the complex issues of causality that beset attempts properly to understand the nature of that relationship.

The technique of emphasising regulation as the key to Europe's growing economic strength promotes the EU's reputation as a source of worthwhile regulatory ideas: 'success', as demonstrated by objective, measurable criteria such as market share, helps to ensure that European views on regulatory design will be taken seriously in international policy circles. Academic literature of the period noted that the US was embracing strategies that are closely associated with the European Union's single market project: convergence, harmonisation and mutual recognition.[17] European Union regulatory policy was seen to have played an 'instrumental' role in moving the SEC forward.[18] Thus, the Union appeared to be well on its way to achieving one of its financial services policy priorities, namely, to strengthen European influence globally.[19]

III. THE FINANCIAL CRISIS AND THE IMMEDIATE AFTERMATH

Then came the financial turmoil of 2007–08. In the most intense period during the autumn of 2008, when the financial system was in crisis and in need of urgent intervention to ensure fundamental stability and soundness, the themes that

15 *Ibid.*

16 C McCreevy, 'Building the Transatlantic Marketplace', 7 March 2007. Text of speech available at <http://www.europa.eu/rapid/pressReleasesAction.do?reference=SPEECH/07/131&format=HTML&aged=0&language=EN&guiLanguage=fr>.

17 EJ Pan, 'The New Internationalization of US Securities Regulation: Improving the Prospects for a Trans-Atlantic Marketplace' (2008) 5 *European Company Law* 73.

18 RS Karmel, 'The EU Challenge to the SEC' (2008) 31 *Fordham International Law Journal* 1692.

19 European Commission, *White Paper—Financial Services Policy 2005–2010* (COM(2005) 629).

had been dominating the capital markets policy debate previously—opening up markets, removing regulatory frictions and facilitating international capital flows, all of which could be associated with the underlying aim of boosting international capital market competitiveness—suddenly seemed, at best, unimportant. They could even be viewed as a significant part of the problem, in that the failure of national regulators to step in earlier in order to curb excess could be attributed to misplaced over-emphasis on shaping regulatory policy so as to enhance competitiveness.[20]

The collapse of the Icelandic banks and the repatriation of foreign assets that it triggered dealt a blow to the previously admired European market-opening regulatory strategy of affording firms a passport to conduct cross-border business subject to home country supervisory control. Member States were said to have 'fallen out of love with the single market concept'[21] because they had discovered that the European system of allocating supervisory responsibility to home States exposed host countries to the risk that home countries would take decisions that could harm host countries' depositors or host countries' markets and economies.[22] The credibility of the European approach as a model for the rest of the world on how to break down barriers to cross-border financial market activity without compromising fundamental market stability and investor protection goals was thus undermined. For a brief period, the robustness of even the most fundamental tenets of the single market philosophy seemed in doubt, as a clear gap opened up between Member States' professions of support for 'a comprehensive and coordinated response to the current situation'[23] and the actual steps that each of them was taking to shore up domestic institutions and to protect their national interests.[24]

Yet by mid-2009 the mood had shifted again, both internationally and regionally. In a reaction to concerns that crisis measures adopted in emergency circumstances to protect domestic interests could harden into a new era of economic nationalism and protectionism, the governments of the world's major economies

[20] PJ Davies and B Masters, 'Regulator to Soften Focus on Keeping City's Edge', *Financial Times*, 10 June 2009, 2, report remarks by Lord Turner (Chairman, FSA) signalling a new approach: 'We are interested in competitive markets rather than competitiveness'. For critical analysis of arguments linking loss of competitiveness to regulatory intensity in the academic literature, see JC Coffee and HA Sale, 'Redesigning the SEC: Does the Treasury Have a Better Idea?'(2009) 95 *Virginia Law Review* 707.

[21] H Davies, 'Europe's Banks Need a Federal Fix', *Financial Times*, 13 January 2009, 9.

[22] T Huertas, 'The Rationale for and Limits of Bank Supervision', 19 January 2009. Text of speech available at <http://www.fsa.gov.uk/pages/Library/Communication/Speeches/2009/0119_th.shtml>.

[23] Council Conclusions—Ecofin Council of 7 October 2008, 'Immediate Responses to Financial Turmoil', available at www.consilium.europa.eu/ueDocs/cms_Data/docs/pressData/en/misc/103202.pdf.

[24] European Commission, *State Aid: Overview of National Measures Adopted as a Response to the Financial/Economic Crisis*, available at <http://www.europa.eu/rapid/pressReleasesAction.do?reference=MEMO/09/305&format=HTML&aged=0&language=EN&guiLanguage=en>. The European legislative institutions have since intervened to impose order: Directive 2009/14/EC, [2009] OJ L68/3 (deposit guarantee schemes).

strongly reaffirmed their commitment to open markets, first at the G7 meeting in February 2009[25] and then at G20 summit meetings in April and September 2009.[26] The G20 (of which the EU is a member) has put itself at the centre of efforts to ensure a strong, sustained and balanced recovery, underpinned by strengthened regulation and more robust oversight and enforcement.[27] Within Europe, EU order and method began to be restored, with EU State aid law providing the mechanism for the European Commission to exert direct control over Member States' support for troubled national financial institutions and with the Commission actively working to re-establish itself at the centre of the regulatory initiation process.[28]

This is not to suggest that with 'open markets' back in favour, the debate on international capital market regulation could simply pick up in 2009 from where it had been before the crisis. The reform agenda for regulating open markets in the aftermath of the cataclysmic events of autumn 2008 was dominated by efforts to repair and strengthen financial regulation to restore trust, not by efficiency-orientated moves to streamline regulation to facilitate international investment activity. The revision of capital requirements, the regulation of 'shadow' banks and of credit rating agencies, consideration of the role and responsibilities of depositaries, improving the transparency and stability of derivatives markets, and curbing executive pay excesses and other perceived corporate governance shortcomings were among the new priorities.[29] There was particular emphasis on the need for reform of the institutional framework for regulation and supervision of financial markets.[30] Indeed,

[25] 'Statement of G7 Finance Ministers and Central Bank Governors', Rome, 14 February 2009. Available at <http://www.g7finance.tesoro.it/export/sites/G8/en/2009ItalianPresidency/Meetings/February/Communiqes/Documents/Communique.pdf>.

[26] *Global Plan for Recovery and Reform* (2 April 2009). The official communiqué issued at the close of the G20 London Summit, available at <http://www.londonsummit.gov.uk/resources/en/news/15766232/communique-020409>. The Leaders' Statement from the Pittsburgh Summit (September 2009) is available at <http://www.g20.org/Documents/pittsburgh_summit_leaders_statement_250909.pdf>.

[27] Communiqué from the Meeting of Finance Ministers and Central Bank Governors (St Andrew's, November 2009), available at <http://www.hm-treasury.gov.uk/d/2009_communique_standrews.pdf>.

[28] The Commission initiated regulatory change in a range of areas, including deposit guarantees (Directive 2009/14/EC), capital requirements (Proposal COM(2008) 602), credit rating agencies (Regulation (EC) 1060/2009), alternative investment funds (Proposal COM(2009) 207) and executive pay (Commission Recommendation C(2009) 3159; Commission Recommendation C(2009) 3177).

[29] See the European Commission's agenda outlined in the previous note and Brussels European Council, *Presidency Conclusions*, 18–19 June 2009. Stronger capital standards, regulation of hedge funds, stronger regulation of credit rating agencies, closing regulatory loopholes, strengthening regulation of securitisation and of derivatives markets, and control of executive pay also feature on the US reform agenda: Department of the US Treasury, *Financial Regulatory Reform A New Foundation: Rebuilding Financial Supervision and Regulation* (June 2009). These national/regional agenda reflect the G20 consensus: G20, *Global Plan*, above n 26.

[30] In the US: US Treasury, *Financial Regulatory Reform* (n 29). In Europe: European Commission: *European Financial Supervision* (COM(2009) 252). Internationally, institutional reform was also part of the G20 consensus in particular, the agreement to broaden the mandate of the Financial Stability Forum to promote financial stability, and to re-establish it with a stronger institutional basis and enhanced capacity as the Financial Stability Board.

of all the issues that had been attracting particular attention in policy debates on international capital market regulation in the mid-2000s, only accounting standards remained in the foreground by mid-2009 and the debate had taken on a somewhat different slant: correcting perceived deficiencies in specific accounting standards, rather than moving quickly to the adoption of a single, universally applicable set of financial disclosure requirements, being the most pressing issue of the day.[31] Nevertheless, there were signs that with some order restored, policy analysis in the area of capital market regulation was returning to the idea that openness of markets, through alleviating complexities, costs and burdens imposed by different national rules, was an objective that still needed to be pursued. More generally, it began to be politically possible to speak seriously again about the desirability of a balanced regulatory system that delivers both high standards of investor protection *and* a framework conducive to innovation and growth.[32]

This resurgence of interest makes it timely to look again at policies aimed at promoting capital market openness.

IV. REGULATORY STRATEGIES FOR OPENING UP INTERNATIONAL CAPITAL MARKETS

Different sets of national regulatory requirements act as barriers to market access for internationally mobile actors, such as issuers seeking to raise capital outside their home market or financial services firms that want to offer services to foreign issuers and investors. If a country sticks rigidly to a national treatment approach—that is, applying the same regulations to foreign issuers and firms as to nationals[33]—it risks damaging the international competitiveness of its capital markets. Furthermore, by limiting the choice that is available to investors in their 'home' market, such a strategy could have precisely the opposite effect to that which was intended, by forcing investors either to restrict their portfolio diversification strategies or to bear in full the risks and costs involved in fending for themselves in seeking out foreign investment opportunities. This implies that it can be both commercially advantageous and compatible with the fundamental goals of securities regulation for countries to provide concessions designed to facilitate cross-border investment and financial services business.

[31] Eg US Treasury, *Financial Regulatory Reform*, above n 29 (1st priority in area of accounting standard: review of fair value; progress on global standards in 3rd place).

[32] President Obama has noted: 'In these efforts [US reform proposals], we seek a careful balance … With the reforms we're proposing today, we seek to put in place rules that will allow our markets to promote innovation while discouraging abuse' ('21st Century Financial Regulatory Reform', 17 June 2009) Text of remarks available at <http://www.whitehouse.gov/the_press_office/Remarks-of-the-President-on-Regulatory-Reform/>.

[33] SK Schmidt 'Mutual Recognition as a New Mode of Governance' (2007) 14(5) *Journal of European Public Policy* 667, 671.

Countries differ in how far they are prepared to go in opening up their markets to foreign actors otherwise than on a full national treatment basis. Moreover, many of the market-opening strategies are not pure alternatives, and systems that are actually in operation often combine elements of several options. This section briefly reviews the main market-opening strategies at a broad level of generality. Later sections discuss more specific examples.

One option is for a country simply to allow foreign actors free access to the entirety of its domestic markets, provided those actors satisfy another country's regulatory requirements and are overseen by the appropriate authorities of that other country.[34] This approach affords choice to foreign actors, and leaves it to the market to make its own determinations as to the quality of the regulation and supervision under which those actors operate. Choice-based models for the development of international securities regulation divide opinion in the academic literature, and the potential for regulatory arbitrage dampens regulators' enthusiasm for them.[35]

A second option is to allow foreign actors limited access to certain parts of the market without having to comply with domestic regulatory requirements and thus becoming subject to associated oversight and enforcement mechanisms. Some liability rules in the 'host' country's laws (such as anti-fraud provisions) may, however, continue to apply. Exemptions-based models tend not to involve detailed conditions relating to the quality of any foreign regulation or supervision that will impinge on the exempt activity. Exemptions from the full brunt of domestic securities laws and supervisory oversight are common in practice, particularly in respect of the wholesale markets. Professionals-only exemptions have liberalised the wholesale segment of the market and led to the development of private institutional markets that account for a very significant portion of international capital market activity.[36]

A third approach is to amend some of the domestic rules governing the public markets so as to accommodate foreign actors. One way of doing this is for one country to deem certain elements of another country's regulatory requirements to be equivalent to its own and, to the extent so deemed, to relieve actors that adhere to the other country's requirements from the need also to comply with first country's requirements. Apart from the areas that have been deemed equivalent, a foreign

[34] S Choi and A Guzman, 'Portable Reciprocity: Rethinking the International Reach of Securities Regulation' (1998) 71 *Southern California Law Review* 903; R Romano, 'Empowering Investors: a Market Approach to Securities Regulation' (1998) 107 *Yale Law Journal* 2359; R Romano, 'The Need for Competition in International Securities Regulation' (2001) 2 *Theoretical Inquiries in Law* 387. Contrast M Fox, 'Retaining Mandatory Disclosure: Why Issuer Choice is not Investor Empowerment' (1999) 85 *Virginia Law Review* 1335.

[35] E Tafara and RJ Peterson, 'A Blueprint for Cross-Border Access to US Investors: A New International Framework' (2007) 48 *Harvard International Law Journal* 31, 52–53.

[36] In particular, the Rule 144A market: see WK Sjostrom, 'The Birth of Rule 144A Equity Offerings' (2008) 56 *UCLA Law Review* 409; L Zingales, 'The Future of Securities Regulation'(2009) *Journal of Accounting Research* 391.

actor's access to the other country's public markets remains subject to compliance in full with that country's domestic laws. 'Equivalence' does not mean that rules have to be exactly the same, provided they achieve comparable outcomes, but, in practical terms, some degree of harmonisation—'a common baseline'[37]—will facilitate determinations of equivalence. Equivalence essentially involves one country trusting another country to regulate the matter in question. As discussed in section VI. below, equivalence-based models have recently become more significant in international securities regulation, particularly with regard to financial disclosures.

A fourth strategy is mutual recognition, a notion with which the EU is very familiar by virtue of its free movement law. 'Substituted compliance' is a term that has been used recently by SEC officials to describe an approach that, broadly speaking, is similar to that implied by the more familiar phrase.[38] Mutual recognition in this context shares with equivalence models the idea that domestic law governing some aspects of securities market activity can be disapplied in favour of foreign actors that are adhering to a comparable regulatory regime; but it goes further in the extent to which the supervisory dimension is addressed, with the 'host' country expecting to look to the 'home' country to discharge substantial oversight functions in respect of the cross-border activity and, as this implies, the host country placing considerable reliance on the quality of the other supervisory regime. Mutual recognition implies a broader acceptance of similarities between systems than equivalence, which is more concerned with the similarities between particular rules.[39]

Global regulatory standardisation is a further relevant strategy. Universally agreed standards that are sufficiently detailed to be practically operational on their own, or which are supported by a transnational body that has exclusive authority to interpret and fill gaps, and which are consistently applied and enforced in all countries, would be the most-evolved system of standardised global regulation. On the securities side, international accounting standards come closest to satisfying these criteria, though even they fall short in certain respects.[40] Progress on accounting standards may be related to the fact that these are highly technical measures in a field where the profession that has frontline responsibility for overseeing their application in practice is itself highly concentrated. In other areas of

[37] Schmidt, above n 33, 676.

[38] Tafara and Peterson, above n 35. The views expressed in this article are those of the authors personally and it is not a statement of official SEC policy.

[39] 'Particular' and 'broad' are terms that others have used (in different ways) to explain the difference between equivalence and mutual recognition: see JP Trachtman, 'Embedding Mutual Recognition at the WTO' (2007) 14 *Journal of European Public Policy* 780.

[40] L Hail, C Leuz and P Wysocki, 'Global Accounting Convergence and the Potential Adoption of IFRS by the United States: An Analysis of Economic and Policy Factors' (Working Paper, February 2009, SSRN abstract=1357331) make the point that a single set of accounting standards by itself does not guarantee the comparability of firms' reporting practices because of differences in approaches to interpretation, etc. See also LA Cunningham, 'The SEC's Global Accounting Vision: A Realistic Appraisal of a Quixotic Quest' (2008) 87 *North Carolina Law Review* 1, 53.

international capital market regulation, the trade-offs and compromises involved in multilateral standard-setting can result in global standards being articulated at too high a level of generality to be immediately operational on a stand-alone basis. Yet generally-worded global standards can still play an important role as a 'starting point'. By adhering to them, countries can establish a common core which may serve as the foundation for equivalence or mutual recognition decisions about sets of national requirements that have different detailed features.[41]

V. MECHANISMS FOR THE DEVELOPMENT OF MARKET-OPENING REGULATORY STRATEGIES

The de Larosière Report, which is a report by a group established in 2008 under the chairmanship of the distinguished financier Jacques de Larosière[42] to give advice to the Commission on the future of European financial regulation and supervision, notes that international regulatory convergence towards a consistent set of rules can be promoted by pursuing two parallel avenues: international standard-setting, and bilateral regulatory dialogues.[43] While the focus of the de Larosière Report is more on repairing weaknesses in the financial regulatory system and reinforcing systemic stability than on reducing compliance burdens and facilitating global business, the two avenues also provide the main routes that have been followed in the development of market-opening regulatory strategies. That the same mechanisms operate across the board is not surprising: particular regulatory measures may have a stronger/weaker enabling/restrictive character, but they are all part of an integrated and mutually-reinforcing system in which safety and soundness measures help to build investor confidence and thus make feasible the possibility of opening markets to the extent that comparability of protective standards can be assured.

A. International Standard-setting

The capital markets, in the narrow sense of markets for equities, bonds and other types of financial instruments, have lagged behind the banking segment of the financial markets in having a comprehensive and detailed regulatory framework set

[41] Eg, Commissioner McCreevy has suggested that the IOSCO principles and standards for securities markets regulation could be a basic reference for EU–US mutual recognition: 'Speech', 18 December 2007. Text of speech available at <http://www.europa.eu/rapid/pressReleasesAction.do?reference=SPEECH/07/836&format=PDF&aged=1&language=EN&guiLanguage=fr>.

[42] Managing Director of the International Monetary Fund (1978–87), Governor of the Banque de France (1987–93) and President of the European Bank for Reconstruction and Development (1993–98).

[43] High-level Group on Financial Supervision in the EU, *Report* (Brussels, European Commission, February 2009) ('de Larosière Report'), para 226.

by a powerful international body. The Basel Committee on Banking Supervision was established by the central bank governors of the G10 countries at the end of 1974 in the aftermath of serious disturbances in international financial markets, in particular the failure of Bankhaus Herstatt in West Germany.[44] The capital adequacy standards, as now set out in the Basel II Framework, are very detailed and carry immense international significance.[45] The most directly equivalent body in capital markets is the International Organisation of Securities Commissions (IOSCO), which grew out of an ancestor inter-American regional association and has been in operation since 1983.[46] Historically, IOSCO standards have tended to be framed in quite general terms and to be designed to function more as best practice benchmarks than as detailed rules that can be translated easily into a legally-enforceable form.[47] Confirming the role of crises as drivers of change,[48] the turmoil in the financial markets has led to an acceleration of the work done by the IOSCO's Technical Committee, as part of the new impetus for raising international regulatory standards and improving international cooperation.[49] (The Technical Committee is effectively the IOSCO's powerhouse, as it is made up of the agencies that regulate some of the world's larger, more developed and internationalised markets, including, as from February 2009, Brazil, China and India.[50]) Nevertheless the IOSCO's regulatory contribution continues to be more that of articulating fundamental standards, principles and best practice recommendations than that of producing exhaustive statements of detailed requirements.[51]

[44] BIS, *History of the Basel Committee and its Membership* (January 2007), available at <http://www.bis.org/bcbs/history.pdf>.

[45] Basel Committee on Banking Supervision, *International Convergence of Capital Measurement and Capital Standards: A Revised Framework* (2006). The Basel Accord 1988 (Basel I) was given legal backing in all G10 countries by 1992. Basel II rules are in the process of being implemented. However, as of June 2009 Basel II rules had not been fully implemented for any US financial institution.

[46] IOSCO, *Historical Background*, available at <http://www.iosco.org/about/index.cfm?section=history>.

[47] This is particularly true of the IOSCO's major contribution, *Objectives and Principles of Securities Regulation* (Madrid, IOSCO, 2003).

[48] The lack, historically, of a Herstatt-style crisis to force cooperation has been mentioned as a factor that could explain why international cooperation in the securities field has taken longer to crystallise: M Brunnermeier, A Crockett, C Goodhart, AD Persaud and H Shin, *The Fundamental Principles of Financial Regulation* (Geneva Reports on the World Economy No 11, 2009) 55, available at <http://www.voxeu.org/reports/Geneva11.pdf>.

[49] IOSCO, *Annual Report 2008*, 10–13, details work by the Technical Committee across a range of matters from accountability of standard setters through to unregulated financial entities.

[50] Membership of the Technical Committee is listed at <http://www.iosco.org/lists/display_committees.cfm?cmtid=3>.

[51] IOSCO, above n 49, 11, describes the use of the IOSCO credit rating agencies' code of conduct standards as a common starting point for credit rating agency regulation around the world. Another example is in the area of short selling, where the IOSCO sees its role as being to develop high-level principles that are designed to assist regulators around the world in their consideration of a regulatory regime for short selling: *Regulation of Short Selling: a Consultation Report* (IOSCO Technical Committee, March 2009), para 1.2.

The limits of the IOSCO's approach can be seen in the context of the new EC Regulation on Credit Rating Agencies.[52] In formulating its proposals, the European Commission drew heavily on the work that the IOSCO had already done in this area:

> However, the code has some limitations that need to be overcome to make its rules fully operational. Some IOSCO rules are quite abstract and generic; they need to be concretised, and consolidated in some cases, to make them easier to apply in practice and more efficient. Most importantly, the code provides no enforcement mechanism but only invites credit rating agencies to give reasons if they do not comply with it (the 'comply or explain' approach). The code itself is open to being complemented by enforceable rules.[53]

The IOSCO's 'predilection towards flexibility'[54] leaves considerable leeway for national adaptations to fit local circumstances. This flexibility could be said to impede progress towards full international regulatory convergence. On the other hand, it avoids the obvious difficulties that would beset any attempt to get sovereign States to adopt international requirements that give them little discretion and which may be a poor fit with local conditions. This point is developed further in section VI. of this chapter in relation to accounting standards.

B. Bilateral Regulatory Dialogues: The Transatlantic Dialogue

The bilateral dialogue that is of particular interest here is the transatlantic financial services regulatory dialogue. An organised framework for financial services regulatory dialogue between the US and the EU emerged in 2002.[55] Its origins lay in regulatory developments on either side of the Atlantic—the EC Financial Conglomerates Directive[56] and the US Sarbanes-Oxley legislation[57]—that threatened unintentional regulatory spillovers for other jurisdictions and companies that could have had damaging repercussions for the international competitiveness of both regions. The prospect of mutual advantages to be gained from the removal of regulatory frictions helped regulators and policymakers on both sides of the Atlantic to find common ground. It coincided with the interests of the

[52] Regulation (EC) No 1060/2009, [2009] OJ L302/1.

[53] *Proposal for a Regulation of the European Parliament and of the Council on Credit Rating Agencies* (COM(2008) 704), 3.

[54] C Kelly and R Karmel, 'The Hardening of Soft Law in Securities Regulation' (2009) 34 *Brooklyn Journal of International Law* 1, 17.

[55] It was established informally in March 2002: 'US–EU Summit: Informal Financial Markets Dialogue Fact Sheet' (White House Press Release, 25 June 2003, available at <useu.usmission.gov/Article.asp?ID=14BF6AE8-E432-4BBE-B916-0989ABEC3C74>.

[56] Directive 2002/87/EC, [2003] OJ L35/1.

[57] Corporate and Auditing and Accountability, Responsibility, and Transparency Act of 2002, Pub L No 107-204.

financial services industry to treat the removal of transatlantic frictions as a policy priority.[58]

The formal aims of this dialogue are to foster a better mutual understanding of EU and US regulatory approaches, to identify potential conflicts in approach as early in the regulatory process as possible, and to discuss regulatory issues of mutual interest.[59] The dialogue is led by the US Treasury Department and the European Commission, but other bodies, including the SEC and the Committee of European Securities Regulators (CESR), also participate.

One notable feature of the transatlantic regulatory dialogue from the European perspective is that it puts Union bodies firmly in the driving seat so far as 'speaking for Europe' in external relations in matters relating to financial regulation is concerned. This clarity contrasts with the position, historically, in respect of many of the international discussion and standard-setting fora for financial markets, where the formal status of Union institutions has tended to vary depending on the nature of the organisation in question and its history.[60] As recently as February 2009, the representation of the European Union in international organisations and other international bodies in the financial field could be described as 'fragmented' and as lacking 'coherence and continuity'.[61] However, this is another area where crisis has had a galvanising effect: the European Commission became an affiliate member of the IOSCO in its own right in June 2009,[62] a change that followed close on the heels of its accession to membership of the Financial Stability Board, which is the body that is now charged with wide-ranging oversight responsibilities relating to international financial stability.[63]

Between 2002 and 2008, the transatlantic regulatory dialogue addressed many issues, including the implementation of the Basel II capital adequacy requirements, the termination of SEC registration by foreign companies and potential frictions in insurance regulation.[64] Accounting convergence and mutual

[58] Eg, that the capital markets led the way in development of IFRS and active support offered by governments, such as the EU adoption, followed behind: G Whittington, 'The Adoption of International Accounting Standards in the European Union' (2005) 14 *European Accounting Review* 127, 128.

[59] Representatives of the European Commission and US Financial Regulators, *EU–US Financial Markets Regulatory Dialogue* (June 2004), available at <http://www.ec.europa.eu/internal_market/finances/docs/general/eu-us-dialogue-report-state-of-play_en.pdf>.

[60] No Union institution is a member of the Basel Committee but several EU Member States are members (membership listed at <http://www.bis.org/bcbs/as>). The European Commission and European Central Bank participate as observers in the Committee itself and in its many working groups, including the Joint Forum, which was established to deal with issues common to the banking, securities and insurance sectors: BIS, above n 44.

[61] de Larosière Report, above n 43, para 256.

[62] 'Final Update 34th Annual Conference of the International Organization of Securities Commissions' (IOSCO Media Statement, IOSCO/MS/06/2009), available at <http://www.iosco.org/library/statements/pdf/statements-6.pdf>.

[63] Financial Stability Forum, 'Financial Stability Forum Decides to Broaden its Membership' (Press Release, 12 March 2009), available at <http://www.financialstabilityboard.org/press/pr_090312b.pdf>.

[64] M Sobel, Treasury Deputy Assistant Secretary, 'Remarks on US–EU Regulatory Cooperation', 30 April 2008. Text of speech available at <useu.usmission.gov/Dossiers/Regulation/Apr3008_Sobel_TEC.asp>.

recognition in securities, the two issues that are discussed in sections VI. and VII. of this chapter, were among the main topics. While much of the emphasis in the dialogue was on finding practical solutions to specific difficulties rather than ambitious grand design projects, it was also associated with more lofty aims. Thus, Commissioner McCreevy of the European Commission spoke of the transatlantic market as serving as the laboratory of globalisation,[65] and SEC Commissioner Casey described the transatlantic dialogue as having 'cooperatively led the way in forging key progress' in the adaptation of regulatory approaches in response to globalisation.[66]

Little was heard of the transatlantic dialogue in the immediate aftermath of the financial crisis; instead, 'global solutions' worked out by international standard-setting bodies were seized upon as the most apt way of addressing a global financial problem. However, as the de Larosière Report acknowledges, bilateral exchanges still have an important role to play. This view is also taken by some on the other side of the Atlantic: the Committee on Capital Market Regulation, an independent research organisation dedicated to improving the regulation of US capital markets, has called specifically for post-crisis regulatory reform to include the strengthening of regional regulatory dialogues, and in particular that of the United States and Europe, because of the important role they can play in resolving transnational regulatory disputes.[67] Bilateral regulatory dialogues hold out the possibility of achieving cross-border results that have more granularity than generally-worded international standards. While the matters discussed in any dialogue will flow with the course of actual events, in broad terms dialogue involving multi-level collaboration and cooperation between officials and agencies from different countries should build trust, which is a foundational element in the development of an effective system of coordinated transnational regulation based on equivalence or mutual recognition.[68]

C. Parallel Avenues …

It may be more accurate to regard international standard setting and bilateral dialogues as routes that often intersect with each other rather than as 'parallel avenues' as they are described in the de Larosière Report. Multilateral regulatory initiatives can help participants in bilateral regulatory dialogues find common ground; bilateral exchanges can help to fill out the detail that is often missing from

[65] McCreevy, above n 16.

[66] KL Casey, SEC Commissioner, 'Sixth Annual Symposium on Building the Financial System of the 21st Century', 3 April 2008. Text of speech available at <http://www.sec.gov/news/speech/2008/spch040308klc.htm>.

[67] *The Global Financial Crisis: A Plan for Regulatory Reform* (May 2009), recommendation 57.

[68] K Nicolaïdis, 'Trusting the Poles? Constructing Europe Through Mutual Recognition' (2007) 14 *Journal of European Public Policy* 682.

international standards, and thus make them practically operational on a cross-border basis. Analysis of recent international progress in relation to accounting standards and mutual recognition demonstrates the close connections between the two routes.

VI. ACCOUNTING STANDARDS

A. International Financial Reporting Standards

The language of financial statements is an area where the development of a truly international detailed regulatory framework is particularly mature. The International Accounting Standard Board (IASB) and its predecessor, the International Accounting Standards Committee, have been working since 1973 on the development of global accounting standards to provide high-quality, transparent and comparable information in financial statements and reports. The IASB's standards, now known as International Financial Reporting Standards (IFRS) (previously International Accounting Standards or IAS), are not directly enforceable but can acquire legal force by being incorporated into countries' domestic law. As of February 2010, 117 jurisdictions permitted or required IFRS for domestic listed companies.[69]

With effect from March 2008, the SEC adopted rules to accept from foreign private issuers in their US filings financial statements prepared in accordance with IFRS as issued by the IASB, without reconciliation to generally accepted accounting principles as used in the United States (US GAAP).[70] The SEC followed this in November 2008 with a formal proposal for a phased-in mandatory introduction of IFRS for US issuers, beginning from financial years from December 2014 onwards (SEC *Roadmap*).[71]

These moves by the SEC were described by one commentator as 'the most revolutionary development in securities regulation since the New Deal',[72] a comment that, in the light of the fundamental overhaul of financial regulation triggered by the financial crisis, may now seem a little overstated but which nevertheless helpfully conveys a sense of the significance of the development. The financial reporting burden on foreign issuers entering the United States had been a stick-

[69] *Use of IFRSs by Jurisdiction*, data available at <http://www.iasplus.com/country/useias.htm>. For further background, see E Ferran, *Principles of Corporate Finance Law* (Oxford, Oxford University Press, 2008) 483–89.

[70] SEC, *Acceptance From Foreign Private Issuers of Financial Statements Prepared in Accordance with International Financial Reporting Standards Without Reconciliation to US GAAP*, Release Nos 33-8879; 34-57026; International Series Release No 1306; File No S7-13-07.

[71] SEC, *Roadmap for the Potential Use of Financial Statements Prepared in Accordance with International Financial Reporting Standards by US Issuers*, Release Nos 33-8982; 34-58960; File No S7-27-08. Hail *et al*, above n 40, consider the potential implications of adoption of IFRS in the US.

[72] Cunningham, above n 40, 3.

ing point for many years. During the 1980s, the US had sought to accommodate foreign issuers by allowing them to satisfy their US reporting requirements by preparing their financial statements using a body of generally accepted accounting principles other than the US GAAP, but only subject to a requirement to include a reconciliation of significant variations from the US GAAP.[73] When it was introduced, reconciliation was intended to be a concession, but it came to be regarded as an expensive and time-consuming process that served as a barrier to foreign issuers seeking entry to the US markets. Some relatively modest relaxations of the reconciliation requirements were made in the 1990s, but these did not staunch the flow of demands for a single set of high-quality international accounting standards.

The combination of the financial crisis and new US Administration has had an impact on the US transition to IFRS, although in this case the effect of crisis has been to cause a loss of pace rather than an acceleration. In her Senate confirmation hearing in January 2009, the new SEC Chairman, Mary Schapiro, made clear a range of concerns about IFRS standards generally, and emphasised that she would not be bound by the SEC *Roadmap* published by her predecessor.[74] However, in the same hearing Schapiro acknowledged that 'a single set of accounting standards used around the world would be a very beneficial thing'. This aspiration is consistent with the political commitment of the US Government via the G20 to the development of a single set of global accounting standards. So, while there may be more urgent priorities in the short term, global standardisation of the language of financial reporting certainly remains on the regulatory agenda.

What are the factors that brought IFRS to the point of being a credible alternative to US GAAP and, more recently, a strong contender to win the race to be the single set of global accounting standards? Developments in Europe merit particular attention in responding to this question. Since January 2005 the IAS Regulation has required all European companies admitted to trading on regulated markets within the EEA to prepare consolidated accounts in accordance with EU-adopted IFRS.[75] Prospectus and continuous financial disclosure requirements

[73] The history is reviewed in SEC, above n 70.

[74] M Schapiro, 'Testimony', as reported on Financial Market Regulatory Wire, 15 January 2009: 'That said, I have some concerns about the road map that's been published by the SEC and is out for comment now, and I have some concerns about the IFRS standards generally. …they're not as detailed as the U.S. standards. There's a lot left to interpretation. Even if adopted, there would still be a lack of consistency, I believe, around the world in how they're implemented and how they're enforced. The cost to switch from U.S. GAAP to IFRS is going to be extraordinary, and I've seen some estimates that range as high as $30 million for each U.S. company in order to do that. This is time when I think we have to think carefully about whether imposing those sorts of costs on U.S. industry really makes sense. Perhaps one of my greatest concerns is the independence of the International Accounting Standards Board and the ability to have oversight of their process for setting accounting standards and …and the amount of rigor that exists in that process today. So I will tell you that I will take a big deep breath and look at this entire area again carefully and will not necessarily feel bound by the existing road map that's out for comment.'

[75] Regulation (EC) 1606/2002, [2002] OJ L243/1.

under EU law are also now IFRS-based.[76] Foreign issuers are required to present financial disclosures in accordance with EU-adopted IFRS, except where they are drawn up under accounting standards that EU bodies have deemed to be 'equivalent' to EU-adopted IFRS.[77]

There is considerable support for the view that the EU's strong endorsement of IFRS significantly enhanced their international credibility. Karmel, an academic and former SEC Commissioner, describes this as an area where the EU seized the initiative at a time when the SEC was perhaps too preoccupied with dealing with the fallout from Enron and Worldcom and the implementation of the Sarbanes-Oxley legislation.[78] The fallout from those corporate scandals included much criticism of the rules-based US GAAP and unfavourable comparison with the principles-based IFRS. For Nicolaisen, formerly the SEC's chief accountant, the EU's move was a 'bold and critically important decision' in the evolution towards a single set of globally-accepted accounting standards.[79]

Sheer weight of numbers associated with the EU's adoption played a significant role in making IFRS more competitive. Schipper, a member of the US Financial Accounting Standards Board (FASB), notes that the effect of the EU's decision was to increase the number of enterprises that apply IFRS in preparing their financial statements from several hundred to several thousand.[80] Indeed, the total global market capitalisation of exchange-listed companies subject to IFRS-based financial disclosure requirements has been estimated to be approaching £13.4 trillion, or approximately 31 per cent of global stock market capitalisation.[81] In its *Roadmap*, the SEC acknowledged that engagement with IFRS accounts was thus an increasingly unavoidable fact of life for investors seeking international investment opportunities, regardless of whether their home country mandated IFRS or another set of accounting standards, and that these market realities formed the background for its commitment to pursuing consideration of the use of IFRS in the US markets.[82]

Yet it would be an inaccurate over-simplification of a complex situation to present a one-sided picture of the EU as the pioneer and the US in the role of 'follow my leader' in respect of IFRS. An obvious objection to this simplistic interpretation is that the EU is not the standard-setter; it has 'merely' adopted the standards of a third party global standard-setter, though this is not to deny

[76] Commission Regulation 809/2004, [2004] OJ L149/1 (Prospectus Directive Regulation), annex 1, para 20; Directive 2004/109/EC, [2004] OJ L390/38 (Transparency Obligations Directive), arts 4–5.

[77] Commission Regulation (EC) 1289/2008, [2008] OJ L340/17 (equivalence determination); Commission Regulation (EC) 1569/2007, [2007] L340/66 (equivalence mechanism).

[78] Karmel, above, n 12.

[79] DT Nicolaisen, 'A Securities Regulator Looks at Convergence' (2005) 25 *Northwestern Journal of International Law and Business* 661.

[80] K Schipper, 'The Introduction of International Accounting Standards in Europe: Implications for International Convergence' (2005) 14 *European Accounting Review* 101.

[81] SEC, above, n 71.

[82] SEC, above, n 71.

the significance of that endorsement as a boost to the efforts of an international standard-setting 'soft law' body that has no power itself to make binding rules. Moreover, to view the situation in this way would be to ignore the myriad influences relating to the development of IFRS and their interpretation, including many emanating from the United States itself.

The IASB began life as a private-sector committee established by professional accountancy bodies from Australia, Canada, France, Germany, Japan, Mexico, the Netherlands, the United Kingdom and Ireland, and the United States. The idea of such a body had been under development since 1966, when the professional accountancy bodies in Canada, the United Kingdom and the United States agreed to develop comparative studies of accounting and auditing practices in the three nations.[83] The founder members have retained considerable influence. Under new governance arrangements, the aim is that from 2012 there will 16 members, with North America, Europe and the Asia/Oceania countries each having four representatives.[84] Thus, notwithstanding an increasing emphasis on geographical balance, a strong US presence feeding directly into the work of the IASB can be expected to continue.

The US also has indirect input into the work of the IASB via the IOSCO.[85] While the IOSCO does not itself play a frontline role in setting financial reporting standards, its Technical Committee monitors developments in IFRS, comments on proposed changes and discusses standard-setting work with representatives of the IASB. The SEC has said that it participates in the development of IFRS primarily through its participation in the IOSCO.[86] However, it is clear that the SEC has over the years also contributed in more direct ways to the work of the IASB, offering guidance on both standard-setting processes and on the substantive contents of standards.[87]

In responding to the suggestion that IFRS have become more acceptable to US authorities simply because of their growing popularity in the rest of the world, as boosted by the EU endorsement, mention must also be made of the considerable efforts to eliminate differences between those standards and the US GAAP in the convergence process led by the IASB and its US counterpart, the FASB.[88] Although that process remains incomplete,[89] and the persistence of some fundamental differences in approach has had repercussions in the context of the financial crisis because it has precluded complete alignment of the steps taken by the IASB

[83] The chronology and history of the IASB is traced at www.iasplus.com/restruct/chrono.htm.

[84] International Accounting Standards Committee Foundation, *Revised Constitution* (February 2009), para 26.

[85] IOSCO *An Overview of the Work of the IOSCO Technical Committee* (July 2008), 6.

[86] SEC, above, n 70, 14–15. Further on US support, via IOSCO, for the development of IFRS: JD Cox, 'Regulatory Duopoly in U.S. Securities Markets' (1999) 99 *Columbia Law Review* 1200.

[87] Cunningham, above n 40, 9–15.

[88] On the convergence project, see Ferran, above n 69, 483–89.

[89] Hail *et al*, above n 40, § 4.5.2 identifies remaining differences, especially the amount of discretion offered.

and FASB to respond to perceived weaknesses in reporting requirements,[90] there is a strong, longstanding commitment to draw the two systems together, which responses to the crisis, with their emphasis on global coordination, have not impaired.[91] That commitment has, it is said, resulted in the US GAAP and IFRS being 'already fairly close and … expected to be even closer by the time the US might adopt IFRS'.[92]

Yet notwithstanding the well-established substantial US input into IFRS, there is a palpable sense of concern that the balance of power and influence over the IFRS standard-setting process has begun to shift away from the United States. Cunningham refers to the SEC having provided steady support for international accounting standards over several decades but now finding itself in a position where the IASB has risen from humble origins to world leadership as a result of numerous factors, many outside the SEC's control and including political pressure from the EU.[93] Arguably this trend could have been anticipated: that adopting IFRS would strengthen European interests in the international standard-setting process had been openly acknowledged in Community deliberations from at least 1995.[94] The changes lead Hail *et al* to suggest that one of the major current concerns from a US perspective is that foreign governments and interest groups exercise an undue influence on the IASB.[95] They make the point that the IASB's history as an organisation attuned to the needs of an open capital market like that in the US does not guarantee that it will continue to operate in that way in future; they identify as a significant risk for the US that the dynamics of the IASB may change as its constituencies change and the influence of emerging markets like China, India and other developing nations increases. From the US national perspective, there is much to be said for SEC and the FASB aiming for more influence and cooperation in relation to the IASB before ceding rule-making authority.[96] Or, as Cox, a critic of the pace of transition that was envisaged by the SEC's *Roadmap*, puts it:

> It is equally premature to discuss abandoning GAAP without a full understanding what strategies the SEC can employ to influence standard setting in a body located in London rather than Stamford, Connecticut.[97]

The United States does not have a monopoly on political concerns about the ramifications of ceding powers to write the rules governing activities taking place

[90] Sir David Tweedie, 'Prepared Statement', 9 June 2009. Text of speech by Chairman of the IASB, explaining why the IASB could not simply adopt the FASB changes relating to fair value and impairment. Available at <http://www.iasplus.com/crunch/0906tweedieecofin.pdf>.

[91] *Ibid*; see also IASC Foundation, *Annual Report 2008*, describing responses to the global financial crisis.

[92] Hail *et al*, above n 40.

[93] Cunningham, above n 40, 15–16.

[94] 'Commission Proposes a New Strategy for the Improvement of the Financial Reporting Framework for Companies in Europe' (IP/95/1234, 14 November 1995).

[95] Hail *et al*, above n 40.

[96] *Ibid.*

[97] Cox, above n 11, 984.

within its territory to a third party standard-setting body. Particularly for mature economies that have their own robust internal rule-making apparatus that functions within a domestic framework of accountability and transparency, this loss of control is a huge step.[98] While the political sensitivities may be particularly acute for the US because of the historically dominant position of its capital markets, they are not unique to it. Therefore, the EU's experience in dealing with those sensitivities in its evolving relationship with the IASB constitutes a potentially valuable source of insights for the US as it contemplates its options.

The EU has imposed a jurisdictional filter on the application of IFRS by requiring relevant accounts to be drawn up in accordance with IFRS that have been *endorsed by the EU*.[99] At least so long as the EU has this filter in place, it seems politically inconceivable that the US would contemplate transition to IFRS without similar protection. In any event, any attempt to hand over rule-making power without reserving some veto rights would no doubt encounter significant legal objections.

An endorsement mechanism or other veto right performs a valuable role by avoiding constitutional problems and political sensitivities that would be involved in delegating rule-making authority to a private non-governmental authority. The European Commission has noted that 'the EU endorsement process per se ensures technical quality, political legitimacy and relevance to business'.[100] While an endorsement mechanism raises the possibility of regional variant versions of IFRS, an outcome that would be at odds with the aspiration for a single set of global standards, it may be viewed on a more pragmatic basis as an acceptable compromise that enables the system to move forward in an incremental way rather than being held up by intractable problems. Remember that even if IFRS were to be adopted without national veto rights or filters, this would not guarantee uniformity because of the strong likelihood that their interpretation and application would be susceptible to local influences.[101] Whatever the objections in principle, in practical terms the presence of an endorsement mechanism or some other form of veto right could be less of a problem than it might first appear.

However, this depends on how wide the power of veto is, and also on how it is actually used: minor changes would seem relatively untroubling, but frequent refusal to endorse IFRS as produced by the IASB, or threats to do so, would undermine the credibility of a commitment to following international standards and could jeopardise the independence of the standard-setter itself. On this matter, the evidence from Europe is mixed. The endorsement mechanism is designed to operate mainly on the basis of adoption or non-adoption of an IFRS

[98] Cunningham, above n 40, 3.

[99] The operation of the endorsement process is described in European Commission, *Report on the Operation of Regulation (EC) No 1606/2002 of 19 July 2002 on the Application of International Accounting Standards* (COM(2008) 215), para 2.1.

[100] Ibid, para 3.

[101] Hail *et al*, above n 40.

as a whole, but where a standard covers two or more accounting subjects which are entirely autonomous, distinct and separable, the Commission can decide on the partial application of that standard.[102] By July 2007, all extant IASB standards had been endorsed except for limited parts of one controversial IFRS concerning hedging,[103] an outcome that could be interpreted optimistically as indicating that the integrity of IFRS was not in serious danger of being eroded by the operation of the EU's filter. However, a less benign picture emerges from events in 2008, when the IASB found itself drawn into the maelstrom of the EU's political response to the financial crisis. In October 2008 the IASB made a 'fast-track' decision to amend its standards governing the balance sheet recognition of financial derivatives, which was then endorsed by the Commission.[104] Sir David Tweedie, the Chairman of the IASB, later admitted that the IASB's decision was taken under pressure because of EU threats of carve-outs.[105] The strains demonstrated by this incident were still present well into 2009, as the IASB continued to find itself under attack from the EU, facing accusations of being inflexible, slow, over-academic and out of touch,[106] and having to battle against pressure to bow to political demands for revisions of certain standards.[107] A new low point was reached in November 2009, when the EU delayed endorsement of post-crisis revisions of IFRS standards relating to the measurement of financial instruments. This clash revealed not only difficulties in the relations between the EU and the IASB, with reports of EU officials being 'furious' that the IASB did not give them due weight in the negotiations as its main sponsor,[108] but also signs of a fragmentation within the EU along national lines.[109]

The financial crisis has thus revealed a fundamental tension in the relationship between the EU and the IASB. On the one hand the EU professes support for

[102] European Commission, *Explanatory Memorandum of the Commission Services on the Proposal for a Regulation Adopting IAS 39* (Brussels, European Commission, 24 September 2004).

[103] IAS 39.

[104] Commission Regulation (EC) No 1004/2008, [2008] OJ L275/37.

[105] Uncorrected transcript of oral evidence before Treasury Committee, 11 November 2008. Published in Treasury Committee, *Banking Crisis: Oral Evidence Transcripts* (HC 1167-ii, London, November 2009) Qs 185–239. On the implications of the IASB's emergency decision for a commitment to proper processes, see IASC Foundation, *Annual Report 2008*, 5–6.

[106] C McCreevy, 'Financial Reporting in a Changing World: Keynote Address', 7 May 2009. Text of speech available at <http://www.iasplus.com/europe/0905mccreevy.pdf>.

[107] The EU Finance Ministers and Central Bank Governors (ECOFIN) issued a statement in April 2009 urging the IASB to adopt certain changes mirroring those that had been made the week before by FASB. The statement is available at <http://www.iasplus.com/europe/0904ecofinstatement.pdf>. The IASB's reponse—explaining why simply following the FASB's approach was not the best strategy—can be found in Tweedie, above n 90.

[108] R Sanderson, 'Europe's Schism Threatens Global Accounting Rules', *Financial Times*, 16 November 2009, 6.

[109] An extract from the record of a meeting of the accounting regulatory committee and contact committee of 11 November 2009 reports a difference of views among Member States on whether there should be an accelerated endorsement process. See extract at <http://www.europa.eu/internal_market/accounting/docs/arc/2009-11-11_ARC_IFRS9_en.pdf>.

global accounting standards made by an independent body.[110] Indeed, it could be thought remarkable that it has already vested so much trust in the IASB, a body that, despite many changes to its governance structure over the years that have sought to meet expectations with regard to independence, transparency, legitimacy and accountability that have become more stringent as the IASB's public role has become more significant, still has legitimacy gaps that are rooted in its private sector origins and a funding structure that continues to depend in part on voluntary contributions from commercial organisations.[111] The EU has a good record of supporting such changes, the most recent example of this activity being its joint effort with US and Japanese authorities and the IOSCO, to secure the establishment of a public sector monitoring board to which the trustees of the International Accounting Standards Committee Foundation, which oversees the IASB, are publically accountable.[112] On the other hand, the EU is not averse to applying pressure to advance its own political agenda, even to the point where this threatens to compromise the standard-setter's independence. This suggests that a workable accommodation between regional interests and global concerns is not yet firmly established.

The strains in the EU–IASB relationship exposed by the financial crisis add to many other concerns voiced in relation to the SEC *Roadmap*. Also, one particularly significant difference between the position of the EU and that of the US merits emphasis: adoption of IFRS filled an important gap for the EU by providing Union-wide standardisation in an area where previous harmonisation efforts via company law directives had had only limited effect, but that gap does not exist across the Atlantic because the US GAAP already ensures standardisation. In other words, the gain for the US from rapid transition to IFRS is much less obvious than it was for the EU. Those who are advocating that the US should proceed cautiously in moving to IFRS for domestic issuers thus appear currently to have the weight of the argument on their side. Less radical alternatives to full transition, such as allowing a choice between IFRS and the US GAAP for domestic issuers, may be the incremental way forward in the short to medium term.

For proponents of global standardisation, a correction in the pace of US transition to IFRS could seem like a setback, but there are possible benefits for the international community. Recent events suggest that it may be over-optimistic to suppose that the IASB has a sufficiently secure foundation to be able currently to cope with two (the EU and the US) particularly demanding users rather than just one (the EU). A breathing space leaves room for the further reinforcement of the

[110] Eg, McCreevy, above n 106.

[111] Funding comes from a number of sources, including individual countries, central banks and international organisations and accounting firms. See IASC Foundation, *Annual Report 2008*, 16–17. EU institutions currently do not contribute to the funding of the IASB, but the European Commission has suggested that it should provide funding directly to the IASB: COM(2009) 14. The Commission suggests that this would strengthen independence: *ibid.*

[112] The Basel Committee on Banking Supervision will sit as a formal observer at Monitoring Board meetings. See generally IASC Foundation, *Annual Report 2008*, 2–3.

independence of the international financial reporting institutional framework, so that it is better equipped to manage the formidably complicated balancing act of giving important regions a fair say in the standard-setting process and yet not allowing them to dominate. The IASB can function effectively as a global standard setter only if it is, and is seen to be, an impartial and neutral general international body that complies with due process and makes fully-informed decisions that reflect in an unbiased way views from all over the world, and which is accountable to all of its stakeholders.

B. Equivalence: An Alternative Way Forward

If the possibility of IFRS becoming the universal language of international financial reporting looks more remote than it may have done before the crisis, a more positive assessment can be made in relation to another level of international activity that has also been aiming at the goal of removing unnecessary reporting burdens associated with cross-border capital market activity. This level is the transatlantic dialogue on equivalence of accounting standards. As noted earlier, equivalence can be thought of as a halfway house or compromise that falls short of full convergence to a single global set of standards but which can be effective to open up foreign access to a market because it relieves entrants from the burden of having to comply with selected local requirements.

The transatlantic dialogue on equivalence has not been entirely easy.[113] Each side has pursued its own agenda and often put pressure on the other—understandably so, since national/regional financial authorities enter into dialogues and cooperative alliances with their foreign counterparts to fulfil their fundamental domestic duties to maintain confidence in their own markets and to protect their own investors, and not because those duties have been displaced by some other goal. For a while, the threat that foreign companies operating in the EEA might be required by the disclosure framework mandated by the Prospectus and Transparency Obligations Directives[114] to use IFRS unless their accounts had been drawn up under a system that EU bodies deemed to be equivalent appeared to put Europe into the ascendancy.[115] The timetable originally envisaged by these Directives was for the requirements for third-country issuers to come into effect from 2007. One commentator has argued that the political pressure exerted by this threat goaded the SEC into action.[116] Yet with the announcement in 2005

[113] E Tafara, 'The Road to Regulatory Convergence: Where are We and Where are We Going?', 27 April 2005, gives an account of areas of controversy and how they were resolved. Text of speech available at <http://www.sec.gov/news/speech/spch042705et.htm>.

[114] Prospectus Directive 2003/71/EC, [2003] OJ l345/64; Transparency Obligations Directive 2004/109/EC, [2004] L390/38.

[115] The events described in this paragraph are discussed further in Ferran, above n 69, 484–89.

[116] Cunningham, above n 40.

that the European Commission and the SEC had agreed on a 'roadmap' towards equivalence between IFRS and the US GAAP, the initiative began to shift back across the Atlantic and was seized decisively by the SEC in its earlier-than-expected decision in 2008 to abolish reconciliation requirements for foreign issuers that prepare financial statements under IFRS. The SEC's ruling effectively made the European decision on US GAAP–IFRS equivalence, for which in the intervening period the deadline had been postponed, a foregone conclusion: with the need to hold on to a bargaining chip now eliminated by the SEC's decision to abolish reconciliation, and with major differences having been addressed though the convergence process, it was appropriate to regard the US GAAP as equivalent to IFRS as adopted in the Union.[117]

So, notwithstanding various spats along the way, bilateral dialogue eventually resulted in a major breakthrough. That some of the groundwork had been done by the IFRS–US GAAP convergence project serves to illustrate the point that different market-opening strategies often complement and interact with each other rather than being two truly parallel avenues. Looking forward, the equivalence framework could well prove to be a major milestone on the route to eventual full convergence around a set of global standards. One detail of the equivalence determinations is worth highlighting in this regard. The SEC's concession for foreign issuers does not extend to issuers using regional variants of IFRS, because the SEC felt that allowing the use of IFRS as adopted by the EU or other variants would be less effective in fostering the development and use of a single set of high-quality global accounting standards.[118] The SEC's stance puts pressure on its European counterparts not to deviate from the IASB version of IFRS.[119] As such, it has the potential to encourage restrained use of jurisdictional filters, which could benefit the international standard-setting process by neutralising a significant threat to its overall integrity.

VII. INTERNATIONAL MUTUAL RECOGNITION

In June 2009, the CESR issued a call for evidence on mutual recognition with non-EU jurisdictions.[120] The Committee acknowledged that work on mutual recognition with the US, a project that had been on the agenda since early 2007, had been delayed by the financial crisis and the change in the US Administration. However, the CESR argued that it was important to continue investigating the opportunities

[117] Commission Regulation (EC) No 1289/2008, rec 7; Commission Decision 2008/961/EC, [2008] OJ L340/112, rec 8.

[118] SEC, above n 70, 33.

[119] The SEC has given a temporary accommodation in respect of the EU's carve out in respect of IAS 39 covering only the first two financial years ending after 15 November 2007.

[120] CESR, *Call for Evidence on Mutual Recognition with Non-EU Jurisdictions* (CESR/09-406b).

of mutual recognition with third countries as a way of reducing the complexities, burdens and costs associated with cross-border capital market activity.

Given the EU's familiarity with mutual recognition, and also the extent to which deepening EU–US cooperation has been seen to be key to boosting the competitiveness of both regions' economies, it is unsurprising that mutual recognition was a topic on the pre-crisis transatlantic bilateral regulatory agenda and that European bodies are keen to revive interest in it. Yet from the European perspective, one striking fact about the pre-crisis period is that it was not between the US and the EU where the most significant developments in international mutual recognition were taking place. This is worth exploring, as it sets the background for consideration of the prospects for meaningful progress in EU–US mutual recognition going forward.

The CESR traces the emergence of recent interest in international mutual recognition back to 2007. Proposals gathered pace in early 2008 with a number of significant developments, including an SEC–European Commission joint press statement indicating an intention to work towards an EU–US mutual recognition arrangement,[121] an announcement by the SEC of a series of actions it intended to take to further the implementation of the concept of mutual recognition for high-quality regulatory regimes in other countries,[122] and the commencement of a process aimed at paving the way for discussions on a potential US–Canada mutual recognition arrangement for exchanges and financial firms.[123] However, it was with Australia that the first formal agreement under the new initiative was concluded.[124] The agreement provides a framework for the parties to consider regulatory exemptions that would permit eligible US and Australian stock exchanges and broker-dealers to operate in both jurisdictions in respect of certain types of investor, without the need for these entities (in certain aspects) to be regulated separately in both countries.

The SEC's heightened interest in mutual recognition during 2007 and early 2008 was widely regarded as a significant shift in the agency's approach to external relations.[125] Although other US financial regulatory agencies have operated mutual recognition arrangements for some time,[126] the SEC's only previous

[121] SEC-European Commission Press Release, 1 February 2008, available at <http://www.sec.gov/news/press/2008/2008-9.htm>.

[122] Press Release, 24 March 2008, available at <http://www.sec.gov/news/press/2008/2008-9.htm>.

[123] SEC-Canadian Securities Administrators Press Release, 29 May 2008, available at <http://www.sec.gov/news/press/2008/2008-98.htm>.

[124] *Mutual Recognition Arrangement Between the United States Securities and Exchange Commission and the Australian Securities and Investments Commission, Together with the Australian Minister for Superannuation and Corporate Law*, discussed in P Schammo, 'Regulating Stock Exchanges' (2008) 57 *International and Comparative Law Quarterly* 827.

[125] There was also a related (some would say competing) SEC proposal to reform its Rule 15a-6, which provides conditional exemptions from registration under US law for foreign broker-dealers. See <http://www.sec.gov/rules/proposed/2008/34-58047.pdf>.

[126] The Chicago-based Commodity Futures Trading Commission (CFTC) has employed the mutual recognition concept in derivatives markets and has operated it with a number of European regulators for over a decade. The home-country principle is also well established in US banking regulation. See EF Greene, 'Beyond Borders: Time To Tear Down the Barriers to Global Investing' (2007) 48 *Harvard International Law Journal* 85, 87.

foray into mutual recognition as a practical reality (rather than a concept in principle)[127] was a 1991 agreement with Canada.[128] That agreement was intended to remove barriers to cross-border issuance activity, but it was subject to various limitations that reduced its practical value.[129]

Why was the EU not the US's first partner in the new push on mutual recognition? One reason for asking this question is that it has been said that European law, in the form of the Markets in Financial Instruments Directive (MiFID),[130] offers 'a blueprint for a mutual recognition regime between the United States and other jurisdictions'.[131] On the surface, the EU's particularly rich experience could be thought to have made it the obvious candidate for the pioneering role. However, on closer examination, it becomes apparent that there are several considerations that have explanatory force in understanding why the first framework agreement was struck elsewhere.

First, the idea that European law in the form of MiFID provides a 'blueprint' for international mutual recognition is open to question, because if 'blueprint' is understood to denote a detailed plan, this overstates MiFID's suitability for export. The Directive's success as a Union-wide market-opening mechanism is built on the foundation of a mature, complex internal market regulatory and institutional framework at both national and regional level, and, as such, it contains certain features that could not easily be replicated internationally. It may be more accurate to describe it as a 'prototype'—that is, a model that serves as the basis for the development of later versions.

Under MiFID, described by Moloney as the 'leviathan' of the Financial Services Action Plan,[132] Union-incorporated regulated firms and markets and multilateral trading facilities that are authorised in one Member State enjoy an unlimited passport to operate elsewhere in the Union without the need for reauthorisation.[133] The distribution of supervisory responsibilities under the MiFID passport is that these are located in a firm's home State irrespective of where services are provided.[134] As this implies, home State control extends to conduct of business regulation subject only to quite limited exceptions.[135]

The operation of the MiFID passport is tied to a very detailed substantive regulatory framework governing the organisation and conduct of investment business,

[127] *Ibid*, fn 12 notes previous consideration by the SEC of similar approaches.

[128] Securities Act Release No 6902 (June 21, 1991).

[129] HS Scott, *International Finance: Law and Regulation* (London, Sweet & Maxwell, 2004) 53.

[130] Directive 2004/39/EC, [2004] OJ L145/1.

[131] EJ Pan, 'A European Solution to the Regulation of Cross-Border Markets' (2007) 2 *Brooklyn Journal of Corporate, Financial & Commercial Law* 133.

[132] N Moloney, *EC Securities Regulation*, 2nd edn (Oxford, Oxford University Press, 2008) 356.

[133] *Ibid*, 392, 806 and 813. The passport does not extend to branches (rather than subsidiaries) of third country firms and operators, which can operate in the Union only on the basis of State-by-State authorisation: MiFID, rec 28.

[134] Moloney, above n 132, p 392.

[135] There is an exception in relation to branches that enables host States to retain some control: *ibid*, 392. Cross-border activity by regulated markets is subject to certain arrangements for cooperation between home and host States: *ibid*, 806.

which is set out in MiFID and accompanying Level 2 rules.[136] The extent to which MiFID imposes regulatory uniformity on Member States is apparent from Article 4 of the MiFID Level 2 Directive, which sets out conditions for creating or retaining national requirements that go beyond MiFID: Member States must notify the European Commission of these additional requirements and must be able to justify them.[137] The CESR supports the task of ensuring that MiFID is implemented consistently across the Union. In EU financial law parlance, coordination of Member States' implementation of Level 1 and Level 2 measures and efforts to promote supervisory convergence are known as 'Level 3' activity.

It is hard to conceive of anything akin to the EU system being closely replicated at the international level. Realistically, mutual recognition at the international level is more likely to take the form of broad, but not unlimited, exemptions from 'host' country laws, and to depend on the partner jurisdictions being satisfied that there is enough common ground (in other words, equivalence) between their regulatory rules and their supervisory practices and philosophy to ensure broadly similar outcomes, and being willing to commit to more cooperation and coordination between their supervisory authorities.

Certainly the SEC's preconditions for entry into mutual recognition arrangements with other countries, though demanding, are not as stringent as those that are now established in the EU legal framework. The new mutual recognition scheme is based on comparability assessments by both regulators of each other's regulatory structures taking place before the mutual recognition scheme comes into operation. The comparability assessment, as envisaged by the SEC, is aimed at determining whether regulation of markets and intermediaries in the foreign jurisdiction is comparable to that in the home jurisdiction, but it need not be exactly the same. Also integral to the comparability assessment as outlined by the SEC is the quality of oversight and enforcement in the foreign jurisdiction. Again, comparability of outcomes rather than identical approaches is the touchstone. (However, in seeking to understand why Australia was the country with which the US commenced its new mutual recognition venture, it is worth noting that it is the jurisdiction that on various measurements comes closest to the United States in the level of its enforcement intensity.[138]) As for home State control, that an international arrangement is likely to involve much less deferral by the 'host' country to the home State than is now mandated by EU law is also supported by the US–Australia arrangement, which reserves to the partner jurisdictions full power to pursue violations of their own anti-fraud laws and regulations.

[136] Level 2 refers to technical implementing measures for framework (Level 1) directives.

[137] Directive 2006/73/EC.

[138] HE Jackson, 'Variation in the Intensity of Financial Regulation: Preliminary Evidence and Potential Implications' (2007) 24 *Yale Journal on Regulation* 101.

In the European securities law context, the pragmatic compromises[139] involved in having similarity between regimes via a minimum harmonisation programme and a division of responsibilities between home and host States eventually failed to deliver the desired outcomes and had to be replaced by MiFID and the institutional overhaul that led to the CESR. European experience could thus be taken to suggest that the model that is emerging at the international level is one that could be subject to serious limitations. However, a minimalist approach may be less problematic where what is at stake is 'merely' the removal of barriers to cross-border investment rather than the establishment of a fully-integrated single market. Furthermore, also evident from the European experience is that systems evolve, and that an arrangement that is limited in scope and effect can serve as a foundation for something more ambitious in the longer term.

A set of factors that would complicate the task of striking a mutual recognition arrangement that involves the EU, flows from its status as a regional grouping that locates responsibility for supervision with national agencies rather than with a single pan-European authority.[140] Questions arise about the levels at which comparability exercises should be conducted. Should the SEC focus initially on the quality of European regulation and supervision as a whole; and likewise the European Commission supported by the CESR in respect of US supervision? Assuming a favourable decision by both sides, this approach would pave the way for the supervisory authorities of individual Member States to conclude bilateral supervisory and enforcement memoranda of understanding with the SEC, thereby completing the steps for mutual recognition to come into effect. This approach would give Union institutions a controlling role in establishing the methodology to govern discussions between the SEC and interested Member States. Alternatively, should the SEC bypass Union institutions and direct its inquiries to the quality of regulation and supervision in individual Member States, since that is where responsibility for supervision and enforcement actually lies, and work bilaterally with that State's supervisory agency to determine the comparative quality of each other's system? But would Member States be free to pursue the possibility of a stand-alone bilateral mutual recognition arrangement with the US outside an EU-approved framework, or would this conflict with the distribution of competencies between Member States and the Union or with obligations on Member States to ensure that their bilateral external relations are conducted in a manner that is compatible with Union obligations?[141] These

[139] B Steil, 'Regional Financial Market Integration: Learning from the European Experience' (1999) 12 *Tokyo Club Papers* 99, notes that minimum harmonisation-based mutual recognition was chosen as the basis for Single Market legislation primarily on pragmatic grounds.

[140] Canada is also a regional grouping without a single regulator, but its set-up is less complex than that in the EU.

[141] On this topic see M Cremona, 'Defending the Community Interest: the Duties of Cooperation and Compliance' in M Cremona and B de Witte (eds), *EU Foreign Relations Law* (Oxford, Hart Publishing, 2008) 125; and more generally P Koutrakos, *EU International Relations Law* (Oxford, Hart Publishing, 2006).

issues must, ultimately, be viewed against the broader background, in which the external interests of the single market in terms of international competitiveness are increasingly important.[142]

Uncertainty and controversy surrounded these issues in the early stages of the renewed interest in international mutual recognition. During 2007, the CESR warned that stand-alone bilateral negotiations between the US and individual Member States law regarding third countries market participants' access to the Single Market could be detrimental to the mutual trust between supervisory authorities in Europe, and challenge the credibility and the efficiency of the whole EU supervisory system.[143] Commissioner McCreevy felt it necessary to set out a set of principles or 'red lines' for the development of mutual recognition between the EU and the US that included an emphasis on a genuine, mutually-agreed cooperative approach that was multilateral rather than unilateral or bilateral, and an insistence that it should apply equally across the EU.[144] The desirability of Europe 'sticking together' in this matter was also discussed in the European Securities Committee.[145]

The joint SEC–Commission announcement in February 2008, that the US had agreed that the first step should be a framework for mutual recognition discussions developed by the SEC and the European Commission staff, assisted by the CESR, seems to indicate that the EU institutions 'won' the argument to promote a Union-first approach. Presumably it was only after the issues of lead responsibility had been settled in this way that serious work on the substantive issues involved in an EU–US comparability assessment could properly begin. The CESR call for evidence in June 2009 creates an impression that this work is still in its early stages, but in the absence of detailed, publicly-available information, it is impossible to be sure how much progress has actually been made.

In principle a comparability exercise involving an assessment of the quality of EU regulation compared to US regulation should be relatively straightforward. One of the guiding principles that underpinned recent EU securities law reform, in particular MiFID, was that European markets should be well placed to take advantage of the globalisation of securities markets.[146] In other words, the recent European reforms can be viewed as having been deliberately designed to be

[142] M Cremona, 'The External Dimension of the Single Market: Builiding (on) the Foundations' in C Barnard and J Scott (eds), *The Law of the Single Market—Unpacking the Premises* (Oxford, Hart Publishing, 2002), ch 14.

[143] CESR, *A Proposed Evolution of EU Securities Supervision Beyond 2007* (07-783, November 2007), 5.

[144] C McCreevy, 'Security Markets Consolidation and its Implications', 30 November 2007. Text of speech available at <http://www.europa.eu/rapid/pressReleasesAction.do?reference=SPEECH/07/776&format=HTML&aged=0&language=en>.

[145] Draft Summary Record of the 53rd Meeting of the European Securities Committee (12 July 2007), Working Document ESC-31-2007.

[146] European Commission, *Communication from the Commission to the European Parliament and the Council: Upgrading The Investment Services Directive* (COM(2000) 729), para 5.2.

'mutual recognition friendly'.[147] Thus, while a comparability assessment between the US and EU approach to the regulation of investment firms, markets and trading platforms would no doubt identify many differences in the detailed rules,[148] it seems unlikely that one side's regulatory framework would be found by the other to fall short of world standards, judged by reference to comparability of outcomes. That internationally-agreed standards should serve as the reference point for such evaluations appears uncontentious.[149]

Comparability of supervision presents more controversial issues. Even in the simplest case where the comparison is between two countries that each has a nationwide system of capital market regulation, difficulties abound because different countries organise things in different ways. To make sense of these differences and to evaluate their significance, there is a need for an assessment methodology that operates at a level of intensity that is sufficient to enable each of the participating countries to defend robustly to potentially hostile local constituencies their assessment that the other regime can be relied upon to deliver comparable standards, despite differences in how supervision is conducted, but which does not become too preoccupied with trivial details and which does not risk undermining established cooperative relationships by offensively intruding into areas of national sovereignty. Objective, verifiable data, such as supervisory budgets, staffing levels and enforcement activity (actions brought, fees levied, etc), could have an important role in this, but a quantitative approach may not fully capture all of the relevant considerations.[150] Regulators with frontline responsibility for conducting such exercises appear to be feeling their way, and a standard approach has yet to emerge.[151]

An already challenging task becomes even more complicated where what is involved is not a country-to-country comparison but an exercise in comparing one country to a regional grouping of 27 individual countries, each of which has its own separate arrangements for capital market supervision. First, while EU-wide supervision of securities markets is now more coordinated, it remains

[147] K Nicolaïdis and G Shaffer, 'Transnational Mutual Recognition Regimes: Governance without Global Government' (2005) 68 *Law and Contemporary Problems* 263, 265.

[148] G Petrella, 'MiFID, Reg NMS and competition across trading venues in Europe and the USA' (2010) 18 *Journal of Financial Regulation and Compliance* 257; K Lannoo, *MiFID and Reg NMS A test-case for 'substituted compliance'?*, ECMI Policy Brief No 8 (July 2007).

[149] See J White, SEC Director of Corporation Finance, 'Corporation Finance in 2008—International Initiatives', 14 January 2008. Text of speech available at <http://www.sec.gov/news/speech/2008/spch011408jww.htm>.

[150] HE Jackson, 'Toward a New Regulatory Paradigm for the Trans-Atlantic Financial Market and Beyond: Legal and Economic Perspectives' (2011) 12 *European Business Organization Law Review* (forthcoming).

[151] Even in respect of the US–Australia arrangement, no formal statement as to the criteria and methodology for the comparability assessment is in the public domain at the time of writing. For an informal indication of what a comparability assessment might examine, see ER Sirri, Director, SEC's Division of Trading and Markets, 'Foreign Issuers & the US Securities Laws 2008: Strategies for the Changing Regulatory Environment', 30 April 2008. Text of speech available at <http://www.sec.gov/news/speech/2008/spch043008ers.htm>.

implausible to suggest there is a consistent EU-wide standard of supervision that is comparable to that achieved in the US. Secondly, since supervision is a Member State responsibility, a mutual recognition framework at EU–US level would not suffice on its own; US–individual Member State dialogues would also be needed to put in place the enhanced arrangements for supervisory cooperation that are central to the SEC's mutual recognition scheme and to work out the precise access arrangements for firms and products from the other country. Complex questions of European law could arise as to what Member States can agree to in respect of access. For example, there is a suggestion in the academic literature that SEC mutual recognition in respect of Member States might be limited to financial products fully overseen by the signature Member State and might not extend to products passported into that State from elsewhere in the Union.[152] However, such an arrangement looks quite similar to the nationality clauses in bilateral aviation agreements between the US and various Member States that restricted international traffic rights to the national flag carriers of the countries concerned; as such, it would seem to give rise to problems under EU law.[153]

Taking all of these factors together, it is not hard to see why the EU was not a suitable partner for the SEC's pilot mutual recognition scheme. Even without a financial crisis to stall the process, it is quite likely that working out a US–EU mutual recognition framework would have taken quite some time to achieve.

Where do things stand in the aftermath of the crisis? The reorientation of policy priorities engendered by the financial turmoil has undoubtedly led to a loss of momentum in relation to international mutual recognition. Some of this delay can be attributed to practicalities—ie, the emergence of other, more pressing, short-term regulatory demands—but there are signs that suggest a reassessment on the American side of the fundamental merits of international mutual recognition.

Thinking within the SEC that underpinned the shift towards making more use of international mutual recognition employed an ingenious argument that emphasised the position of retail investors and their greater propensity to seek out international investment opportunities.[154] It was argued that regulation needed to catch up with the technological developments that had made global markets a reality even for less sophisticated investors. Such developments created a need for a framework that would lower the transaction costs of investing in foreign securities and protect all investors by providing them with reliable information about

[152] Jackson, above n 150.

[153] *Commission v United Kingdom, Denmark, Sweden, Finland, Belgium, Luxembourg, Austria, Germany*, Cases C-466/98, [2002] ECR I-9427, C-467/98, [2002] ECR I-9519, C-468/98, [2002] ECR I-9575, C-469/98, [2002] ECR I-9627, C-471/98, [2002] ECR I-9681, C-472/98, [2002] ECR I-9741, C-475/98, [2002] ECR I-9797 and C-476/98, [2002] ECR I-9855.

[154] Tafara and Peterson, above n 35.

the quality of protection different jurisdictions offer investors.[155] However, not everyone has found this analysis convincing. Recent scholarship has been sceptical about the claim that international mutual recognition would benefit retail investors.[156] In particular, it has been said that 'mutual recognition *vis-à-vis* European and similar regulatory regimes cannot be justified if what we are looking for is true comparability'[157] because European regulation has developed by reference to markets that are dominated by institutional investors, whereas the US system relates to markets that have a strong retail base. Langevoort suggests that, in reality, the benefits in international mutual recognition would accrue to the financial services industry, but only at the cost of increased risk to less well-diversified retail investors.

The new top officers of the SEC appear to share the doubts about international mutual recognition's capacity to strengthen investor protection. In her confirmation hearing, new SEC Chairman Schapiro said that mutual recognition was

> another area where I think you take a big step back and look at whether we're headed in the right direction. I want to ensure that US investors' protections are maximized going forward, not that they're compromised.[158]

Practical concerns about the labour-intensive nature of putting an international mutual recognition scheme into effect and monitoring its operation have also been attributed to the top level of the current SEC.[159]

So the signs are that, for now, the US authorities, which can be viewed as a key target market for the EU's biggest regulatory export—mutual recognition—have lost interest. The likelihood is that the CESR will face an uphill task in seeking to revive the project. Since one of the effects of the crisis has been to focus the attention of governments on the need to reform and strengthen their domestic regulatory institutions, it may indeed seem quite odd that the CESR is continuing to push a scheme that involves making judgements on the quality of other countries' regimes. A possible explanation is that the Union institutions are in this for the long haul.[160] International mutual recognition has the capacity to promote regulatory and supervisory convergence around world-class standards.[161] As such, it is worth not giving up on it completely.

[155] *Ibid.*

[156] DC Langevoort, 'The SEC, Retail Investors, and the Institutionalization of the Securities Markets' (2009) 95 *Virginia Law Review* 1025.

[157] *Ibid*, 1075.

[158] Schapiro, above n 74.

[159] *Accounting & Compliance Alert* (4 March 2009) reports remarks by SEC Commissioner Walter to this effect.

[160] CESR, above n 143, acknowledges mutual recognition dialogue with US authorities as part of political efforts to advocate the interest of Europe and promote an EU model of regulation.

[161] C Cox, SEC Chairman, 'The Future of International Standards and Cooperation in Light of the Credit Crisis', 18 November 2008. Text of speech available at <http://www.iasplus.com/usa/sec/0811coxifrs.pdf>.

VIII. CONCLUSIONS

After a brief period during the financial crisis when countries appeared to be lurching towards economic nationalism, the international community has reaffirmed its commitment to open markets that are regulated in balanced ways that promote innovation while discouraging abuse. Hence, it remains important to look closely at market-opening regulatory strategies.

Before the crisis, a lot of momentum had built up behind flagship projects in financial reporting and mutual recognition. This chapter has looked at those projects through a post-crisis lens. Much has changed. The United States has stepped back from transition to IFRS, thereby making universal adoption of IFRS as the language of international financial reporting a more distant prospect. A cooling of US interest in international mutual recognition has also made rapid progress on that front unlikely, notwithstanding efforts by European Union bodies to keep things moving.

Irrespective of what happens to the flagship projects, international capital market regulation can be expected to remain dynamic. One of its strengths is its creative ability to employ a range of different strategies to achieve its underlying goals; this multifaceted approach helps progress to continue in the direction of the creation of a broadly consistent global framework that is conducive to cross-border investment activity, even when certain mechanisms hit difficulties. One illustration is that regulatory equivalence agreements between countries can alleviate significantly the burden of regulatory duplication; but unlike universal standards, which would also perform that role, they do not raise contentious issues about delegating rule-making powers to a third party.

International standard setting and bilateral regulatory dialogues are the two key routes that lead to international regulatory convergence towards a consistent set of rules. Post-crisis, 'global solutions' worked out by international standard-setting bodies have assumed particular prominence, but this chapter argues that bilateral exchanges still have an important role to play and that the two routes complement each other. It focuses, in particular, on the bilateral regulatory dialogue between the United States and the European Union. A well-functioning transatlantic securities regulation bilateral dialogue arrangement has the capacity to support global regulation by providing a forum in which generally-worded world standards acquire more content so as to become practically operational on a cross-border basis. A stronger, more independent global institutional framework for securities regulation could also be good for EU–US relations by providing a buffer that can smooth out frictions in their bilateral relations.

3

When is Migration not Migration? Examining Services in the EU and GATS

ELSPETH GUILD

I. INTRODUCTION

MIGRATION POLICY AND law have become a political minefield in many European and developed-world countries. Whether it is the spectre of overcrowded little boats arriving on the northern shores of the Mediterranean, asylum seekers from Afghanistan and Iraq making claims for protection against return, or labour migrants obtaining work permits in times of rising unemployment, there is rarely an opportunity for politicians to come out of a debate on migration in a winning position. Yet the world economy depends upon many sorts of migration, whether in a short form such as tourism, where people from one country travel to another to enjoy a holiday, longer-term movement such as that of students in an increasingly international academic world, or potentially even long-term movement where enterprises send their personnel across the world following investments, expansion opportunities and career openings. As the word 'migration' is increasingly associated with negative images and poverty, a new language has developed to encompass politically acceptable forms of migration.

The concept of migration depends on the existence of inter-State borders which are the object of sovereignty claims by States regarding their citizens and others. Thereafter, there needs to be a possibility that the individual may travel beyond the borders of the State (or States) of which he or she is a citizen. The cross-border movement of individuals must be accompanied both by the allocation of a citizenship status to the individual which is evidenced in some form or is otherwise discernible, and by an administrative system—at least in the country to which the individual is going—which recognises the individual as foreign and differentiates its treatment of him or her accordingly. Normally this means that the individual is entitled to fewer rights (and possibly subject to few duties, for instance in the case of military service or taxes) than citizens of the State.

Once the individual falls into the general category of 'foreigner', the variety of possible statuses which may be applied to him or her multiplies. Depending on how the individual is categorised, he or she may acquire quite different and normatively charged titles. For instance, so long as the individual is a foreigner or an alien, this defines the individual as the responsibility of another State in general terms. However, once the individual is categorised as an immigrant or a migrant, a different relationship with the host State comes into existence. Both terms are meant to define foreigners, and both relate to the degree of social and economic insertion the individual plans or hopes to have. But nationals of some countries are more easily defined as immigrants or migrants than those of others. For instance, it is rare to come across US citizens being described as migrants or immigrants (except by statisticians). On the other hand, Moroccans or Malians in many parts of Europe are almost always described as immigrants or migrants. Further, the children of immigrants who have acquired citizenship of the host State are often described in European discussions as 'second generation immigrants'.[1] This discourse was particularly evident (and problematic) during the 2005 social disturbances in the suburbs of Paris, where the categorisation of young French citizens as 'immigrants' provided a mechanism to speak of ethnicity without using the term. The allocation of the terms 'immigrant' or 'migrant' is not necessarily neutral, but in many circumstances, particularly in Europe, is already normatively loaded.

The first separation which western liberal democracies make is between foreigners who are legally on the territory and those who are present irregularly. Here the force of the use of the terms 'immigrant' and 'migrant' is particularly clear: if someone were to be described as an 'irregular foreigner', it would be uncertain exactly what aspect of the foreigner was irregular: His or her behaviour? His or her dress? One would not be sure. As soon as the term 'migrant' or 'immigrant' is used there is no long any doubt—an image is evoked which relates to the decision of the State whether to admit or refuse admission to the individual. While the European Union exclusively uses the term 'illegal migrant', most international fora prefer less normative terms, such as 'irregular' or 'undocumented' migrants.

This division of foreigners into legal and irregular is made exclusively on the basis of the host State's knowledge of the individual. A 'regular migrant' is someone who has passed through the formal processes of the State and whom the State recognises as an individual who is entitled to be on the territory. It is a State-centric division which reinforces States' claim to a monopoly on the legitimacy of movement across borders. Most commonly these processes take place at borders and require the formal presentation of documents. Particularly in the context of the European Union, this paradigm of the border as the place where the State and the individual meet is subject to change. An 'illegal immigrant' is someone who

[1] A good example of this is the press release of the Bertelsmann Foundation regarding the award of a prize in education for children of immigrants, available at <http://www.bertelsmann-stiftung.de/cps/rde/xchg/SID-0A000F0A-CF63108F/bst_engl/hs.xsl/nachrichten_86840.htm>.

has not fulfilled the State's rules on admission or stay. This group may be further divided into 'clandestine immigrants'—a term usually used to describe persons who crossed the border surreptitiously, avoiding all contact with State officials who would refuse them entry—and 'irregular immigrants'. The latter term may be used to include clandestine immigrants, but it also covers those who arrived lawfully but who overstayed the period of time they were permitted to be on the territory, or who engaged in activities which were prohibited by the immigration status which the State had given them. The most common example of this is the foreigner who arrives as a tourist and then stays on beyond the end of his or her permitted stay and takes a job. While the content of the term 'illegal immigrant' may be clear, many people who fit into the category will not be considered or treated as such by State officials.

Australia has excellent statistics on entry and exit from its territory, as it has a mandatory registration system which is tied to the transport companies. According to the Australian Government's publication *Immigration Compliance* (2005),[2] the highest number of visitors to Australia were British citizens. Of those foreign nationals who stayed beyond the period permitted by their visas (set out in the delicately named 'Visitor Non Return Rates'), the global average is 1.22 per cent but the average for British citizens in Australia is 1.58 per cent. Thus the country whose nationals, objectively both in numeric and percentage terms, represent the greatest risk of overstaying their visit visa in Australia is Britain. If the category of 'illegal immigrant' were one neutral of normative content then the efforts of the Australian authorities to reduce overstaying of visit visas would be directed principally against British citizens. Instead, the Australian report itself obscures the issue by grouping the statistics in such a way that the category of overstayers described as 'a considerable burden to the community because of the cost of their location and removal from Australia'[3] is separate from the Visitor Non Return Rates (by including all sorts of other categories of persons in the first, but only visitors in the second), thereby providing an overstaying rate which puts nationals of Kiribati at the top of the list—the result of Kiribati having a tiny population from which even one individual overstaying will change the statistics.[4]

Irregular migrants, overstayers and 'visitor non returners' do not remain in their categories indefinitely. As the Australian authorities note in the 2005 report, 'most overstayers only overstay in Australia for a few days'.[5] Because the status is one allocated by the host State by reference exclusively to its own rules, once the individual leaves the State, he or she ceases to come within the category. The same individual

[2] Available at <http://www.immi.gov.au/media/publications/compliance/managing-the-border/pdf/mtb-chapter5.pdf>.

[3] *Ibid*, 37.

[4] According to the Australian Government, the total population of Kiribati is 88,500; see <http://www.ausaid.gov.au/country/country.cfm?CountryId=20>.

[5] *Immigration Compliance*, above n 2, 37.

may return to the State and overstay again, or go to another country and overstay there as a result of very different rules applicable to that State. Or the individual may go to his or her country of origin and never fall into the category again. These are the options immediately available to the individual as the result of his or her own actions. It is also open to the State to remove the individual from the status of irregularity. This may happen in many different ways. First, the State may change its rules, eg extend the period of time generally available for visitors to remain on the territory. As a result of an international agreement, nationals of one State may cease to be irregular on the territory of another State and enjoy a right of residence there. This happened in the EU in 2004 and again in 2007, when, by reason of their States of nationality joining the EU, nationals of 10 countries in 2004 and two countries in 2007 gained a right of residence which reduced to a very low level the possibility that they would become irregularly present in other EU States. The State may take a decision in respect of the individual to extend his or her permission to be on the territory after a period of irregular residence, for instance on the basis of marriage to a national or successful studies. Alternatively, the State may open a wider regularisation programme to bring classes of foreigners irregularly on the territory into regularity. Lastly, the State may seek to force the foreigner to leave the territory ultimately by expulsion, a more or less expensive option depending on how far the country of nationality is from the host country.[6]

In view of the highly-contested territory which is the political discussion on migration, it is not surprising that when the international community came to touch upon the subject of movement of persons across international borders in the context of service provision, every effort was made to ring-fence the field from contamination by the immigration debate. In this chapter, I examine how EU law relating to the free movement of services has come to include what some Member States have sought to qualify as labour migration, and the mechanisms of interpretation of the European Court of Justice used to safeguard service provision from the migration debate. One of the consequences of the ring-fencing of the right of service provision has been the displacement of the political discussion on the consequences of movement of workers in the form of service provision from a 'migration' debate to one dominated by challenges regarding the protection of labour standards and social contributions.[7] This chapter will look at how that process of separating migration from service provision, even where service provision involves movement of persons across international borders for the purpose of economic activity, has taken place first in the EU and secondly in the WTO. In this sense the chapter constitutes a case study on the parallel mechanisms for privileging labour migration by removing it from the field of migration politics first in the EU and then in the WTO.

[6] I have developed further on this area in the first chapter of my book, E Guild, *Security and Migration in the 21st Century* (Cambridge, Polity Press, 2009).

[7] See, eg, the ECJ's judgments in Case C-341/05 *Laval* [2007] ECR I-11767 and Case C-438/05 *Viking* [2007] ECR I-10779.

That the mechanisms mirror one another in their legal approaches bears attention, notwithstanding the rather different institutional structures of the EU and the WTO. The need to find a mechanism to avoid interior ministry control over types of labour migration central to the capacity of companies to carry out business across borders, results in both cases in a privileging of the right of service provision over the status of the individual. One might say that by making the individual worker 'invisible' to interior ministries by subsuming him or her to the employer through the categorisation of the activity as service provision and not migration, renders the individual fundamentally voiceless before the authorities of the State where he or she will be carrying out the activities.

To reveal the tensions, I shall, in this chapter, juxtapose against the EU experience in service provision the WTO's General Agreement on Trade in Services (GATS), which acknowledges in mode 4 the necessity for natural persons to move in order to provide services, either on their own account or on the account of their employers. The objective of GATS to reduce obstacles to the international movement of services comes up against the same issues that trouble the EU, and with which it continues to struggle, as regards protectionism in respect of the movement of persons for service provision. The mechanisms adopted in the GATS mirror, with important differences, the EU approaches, permitting the continuation of obstacles to movement of services where this includes the movement of persons in respect of categories of activities. The chapter ends with an overview of the GATS approaches to the issues of labour standards and social protection, and the lessons which the EU experiences can provide.

Institutionally, it is important to remember that the EU enjoys very strong mechanisms which encourage Member States, correctly, to apply EU law. The supremacy of EU law over national law is generally accepted throughout the Union. The European Commission has among its tasks the power to take infringement proceedings against recalcitrant Member States where they fail properly to apply EU law (which, as this case study will show, is frequently). The Court of Justice has the power to hand down binding judgments which the courts in the Member States by and large apply fairly faithfully. The whole structure of the EU is designed teleologically—there is an end in sight, the completion of the internal market, to which all measures should contribute. There are four fundamental freedoms which form the internal market, one of which is free movement of services. So service provision is at the constitutional heart of the EU and enjoys fierce protection by all the EU institutions (as the case study will demonstrate). The WTO is a multilateral organisation whose objective is to encourage the favourable conditions of cross-border trade. While it has institutions which are shadows of the EU institutions, its power to assure obedience by its Member States is much more limited. The judicial capacity of the WTO is only just beginning to make an impact, and as yet only one important decision has been handed down in the field of service provision which relates to gambling and has no impact on migration. There is no 'holy grail', like the four freedoms of the EU, to give direction to the WTO—or at least so far these have not emerged clearly.

Free movement of services in EU law includes the right of natural persons to move freely to provide services anywhere in the Member States. Where the service provider is a company, it has a right to send its third country national employees from one Member State to another to fulfil a service contract.[8] So far, third country nationals who are resident in the EU do not have a personal right to move across borders to provide services unless they come within the scope of the Directive on long-term resident third country nationals.[9] The right of businesses to send third country nationals across EU borders for service provision has been challenged by a number of Member States, though it has been firmly established by the European Court of Justice. Clearly there is a conceptual difficulty in imagining the employees of service providers as the extension of the business's right to service provision, rather than as workers who require work permits or whose presence constitutes access to the labour market. This chapter examines the tension between service provision and movement of workers in the EU as follows:

- Service provision among the Member States and third country nationals.
- The EU Services Directive and third country nationals.
- Member State mode 4 practices, labour migration and EU service provision.
- Conclusions.

II. SERVICE PROVISION AMONG THE MEMBER STATES AND THIRD COUNTRY NATIONALS

The right to provide services across the borders of the Member States is one of the fundamental freedoms of the internal market, the heart of the EU. It is contained in Article 56 TFEU (ex Article 49 EC) and applies to all nationals of the Member States, whether they are natural persons or businesses. This provision permits the EU institutions to extend the right to provide services to third country nationals who are established within the EU. The Commission proposed legislation to give effect to this power, but the Member States, in the form of the Council, rejected the proposal and eventually the Commission withdrew it.[10] A second attempt was made in the context of the negotiations on the Services Directive,[11] but this was not received favourably by the Council.

The Court of Justice has held that, so long as the Council has not adopted implementing legislation regarding the right of third country nationals to provide services in the EU, no such right exists. Third country nationals are not entitled to

[8] C Barnard, *Substantive Law of the EU: the Four Freedoms*, 2nd edn (Oxford, Oxford University Press, 2007) 254–408.

[9] Directive 2003/109, [2004] OJ L 16/44.

[10] COM(1999) 3.

[11] Directive 2006/123, [2006] OJ L376/36.

rely on Article 56 TFEU (ex Article 49 EC) to provide services across EU borders.[12] Where, however, the service provider is a business established in the EU,[13] so long as the service meets the requisite criterion (ie comprises activities of an industrial, commercial, craft or professional character), the business has the right to send its employees across EU borders to provide services, whether or not those workers have free movement rights themselves or are third country nationals.

The key challenge to such movement of persons took place in 1990 in respect of Portuguese workers who were deployed in France to carry out service provision for their employer. At the time, transitional provisions prohibiting the free movement of workers from Portugal had not yet expired.[14] The French labour inspectorate fined the employer for employing persons without the right to work in France without work permits. The European Court of Justice (ECJ) held that the fines were contrary to the right of free movement of services. The logic of the ECJ was that the right to provide services must include the right, where necessary, to move personnel to do so. If it did not, the service provider based in another Member State would be under a disadvantage, indeed suffer discrimination on the basis of nationality, in comparison with the national service provider which is its competitor and can move its personnel within the territory.

Additionally, the ECJ found that where there is a temporary movement of workers who are sent to another Member State to carry out a service contract, such workers return to their country of residence and employment at the completion of the job 'without at any time gaining access to the labour market'.[15] The key, then, to movement of personnel of any nationality across EU borders for service provision is the fact that the workers, according to the ECJ, do not gain access to the labour market. Hence there is no competition with domestic workers and no need for the business to obtain labour permits for third country national staff. The ECJ made an exception in respect of temporary employment agencies, which it found to be caught by the transitional provisions, as the purpose of such contracts was to provide labour. In response to the French Government's concern about social dumping, ie the movement of labour under conditions which do not comply with national rules of working conditions and wages, the ECJ found that Member States could apply their national law to such situations.

While the *Rush Portuguesa* judgment involved EU nationals who had not yet acquired a right to free movement as workers, the next important decision was about Moroccan workers resident in Belgium who were sent to France to carry

[12] Case C-290/04 *Scorpio* [2006] ECR I-9461.

[13] This is defined in Art 54 TFEU (ex Art 48 EC) as 'companies or firms formed in accordance with the law of a Member State and having their registered office, central administration or principal place of business within the [Union] ...'. It includes companies or firms constituted under civil or commercial law, including cooperative societies and other legal persons governed by public or private law save for those which are non-profit-making.

[14] Case C-113/89 *Rush Portuguesa* [1990] ECR I-1417.

[15] *Ibid*, para 15.

out a job (together with a number of Belgian colleagues).[16] The situation was broadly similar to that in the earlier case—this time a Belgian employer sent his work force (four Belgians and four Moroccans) to France to carry out a demolition job. The employer had taken the precaution of obtaining short-stay visas for the Moroccans from the French Consulate in Brussels. Nonetheless, the French labour inspectorate fined him for employing third country nationals in France without work permits. The ECJ again underlined that the right to provide services across the EU is a fundamental principle of the Union. Any interference with such a right could only be justified by overriding reasons in the general interest which are applied to all service providers irrespective of their nationality. The ECJ also noted that the Moroccans were lawfully resident in Belgium and in possession of visas which made their presence in France lawful. Once again the ECJ rejected the French Government's argument that the workers were participating in the labour force when they were not entitled to do so. It stated that workers, employed by an undertaking in one Member State, who are temporarily sent to another Member State to provide services, do not in any way seek access to the labour market in that second State if they return to their country of origin or residence after completion of their work. The ECJ permitted the host Member State to apply its national laws on collective labour agreements relating to minimum wages.

The Member States have not been particularly at ease with the result. In many Member States, legislation was maintained (contrary to the ECJ's judgments) which required businesses to obtain work permits for third country national employees being sent temporarily to another Member State for service provision. While a number of groups representing lawyers, such as the Immigration Law Practitioners Association in the UK and the Meijers Committee in The Netherlands, made submissions requesting better control over the implementation in the Member States of the *Vander Elst* judgment, little happened. The lack of progress on third country nationals and service provision was overtaken by a variety of other events in the EU, not least the abolition of intra-Member State border controls (leaving aside the UK and Ireland) in 1995 in the context of an intergovernmental agreement (the Schengen Agreements incorporated into the EU treaties in 1999). This at least meant that for most businesses in the EU, service provision, whether using nationals of the State or third country national employees, was not impeded by a passport check at an internal border. The French authorities, which had been the defendants in both cases which had come before the ECJ, began to adjust their system of controls to require only an *ex post* declaration from the business when a service provider who was a third country national commenced a service contract.

The legitimate concern of a number of Member States that provision of services might be used to undermine national wage and working conditions was,

[16] Case C-43/93 *Vander Elst* [1994] ECR I-3803.

in the meantime, addressed by the Posted Workers Directive.[17] This Directive applies to all posted workers moving within the EU, whether they are EU or third country nationals. Adopted in 1997, it provides that Member States shall ensure that, whatever the applicable law of the employment relationship, workers posted to their territory are guaranteed equal treatment with the State's own nationals (whether by way of regulation or collective agreement) regarding:

a) maximum working and minimum rest periods;
b) minimum paid annual holidays;
c) minimum rates of pay including overtime rates;
d) conditions of hiring out workers;
e) health, safety and hygiene at work;
f) protection of pregnant women at work;
g) equal treatment between men and women.

On the entry into force of this Directive, the issue of social dumping ought to have been resolved. The fact that it has continued to be a concern in the context of the Services Directive indicates that perhaps not all Member States are applying it in full.

In 2004 the European Commission proposed a directive to regulate the cross-border provision of services. The proposal was quite radical, not least as it included the principle that the regulation of service providers should take place in the State where they are based, not in the State where the service is provided. Substantial concerns were raised in a number of sectors, not least among trade unions regarding the extent to which this would provide adequate protection for workers and provide sufficient guarantees against social dumping. The Directive finally adopted in 2006 abandoned the more radical aspects which the Commission had proposed while still providing a new framework for the movement of services across the EU.[18]

The Directive was originally planned to include the movement of third country national employees of service providers based in the Union to fulfil service contracts in other Member States. The original proposal of the Commission included Article 25, which stated:

Article 25 Posting of third country nationals

1. Subject to the possibility of derogation as referred to in paragraph 2, where a provider posts a worker who is a national of a third country to the territory of another Member State in order to provide a service there, the Member State of posting may not require the provider or the worker posted by the latter to hold an entry, exit, residence or work permit, or to satisfy other equivalent conditions.

[17] Directive 96/71, [1997] OJ L18/1.
[18] Directive 2006/123, [2006] OJ L376/36.

2. Paragraph 1 does not prejudice the possibility for Member States to require a short-term visa for third country nationals who are not covered by the mutual recognition regime provided for in Article 21 of the Convention implementing the Schengen Agreement.
3. In the circumstances referred to in paragraph 1, the Member State of origin shall ensure that a provider posts only a worker who is resident in its territory in accordance with its own national rules and who is lawfully employed in its territory.
   The Member State of origin shall not regard a posting made in order to provide a service in another Member State as interrupting the residence or activity of the posted worker and shall not refuse to readmit the posted worker to its territory on the basis of its national rules.
   The Member State of origin shall communicate to the Member State of posting, upon its request and in the shortest possible time, information and guarantees regarding compliance with the first subparagraph and shall impose the appropriate penalties in cases of non-compliance.

The main issue, which received wide media interest regarding the European Parliament's vote on the Directive in February 2006, was the country of origin principle, ie the provision applying the regulatory law of the country of origin of the service provider to the conditions of the provision of the service. The European Parliament rejected this principle in favour of country of provision regulation. However, the European Parliament's report[19] on the Directive also proposed that Article 25 should be deleted, on the basis that the matter of third country national posted workers should be dealt with in the context of the protection of posted workers under Directive 96/71. This was incorporated into the final version.

At the same time as trying to get a legislative move on the issue, the Commission commenced a series of infringement proceedings against those Member States still applying restrictions on service provision by third country national employees which exceeded those permitted by the ECJ's judgments. These cases[20] reveal the inconsistencies in the Member States as regards the provision of services and exemplify State resistance to the argument that these economic actors are outside the labour market.

III. LABOUR MIGRATION AND EU SERVICE PROVISION

The main bone of contention between the Commission, on the one hand, and the Member States, on the other, regarding third country national employees of service providers, is whether these persons should be treated as foreigners seeking

[19] [2006] OJ C270E.

[20] Cases C-445/03 *Commission v Luxembourg* [2004] ECR I-10191; C-244/04 *Commission v Germany* [2006] ECR I-885; C-168/04 *Commission v Austria* [2006] ECR I-9041; C-219/08 *Commission v Belgium*, judgment of 1 October 2009, *nyr*. I shall examine each of these cases in section III. below.

access to the labour market or whether they should be treated as the mechanism by which a service provider exercises its right under Article 57 TFEU (ex Article 49 EC). In order better to understand the difference of opinion, it is useful to examine the cases which the Commission brought before the ECJ against the Member States. These reveal what controls the Member States variously would like to maintain on third country nationals who are employed by service providers in the way of immigration measures to regulate their activities in the Member States, and the ECJ's view of their compatibility with the right to service provision.

In the first decision, *Commission v Luxembourg*,[21] the Luxembourg authorities sought to defend their practices of treating third country national employees of EU service providers in accordance with their general rules on access to the labour market for third country nationals. The Commission attacked the specific requirements which the Luxembourg authorities considered necessary to control economic activities on their territory. These were:

a) A work permit. The Luxembourg authorities argued that the only effective way they had to ensure compliance with social welfare rules, including strict limits of minimum wages, safety in the workplace and duration of contracts, was through monitoring on the basis of administrative permits for all third country nationals. The objective of the system was, according to the officials, to protect the workers by seeking to eliminate the risk of exploitation; and in any event, the same requirements were placed on Luxembourg companies.
b) The work permit had to be obtained in advance of the arrival of the third country national. This was necessary, according to the authorities, to ensure that priority was given to EU national workers for any jobs or contracts which were available in Luxembourg.
c) The employment contract had to be of an indefinite duration and have been in existence for six months before the employee was posted. The authorities argued that this was necessary to ensure that the employee had a stable link with the Member State of origin and with the company in order to reduce the risk of exploitation. This was also needed, according to the authorities, in order to prevent distortion of competition through social dumping, and to ensure that the employee did not seek to remain in Luxembourg after the end of the service provision.
d) A bank guarantee from a Luxembourg bank was required to cover the cost of repatriation at the end of the contract. The authorities argued that this was not an onerous requirement and provided security for the employees.

The ECJ was unimpressed with the Luxembourg authorities' arguments. It repeated its previous case law on the centrality of the right to provide services

[21] Case C-445/03 [2004] ECR I-10191.

across EU internal borders. As regards the justification of the restrictions on this right, while enforcement of labour protection rules is a laudable objective, the mechanism of a system of work permits is not an appropriate means to achieve that end, particularly in light of the obstacle which it constitutes for service provision. The Court suggested that a simple declaration by the employer of the presence of the employees would be equally effective to achieve this end. Similarly, the ECJ rejected the Luxembourg authorities' argument regarding indefinite contracts of employment and six months employment before the posting. It merely stated that this exceeded the objective of social welfare protection. It accepted the Commission's argument that such a requirement was an obstacle, particularly in sectors where short-term and service-specific contracts are the norm. Further, the ECJ noted that such a requirement ignored the labour standards applicable in the country of origin of the workers which required their protection.

On the argument that the measures were necessary to prevent disruption of the domestic labour market, the ECJ once again insisted that employees deployed to carry out service contracts in other Member States do not gain access to the labour market of the second State as they return to their country of origin or residence on completion of the job. Any legitimate checks which a Member State might put into place to ensure that such employees do not move into the labour market cannot have the effect of rendering illusory the right of the business, and may not be made subject to the discretion of the authorities. Similarly, the argument regarding the priority of EU nationals was irrelevant because the third country nationals were not accessing the labour market. Regarding the bank guarantee, again the ECJ found that this was excessive, as a simple requirement after the fact to recover the costs of repatriation from the business would be more than sufficient.

The second decision was in respect of Germany.[22] Here the arguments were more refined, as the German authorities distinguished their restrictions on third country nationals from those which had been found incompatible with Article 57 TFEU (ex Article 49 EC) in the *Luxembourg* case. The restrictions which Germany applied included the following:

a) A specific posting visa had to be obtained from a German consulate before the posting. The Germany authorities argued that this was necessary to check that the provider had the right to provide services in Germany in connection with the posting, and to prevent the evasion of EU and national requirements in the employment of third country nationals.
b) The dates of the beginning and end of the posting had to be supplied.

[22] Case C-244/04 *Commission v Germany* [2006] ECR I-885.

c) Evidence was required that the worker had been employed by the business for more than a year before the posting. The authorities argued that this was necessary to show that the employee had lawful and regular employment in the State of residence. According to the authorities, this ensured that businesses did not employ staff only for the purpose of the posting, thus protecting the national labour market.
d) The residence and work visas of the State where the employee was engaged were required, to show that the employee could return to the State of residence after the posting. This requirement, according to the authorities, was necessary to ensure that the third country national would not enter the national labour market.
e) Evidence was necessary of affiliation to the national social security scheme, or of private insurance sufficient to cover all risks of sickness and accident. The authorities argued that this was required to prevent social dumping.
f) A passport valid for the period of residence.

The German authorities argued that the requirements were not a significant restriction on the right to provide services as they affected only a limited number of cases since most third country nationals would either have a Schengen visa already or be posted for less than three months, in which cases they would not need the authorisation. They maintained that the issue of the posting visa was almost automatic, very quick and there was no discretion involved. They argued that a post-entry check would not be sufficient because of the constitutional arrangements in Germany that gave this responsibility to the *Länder*. Thus, the prior check provided necessary legal certainty to the business. As regards the requirement to be employed for more than a year, the German authorities were aware that this had already been found unnecessary in the *Luxembourg* case, so offered, during the proceedings, to reduce the period to six months.

Once again, the ECJ was not convinced that the restrictions were consistent with a right to provide services. It found that the small number of persons affected was irrelevant to the legality of the restrictions. It held that the issue of an administrative visa constituted a restriction on the freedom to provide services. Such a procedure might make it more difficult, or even impossible, to exercise the freedom of services through posted workers where the services to be provided required a certain speed of action. It stressed that Member States were not permitted to use their power to verify compliance so as to render the freedom to provide services illusory. The ECJ suggested that a simple prior declaration certifying the situation of the employee would be more than sufficient for the host State and, in so doing, found that the prior visa requirement exceeded what was necessary to prevent abuse. On the requirement of a year's employment, the ECJ confirmed its finding in the case against Luxembourg. As regards requirement for evidence of social security insurance, the ECJ found, again, that a simple declaration would be sufficient and less restrictive for the business. Such a declaration would enable the local authorities to check whether national wages and working conditions were being respected.

The third case in this line was against Austria.[23] The Austrian requirements for service provision by a business in another Member State by means of a third country national employee included the following:

a) An EU Posting Confirmation, issued before the employee was posted. The Austrian authorities claimed that this was a declaratory procedure which was not onerous, and that it did not constitute a dual procedure with the visa and residence permit as each procedure pursued a different aim. The Posting Confirmation took on average six weeks to be issued.
b) A visa and residence permit to enter and reside in Austria. The authorities argued that these documents were also needed since legality on the territory of Austria depended not only on the legality of the posting, but also on other factors linked to the control of aliens.
c) Employment of the worker for at least a year before the posting or on an unlimited contract. The arguments here were similar to those used by the Luxembourg and German authorities; the Austrian authorities stressed that this requirement was necessary to protect the worker from unlawful treatment.
d) Evidence that wage and employment conditions and social security provisions of Austria would be met for the duration of the posting. This requirement, according to the authorities, was to ensure the protection of the posted workers before the posting began.
e) Where the third country national entered irregularly, a ban on regularising his or her position thereafter from within the State. The authorities considered that it was not expedient to enact a measure prohibiting residence where the person making the request was already in Austria.
f) The provision of a declaration by the employer to the Austrian authorities a week before the posting commenced, stating the identity of the posted workers and the duration of the posting.
g) Information about the business, its clients in Austria and the identities of the employees to be posted, their activities and remuneration, with a liability to fines if any information was missing.

In general, the Austrian authorities argued that all the restrictions were justified as overriding requirements relating to the general interest, in particular the protection of workers and the safeguarding of public policy and security. They further claimed that all the restrictions were proportionate to the objectives pursued.

The ECJ considered the requirements one by one against the right to provide services contained in the EC Treaty. It rejected the Austrian authorities' argument that the Posting Confirmation procedure was merely declaratory. It found the

[23] Case C-168/04 *Commission v Austria* [2006] ECR I-9041.

procedure likely to render difficult, if not impossible, the provision of services using third country national posted workers. The measure was, in the opinion of the ECJ, disproportionate to the aim and thus not consistent with the Treaty. The one-year employment requirement was also rejected. Further, the ECJ considered that making it impossible to regularise the situation of a third country national worker lawfully posted by an EU business to Austria where the individual had entered Austria without a visa contrary to Austrian law, imposed a restriction on the right to provide services. As the Austrian provision exposed the employee to the risk of being excluded from the national territory, this was liable to jeopardise the planned posting.

The Austrian authorities sought to justify the prohibition on regularising workers arriving illegally without success. They claimed that this was necessary to avoid a genuine and sufficiently serious threat to a fundamental interest of society. The ECJ nonetheless considered it disproportionate to the gravity of the offence, inasmuch as it disregarded the fact that the posted worker, who did not possess a visa, was in a lawful position in the Member State from which he or she had been posted as well as under Austrian rules on postings, and therefore did not pose a threat to public policy or security. The ECJ held that the automatic nature of the refusal to issue an entry and residence permit to a posted third country national worker in the event of entry without a visa must be considered to be disproportionate in relation to the objective which it was intended to attain.

In something of a departure from the constant jurisprudence on the matter, the ECJ held in an infringement proceeding against Belgium that obstacles which the Belgian authorities placed in the way of employers from other Member States seeking to post third country national workers to Belgium for service provision were permissible.[24] The Commission had argued that the requirement to produce a form E101 (on health coverage) and delays in the issue of visas were obstacles to businesses contrary to the earlier jurisprudence of the ECJ. However, in this case the ECJ accepted that the production of an E101 form was a simpler requirement than the production of a declaration which the ECJ had accepted as proportionate. Further, the ECJ was not satisfied that the Commission's information on delay was accurate.

IV. WORKING CONDITIONS AND POSTED WORKERS IN THE EU

The issue of posted workers and their impact on working conditions became the object of substantial concern, particularly in the Nordic countries, following the accession of 10 Member States in Central and Eastern Europe, the Baltic States and the Mediterranean. In 2004, while the pre-2004 Member States were permitted to exclude nationals of eight of the 10 acceding States (Cyprus and Malta had no

[24] Case C-219/08 *Commission v Belgium*, judgment of 1 October 2009, *nyr*.

transitional restrictions on free movement of workers) from provisions on the free movement of workers, there were no transitional restrictions on rights to establishment or service provision. The issue which came before the ECJ, then, was about applicable wages and working conditions.

In the framework of EU law, this problem was supposed to have been resolved by Directive 96/71, discussed in section II. above. But the problem for Sweden and Finland was that their industrial relations models were not compatible with the Directive in ways that would permit the national authorities to apply local wages and working conditions provisions.[25] Notwithstanding the fact that Sweden did not apply any transitional restrictions on the free movement of workers from the new Member States (as some other Member States had), problems arose as regards the posting of workers from the Baltic States to Sweden (and Finland) where the pay and working conditions were those applicable in the State of origin. The result was that companies posting workers from Latvia, Estonia or Lithuania were able to tender for contracts in Sweden and Finland more cheaply, as their labour costs were significantly lower than those in the destination States.

The issue came before the ECJ in 2007 in two cases with different facts but similar problems: *Laval*[26] and *Viking*.[27] The facts of the two cases are complex, but in both instances companies established in Latvia or Estonia used contract workers from their labour force to carry out work respectively in Sweden and Finland at significantly lower rates of pay than provided to domestic workers. Trade unions objected, and in the *Laval* case went on strike. The two matters came before the national courts, which referred to the ECJ the question of the validity of the posting of workers. The ECJ maintained its case law. It found that the mechanism for resolving the issue of application of national working and wage conditions to posted workers is through Directive 96/71 on the conditions applicable to posted workers. The fact that the Swedish (or Finnish) labour regulation system did not fit within the Directive was not a reason to find that the right to provide services must be curtailed.[28] The ECJ held that Member States are prohibited from applying restrictions to movement of other Member States' service providers' personnel where such restrictions do not apply to their own service providers. However, Member States may apply their collective labour agreements to any employed person, including posted workers temporarily on their territory. But these rules can be applied only if they are suitable to achieve the objective pursued—the protection of workers—and do not go beyond what is necessary to achieve that aim. As the Swedish (and Finnish) industrial relations systems did not set minimum

[25] O Edstrom, 'The free movement of services in conflict with Swedish industrial relations model—or was it the other way around?' in N Wahl and P Cramer (eds) (2006) 1 *Swedish Studies in European Law* 120.

[26] Case C-341/05 *Laval* [2007] ECR I-11767.

[27] Case C-438/05 *Viking* [2007] ECR I-10779.

[28] S Tans, 'Case note on the *Laval* Judgment' (2009) 11 *European Journal of Migration and Law* 2009.

rates of pay as specified in Directive 96/71, the authorities could not use the Directive to apply their own nationals rules as these were based on a case-by-case wage negotiation. In such a situation, this conflicted with the Article 57 TFEU (ex Article 49 EC) right.

The EU's experience with service provision and the movement of personnel of service providers across international borders throws an interesting light on the issues which are arising in the WTO context of the GATS. The objective of the GATS is liberalisation of service provision, including what GATS defines as mode 4, namely the movement of natural persons across international borders for the purpose of service provision. In the next section I shall examine the WTO rules before drawing some conclusions on the issues.

V. GATS AND THE WORKER/PERSONNEL DIVISION[29]

The objective of the WTO is to ensure that international trade is as fair as possible and as free as practical. The first of the agreements which over time led to the establishment of the WTO was signed in 1947, though the WTO itself did not come into existence until 1995. It is the only organisation which deals with the rules of trade between nations (and it is not part of the UN system). Its goal is to help producers of goods and services, exporters and importers conduct their business.[30] The WTO rule book on international trade comprises over 30,000 pages and 30 agreements.

The WTO focuses on six main activities:

a) the administration of trade agreements;
b) acting as a forum for trade negotiations (an area in which it has been particularly active and successful);
c) acting as a dispute settlement mechanism for international trade disputes (the Dispute Settlement Body);
d) providing a policing mechanism in respect of national trade policies (the Trade Policy Review Body);
e) providing a venue for technical assistance to developing countries;
f) acting as a participant in the system of international organisations.

Approximately 97 per cent of the world's trade takes place among States which are parties to the WTO agreements. The decision making-bodies of the WTO consist of a Ministerial Conference, including delegates from all the members, which meets every two years; and a General Council, which is made up of ambassadors and heads of delegation based in Geneva, which meets several times a year. The latter body also sits as the Trade Policy Review Body and the Dispute Settlement

[29] In this section I rely on work I have done in the volume cited in n 6 above.

[30] See <http://www.wto.org/english/thewto_e/whatis_e/whatis_e.htm>, last consulted 20 August 2008.

Body. Under these bodies, one finds the three sector-specific councils—the Goods Council, the Services Council and the Intellectual Property Council—all of which report to the General Council.

A. The International Community Opens Borders?

Of particular interest to the issue of individuals is the Services Council. Among the many agreements which constitute the WTO system, the GATS is the one which most directly touches individuals crossing international borders. A late-comer to the WTO system, it was only in 1995 that services acquired their own agreement. While many services can be provided without the movement of persons, such as telecommunications, many others cannot. This is particularly the case for services which are created and consumed simultaneously, for instance most kinds of installation or repair work, where the service cannot be provided if a person is not physically able to be on the site where it is to be so provided. This is called mode 4 service provision.[31] The whole system is designed to regulate cross-border economic activities; and as the decision was taken to extend the system to services, including those which can be carried out only if a foreigner is permitted entry to the State, this accommodation of service provision and national immigration rules was going to be required. The international rule book and State sensitivities about movement of persons is illustrated by that fact that on the GATS website the second paragraph on mode 4 deals with immigration worries:

> Movement of 'natural persons' refers to the entry and temporary stay of persons for the purpose of providing a service. It does not relate to persons seeking citizenship, permanent employment or permanent residence in a country.[32]

The GATS system is based on a number of basic principles in respect of which Member countries are entitled to retain exceptions listed in the annexes, or to which they may sign up in accordance with sectoral annexes. There are two key principles which have a direct impact on State control over migration:

a) *The general obligations*
   i) Member countries will provide to one another most favoured nation (MFN) treatment for access to the market, *viz*, the territory (Article

[31] The other three modes are: i) The cross-border delivery of services (mode 1), eg the transmission of consultancy advice from country A to country B without any physical travel by either party. Electronic commerce has led to major developments in the opportunities for cross-border trade. ii) Consumption abroad (mode 2), where the consumer in country B goes to country A to use the service. Examples include tourism and dispatching ships to a foreign port for repairs. iii) Commercial presence (mode 3), the creation of a subsidiary in country A by a company from country B.

[32] Available at <http://www.wto.org/english/tratop_e/serv_e/mouvement_persons_e/mouvement_persons_e.htm>, visited 14 February 2010.

XVI GATS). For included sectors, the best treatment which one Member provides to another country must be extended to all GATS Member countries. Exceptions to and exemptions from the MFN treatment were permitted but had to be tabled at the time of adoption, and could not be added to subsequently. This principle applies to the three types of movement of persons within the GATS framework: access by persons seeking to use services, access to provide services on a one-off basis or access to set up a commercial presence. Where States wished to preserve special treatment for nationals of certain countries, these exceptions had to be listed in a schedule.

ii) Transparency. Rules must be published which are available to all economic actors on the limitations which have been placed on market access (if any).

b) *The specific commitments*

i) Market access. This is negotiated sector by sector to determine which sectors are opened to economic actors from other Members and on which conditions, and which remain closed.

ii) Treatment 'no less favourable than that [the country] accords to its own like services and service suppliers', ie national treatment (Article XVII GATS). This equal treatment provision covers both direct and indirect discrimination. Formally, different treatment is permitted only so long as it does not modify the conditions of competition in favour of the services of service providers of the host country. Exceptions and limitations to this equal treatment provision are permitted but must be made public through inclusion in the schedule of specific commitments. Again, these are submitted for each State individually.

Leaving aside, then, the exceptions, exemptions and limitations contained in the annexes (which restrict the impact of the GATS), what are the consequences of these two principles? First, if economic actors are to have a right to market access then they need to be able to cross borders to enjoy this. Economic actors may either be individuals who are, as self-employed persons, carrying out contracts they have won on the territory of another State, or they may be companies which seek to move their employees to carry out contracts elsewhere. In either case, in mode 4, people will need to cross borders in order that the promises of the GATS are fulfilled. The GATS mechanism for achieving this is to permit Members to maintain their systems of immigration control; but whatever regime applies to the most favoured country, that regime must apply to all GATS Members' economic actors. This is a sort of lock-step arrangement—whatever is agreed for the closest trading partner must be extended to all.

The second principle is also challenging in the migration context. If equality with domestic actors is guaranteed then, as soon as the foreign economic actor has access to the market, obstacles to the exercise of economic activities must be abolished. In principle, this should include restrictions on the immigration status of the individual who is carrying out the economic activity which would operate as a constraint on the completion of the service provision. These come in the form of time restrictions on the individual's lawful presence on the territory and on the type of activity which can be carried out. Equal treatment also raises the question of recognition of professional qualifications and compliance with national rules on consumer protection. Additionally, equal treatment with national economic actors engages the issues of working conditions, wages and social protection—to what extent are service providers, in the form either of individuals who are providing services themselves, or companies which are service providers and provide the services through their employees, obliged to comply with national rules?

The GATS expressly permits States to contravene their obligations if this is necessary to protect public morals or maintain public order; to protect human or plant life or health; or to secure compliance with laws or regulations not inconsistent with the GATS, in particular those necessary to prevent deceptive or fraudulent practices.[33] There is no jurisprudence on the meaning of these terms, but academic authorities tend to consider that it must be interpreted restrictively.[34]

The GATS framework of economic migration is based on the principle that private enterprises are the determiners: if they are self-employed they move to where the work is; if they are corporate entities they select, recruit and move workers depending on the demands of the market as determined by themselves. The provisions of the GATS are designed to ensure market access for service providers—in other words, to restrict the power of States to impede access to their territory by foreign competitors in the services field through the use of restrictive economic migration laws. The provisions are written in terms of the rights of service providers based in one of the contracting parties.

B. Migrants and GATS

The question of market access for natural persons has been a matter of substantial negotiation within the GATS. As mentioned above, the principles of the GATS—access to the territory on the same basis as the most privileged of foreigners, and equal access to the market once within the State—immediately come into conflict with the principle of national immigration control. Immigration control is based on the principle that sovereignty gives States the right to discriminate against foreigners in comparison with their own nationals—this is why it is possible to have border controls on persons. This right to control the entry of foreigners onto the territory is not tempered by any obligation to treat all foreigners the same way (otherwise it would not be possible to submit the nationals of some countries

[33] Art XIV(c)(1) GATS.

[34] See AB Overby, 'Consumer protection after Accession to the WTO' (2006) 33 *Syracuse Journal of International Law & Commerce* 347.

to mandatory visa requirements while exempting nationals of others). Thus, immigration control is based on the right of State officials, in the exercise of sovereign powers, to discriminate against foreigners and among different groups of foreigners. It remains an open question to what extent the exercise of sovereign powers is subject even to a duty to provide reasons for the decision of the immigration official, be it at the consulate on a visa application or at the border.[35]

Equal treatment with nationals as regards market access within the State is also complicated from the perspective of immigration controls. Immigration controls in liberal democracies are based on limiting two main aspects of the individual's presence:

a) the length of time which the individual can spend on the territory (eg, tourists and visitors are limited to three months out of every six in the EU); and
b) the economic activities into which the individual can enter (under EU law, tourists and visitors are prohibited from engaging in economic activities except in very limited ways).

Both of these principles of immigration control are potentially in conflict with the GATS principle of equal treatment with a State's own nationals.

In order to resolve, at least in part, these conflicts, there is an Annex to the GATS on the movement of natural persons supplying services.[36] It applies both to individuals who provide services themselves and to the employees of companies which are providing services via those employees. The Annex specifies that the GATS does not apply to:

a) measures affecting natural persons seeking access to the employment market;
b) citizenship, residence or employment on a permanent basis.

There are a number of points of difficulty in these exclusions. The first, which has arisen in the context of the EU, is whether the employees of service providers who arrive to carry out work in a State are seeking access to the employment market. As discussed above, the ECJ has answered this question with a decisive 'No'. However, the EU is only one collection of Members of GATS, and its decision is not decisive as to the meaning of GATS commitments. The second point of difficulty relates to residence or employment on a permanent basis. While the exclusion of citizenship does not raise any particular problems, the exclusion of residence and employment does. Clearly, if an individual does not have access

[35] The EU Schengen Borders Code (Regulation 562/2006, [2006] OJ L105), which applies to all persons seeking entry to an EU State (with the exception of Denmark, Ireland and the UK), provides that if an immigration official refuses admission, that decision must be motivated on grounds within the Regulation and give rise to a right of appeal. This is an innovation of the Regulation, which was included only as a result of pressure from the European Parliament and at the last minute.

[36] Available at <http://www.wto.org/english/tratop_e/serv_e/8-anmvnt_e.htm>, visited 21 August 2008.

to residence on the territory, he or she is unlikely to be able to provide services which require personal presence. Thus, the meaning of 'residence' needs to be modified so that it does not mean temporary residence for the purpose of the service contract but something else. In this way, for the GATS 'residence' becomes assimilated to an independent right of residence disconnected from service provision. The residence which is necessary for the service provision is defined out. 'Employment' as a term also undergoes a similar change. Employment is not only divorced from access to the labour market, but is also divided into two kinds, temporary and permanent. Thus temporality is the key which permits differentiation of labour between the GATS-permitted kind—temporary employment on the territory—and the GATS-excluded kind—which is associated with rights to individuals regarding long-term residence on the territory independent of the economic activity undertaken.

Further, the Annex specifies that Members are free to negotiate specific commitments which apply to all categories of natural persons providing services under the Agreement, and the provision of the commitment then applies in respect of the activity. This provision of the Annex permits the inclusion in the schedules relating to different sectors of limitations such as professional qualifications, etc.

Lastly, the third provision of the Annex states that the Agreement does not prevent Members from applying their measures to regulate the entry of natural persons into, or temporary stays in, their territories. A Member is also entitled to retain measures which

> ensure the orderly movement of natural persons across its borders provided that such measures are not applied in such a manner as to nullify or impair the benefits accruing to any Member under the terms of a specific commitment.[37]

This provision more than any other evidences the difficulty between the objective of the Agreement and the sovereignty claims of the Members regarding border controls. It recognises the sovereign power of Members to apply immigration measures, while at the same time it seeks to limit those powers by reference to the GATS obligations of market access and equality within the market. Thus, national sovereign powers are consistent with the GATS commitments only so long as they do not interfere too substantially with (ie nullify or impair) the benefits to which other Members are entitled under the Agreement. These benefits comprise, of course, the possibility for nationals of the Member or companies based in the Member to have access to the territory and market of other Members. It is difficult to argue that immigration controls do not impair access by individuals to the territory. Indeed, the purpose of immigration controls is to do exactly that—to make it more difficult for some people rather than others to have access to the territory of a State. It is, then, interesting to return to the formulation of the GATS Annex—the right of the State to apply immigration controls ends at the

[37] Annex 1B on Article II Exemptions, GATS.

place where the GATS commitment to other States starts. But there is no clarity as to where the rights of individuals who claim a benefit to their State under the GATS start in comparison with where the sovereignty of a State ends in respect of immigration controls. Nonetheless, the principle is one of access, against which obstacles must be weighted.

VI. CONCLUSIONS

There is a tension between the movement of persons for service provision and national law and policy on economic immigration. This tension has been the subject of substantial attention in the EU, focusing primarily on service provision by third country nationals in the Member States. While Member States are entitled to place such restrictions as they consider necessary on access to the labour market of third country nationals coming directly to their State from outside the EU, and are constrained only by their GATS commitments regarding the admission of third country nationals for service provision coming from outside the EU, the same is not true as regards intra-EU movement. The right to provide services contained in the EC Treaty has been interpreted as meaning that businesses based in the EU also have the right to move their third country national personnel from one Member State to another to carry out service provision.

The concerns of a number of Member States regarding this kind of movement of persons for service provision fall into two main categories:

a) the risk of abuse of service provision to gain access to the labour market for third country nationals who are not entitled to such access;
b) the risk of exploitation of the employees who are posted and adverse competition *vis-à-vis* its own nationals where working conditions and wages of foreign competitors provide a basis for lower costs.

The mechanisms which EU States have deployed to avoid these two risks have nevertheless been found to go far beyond what is necessary and proportionate to address the problems. As regards illegal access to the labour market, in the EU context the ECJ has not accepted that heavy prior visa and residence requirements are necessary to this end. In more than one case, the Court has stressed that simple declarations by the business as to its identity, the identity of the posted employees and the place of the posting should be sufficient for the host State to control, as needs be, the legality of the posting. Following the same logic, the ECJ has found that protection of workers is something which takes place on the territory of the host State, not something which can effectively be regulated by prior visa requirements. In one case, the ECJ has held that regularisation of posted workers who have entered irregularly is not only consistent but necessary to give full effect to the intra-EU right of service provision for businesses.

The issue of wages and working conditions has been more problematic in the EU system. While on the one hand the legislator and ECJ approve of the application of nationally set wages and working condition requirements, the ECJ ruled out agreements which lack transparency as they are negotiated on a case-by-case basis, since this effectively excluded foreign competitors. In the international trading system, the issues are still only just beginning to be addressed. For the moment, most developed countries limit the application of the GATS to highly-skilled sectors such as accountancy and banking through the listing procedures. The argument is that these are highly-paid sectors where markets are fairly self-regulating. In the current GATS negotiations on widening the scope of the application of the Agreement, developing countries have been particularly interested in widening its scope to include economic sectors where their nationals and companies have competence and capacity but are excluded from service provision in developed countries, not least by immigration requirements. The 2008/09 turbulence in world markets has temporarily slowed progress towards market liberalisation in services. It will be interesting to see whether, with the advent of greater stability into the world trading system, new impetus will be injected into the GATS negotiations.

Lastly, in the EU system on free movement of services, the role of the ECJ has been of great importance in interpreting the scope of the service obligation and resolving issues around claims of 'social dumping'. Without a strong judicial body, it is unlikely that the EU would have been able to move as far as it has in liberalisation of services where the movement of natural persons is engaged. For the moment, in the WTO system, it is not clear that the Dispute Settlement Body (the Panel and the Appellate Body) has a similar authority. Further, the inter-State limitation on access to the Body means that interpretation of the GATS rules on mode 4 will require a State to commence an action against another party. The politics of market access in an area as sensitive as border controls may mean that we shall have to wait quite a while for such an action to materialise.

The development of service provision by third country national employees in the EU provides a useful indicator of the kinds of concerns of some EU Member States regarding mode 4 movement. It also reveals the kinds of measures which Member States take to seek to control mode 4 movement. The robust approach of the ECJ on the proportionality of those measures in actually achieving the ends sought may provide some useful pointers for negotiators in the international domain where the same measures (and indeed more) are maintained by the Member States, which may have the effect of making more difficult, if not impossible, service provision within the GATS.

4

Diplomacy by Directive? An Analysis of the International Context of the Emissions Trading Scheme Directive

HANS VEDDER

I. A TRAGEDY OF THE COMMONS AND CLIMATE CHANGE

CLIMATE CHANGE IS without a shadow of a doubt a transboundary problem. As a result, it can only be addressed through a global effort. The United Nations Framework Convention on Climate Change sets the scene for just such international cooperation.[1] However, the implementation of this Convention has been slow, and even in the face of overwhelming evidence of the disastrous effects of climate change,[2] the parties to the Convention have only been inching towards hard and binding international targets, making climate change a classic 'tragedy of the commons', with the climate as an overexploited common resource and all the users of this resource finding themselves unable to address the overexploitation.[3]

In the midst of limp-wristed international progress, the European Union has refused to surrender, and has committed itself to ambitious and binding emissions abatement goals. In view of the probability that climate change will become the next *locus classicus* of a tragedy of the commons, these ambitious goals seem without explanation, and perhaps even foolish in view of their effect on the competitiveness

[1] Hereafter the 'UNFCCC'. This chapter will not deal with the UNFCCC or the negotiations as such. For an account, see WT Douma, L Massai and M Montini (eds), *The Kyoto Protocol and Beyond: Legal and Policy Challenges of Climate Change* (The Hague, TMC Asser Press, 2007).

[2] See eg the Stern Report, available from <http://www.hm-treasury.gov.uk/sternreview_index.htm>.

[3] G Hardin, 'The Tragedy of the Commons' (1968) 162 *Science* 1243. Hardin actually uses the example of a common grazing ground that is used by several herders. Each of the herders will gain individually from allowing his livestock to graze there, even though that results in overgrazing and thus a reduction in the value of the common pasture. Since the individual benefit from allowing the cattle to graze without limits outweighs an individual herder's share in the collective costs, there is an incentive to overexploit. Despite criticism, the underlying idea is widely accepted among economists who study externalities and common pool resource problems, and is visible in the example of overfishing.

of European industry. However, Hardin has already contrasted 'his' tragedy of the commons with the 'invisible hand' that Adam Smith claimed would guide all those pursuing nothing but their private interests in the direction of the public good.[4] This does rely on two things: the availability of property rights, and enlightened self-interest. Whereas the former should appeal to lawyers (but may be hard to implement for climate), the latter is outside law's realm. Similarly, Hardin's solution, in the form of mutually-agreed coercion, or enlightened self-interest, takes us to the fringes of the legal domain, right up to the political, if not philosophical, arena.[5] It presupposes the creation of social arrangements that result in a global responsibility for the climate. In short, we all accept restrictions on our individual and short-term freedom to act in return for collective freedom to act in the longer term. The question is whether and to what extent this works for something as incomprehensibly all-encompassing as climate change? In the current world order, effectively curbing climate change essentially requires solidarity on a global scale, with developed countries contributing not only to greenhouse gas reductions, but also to the low-carbon development of developing countries.

Nevertheless, Hardin's observations seem quite appropriate to understand the European Union's climate change policy, and notably the European Commission's involvement in shaping this policy. In a nutshell, enlightened self-interest may be said to have shaped this audacious policy. This self-interest undoubtedly has its roots in a sincere wish to save our planet from climate change. At the same time, much more mundane economic and political interests play a role as well. Europe wants to be the world leader in climate change and, in addition, create a comfortable position for itself as a technology leader in the field of climate change abatement equipment.[6]

However, demand for low-carbon technology will probably increase only if there is an internationally-shared belief that greenhouse gas emissions need to be reduced, and thus Europe's climate change policy must result in more mutually-agreed coercion if we are to prevent an international tragedy of the commons in climate change.

Interestingly, Europe's climate package contains just those elements that may result in mutually agreed coercion. In brief, the EU has committed itself to strict climate change targets in the form of the '20, 20 by 2020' goal. In other words, Europe wants to reduce emissions of greenhouse gases by 20 per cent and increase energy efficiency by 20 per cent by the year 2020.[7] In making this commitment, the European Council also indicated that it has set itself these objectives in view

[4] *Ibid*, 1244.

[5] *Ibid*, 1247.

[6] The Zero Emissions Power Plant (ZEPP) project and carbon capture and storage (CCS) technology are important potential technology export products; see eg W Renzenbrink *et al*, 'RWE's 450 MW IGCC/CCS project—Status and outlook' (2009) *Energy Procedia* 615, 616.

[7] Presidency Conclusions 8/9 March 2007, points 29 *et seq*.

of the international negotiations regarding the successor to the Kyoto Protocol.[8] Moreover, the EU indicates that it will go beyond these targets if there is an international agreement signed in Copenhagen[9] in which developed countries commit themselves to similar reductions targets.[10] Between these political messages, the European Council indicates that it is aware of the effects on the competitiveness of European industry of having a stringent internal environmental policy.[11] In other words, the European Union must carefully balance its climate change policy with the international climate change policy; and in doing so, it is perfectly aware of the imperfect interrelation between these two policy levels.

We find this delicate balancing act back in the December 2008 Energy and Climate Package.[12] This consists of an Effort Sharing Decision, an amendment of the Emissions Trading Scheme Directive and a Renewables Directive, all of which show concern with the external impact of this EU policy.[13] The most prominent role in this balancing act is performed by the amended ETS Directive, in which the EU has included provisions on so-called carbon leakage.[14] This refers to the export of greenhouse gas emissions to non-EU States as a result of higher costs imposed on EU industry. It indicates that carbon leakage is an environmental issue as well as a competitiveness and employment issue.

This prominence is only confirmed by the fact that the package was ultimately agreed upon by the European Council. This is particularly interesting in view of the fact that the then applicable co-decision procedure[15] normally envisaged decision-making by the Council, and not the European Council.[16] This pivotal role for the European Council, a body that is primarily active in the EU's external policy, signals the external component of this European policy.

This chapter will analyse the Energy and Climate Package and, notably, the amended ETS Directive from this external perspective. It will do so by, first, providing a short overview of the external dimension of EU environmental action in general. It will then analyse the Package as a whole. This will reveal the pivotal role played by the ETS Directive. This Directive will then be analysed in greater

[8] Presidency Conclusions 8/9 March 2007, points 29 and 31.

[9] Copenhagen is the location of 15th Conference of the Parties to the United Nations Framework Convention on Climate Change, see <http://www.unfccc.org>. In the meantime the 16th Conference of the Parties has been held in Cancun. Also for this Conference, the EU has repeated its conditional offer to move to a 30% abatement target, Council Conclusions of 14 October 2010, 14957/10, at point 9.

[10] Presidency Conclusions 11/12 December 2008, point 22.

[11] Presidency Conclusions 21/22 June 2007, point 40, and Presidency Conclusions, 13/14 March 2008, point 19.

[12] Presidency Conclusions 11/12 December 2008, points 19 *et seq*.

[13] Energy and Climate Change—Elements of the final compromise referred to in Point 20 of Presidency Conclusions 11/12 December 2008. The elements of the Energy and Climate Package will be discussed more extensively in section III. below.

[14] *Ibid*, points 1 and 2. See further Article 10a(15) and 10b of the amended ETS Directive.

[15] Art 251 EC. The Treaty of Lisbon has renamed this procedure the 'ordinary legislative procedure' (Arts 289 and 294 TFEU).

[16] In fact, the Treaty on European Union, as amended by the Treaty of Lisbon, explicitly rules out a legislative role for the European Council, Art 15(1) TEU.

detail, at which point we shall focus on the areas in which the external component is visible. Lastly, the relation between the ETS Directive and the international negotiations will be analysed, taking into account the very limited progress made in Copenhagen.

II. THE EXTERNAL DIMENSION OF EU ENVIRONMENTAL POLICY

From its inception onwards, the external dimension of the EU's environmental policy was a matter of debate, with the Commission arguing for an external competence and Member States being by and large opposed to this idea.[17] Treaty amendments have, however, included an explicit reference to 'promoting measures at international level to deal with regional or worldwide environmental problems'.[18] The Treaty of Lisbon included 'combating climate change' as an explicit objective of the European Union's external environmental competence.[19]

The EU not only participates actively in many international environmental agreements, it further envisages a leadership role for itself at the international level. This follows from, *inter alia*, the Sixth Environmental Action Programme, which states that the Programme shall stimulate 'the positive and constructive role of the European Union as a *leading partner* in the protection of the global environment and in the pursuit of a sustainable development'.[20]

This can logically be explained by the fact that the EU aims for a relatively high level of environmental protection whilst being acutely aware of the impossibility of an environmental *alleingang* in view of WTO law and the competitiveness of European industry.[21] The solution to this conundrum was to try to achieve an international level of protection that was in line with European aspirations, which requires the EU to position itself as a leader in international discussions. Whilst this may be true for all environmental problems that ultimately have a transboundary or even global scope, it is the cross-cutting and fundamental nature of climate change that sets this environmental challenge apart from all other ecological problems that are addressed internationally.[22] The required shift towards a low-carbon society

[17] For an overview, see JH Jans and HHB Vedder, *European Environmental Law* (Groningen, Europa Law Publishing, 2008), 31 *et seq.*

[18] Ex Art 174(1) EC, fourth indent, and currently Art 191(1) TFEU, fourth indent.

[19] It is submitted, however, that this entails nothing more than a confirmation of the status quo; cf HHB Vedder, 'The Treaty of Lisbon and European Environmental Law and Policy' (2010) 22(2) *Journal of Environmental Law* 285.

[20] Decision 1600/2002 of the European Parliament and of the Council of 22 July 2002 laying down the Sixth Community Environment Action Programme [2002] OJ L242/1, Art 2(6) (emphasis added). References to climate change as a factor influencing European energy policy could already be found in the Fourth Environmental Action Programme (1987–93), [1987] OJ C328/1, at 2.3.20.

[21] See, on the (im)possibility of unilateral and extraterritorial environmental measures, J Wiers, *Trade and Environment in the EC and the WTO* (Groningen, Europa Law Publishing, 2002) 347 *et seq.*

[22] Long-range transboundary air pollution and ozone-depleting substances, for example, have similar transboundary environmental effects, and thus result in international action as well as European

poses an immense challenge to industrial competitiveness and organisation, and the EU's climate policy is thus firmly situated in its equally topical and central energy policy.[23]

This makes the EU position in the international climate change negotiations different from that in other international environmental fora. In the latter, we are unlikely to find internal European rules that are (partly) designed to influence the outcome of international negotiations. We are similarly unlikely to find rules that allow for a structural interaction with international legal structures. Already from 2004 onwards, the EU Emissions Trading System (ETS) was linked to the flexible mechanisms in the Kyoto Protocol that allow for international emissions trading with developed as well as developing counties.[24] This ties the EU ETS firmly to international climate change rules and can be seen not only as the completion of the EU ETS, but also as a measure in support of the Kyoto Protocol.[25] This, in turn, can be seen as a measure to increase the EU's leadership on climate change issues. Following the Bush administration's decision not to ratify the Kyoto Protocol, intellectual and political leadership on climate change shifted in the direction of the EU.[26] The EU's political effort to get Russia to ratify the Protocol and thus ensure its entry into force only reconfirms this leadership, as does its linking with the world's biggest greenhouse gas trading scheme, the EU ETS.

III. THE ENERGY AND CLIMATE PACKAGE

The Energy and Climate Package was effectively adopted in the December 2008 European Council,[27] and formally adopted by the Council and European Parliament on 23 April 2009. It consists of the following elements:

- Decision No 406/2009/EC on the effort of Member States to reduce their greenhouse gas emissions to meet the Community's greenhouse gas emission reduction commitments up to 2020;[28]
- Directive 2009/31/EC on the geological storage of carbon dioxide;[29]

policy. Yet they differ fundamentally from climate change with regard to the effect the implementation of this international action has on industry, or even the organisation of economies worldwide.

[23] It further entails elements of industrial policy, with the EU seeking to change the structure of its energy sector and trying to become a technology leader for low-carbon and carbon abatement technologies.

[24] Directive 2004/101, OJ 2004 L 338/1, this concerns Joint Implementation and the Clean Development Mechanism.

[25] C Streck and D Freestone, 'The EU and Climate Change' in R Macrory (ed), *Reflections on 30 Years of EU Environmental Law* (Groningen, Europa Law Publishing, 2006) 105.

[26] *Ibid*, 96.

[27] Presidency Conclusions 11/12 December 2008, points 19 *et seq*.

[28] [2009] OJ L140/136, hereafter referred to as the 'Effort Sharing Decision'.

[29] [2009] OJ L140/114, hereafter referred to as the 'CCS Directive'.

— Directive 2009/30/EC as regards the specification of petrol, diesel and gas-oil and introducing a mechanism to monitor and reduce greenhouse gas emissions;[30]
— Directive 2009/29/EC amending Directive 2003/87/EC so as to improve and extend the greenhouse gas emission allowance trading scheme of the Community;[31]
— Directive 2009/28/EC on the promotion of the use of energy from renewable sources;[32]
— Regulation (EC) No 443/2009 setting emission performance standards for new passenger cars as part of the Community's integrated approach to reduce CO_2 emissions from light-duty vehicles.[33]

As these instruments are all part of the Energy and Climate Package, they all refer to the conundrum which faces the EU when it commits to strict environmental targets, while it is unlikely that many third countries will impose similar standards on their industry.[34] Nevertheless, the external dimension of intra-EU climate change policy is most prominent in the Effort Sharing Decision, the New ETS Directive and the Biofuels Directive.[35] The entire package is interrelated, in that the EU seeks to combat climate change through changes in (primary) energy sources,[36] efficiency of fuel use, capture of resulting carbon dioxide emissions and the trading of emissions allowances.

As regards changes in primary energy sources, the New Renewables and Biofuels Directives both seek to reduce the carbon footprint of the energy sources concerned. The Biofuels Directive does this by incentivising the production of biofuels worldwide[37] and laying down standards for petrol and diesel fuels,[38] as well as a reduction of the life-cycle greenhouse gas emissions.[39] The latter aspect is particularly interesting as it entails a duty on the part of the suppliers of fuels to monitor and reduce, as gradually as possible, the life-cycle greenhouse gas emissions up to 10 per cent by 2020.[40] The concept of the life-cycle greenhouse

30 [2009] OJ L140/88, hereafter referred to as the 'Biofuels Directive'.

31 [2009] OJ L140/63, hereafter referred to as the 'New ETS Directive'.

32 [2009] OJ L140/16, hereafter referred to as the 'New Renewables Directive'.

33 [2009] OJ L140/1, hereafter referred to as the 'Passenger Car Emissions Regulation'.

34 The Preambles invariably refer to the EU negotiation position in the UNFCCC.

35 The Passenger Car Emissions Regulation and the CCS Directive by definition have a much smaller external component. Imposing stricter energy efficiency standards on cars imported into the EU may result in challenges on the basis of the GATT/WTO Agreements, but these are outside the scope of this chapter. Similarly, the CCS Directive is intended to enable this technology only within the EU.

36 'Primary energy sources' refers to energy carriers (substances) or processes that carry sufficient energy to be converted to energy for human use. Fossil and nuclear fuels, as well as solar and wind energy, are examples of primary energy sources.

37 Biofuels Directive, above n 30, Preamble, recital 15.

38 *Ibid*, Arts 3 and 4 in connection with Annexes I and II.

39 *Ibid*, Art 7a.

40 *Ibid*, Art 7a(2). Rules on the verification, calculation and reporting of these sustainability criteria and the life-cycle greenhouse gas emissions are laid down *ibid*, Arts 7c, 7d and 7e.

gas emissions refers to all greenhouse gas emissions associated with a unit of fuel. As this includes biofuels, ie fuels produced from biomass, this life-cycle should include the greenhouse gas impact of the production of this biomass.[41] According to the Biofuels Directive, this life-cycle includes the emissions that can be assigned to the fuel, including extraction or cultivation (land-use changes, transport and distribution), processing and combustion. Given the global nature of biomass production and climate change, it is only logical that the Biofuels Directive should explicitly include an extraterritorial element when it states that the location where these emissions occur is irrelevant.[42] The sustainability criteria of Article 7b of the Biofuels Directive apply similarly irrespective of where the biomass was cultivated. These sustainability criteria appear primarily to be intended to ensure that biomass production in third States takes place in a sustainable manner.[43] This is achieved in two ways. First, the Directive contains a list of circumstances and conditions in which biomass production cannot be taken into account for the purpose of the Biofuels Directive. In a nutshell, these circumstances and conditions attempt to prevent deforestation and drainage of soils.[44] Secondly, the Directive contains a reporting obligation on the part of the European Commission concerning the ratification and implementation of a number of social and environmental international conventions.[45] In these reports the Commission will have to indicate the effect of biomass production on foodstuff availability and food prices, and it may propose corrective action to the European Parliament and Council.[46]

The New Renewables Directive contains similar semi-extraterritorial elements and adopts a similar approach to greening primary energy sources. The central provision is a duty on the part of the Member States to ensure that they achieve certain minimum percentages of renewable energy use by 2020.[47] These national renewable targets should enable the Union as a whole to achieve the 20 per cent objective set in the Energy and Climate Package. Apart from a separate 10 per cent renewables obligation for energy consumption in transport,[48] the Member States are free as regards the sector in which they would like to achieve their renewables target.[49] In addition, the New Renewables Directive allows for

[41] *Ibid*, Art 2(6), in connection with the New Renewables Directive, above n 31, Art 2(i).

[42] Biofuels Directive, above n 30, Art 2(6).

[43] Note that the sustainability criteria in the Biofuels Directive (above n 30) are nearly identical to those in Arts 17–19 of the New Renewables Directive (above n 32), with the exception that the latter refers to the term 'greenhouse gas impact' rather than 'life cycle greenhouse gas emissions' used in the former.

[44] Needless to say, cutting down rainforest in order to plant biomass is counterproductive from an environmental perspective, as is drainage of (peatlike) soils; cf A Hooijer, M Silvius, H Wösten and S Page, PEAT-CO2, *Assessment of CO_2 emissions from drained peatlands in SE Asia*, Delft Hydraulics Report Q3943 (2006). See further recital 70 of the Preamble to the New Renewables Directive, above n 32.

[45] Biofuels Directive, above n 30, Art 7b(7).

[46] *Ibid*, Art 7b(7), last paragraph.

[47] New Renewables Directive, above n 32, Art 3(1) in connection with Annex I, part A.

[48] *Ibid*, Art 3(4).

[49] *Ibid*, Preamble, recital 15.

joint projects between Member States,[50] as well as between Member States and third countries.[51] Furthermore, the Member States are required to ensure access to transmission and distribution grids for renewable energy.[52] Such access shall be on non-discriminatory and transparent terms subject to the reliable and safe operation of the grid. The latter proviso is particularly interesting, as currently most grids are not designed for the decentralised generation that characterises renewable energy generation. As a result, the New Renewables Directive includes a duty, albeit loosely formulated, for the Member States to take the appropriate steps to develop grid infrastructure in order to allow the secure operation of the grid in view of increasing renewable energy production.[53] As already alluded to above, the sustainability criteria for renewables are identical to those imposed under the Biofuels Directive.[54] The renewables targets imposed on the Member States may be achieved in various ways, but just as with the Biofuels Directive, the idea is that renewable energy commands a price premium, thus incentivising its production.[55]

Whereas the New Renewables and Biofuels Directives clearly impose requirements on the suppliers of primary fuels and the Member States, the centrepiece of the European Union's climate change policy consists of the Effort Sharing Decision[56] and the Emissions Trading Scheme Directive.[57]

The Effort Sharing Decision lays down the minimum emissions reductions obligations per Member State which will allow the European Union as a whole to reduce its emissions by 20 per cent. It also lays down the provisions for a possible further greenhouse gas emissions reduction if an international agreement on climate change has been reached.[58] The exact emissions reductions targets for the individual Member States are laid down in Annex II to the Effort Sharing Decision. In addition to the flexible mechanisms or project activities already provided for in the Kyoto Protocol,[59] the Effort Sharing Decision allows Member States to achieve part of their emissions reductions target in another Member State.[60] To implement the Kyoto flexible mechanisms further, the Effort Sharing Decision also contains provisions on the use of credits generated in the project

[50] *Ibid*, Arts 7 and 8.

[51] *Ibid*, Arts 9 and 10.

[52] *Ibid*, Art 16(2). These rules are most elaborate for renewable electricity. For 'green gas' the regime is embryonic at best; cf *ibid*, Art 16(9) and (10).

[53] *Ibid*, Art 16(1).

[54] See above n 30. Cf New Renewables Directive, above n 31, Arts 17–19 on the verification and calculation of sustainability.

[55] Recitals 74 and 76 of the preamble to the Renewables Directive (n32 above).

[56] Above n 28.

[57] Above n 31.

[58] Effort Sharing Decision, above n 28, Art 1, second paragraph.

[59] This refers to the Clean Development Mechanism (CDM) and Joint Implementation (JI), which allow developed countries to use emissions reductions achieved in developing countries (CDM) and developed countries (JI). See Douma *et al* (eds), above n 1, 39 *et seq*.

[60] Effort Sharing Decision, above n 28, Art 3(4) and (5).

activities.[61] Here we also find (semi-)extraterritorial elements in that, for example, Member States 'should ensure that their purchase of credits enhance(s) the equitable geographic distribution of projects and the achievement of an international agreement on climate change'.[62] Lastly, Articles 8 and 9 explicitly address the possibility of adjustments, depending on whether an international agreement does or does not come about.

The Effort Sharing Decision can be said to constitute the intergovernmental side of the emissions reductions obligations as it contains such obligations for the Member States. In view of the fact that the Member States themselves actually contribute only minimally to greenhouse gas emissions, an instrument is needed that will translate their emission reductions obligations into emissions reductions by industry. The ETS is just such an instrument.

The ETS was implemented in the European Union by way of Directive 2003/87.[63] In this regard, a distinction must be made between the ETS as it operates at the moment and the ETS after 2012. In both cases, big stationary emitters of greenhouse gasses require a greenhouse gas emissions permit.[64] This permit should impose upon the permit holder a duty to monitor and report greenhouse gas emissions, and, crucially, surrender an amount of so-called allowances equal to the amount of greenhouse gases emitted in the preceding year.[65] The amount of available allowances is then reduced every year in order to create scarcity of these allowances. The allowances may be traded with other participants in the ETS. This enables the most efficient emissions reductions to be achieved, while less efficient emitters may simply buy the allowances they need to surrender in view of their certified emissions.[66]

The inclusion of the aviation industry in the ETS has been quite eventful, and clearly illustrates the external dimension of this European climate change instrument. Most notable in this regard has been US opposition to the inclusion of international aviation. In a nutshell, the US indicated that it would retaliate against any inclusion of international aviation in the ETS. This US opposition was partly responsible for the adoption of an ICAO Resolution that would, for all practical purposes, make the inclusion of international aviation impossible.[67] A reservation entered by Portugal on behalf of the EU ensured, however, that this

[61] *Ibid*, Art 5.

[62] *Ibid*, Art 5(1), last paragraph.

[63] [2003] OJ L275/32, later amended by Directive 2004/101 (Enabling Kyoto Project Mechanisms), [2004] OJ L338/18, Directive 2008/101 (Inclusion of aviation), [2008] OJ L8/3 and, with effect from 25 June 2009, the New ETS Directive, above n 31.

[64] New ETS Directive, above n 31, Art 4.

[65] *Ibid*, Art 6(2)(c), (d) and (e).

[66] Failure to surrender sufficient allowances attracts a fine of €100 per tonne of CO2, as well as publication of the offender's identity in a naming and shaming list, *ibid*, Art 16(2) and (3). For aircraft operators, an operating ban may be imposed as an ultimate sanction, *ibid*, Art 16(5).

[67] Resolution A36-22, Appendix L. Available at <http://www.icao.int>.

Resolution did not enter into force.[68] International aviation was finally included in the EU ETS, but the compromise clearly bears the scars of this external dimension that manifested itself not only as US opposition, but also as European concern over the competitiveness of EU airlines. The Commission's proposal to apply the ETS only to European operators was relinquished for fear that this would reduce the European carriers' competitiveness *vis-à-vis* other airlines.[69] At the same time the initial allocation and distribution of allowances were amended to reduce the costs, and thus risks to competitiveness, imposed by the ETS.[70]

As regards the initial allocation of allowances, there is a major change as between the current ETS and the post-2012 ETS. In the current ETS, or, better, until the start of the 2012 trading period, allowances have been overwhelmingly 'grandfathered' by means of a National Allocation Plan (NAP).[71] This effectively means that the Member States have been, subject to a Commission approval procedure, allowed to decide on the quantity of allowances initially available, as well as on the distribution of these allowances.[72] In effect, Commission supervision of these so-called NAPs was limited at best, which resulted in over-allocation of allowances and a corresponding lack of scarcity and low prices.[73] As it turned out, regulatory competition between the Member States resulted, certainly during the learning curve of the 2005–08 trading period, in over-allocation that hampered the environmental effectiveness of the scheme. Commission scrutiny of NAPs was already more stringent by the current, 2008–12 trading period, but the solution to this problem adopted by the EU goes beyond just stricter supervision of NAPs. In order to reduce and ideally completely rule out regulatory competition in allocating allowances, it was decided to replace the NAPs with a Europe-wide allocation of allowances.

From 2013 onwards there will thus be only a Community-wide quantity of allowances, to be published by the Commission and subject to a linear yearly reduction that will ensure that the 20 per cent target is met.[74] Moreover, these allowances will no longer be grandfathered as a rule; rather, auctioning will be

[68] Extracts of A36-Min Ex/11 and A36-Min Ex/10 (Minutes of the Eleventh and Tenth Meetings of the Executive Committee) Reservations Made to Assembly Resolutions A36-22 and A36-28. See also Extracts of A36-Min P/9 (Minutes of the Ninth Plenary Meeting)—Reservations made to Assembly Resolutions A36-22, A36-24 and A36-28. Both available at <http://www.icao.int>.

[69] COM(2006) 818 final, p 6.

[70] For an overview, see G Schwarze, 'Including Aviation into the European Union's Emissions Trading Scheme' (2007) 16 *European Energy and Environmental Law Review* 10.

[71] 'Grandfathering' refers to the practice of handing out permits or rights free of charge; see Directive 2003/87, above n 63.

[72] Directive 2003/87 [2003] OJ L275/32. This Directive envisaged so-called NAPs for the initial allocation of allowances to be drawn up by the Member States (Art 9(1)). However, such NAPs were subject to guidance (Art 9(1)) as well as scrutiny by the Commission (Art 9(1) and (3)).

[73] For an overview of this problem and how it could be dealt with through a strict application of competition law, see HHB Vedder, 'Of Jurisdiction and Justification' (2010) 6 *Competition Law Review* 1 (available at <http://www.clasf.org>).

[74] New ETS Directive, above n 31, Art 9.

the main instrument of distribution.[75] As allowances will command a market price from 2013 onwards, the abolition of grandfathering met with considerable opposition from industry which feared for its competitive position. The New ETS Directive accommodates these fears by including provisions on carbon leakage[76] and transitional rules on harmonised free allocation.[77] These rules allow for compensation or exclusion of certain industries from the auctioning principle, and will thus minimise the impact on international competitiveness arising from bearing climate costs. Further to this external dimension, the New ETS Directive contains rules on the use of credits obtained through the Kyoto Protocol's flexible or project mechanisms.[78] Lastly, the Directive provides for the possibility to link the EU ETS with other greenhouse gas emissions schemes[79] and the possibility to take into account third-country measures to combat climate change resulting from aviation.[80] Most prominent in this regard, however, is the provision included in the New ETS Directive on the procedure for increasing the emissions reduction target to 30 per cent following an international agreement.[81]

IV. THE EXTERNAL DIMENSION OF THE EMISSIONS TRADING SCHEME DIRECTIVE

The short overview of the New ETS Directive has already revealed a number of (interrelated) external dimensions of the EU energy and climate policy. These dimensions may be said to manifest themselves on a number of levels: the extraterritorial protective level; the strategic negotiation level; and the competitiveness level.

The extraterritorial protective level relates to the attempts by the EU to influence environmental governance in third States. The negotiation level refers to those aspects of the package that basically adopt a stick-and-carrot approach in order to ensure that both the EU and third countries sign an international climate change agreement. Lastly, the competitiveness level relates to the impact of EU policies on national industries, and notably on their competitiveness.

A. Extraterritorial Protective Elements

In relation to the Kyoto Protocol flexible mechanisms in particular, extraterritorial protective elements can be discerned in the EU ETS and, more generally, the

[75] *Ibid*, Art 10.
[76] *Ibid*, Art 10b.
[77] *Ibid*, Art 10a. In addition Art 10c contains rules for transitional free allocation for electricity generation.
[78] *Ibid*, Art 11a.
[79] *Ibid*, Art 25.
[80] *Ibid*, Art 26.
[81] *Ibid*, Art 28.

Energy and Climate Package. The New ETS Directive requires the Member States to ensure that the relevant international criteria and guidelines, including those contained in the World Commission on Dams November 2000 Report, *Dams and Development A New Framework for Decision-Making*, are respected during the development of large hydroelectric power production project activities.[82] This requirement, which limits the use of the Kyoto project mechanisms, functions in a manner that is similar to the functioning of the sustainability criteria in the Biofuels and New Renewables Directives. In essence, Union law attempts to influence environmental governance in third countries. Whether they relate to the construction of hydroelectric power plants or the growing of biomass, these activities can have negative environmental and social consequences in the third States where they are implemented. The complete flooding of valleys and disappearance of rivers as a result of hydrological interferences, as well as clear-cutting forests to create oil-palm plantations, are just two examples.

In view of their subject-matter, it should not come as a surprise that the Biofuels and New Renewables Directives contain more extensive rules on this extraterritorial protective element. Article 17 of the New Renewables Directive contains such extraterritorial elements on the incentivisation and reporting level in the form of the sustainability criteria. First, as regards the incentivisation level, certain sources of raw materials are completely excluded from the Directive. This affects and regulates the incentivisation effect that the New Renewables Directive intends to have.[83] This refers to raw materials coming from primary forests, nature reserves, highly biodiverse grassland and land with high carbon stock.[84] Similarly, raw materials grown on peatlands will be taken into account only if there is evidence that their production does not involve drainage of land that was undrained before January 2008.[85] As a result, the biofuels resulting from these raw materials will not count towards the renewables targets of the Members States and will not command the price premium. The New Renewables Directive thus tries to protect these aspects of nature in the Union as well as in third countries.

The second level does not involve the incentivisation of biomass production through the Member States but rather the reporting by the EU itself of compliance by Member States[86] and third countries with certain international

[82] *Ibid*, Art 11b(6).

[83] New Renewables Directive, above n 31, Preamble, recital 74.

[84] *Ibid*, Art 17(3)(a), (b), (c) and (4).

[85] *Ibid*, Art 17(5).

[86] This applies to third countries as well as Member States. Concerning the latter, this has the awkward consequence that the Commission will have to report on the application of the CITES Regulation, Council Regulation (EC) No 338/97 of 9 December 1996 on the protection of species of wild fauna and flora by regulating trade therein, [1997] OJ L61/1, in order to control whether or not the Convention on International Trade in Endangered Species of Wild Fauna and Flora has been implemented; cf New Renewables Directive, above n 31, Art 17(7), tenth indent.

conventions[87] and development standards.[88] This is a much weaker instrument that appears to rely primarily on political declarations. It requires the Commission to report to the European Parliament and Council on the impact of the Union's biofuel policy on food availability and affordability in developing countries. Interestingly, this reporting obligation appears to apply only to countries which are a *significant* source of raw materials for biofuels, thus effectively creating a *de minimis* rule with all the discretionary powers inherent in this. The reporting instrument could be more than a paper tiger depending on the corrective measures envisaged in the last paragraph of Article 17(7) of the New Renewables Directive. It may be noted that these corrective measures are *in particular*, but not exclusively, to be imposed if biofuel production has a significant impact on food prices. Insufficient environmental governance in third countries may thus also trigger the applicability of this procedure. In view of the requirements imposed on the EU by the GATT/WTO rules, these corrective measures would most probably only involve political action, or a further extension or reformulation of the list of items taken into account for the incentivisation effect.

B. Negotiation Elements

As has been mentioned above, this is where the stick-and-carrot approach appears and the EU tries to bind itself, as well as others, to agree on a successor to the Kyoto Protocol. The stick is wielded when the EU announces that it will exclude certain third-party activities from the EU ETS unless those third parties have also signed the new international agreement. The carrot is proffered when the EU promises to go beyond its 20 per cent emissions reduction target if there is an international agreement. Both the stick and carrot will be explored in greater detail below.

The clearest 'stick' for both developing and developed countries may be found in Article 11a(7) of the New ETS Directive. According to this provision, once an international agreement has been reached, only credits for project activities from countries which have ratified that agreement can be taken into account for the purpose of the EU ETS.[89] Given that the EU ETS is at this moment by far the largest emissions trading scheme, this certainly creates an incentive for third countries to ratify the successor to the Kyoto Protocol. Interestingly, the New Renewables and Biofuels Directives, concerning the sustainability

[87] The list of ILO Conventions and environmental treaties (the Cartagena Protocol on Biosafety and the Convention on International Trade in Endangered Species of Wild Fauna and Flora) appears to be exhaustive. It is not clear why other international treaties, such as the Ramsar Convention (on the protection of wetlands), were not included.

[88] New Renewables Directive, above n 32, Art 17(7).

[89] See above n 31.

criteria discussed in the paragraph above, require that third States both ratify and implement international conventions as a check on the sustainability of biomass production in those countries.[90] For participation in the EU ETS following a new international agreement, ratification itself suffices according to Article 11a(7) of the New ETS Directive. In view of the fact that even the EU, the great protagonist of concerted action against climate change, has struggled to meet its Kyoto obligations, moving beyond ratification to check for actual implementation is no minor quibble. Then again, depending on the actual enforcement mechanism available in the successor to the Kyoto Protocol, such implementation matters may perhaps best be left to the international level.[91]

The biggest 'carrot' to entice third countries into signing the new international agreement is to be found in Article 28 of the New ETS Directive.[92] Here we read that, should an international agreement have come about, the Commission shall report on a number of issues so that the EU can decide whether to adopt the 30 per cent target. This provision is particularly interesting because it sets, as far as the EU is concerned, a clear goal for the international agreement: a 20 per cent reduction in 2020 compared to 1990 levels. An international agreement with a lower reduction objective will not trigger the EU's move towards the 30 per cent reduction obligation. Moreover, the EU indicates only that it will move towards the 30 per cent reduction target, thus allowing itself to achieve a more modest objective should the international agreement exceed the 20 per cent benchmark only minimally. It may further be noted that this provision refers only to the signature, and not the ratification (let alone implementation), of the international agreement. The experience with the signature of the Kyoto Protocol by the United States, which was followed by a failure to ratify it, should make the EU careful in deciding upon the move to an even stricter emissions reduction target.

As mentioned above, the entire procedure commences with a report by the Commission on the following items in particular:

a) the nature of the measures agreed upon in the framework of the international negotiations, as well as the commitments made by other developed countries to emission reductions comparable to those of the Union and the commitments made by economically more advanced developing countries to contributing adequately according to their responsibilities and respective capabilities;
b) the implications of the international agreement on climate change and, consequently, options required at Union level, in order to move to the more

[90] See above nn 32 and 30, respectively.

[91] Cf the Kyoto Compliance Mechanism, set up pursuant to Art 18 of the Kyoto Protocol.

[92] Another 'carrot' may be found in Art 10(3)(c) of the New ETS Directive (above n 31), according to which the proceeds of the allowance auctions may be used to fund forestry projects, but only in third countries that have ratified the international agreement. In addition, the amount of auctioned allowances will increase with the strength of the international agreement.

ambitious 30 per cent reduction target in a balanced, transparent and equitable way, taking into account work under the Kyoto Protocol's first commitment period;

c) the Union manufacturing industries' competitiveness in the context of carbon leakage risks;
d) the impact of the international agreement on climate change on other Union economic sectors;
e) the impact on the Union agriculture sector, including carbon leakage risks;
f) the appropriate modalities for including emissions and removals related to land use, land use change and forestry in the Union;
g) afforestation, reforestation, avoided deforestation and forest degradation in third countries in the event of the establishment of any internationally recognised system in this context;
h) the need for additional Union policies and measures in view of the greenhouse gas reduction commitments of the Union and of Member States.

This list of items indicates what the EU is looking for in an international agreement and what *quid pro quo* it would be willing to hand out in return for third countries signing that agreement. Of course, the report should contain a detailed analysis of the agreement (under a) above), so that the EU can check whether or not its direct competitors on the international level playing field, other developed countries, are also committed to combating climate change. The fact, however, that the report should also address the commitments made by more advanced developing countries (India, China) sends out a clear message to these countries. Moreover, the fact that the Commission will also have to report on the modalities for including land use, land use change and forestry (so-called LULUCF) in the EU ETS (under g) above) may be interesting for developing countries.[93] As it stands, the New ETS does not allow for such LULUCF credits to be used in the ETS. This is because LULUCF projects do not offer the absolute certainty that stored carbon dioxide will remain stored.[94] However, LULUCF projects are allowed—albeit subject to strict standards—by the Kyoto Protocol, and they are a popular carbon dioxide reduction option for the least developed countries.[95]

Lastly, the reference to so-called 'carbon leakage' (under c), (e) and implicitly d) above) addresses the fears of most developed countries. This fear relates to the possibility of carbon-intensive industries migrating from developed countries with strict emissions reductions obligations to developing countries subject to less strict abatement standards. As environmental protection generally comes at a cost, the

93 This is often referred to more colloquially as a (carbon) 'sink'.

94 A forest, for example, may burn down and release the stored carbon dioxide; Commission Memo/08/797 on the ETS Revision, p 10.

95 See in general on LULUCF projects and developing countries, NH Ravindranath, JA Sathaye, *Climate Change and Developing Countries* (Dordrecht, Kluwer Academic Publishers, 2002) 258.

stricter standards will invariably have a deleterious effect on the competitiveness of the industry subject to the strictest requirements. This industry could then decide to move production to the jurisdiction with the lowest production (and carbon) costs. This would be bad news for climate change, as well as for national competitiveness and employment. Inclusion of the carbon leakage risks in the Commission report not only helps the EU to identify potential risks to the competitiveness of the EU industry, but it could also help third developed countries to find a method that will enable them to sign a comprehensive, strong, international climate change accord.

As regards the process of moving towards the 30 per cent target, the Commission is to release a proposal for an amending directive together with this report, and this should enter into force alongside approval of the international agreement by the Union.[96] However, this new directive should contain transitory rules that will suspend the entry into force of the 30 per cent target pending the entry into force of the international agreement.[97] Nevertheless, the idea of having the amending directive enter into force together with the approval by the EU will perhaps help to get wavering countries to ratify the accord as they see the clear commitment by the EU.[98]

C. Competitiveness Elements

The short reference to carbon leakage in the paragraph above already shows the major concerns the EU has with conducting an ambitious but unilateral climate change policy. It runs the risk of scaring its industry off, causing it to move elsewhere in order to avoid high production and carbon costs. Given that the EU has committed itself to auctioning the allowances, rather than 'grandfathering' them as is the case currently, the carbon costs to industry resulting from the EU ETS will probably rise considerably. The EU addresses carbon leakage in a number of ways. First, allowances may be handed out free of charge to a large extent. Secondly, importers of products likely to be exposed to carbon leakage may be included in the free allocation scheme. Thirdly, the impact of carbon leakage on energy security shall be assessed in relation to electricity production. The compensation envisaged under the carbon leakage provisions may involve the subsidisation of sectors of industry. This would amount to State aid within the meaning of Article 107(1) TFEU (ex Article 87(1) EC), and the Commission has committed itself to modifying the State aid rules in this regard.[99]

[96] New ETS Directive, above n 31, Art 28(2).

[97] *Ibid*, Art 28(5).

[98] A commitment reiterated in the March 2010 European Council meeting, 25/25 March Presidency Conclusions, under point 5(b).

[99] Commission Memo/08/797 on the ETS Revision, p 8.

The New ETS Directive contains a number of elements that will address this risk in the form of the carbon leakage provisions.[100] Naturally, these are all related to the international accord, as such an accord has an impact on the risk of carbon leakage. For example, the transitional EU-wide rules on harmonised free allocation will be reviewed following the approval by the Union of an international accord.[101] When this agreement leads to mandatory reductions that are comparable to those to which the EU has committed itself, the free allocation will take place only where this is fully justified in the light of that agreement. Similarly, the rules that enable support for energy-intensive industry to combat carbon leakage rely on a Commission review of the international agreement.[102] In this regard, the Commission will take into account

> [a]ny binding sectoral agreements which lead to global greenhouse gas emissions reductions of the magnitude required to effectively address climate change, and which are monitorable, verifiable and subject to mandatory enforcement arrangements ... when considering what measures are appropriate.[103]

This allows the Commission to take into account regional or sectoral agreements other than the one that should follow the Kyoto Protocol. It also offers the Commission more flexibility, in that no clear 20 per cent reductions target is laid down. As carbon leakage measures are inherently protectionist, this possibility to (further) open up the European market may very well entice third countries to enter into an agreement effectively to address climate change. Article 10a(18) of the New ETS Directive contains a similar corrective mechanism, to be applied when the Commission draws up the list of industries exposed to a risk of carbon leakage.[104] In this regard, the Commission must take into account

> the extent to which third countries, representing a decisive share of global production of products in sectors or subsectors deemed to be at risk of carbon leakage, firmly commit to reducing greenhouse gas emissions in the relevant sectors or subsectors to an extent comparable to that of the Community and within the same time-frame;[105]

Again, we see how this provision is more flexible than Article 28 of the New ETS Directive, in that only a firm commitment to a comparable emissions reduction is required. This means that even if such emissions reductions take place in a unilateral setting, ie without a binding sectoral international agreement such as referred to in Article 10b(1), last paragraph, of the New ETS Directive, the Commission will be able to take them into account, thus potentially removing the carbon leakage offsets for a particular industry. Again, this will open up market access for products from those third countries.

[100] New ETS Directive, above n 31, Preamble, recitals 24 and 25.
[101] *Ibid*, Art 10a(1), last paragraph.
[102] *Ibid*, Art 10b(1), first paragraph.
[103] *Ibid*, Art 10b(1), last paragraph.
[104] The Carbon Leakage List has been adopted by Decision 2010/2, [2010] OJ L1/10.
[105] New ETS Directive, above n 31 above, Art 10a(18)(a).

In its May 2010 Communication on the options for moving beyond the 20 per cent target, the Commission takes a rather broad approach to the mandate laid down in the New ETS Directive.[106] Instead of just analysing the international context to see whether it allows for the EU to move towards the 30 per cent target, the Commission undertakes to analyse the impact of this move more generally. It does so in the light of the economic crisis, the need for more climate technology innovation and, most importantly, the failed international negotiations. Concerning the last of these, the Commission notes that the requirements laid down in the New ETS Directive for moving to a 30 per cent abatement target clearly have not been met.[107] Indeed, the Commission does not push for the stricter target, but rather indicates to what extent the impact of the economic crisis could make this stricter target more palatable because abatement costs will generally be lower. Moreover, the Commission introduces the idea of having bilateral crediting agreements with third countries in which international credits emanating from countries 'which are not participating adequately in international climate efforts' would be subject to a multiplier.[108] The would mean that more than one credit (normally representing one tonne of CO_2) would have to be surrendered for a tonne of CO_2 emitted under the EU ETS. This in turn effectively makes cooperation with those States under the Clean Development Mechanism or Joint Implementation far less attractive, and thus constitutes an incentive for those States to participate adequately in the international negotiations.

V. CONCLUSIONS: THE FAILURE OF DIPLOMACY BY DIRECTIVE

The title of this chapter contains a question mark, and this is not without reason. Diplomacy, the process of wheeling and dealing, giving and taking and negotiations in the walkways, seems rather hard to reconcile with the open and unilateral character of a directive. This chapter set out to identify elements of diplomacy in the Energy and Climate Package, using the analogy of mutually-agreed coercion, with the EU 'leading by example'.[109]

The overview of the Package, and notably the New ETS Directive, shows that there are instances where the Union is clearly setting the scene for an international accord on climate change. Moreover, the involvement of the European Council, a body normally not involved in drafting European environmental law but primarily active in external relations of the EU, also highlights the external dimension of this policy area. Furthermore, the central role for the Commission in the drafting

[106] Commission Communication, 'Analysis of options to move beyond 20% greenhouse gas emission reductions and assessing the risk of carbon leakage', COM(2010) 265 final.

[107] *Ibid*, 2.

[108] *Ibid*, 12.

[109] See J Rankin, 'Back to the drawing-board', available at <http://www.europeanvoice.com>.

and implementation of the ETS Directive,[110] an institution similarly active in the external relations of the EU, also evidences these external aspects of the Directive.[111] The most important evidence for the international aspects of the ETS Directive presents itself as the stick and (notably) carrot in the form of the move to the 30 per cent emissions reductions target. This form of diplomacy, however, is imperfect, as the EU's Energy and Climate Package fails to address one crucial question: what will happen if there is no international successor to the Kyoto Protocol? The ETS Directive and the other elements of the Energy and Climate Package remain silent on this matter. This means that the ultimate 'stick' does not exist.

The absence of a stick means that the EU can only do so much, as the Copenhagen negotiations clearly show. It has clearly failed to create mutually-agreed coercion resulting in global responsibility for the climate.[112] However successful the EU may have been in the Kyoto phase, it is clear that its 'leading by example' method did not work to secure a post-Kyoto agreement. In two respects the EU no longer functions as the political leader of international climate change negotiations. Its opening bid of a 20 per cent reduction, as well as an option of upping the ante to 30 per cent to create global responsibility for the climate, was, first, unsuccessful in getting the United States to make a similar commitment as a major developed nation and, secondly, unsuccessful in convincing China as a major developing country. The so-called Copenhagen Accord was ultimately hammered out by the United States, China, India, Brazil and South Africa, thereby effectively sidelining the EU.[113] In the meeting of the Environment Council on 28 January 2010, the EU and its Member States associated themselves with this Copenhagen Accord.[114] This, however, has not kept the EU from continuing to position itself as the political leader on climate change.[115]

Interestingly, the conclusions of the European Council meeting on 10 and 11 December 2009 already contain the first signs of retreat on the part of the EU. Here we read that '[t]he agreement should lead to finalising a legally binding instrument, preferably within six months after the Copenhagen Conference'.[116] As part of this process the EU continues to offer its conditional move to a 30 per cent reduction, but for the moment this remains insufficient to get the US Senate

[110] No fewer than 15 comitology procedures are envisaged in the ETS Directive alone.

[111] As does the fact that the Danish Environment Minister, who initially chaired the Copenhagen negotiations, is now nominated to become European Commissioner for Climate Change.

[112] Whether this results from an insufficiently ambitious abatement target for the EU, insufficient funding for the climate change fund for developing countries or requesting too much greenhouse gas abatement from developing countries is unclear.

[113] For an account, see 'EU looks beyond weak Copenhagen climate deal', available at <http://www.euractiv.com>.

[114] Document No 5762/10.

[115] Press release of Environment Council meeting on 22 December 2009, Document No 17764/2/09 REV 2, at 12.

[116] European Council, Conclusions from the meeting on 10 and 11 December 2009, EUCO 6/09, point 34.

to approve the Obama administration's Climate Bill.[117] The EU's conditional contribution of €2.4 billion of fast-start funding to the Copenhagen Green Climate Fund to aid developing countries in implementing the accord similarly fails to impress India and China.[118] Again, the Commission very much puts itself at the forefront of the actual implementation of this pledge, an effort clearly placed in the wider context of brokering an international climate deal in Cancun.[119] However, later European Council meetings fail to give the Commission the central role in implementing the external aspects of the EU's climate policy, reiterating the role played by the Member States.[120] Indeed, while the Commission may prepare the decision on the move to a 30 per cent reduction target, the actual decision will be taken in the spring 2011 European Council meeting.[121] Particularly in view of the fact that this decision is so closely connected to the EU's negotiation position in Cancun, this increased role for the Member States may well reduce the effectiveness of the EU's negotiation strategy.

This forces the EU to think not only about whether it will actually up the ante to a 30 per cent reduction, but more fundamentally about this method of ensuring leadership.[122] In the wake of Copenhagen essentially two European responses were voiced. One argues that the EU should be extra sensitive about carbon leakage; the other urges the EU to reconsider a carbon tariff.[123] The latter could well seem to be the stick needed to ensure a climate deal, but it may also be the spark that sets off another round of trade wars and failed trade liberalisation talks resulting only in less global responsibility. These arguments are clearly inspired by competitiveness concerns and hide the fact that even a 30 per cent reduction still puts the EU a long way from realising the 2°C target, the inclusion of which in the Copenhagen Accord is heralded as an EU feat of negotiation. While the outcome of Cancun may have exceeded the expectations of many, myriad hurdles remain to be overcome before a binding successor to the Kyoto Protocol is agreed upon in Durban in November 2011.[124] For the moment it seems likely that the global climate will indeed end up as the next tragedy of the commons.

[117] For the status quo, see <http://thomas.loc.gov/cgi-bin/bdquery/z?d111:HR02454:@@@S>.

[118] See 'EU official warns climate aid 'will not come for free', available at <http://www.euractiv.com/en/climate-environment/eu-official-warns-climate-aid-will-not-come-free-news-286013>.

[119] Commission Communication, 'International climate policy post-Copenhagen: Acting now to reinvigorate global action on climate change', COM(2010) 86, at 3.2.3.

[120] European Council, Conclusions from the meeting on 25 and 26 March 2010, EUCO 7/10, point 13.

[121] Council, Conclusions from the meeting on 14 October 2010, 14825/10, at 9.

[122] In an informal meeting of the European Council on 11 February it was decided to adhere to the existing strategy of offering a 20% reduction now and a conditional 30% reduction.

[123] See Rankin, above n 108. See further the debate in the European Affairs Committee of the French Senate of 17 November 2009, available at <http://www.senat.fr/europe/r17112009.html#toc0>.

[124] It is interesting to see that the EU is no longer pushing as hard for a single legal framework, but adopts a more flexible attitude that could include non-binding commitments by developing countries, Council Conclusions of 14 October 2010, 14957/10, at points 10 and 11.

Part Two

Political Governance

5

The EU and the International Legal Order: The Case of Human Rights

BRUNO DE WITTE

I. INTRODUCTION

IN THE FIELD of human rights, the policy interconnections between the European Union and the rest of the world have primarily been viewed, in the legal literature, as *judicial interconnections*. Much attention has been paid to the manner in which the Court of Justice of the European Union has used international human rights norms, and their interpretation by international courts and treaty bodies, in the construction of an EU law regime of fundamental rights protection.[1] The main question, in this judicial context, is the extent to which international human rights norms inform and determine the fundamental rights standard applied by the Court of Justice and the General Court in reviewing and interpreting EU law, and in reviewing Member State action that comes within the scope of EU law. More recently, and to a much lesser extent, there has also been some scholarly interest for the reverse side of this judicial or quasi-judicial interconnection, namely the influence of the Court of Justice's fundamental rights case law on the interpretative practice of the European Court of Human Rights (ECtHR) and other international bodies.[2] Section II. of this chapter will focus on the development, and especially the most recent features, of judicial policy interconnections in the human rights field.

However, human rights interconnections between the EU and the outside world also, and increasingly, happen outside the judicial or quasi-judicial arena. The political institutions of the European Union have increasingly resorted to international human rights norms as an inspiration for the development of their

[1] See, from among a very rich literature: D Spielmann, 'Human Rights Case Law in the Strasbourg and Luxembourg Courts: Conflicts, Inconsistencies, and Complementarities' in P Alston, M Bustelo and J Heenan (eds), *The EU and Human Rights* (Oxford, Oxford University Press, 1999) 757–80; A Rosas, 'The European Union and International Human Rights Instruments' in V Kronenberger (ed), *The European Union and the International Legal Order: Discord or Harmony?* (The Hague, TMC Asser Press, 2001) 53–67.

[2] See n 13 below, and the accompanying text.

own laws and policies; they have also taken a more active role, as human rights norm *makers* rather than norm *takers*, by participating in the adoption of international human rights instruments and by the active 'exportation' of international human rights norms to third countries in the framework of the EU's external relations. These various *legislative and executive* approaches to the interconnection between EU law and international human rights law will be mapped in section III. of this chapter.

II. JUDICIAL INTERCONNECTIONS: THE EUROPEAN COURT OF JUSTICE AS A HUMAN RIGHTS ACTOR

A. Judicial Reference to the European Convention on Human Rights

Neither the European Community nor the European Union has become party to any of the core regional and universal human rights instruments: the European Convention on Human Rights (ECHR), the European Social Charter, the two UN Covenants, the UN Conventions on Race Discrimination, on Discrimination against Women and on the Rights of Children, or the main conventions of the International Labour Organisation. In this respect, the European Union finds itself in a very different position from that of its Member States. To the extent that those Member States have transferred many powers to the EU in fields covered by those international instruments, they can no longer fully ensure compliance with their international obligations, and there arises a potential gap in the protection of human rights.

The gap has been plugged, to some extent, by the Court of Justice through its well-established use of international human rights instruments as 'sources of inspiration' for the development of the unwritten general principles of Community law (now to be called, after the entry into force of the Treaty of Lisbon, general principles of Union law). These principles are part of primary EU law and a frequently used basis for the judicial review and interpretation of EU acts, and of Member State measures coming within the scope of EU law. The Court of Justice presents this rather complex legal situation in the following typical way:

> [I]t should be recalled that, according to settled case-law, fundamental rights form an integral part of the general principles of law the observance of which the Court ensures, and that, for that purpose, the Court draws inspiration from the constitutional traditions common to the Member States and from the guidelines supplied by international treaties for the protection of human rights on which the Member States have collaborated or to which they are signatories. The ECHR has special significance in that respect.[3]

[3] Case C-479/04, *Laserdisken ApS v Kulturministeriet* [2006] ECR I-8089, para 61; identical or almost identical paragraphs appear in most ECJ judgments dealing with fundamental rights, including in the famous *Kadi* judgment: Joined Cases C-402/05 P and C-415/05 P, *Kadi and Al Barakaat v Council* [2008] ECR I-6531, para 283.

One may note, in this hallowed formula, that the ECHR is given 'special significance', but that its formal status seems to be the same as that of other international instruments, namely the rather vague status of supplying 'guidelines' from which the Court 'draws inspiration' in fine-tuning its own general principles of EU law.

This is also the accepted view in the legal literature. Most authors praise the CJEU for making frequent reference not just to the text of the Convention but also to the Strasbourg case law, but add that the ECHR is still not formally binding on the EU institutions, as long as the Union has not acceded to the Convention.[4] The President of the ECtHR seems to be in perfect agreement with this interpretation. In a lecture at King's College London in October 2008, he stated: 'It is of course true that formally speaking the Convention is not binding under European Union law.'[5]

Even though this is the received wisdom, it does not seem a very satisfactory account of the current state of the law, in the light of the wording of Article 6(3) TEU, which states:

> Fundamental rights, as guaranteed by the European Convention for the Protection of Human Rights and Fundamental Freedoms and as they result from the constitutional traditions common to the Member States, shall constitute general principles of the Union's law.

Although this sentence was slightly rephrased compared to its pre-Lisbon version (when it figured in Article 6(2) EU Treaty), the wording of its core normative statement has remained unaltered ever since the Maastricht Treaty, when the sentence was first introduced in the EU Treaty. That statement signals that the rights of the Convention *are* general principles of EU law and not just a *source of inspiration* for those principles. So the language of the EU Treaty seems very clearly to express the will of the Member States to make the ECHR formally binding—by reference—on the EU institutions, rather than just a source of inspiration which the Court *may decide* to use in shaping 'its' unwritten general principles. At the time of the Maastricht Treaty, the expression of that will of the Member States was rather half-hearted, since Article F(2) (as it then was) was not listed among the provisions of the EU Treaty which the Court was allowed to apply and enforce. This anomaly was corrected by the Treaty of Amsterdam, which made Article 6(2)—as it was then renumbered—judicially enforceable. It is true that Article 6(2) EU Treaty then, and Article 6(3) TEU now, did not make the Convention

[4] A Rosas, 'The European Union and Fundamental Rights/Human Rights', in C Krause and M Scheinin (eds), *International Protection of Human Rights—A Textbook* (Institute for Human Rights, Åbo Akademi University, 2009) 443, at 457–58; G Harpaz, 'The European Court of Justice and its Relations with the European Court of Human Rights: The Quest for Enhanced Reliance, Coherence and Legitimacy' (2009) 46 *CML Rev* 105, at 108–15.

[5] JP Costa, 'The Relationship between the European Convention on Human Rights and European Union Law—A Jurisprudential Dialogue between the European Court of Human Rights and the European Court of Justice', Lecture at King's College London, 7 October 2008, p 2 (available on the website of the ECtHR, www.echr.coe.int).

applicable *as such* within the EU legal order, but only through the formal intermediary of the general principles of Community law. But the text makes it clear that the Convention rights *are being* incorporated within the category of general principles without leaving any discretion in this regard to the ECJ; one could say that the Court's traditional power to define the content of the unwritten general principles has been partially taken away by the Member States when adopting the Maastricht Treaty.

There is therefore no doubt, in my view, that Article 6(3) TEU gives formal binding status to the ECHR within the EU legal order, and it is quite curious that the Court of Justice and most of the legal literature have failed to draw that conclusion; perhaps this is due to a confusion between two separate legal questions: the question whether the European Union (and, until its recent demise, the European Community) is bound by the ECHR *under international law* (it is not, since it has not signed and ratified the Convention) and the question whether the ECHR is binding for the EU institutions *as a matter of European Union law* (this is so, in view of the unambiguous language of Article 6 TEU). A similar distinction can be made with regard to the Geneva Convention Relating to the Status of Refugees. Neither the EC nor the EU has become a party to that Convention, so that the European Union, as an *international* subject, is not bound by it; but the Convention has been made binding *internally* for the EU institutions when developing their asylum policy, by means of Article 78(1) TFEU.[6]

On a closer look, one does find judgments of the Court of Justice in which it drops the 'special significance' terminology and refers directly to the ECHR as if it considered the Convention to be formally binding. Among the examples of this approach which, as I argued above, is based on a more correct reading of current EU law, one could mention the recent *Elgafaji* judgment, in which the Court stated *obiter* that 'the ECHR forms part of the general principles of Community law, observance of which is ensured by the Court'.[7] In the *Varec* judgment of 2008, the ECJ applied both Articles 6 and 8 ECHR in a straightforward manner without mentioning the 'general principles' construction at all.[8] In *Schneider Electric* (a competition case), the Court of First Instance held simply that

> observance of all persons' right to a hearing before an independent and impartial tribunal is guaranteed by Article 6(1) of the Convention, to which reference is made by Article 6(2) of the Treaty on European Union, and which was reaffirmed by the second paragraph of Article 47 of the Charter of Fundamental rights of the European Union.[9]

[6] Art 78(1) TFEU: 'The Union shall develop a common policy on asylum, subsidiary protection and temporary protection with a view to offering appropriate status to any third-country national requiring international protection and ensuring compliance with the principle of *non-refoulement*. This policy must be in accordance with the Geneva Convention of 28 July 1951 and the Protocol of 31 January 1967 relating to the status of refugees, and other relevant treaties.' Before the entry into force of the Lisbon Treaty, a quasi-identical provision was to be found in Art 63(1) EC Treaty.

[7] Case C-465/07, *Meki Elgafaji, Noor Elgafaji v Staatssecretaris van Justitie* [2009] ECR I-921, para 28.

[8] Case C-450/06, *Varec v Etat belge* [2008] ECR I-581, paras 44 ff.

[9] Case T-351/03, *Schneider Electric v Commission* [2007] ECR II-2237, para 181.

Here, as in *Varec*, the passage through the general principles channel is completely elided.

This tendency of the European Courts to anchor the ECHR more strongly into the EU legal order is pursued with some hesitation (in many other recent cases, the Court reverts to the 'special significance' formula which I quoted above), but it should be pursued more vigorously, since it corresponds to the wording of Article 6 EU Treaty. It would also make the EU's future accession to the ECHR (now imposed by Article 6(2) TEU) an easy step from the 'domestic' EU perspective. Indeed, if the Court of Justice of the European Union were to recognise that the ECHR is already formally binding on the EU institutions now, then the future accession would not cause any major change in the Court's use of the Convention. That would not render the accession meaningless, of course. Whereas the current reference to the ECHR, in Article 6 TEU, is quite generic, accession would require the EU to nail its colours to the mast by deciding which Protocols of the Convention to ratify (for example, should it ratify Protocol No 12 containing a general prohibition of discrimination, which few of its Member States have ratified so far?) and whether or not to make reservations upon ratification. As regards the role of the Court of Justice, accession would make EU acts directly reviewable by the ECtHR, and might thus 'concentrate the mind' of the Court of Justice to shadow the Strasbourg case law even more closely than today, so as to avoid being second-guessed or overruled by the Strasbourg court in human rights cases. Indeed, the current practice of the CJEU—despite the friendly rhetoric—does not always follow closely the case law of the ECtHR. In some of its judgments, fundamental rights issues are decided without any reference to the ECHR, despite the existence of relevant precedents in Strasbourg. This happens, for example, in the field of data protection, in which the Court of Justice now tends to omit any reference to the ECtHR whilst recognising that the EC Data Protection Directive of 1995[10] aims at protecting the right to privacy, a Convention right.[11] In other situations, the Court of Justice does refer to Strasbourg case law, but in an ancillary way, using it to reinforce a conclusion which the Court had reached on the basis of its own fundamental rights precedents. The *Kadi* judgment is a good illustration of this.[12]

[10] Directive 95/46 of the European Parliament and of the Council of 24 October 1995 on the protection of individuals with regard to the processing of personal data and on the free movement of such data, [1995] OJ L281/31.

[11] See, eg, Case C-553/07, *College van burgemeesters en wethouders van Rotterdam v MEE Rijkeboer*, [2009] ECR I-3889. In para 46 of the judgment, the Court states that the purpose of Directive 95/46 'is to protect the fundamental rights and freedoms of natural persons, and in particular their right to privacy with respect to the processing of personal data', but it does not refer to Art 8 of the ECHR, nor to the rather abundant case law of the ECtHR on the data protection dimension of the right to privacy (most notably its Grand Chamber judgment of 4 December 2008, *S and Marper v United Kingdom*, 30562/04 [2008] ECHR 1581).

[12] In *Kadi and Al Barakaat*, above n 3, the long assessment of the human rights compatibility of the Council Regulation freezing the assets of suspected terrorists, in paras 331 to 372 of the judgment, includes references to four judgments of the ECtHR, but the backbone of the ECJ's argument is formed by its own fundamental rights case law. This seminal judgment is analysed in detail in ch 7 of this volume.

It is worth noting that the Court of Justice's generally friendly attitude towards the ECHR has been matched in recent years by a willingness of the ECtHR to borrow from EU law in its interpretation of Convention rights, thus establishing a mutual interconnection between the Luxembourg and Strasbourg courts.[13] In the field of anti-discrimination, in particular, the ECtHR has become more of a follower of EU law than the other way round; for example, in its judgment in *DH and others v Czech Republic* (a case dealing with school segregation of Roma children), the Strasbourg court made extensive reference to 'Community law and practice', and it made use of the concept of indirect discrimination as developed in EC law.[14] The process of mutual borrowing between the two courts is facilitated by the informal interaction between its members at conferences and special meetings, as well as by the fact that some judges of the Strasbourg court have later been appointed to the Court of Justice.[15] One may also note, as another linkage between the two systems, the interventions of representatives of the European Commission in ECtHR cases with an important European Union dimension, where they present the EU law perspective.[16]

B. Judicial Reference to other International Instruments

The privileged position accorded to the ECHR in Article 6(3) TEU contrasts with the precarious legal position of other international human rights conventions. No other human rights conventions are explicitly mentioned in Article 6 TEU. At some point during the 1996–97 negotiations of the Amsterdam Treaty, the European Social Charter figured alongside the ECHR in the draft text of the future Article 6 EU, but it was demoted, later on in the same Intergovernmental Conference, to the (non-binding) Preamble of the Amsterdam Treaty. In that Preamble, the Member States confirmed their 'attachment to fundamental rights as defined in the European Social Charter … and in the 1989 Community Charter of the Fundamental Social Rights of Workers'. Both these legal documents were also mentioned in the body of the EC Treaty—not in a prominent position comparable to that of Article 6 EU, but in the

[13] See R Lawson, '*Ex Boreale Lux*: On the Influence of the ECJ on Interpretation of the ECHR' in M Bulterman, L Hancher, A McDonnell, HG Sevenster (eds), *Views of European Law from the Mountain—Liber Amicorum Piet Jan Slot* (The Hague, Kluwer Law International, 2009) 439.

[14] European Court of Human Rights, Grand Chamber judgment of 13 November 2007, Application 57325/00, *DH and others v Czech Republic*, respectively at paras 81–91 and para 184.

[15] On this out-of-court dialogue, and on the 'joint diplomacy' of the two courts, see L Scheeck, 'La diplomatie commune des cours européennes' in A Mbongo and B Vauchez (eds), *Dans la fabrique du droit européen* (Bruxelles, Bruylant, 2009) 105.

[16] F Hoffmeister, 'The Contribution of EU Practice to International Law' in M Cremona (ed), *Developments in EU External Relations Law* (Oxford, Oxford University Press, 2008) 37, at 112.

small 'niche'[17] of the social policy chapter. Indeed, Article 136 EC, after its amendment in Amsterdam, stated that the 'Community and the Member States' should pursue the social policy objectives listed in that article,

> having in mind fundamental social rights such as those set out in the European Social Charter signed at Turin on 18 October 1961 and in the Community Charter of the Fundamental Social Rights of Workers.

One of the questions raised by this enigmatic phrase (which is now, under the Lisbon Treaty, contained in Article 151 TFEU) is the meaning of 'having in mind'. These words make clear that the fundamental social rights contained in those instruments are not directly enforceable as a matter of EU law. But could they imply that, if EU social legislation were obviously to run counter to the rights guaranteed by the European Social Charter and the Community Charter, it could be declared invalid because its authors had not kept those rights 'in mind'?

In the judicial practice of the European Courts, the human rights treaties other than the ECHR are mentioned only very sporadically. An old example is *Defrenne v Sabena III*, where the Court, in reaching the conclusion that protection against sex discrimination was a fundamental Community right, found support in the fact that

> the same concepts are recognized by the European Social Charter of 18 November 1961 and by Convention No 111 of the International Labour Organization of 25 June 1958 concerning discrimination in respect of employment and occupation.[18]

In later cases, occasional references were made by the Court, for example to the UN Civil and Political Rights Covenant, and to the UN Convention for the Elimination of Discrimination angaisnt Women, but they were never decisive for the outcome of the case.[19]

In its more recent fundamental rights case law, however, especially when no ECHR right is readily available, the Court of Justice adopts a true 'melting pot' approach, distilling a general principle from a combination of international instruments. A striking example of this is the convoluted way in which the Court identified the right to take collective action as a general principle of EC law in *Laval* and *Viking*:

> [T]he right to take collective action, including the right to strike, is recognised both by various international instruments which the Member States have signed or cooperated in, such as the European Social Charter, signed at Turin on 18 October 1961—to which, moreover, express reference is made in Article 136 EC—and Convention No 87

[17] The term is borrowed from S Sciarra, 'From Strasbourg to Amsterdam: Prospects for the Convergence of European Social Rights Policy' in Alston *et al* (eds), above n 1, at 496.

[18] Case 149/77, *Defrenne v Sabena* [1978] ECR 1365, para 26.

[19] See P Craig and G de Búrca, *EU Law. Text, Cases and Materials*, 4th edn (Oxford, Oxford University Press, 2008) at 383–86.

> concerning Freedom of Association and Protection of the Right to Organise, adopted on 9 July 1948 by the International Labour Organisation—and by instruments developed by those Member States at Community level or in the context of the European Union, such as the Community Charter of the Fundamental Social Rights of Workers adopted at the meeting of the European Council held in Strasbourg on 9 December 1989, which is also referred to in Article 136 EC, and the Charter of Fundamental Rights of the European Union proclaimed in Nice on 7 December 2000 … [T]he right to take collective action, including the right to strike, must therefore be recognised as a fundamental right which forms an integral part of the general principles of Community law … [20]

One may note that the Court, here, uses a mixture of binding and non-binding legal instruments (the EU Charter was, of course, not yet binding at the time of the *Viking* and *Laval* judgments), and that, moreover, some Member States (such as the United Kingdom) had not accepted to be bound by *any* of the international instruments listed by the Court. The Court thus uses the 'transmutation' of the international standards into general principles of EU law as a way of developing *new* legal obligations for (some) States when acting within the scope of EU law. One may also note that no further reference was made, in *Laval* and *Viking*, to the practice of the international monitoring bodies, especially those of the International Labour Organisation, when the Court went on to balance the right to take collective action against other values (*in casu*, the freedom of establishment and freedom to provide services).[21]

One could say, in the light of these cases, that the general principles of Union law are being put to a use which is strikingly different from their original use. They were 'invented' by the ECJ in the 1950s (in the context of the ECSC Treaty) in order to provide structure and hierarchy to a primitive system of Community administrative law. They are now used to de-structure the traditional formal distinction between legal orders, by transforming a network of non-binding or half-binding norms developed at the international level into binding sources of EU law. The question arising today is to what extent the Court of Justice will continue to develop its general principles case law (and use international sources in that context), or instead start to refer mainly or exclusively to the now binding EU Charter of Rights. If that were the case, the influence of international human rights on the Court's jurisprudence would also dwindle.

[20] Case C-438/05, *Viking Line* [2007] ECR I-10779, paras 43–44; Case C-341/05, *Laval* [2007[ECR I-11767, paras 90–91. See also, in the same vein, Case C-540/03, *European Parliament v Council* (*re: family reunification*) [2006] ECR I-5769, paras 37–39, where the ECJ referred to the European Social Charter, the Civil Covenant and the Convention on the Rights of the Child.

[21] See T Novitz, 'A Human Rights Analysis of the *Viking* and *Laval* Judgments' (2007–08) 10 *Cambridge Yearbook of European Legal Studies* 541, at 559: 'While the Court was prepared to make reference to ILO Convention No 87 when holding that the right to take collective action constituted a fundamental right, it seems that it adopted a peculiarly restrictive interpretation of that right which neglects ILO jurisprudence.'

III. NON-JUDICIAL INTERCONNECTIONS: THE ROLE OF INTERNATIONAL HUMAN RIGHTS IN THE EXTERNAL AND INTERNAL POLICIES OF THE EU INSTITUTIONS

A. The European Union as a Party to International Human Rights Treaties

The most obvious interconnection between the EU and the rest of the world in the field of human rights is the fact that the EU has recently become involved in human rights standard-setting on the international scene. The EC had, in its final years, started to participate in the adoption of multilateral human rights treaties, and one may expect its successor to continue doing so when the occasion arises (apart from performing its Treaty duty to seek accession to the ECHR). Since the EC and the EU are unusual subjects of international law, their participation in multilateral human rights conventions requires those conventions to have a clause allowing for accession not only by States but also by 'regional integration organisations' (or similar expressions). The classical international human rights conventions do not have such clauses, but when new initiatives are taken, the EU is able to appear on the negotiation scene and try to insist on their inclusion. Thus, the EC helped to negotiate, and signed, the UN Convention on the Rights of Persons with Disabilities, which was adopted by the United Nations General Assembly on 13 December 2006. This Convention does indeed contain a 'regional integration organisations' clause. The competence of the EC to sign the Convention was based, by the Commission, on Articles 13 and 95 EC Treaty, thus connecting the Convention to both the anti-discrimination and internal market competences of the EC.[22] The EU has recently decided to ratify this Convention without waiting for most or all of its Member States to take that step.[23] Ratification not only entails the binding effect of this Convention for the EU institutions, and possibly its direct effect in the EU and national legal orders, but also the submission by the Union to the international monitoring mechanism set in place by the Convention.

The Disability Convention is hailed as the first human rights convention ever concluded by either the EU or the EC. But that qualification depends on how one defines a human rights convention—there is no authoritative definition of that term. On a broader view, one could say that the EC and EU had already signed and ratified some human rights treaties earlier on. One candidate for receiving this human rights label is the Aarhus Convention on Access to Information, Public

[22] Proposal for a Council Decision on the signing, on behalf of the European Community, of the United Nations Convention on the Rights of Persons with Disabilities and its Optional Protocol, COM(2007) 77 of 27 February 2007.

[23] Council of the European Union, Press release of the session of 26 November 2009. For a discussion of the role of the EC in the negotiation of the Convention and its possible impact on EU law after its ratification, see L Waddington, 'Breaking New Ground: The Implications of Ratification of the UN Convention on the Rights of Persons with Disabilities for the European Community' in OM Arnardottir and G Quinn (eds), *The UN Convention on the Rights of Persons with Disabilities—European and Scandinavian Perspectives* (Leiden, Brill, 2009) 111–40.

Participation in Decision-making and Access to Justice in Environmental Matters of 25 June 1998. It was declared open for signature (in Article 17)

> by regional economic integration organizations constituted by sovereign States members of the Economic Commission for Europe to which their member States have transferred competence over matters governed by this Convention…

which was a very cumbersome way of referring to the European Community! The EC duly signed and ratified the Aarhus Convention, and implemented it both for its own institutions (by means of Regulation 1376/2006[24]) and for its Member States by means of two Directives of 2003 dealing respectively with the first two elements mentioned in the title of the Convention, namely access to information and public participation.[25] On the other hand, the Commission's proposal for a Directive on access to justice in environmental matters (the 'third pillar' of the Aarhus Convention) has been blocked in the Council since 2003, probably because of the major impact it would have on national regimes of civil procedure.[26]

Further examples could be mentioned, such as the Council of Europe Convention on the Protection of Children against Sexual Exploitation and Sexual Abuse,[27] Article 45(1) of which specifies clearly that it is open for signature by the EC alongside its Member States. That reference should now be held to refer to the EU, following its succession to the EC. One may expect further examples in the future. This development is linked to the extension of the EU's internal competences way beyond economic life into human rights-sensitive policy areas. The existence and use of internal EU competences in fields such as non-discrimination, employment and social policy, immigration and asylum are likely to raise the question, sooner or later, whether the Union should adhere to existing human rights instruments related to those policy fields, or participate in new drafting initiatives. For example, both the United Nations and the Council of Europe have adopted conventions for the protection of the rights of migrant workers. Those conventions suffer from a lack of ratification by immigration countries.[28] One may wonder whether the EU, if it takes its commitment to guarantee the fundamental

[24] Regulation 1367/2006 of the European Parliament and of the Council of 6 September 2006 on the application of the provisions of the Aarhus Convention on Access to Information, Public Participation in Decision-making and Access to Justice in Environmental Matters to Community institutions and bodies, [2006] OJ L264/13.

[25] Directive 2003/4 of the European Parliament and of the Council of 28 January 2003 on public access to environmental information, [2003] OJ L41/26; Directive 2003/35 of the European Parliament and of the Council of 26 May 2003 providing for public participation in respect of the drawing up of certain plans and programmes relating to the environment, [2003] OJ L156/17.

[26] See, for general discussion, C Redgwell, 'Access to Environmental Justice' in F Francioni (ed), *Access to Justice as a Human Right* (Oxford, Oxford University Press, 2007) 153.

[27] Convention adopted in Lanzarote on 25 October 2007, CETS No 201.

[28] The International Convention on the Protection of the Rights of All Migrant Workers and Members of their Families, of 18 December 1990, has 42 Contracting Parties, among which there is not a single EU State. The European Convention on the Legal Status of Migrant Workers, adopted on 24 November 1977 (CETS No 93), has been ratified by only six EU Member States so far (France, Italy, The Netherlands, Portugal, Spain and Sweden) and Norway.

rights of all persons seriously, and in view of its growing body of migration law, should seek to become a party to one or both of those Conventions or, if this is practically difficult, require all its Member States to ratify them.

Anyway, it seems now clearly established that the Union possesses the necessary *competence* to conclude at least some types of human treaties. For a long time, this question was much disputed, particularly after the unfortunate *Opinion 2/94*, in which the Court of Justice denied the EC the competence to accede to the ECHR and stated that 'no Treaty provision confers on the Community institutions any general power to enact rules on human rights or to conclude international conventions in this field'.[29]

In fact, paragraph 27 of the *Opinion* merely denied that the Community had any *express* power to enact *general* rules on human rights. However, later practice by the Council denoted the view shared by all Member State governments that there was an *implied* competence to adopt general measures in the field of fundamental rights, based on Article 308 EC Treaty (the predecessor of the current Article 352 TFEU). One prominent example of an internal act based on Article 308 is the Council Regulation of 15 February 2007 establishing a European Union Agency for Fundamental Rights.[30] Externally, Article 308 served as a legal basis for the agreement subsequently concluded between the EC and the Council of Europe on cooperation between the Agency and the Council of Europe bodies.[31]

In addition, later decisions of the Court made clear that the EC did possess *specific* treaty-making powers in the field of human rights, especially the *ancillary* power to introduce human rights provisions or concerns into international agreements of the EC dealing with trade or development, or other policy matters falling squarely within the EC's powers. In *Portugal v Council*, the applicant government objected to the fact that the EC's Cooperation Agreement with India contained a provision in its Article 1(1) that respect for human rights and democratic principles was 'the basis for the cooperation between the contracting parties' and 'constitutes an essential element of the agreement'. This so-called 'essential elements clause', which the EC started to insert in most of its external agreements from the 1990s onwards, was considered acceptable by the ECJ from the competence perspective, due to its ancillary nature: it did not constitute a separate field of cooperation but rather a horizontal dimension to be taken into account in the application of the agreement.[32]

[29] *Opinion 2/9 (re Accession of the Community to the European Human Rights Convention)* [1996] ECR I-1759, para 27.

[30] [2007] OJ L53/1. Another internal EC act based on Art 308 EC is the Council Decision of 19 April 2007 establishing the action programme 'Fundamental rights and citizenship', [2007] OJ L110/33.

[31] [2008] OJ L186/6.

[32] Case C-268/94, *Portugal v Council* [1996] ECR I-6177. For a discussion of the case and the evolution of the competence debate, see P Eeckhout, *External Relations of the European Union—Legal and Constitutional Foundations* (Oxford, Oxford University Press, 2004) at 470–73; also E Cannizzaro, 'The scope of EU foreign power. Is the EC competent to conclude agreements with third states including human rights clauses?' in E Cannizzaro (ed), *The European Union as an Actor in International Relations* (The Hague, Kluwer Law International, 2002) 297.

Since then, the practice of the EU has moved on, towards the conclusion of fully-fledged human rights treaties. In the case of the UN Disability Convention, the competence of the EU was argued to be the wish to 'export' and further develop its own domestic policy, particularly its anti-discrimination policy. Although the Court of Justice has not yet had the opportunity to approve this competence argument, it seems to be soundly based. It is still somewhat uncertain whether, from an internal competence perspective, the EU could become a party to the European Social Charter—which, in human rights policy matters, would seem an obvious companion initiative to the projected accession to the ECHR.[33]

Lastly, the EU can contribute to the implementation of human rights conventions concluded by some or all of its Member States. One example is the Commission's communication, 'An EU strategy on the rights of child', in which the Commission proposes to mainstream children's rights in EU legislation, thereby helping the Member States in their implementation of the UN Convention on the Rights of the Child, to which the EU itself is not a party.[34]

B. Human Rights Policy in the Pre-accession Context

The politically most visible use, so far, of human rights in the Union's external policy occurred in the context of the preparation for accession of new Member States, where human rights became a central element of the elaborate political conditionality mechanism gradually set in place on the basis of the Copenhagen criteria adopted by the European Council in 1993. They continue to be a central element in relation to the current candidates for accession, in particular Turkey, as illustrated in the annual reports devoted to those countries' slow progress towards accession.

The Copenhagen European Council of June 1993 famously stated that

> membership requires that the candidate country must have achieved stability of institutions guaranteeing democracy, the rule of law, human rights and respect for and protection of minorities.[35]

Ever since, the EU institutions have applied a human rights standard to the candidate countries which has proved to be very broad, quite demanding but vaguely

[33] For a powerful argument (written in pre-Lisbon times) that the EU should accede to the European Social Charter, and has the legal competence to do so, see O De Schutter, 'Anchoring the European Union to the European Social Charter: The Case for Accession' in G de Búrca and B De Witte (eds), *Social Rights in Europe* (Oxford, Oxford University Press, 2005) 111.

[34] COM(2006) 367 of 4 July 2006. See O De Schutter, 'Fundamental Rights and the Transformation of Governance in the European Union' (2006–2007) 9 *Cambridge Yearbook of European Legal Studies* 133, at 163–67.

[35] On the overall evolution of political conditionality, beyond the specific case of human rights, see K Smith, 'The Evolution and Application of EU Membership Conditionality' in M Cremona (ed), *The Enlargement of the European Union* (Oxford, Hart Publishing, 2003) 105.

defined. At the time this human rights conditionality was adopted, the then ongoing process of ratification by central and eastern European countries of the ECHR was seen as an important ingredient of their approximation to the EU. Although the Copenhagen criteria refer to human rights in general terms and do not mention the European Convention with so many words, it could seem obvious that compliance with the ECHR would form the primary standard for assessment in the context of accession to the EU. It is, therefore, rather striking to see that the European Commission, in its Regular Reports on progress towards accession, did not use compliance with the ECHR as the primary indicator of the applicant States' human rights performance, and still does not do so with the current candidate countries. It rather refers to a variety of sources of human rights protection, including other Council of Europe conventions (such as the European Social Charter and the Framework Convention on National Minorities) and OSCE documents, while leaving open the relative importance it chooses to give to these various instruments in coming to its assessment. It does not clearly distinguish between those human rights instruments which the candidate country has ratified (and which, therefore, the EU would seem justified in using as a benchmark) and other human rights instruments which the country has—often deliberately—not ratified. This absence of a clear 'legal' criterion in deciding the pertinence of the various human rights instruments shows that the Commission conceives of its accession-reporting role in political rather than quasi-judicial terms.

There may be different reasons for the EU's reluctance to give pride of place to the ECHR in this particular context, but one important reason must be that the *substantive scope* of the European Convention is too narrow, so that it cannot provide a yardstick for judging whether a State offers sufficient protection to all important categories of human rights. The scope of the ECHR is too narrow for the purposes of pre-accession monitoring in two important respects: it includes only a few economic, social and cultural rights; and it does not include minority protection rights. Instead, the Commission's Regular Reports' sections on human rights were systematically subdivided in three parts: civil and political rights; economic, social and cultural rights; and minority rights. It was never specified whether one of these categories was more important than the others.

Minority protection rights are a particularly interesting category. Strictly speaking, if one takes the Copenhagen criteria literally, they are not an element of 'human rights' but form a separate political condition for membership. However, in the practice of the Commission's reports, they are usually cited in the same breath, and rightly so. Indeed, the existence of patterns of discrimination against the Kurdish population in Turkey, to cite one of the most constantly troubling cases, can be ranged under both headings of 'human rights' and 'minority protection'. On the other hand, minority rights are undoubtedly a special category in terms of the EU's internal constitutional law. Whereas respect for minority rights is required under the Copenhagen criteria, it was not (unlike the other political criteria) a formal condition of membership under Article 49 EU Treaty and was not included among the Union's founding values listed in Article 6(1) of the same Treaty. These two points have been modified by the Lisbon Treaty: the new accession clause (still numbered as Article 49 TEU) now refers to respect for the values listed in Article 2 TEU as a condition of membership, and those values—as was mentioned above—now include the rights of minorities.

In actual practice, the impact of the EU's insistence on respect for human rights and minority rights has been rather uneven. In some cases, one could observe specific changes in legislation and administrative practice as a result of the EU's pre-accession pressure.[36] Currently, the cases of Turkey and Croatia prove to be rather problematic. Turkey's minority protection performance, in particular, poses a conundrum. In its latest Progress Reports on that country, the European Commission comments favourably on recent legislative changes, but also expresses strong and detailed criticism about the way in which non-Muslim religions and their associations are treated in practice. While being cautious, the Commission is nonetheless critical of Turkey's performance as regards freedom of expression, linguistic and religious minority rights; and this critical attitude seems justified, for there are many signs that the 'implementation gap' between lofty constitutional proclamation and the situation on the ground is still wide in Turkey.[37]

The priorities imposed on Croatia under the current Accession Partnership include, among other actions in the human rights sphere, also to 'promote respect for and protection of minorities in accordance with international law and best practice in EU Member States'.[38] In its annual Progress Reports on Croatia, the European Commission is quite critical of some aspects of Croatia's performance in this regard,[39]

[36] For a number of different viewpoints on the question of the Union's impact on minority protection in the former candidate States, see the contributions of P Guglielmo, 'Human Rights in the Accession Process: Roma and Muslims in an Enlarging EU' in GN Toggenburg (ed), *Minority Protection and the Enlarged European Union: The Way Forward* (Budapest, Open Society Institute, 2004) 37; G Sasse, ' Minority Rights and EU Enlargement: Normative Overstretch or Effective Conditionality?', *ibid*, 59; and F Hoffmeister, 'Monitoring Minority Rights in the Enlarged European Union', *ibid*, 85.

[37] See the Commission's *Turkey 2008 Progress Report*, SEC (2008) 2699, 11–28, and its *Turkey 2009 Progress Report*, SEC (2009) 1334, 13–33. For a detailed account of the evolution of minority rights in Turkish law in connection with EU membership conditionality, see D Kurban, 'Confronting Equality: The Need for Constitutional Protection of National Minorities in Turkey's Path to the EU' (2003) 32 *Columbia Human Rights Law Review* 101. With reference to Turkey's compliance with the ECHR, see D Kurban, 'Protecting Marginalised Individuals and Minorities in the ECtHR: Litigation and Jurisprudence in Turkey' in D Anagnostou and E Psychogiopoulou (eds), *The European Court of Human Rights and the Rights of Marginalised Individuals and Minorities in National Context* (Budapest, Open Society Institute, 2010) 159.

[38] Council Decision of 12 February 2008, [2008] OJ L42/51, at 54.

[39] See, eg, the various conclusions drawn by the Commission in its *Croatia 2009 Progress Report*, SEC (2009) 1333 of 14 October 2009: 'Overall, with some specific exceptions, civil and political rights continue to be reasonably well respected in Croatia. However, shortcomings as regards impunity for war crimes, access to justice and freedom of expression require further attention' (at 12); 'Overall, legal protection for economic and social rights is partially guaranteed. Implementation of women's and children's rights and protection against all forms of discrimination needs to be further improved in practice' (at 14); 'Overall, the position of minorities in Croatia continues to improve. However, many problems remain for the Serb and Roma minorities. Some progress on outstanding refugee return issues was made but efforts to provide housing solutions and ensure sustainability of refugee return need to be accelerated' (at 16).

but, as in the case of earlier accession rounds, the human rights factor is unlikely to be decisive when the time comes to conclude the accession negotiations.

C. External Human Rights Policy more generally

The incorporation of human rights in the pre-accession context had been preceded by the formulation of a general policy of conditionality in the EC's external relations.[40] Such a general policy was solemnly affirmed in the conclusions of the Luxembourg European Council of June 1991[41] and gradually extended ever since. There are, however, some important legal differences between the recourse to human rights conditionality in external agreements concluded by the EU (and the EC, until December 2009) and in accession negotiations. First, whereas its use in external agreements is subject to the legal limits of EU competence (as discussed above), accession treaties are formally concluded by the Member States (not the EU), so that there are no competence limits to the use of human rights conditions in these negotiations—even though in reality EU institutions are actively participating in the negotiations and the pre-accession reporting *on behalf of* the Member States. Secondly, in the case of EU external agreements, the only sanction at the disposal of the EU is a suspension of the agreement, whereas in accession negotiations the Union can wave the much tastier carrot of membership of the Union. The reward offered by the EU for good behaviour has, arguably, proved to be rather effective in inducing changes in the laws and practices of some of the applicant States, whereas the effectiveness of its human rights policy in other contexts is much more doubtful and contested.

The standard human rights clause, which the Union has included in most of the broad international agreements concluded with third countries since the mid-1990s (but not in the agreements dealing with specific questions), states that respect for democratic principles and human rights, as laid down in the Universal Declaration of Human Rights, constitutes an 'essential element' of the agreement.[42] This is the basis for the EU's right unilaterally to suspend the operation of the agreement in

[40] There is an extremely rich literature on this subject. See, among others, the following book-length studies: F Hoffmeister, *Menschenrechts- und Demokratieklauseln in den vertraglichen Aussenbeziehungen der Europäischen Gemeinschaft* (Wien, Sptringer, 1998); M Bulterman, *Human Rights in the Treaty Relations of the European Community* (Antwerp, Intersentia, 2001); E Fierro Sedano, *The EU's Approach to Human Rights Conditionality in Practice* (Wien, Springer, 2003); L Bartels, *Human Rights Conditionality in the EU's International Agreements* (Oxford, Oxford University Press, 2005). For a synthetic presentation, see P Eeckhout, *External Relations of the European Union—Legal and Constitutional Foundations* (Oxford, Oxford University Press, 2004) 475–81.

[41] European Council, Luxembourg, 28–29 June 1991, Conclusions of the Presidency: '[R]espect, promotion and safeguard of human rights is an essential part of international relations and one of the cornerstones of European cooperation as well as of relations between the Community and its Member States and other countries.'

[42] Eg, Art 1(1) of the Agreement establishing an Association between the European Community and its Member States, of the one part, and the Republic of Chile, of the other part, [2002] OJ L352/3.

case of non-respect for human rights. The EU is careful not to impose extraneous human rights standards on the other countries: by referring to the Universal Declaration it selects a standard which it presumes to be reflecting customary international law, and therefore as binding on the other States irrespective of whether or not they have ratified the classical multilateral human rights conventions. Its treaty practice, accepted by the third countries parties to these agreements, accordingly contributes to the reaffirmation of the Universal Declaration as an expression of general international law.[43]

In practice, unilateral EU suspensions of treaties have occurred in relation to a number of ACP countries, including Zimbabwe, Liberia, Togo, Fiji, Guinea and Mauritania.[44] Occasionally, the EU has also decided trade sanctions for human rights violation without a 'human rights clause' providing for it, as in the case of Myanmar.[45] The compatibility of these unilateral measures with the EU's obligations towards Myanmar under the WTO Agreement has been discussed.[46] Although the WTO Agreement does not provide for a human rights exception, the GATT provides for exceptions that are 'necessary to protect public morals', which may be construed as including human rights-inspired trade sanctions.

More broadly, the EU has sought to advance the human rights agenda through 'positive' trade measures (ie by making extra trade benefits conditional on compliance with human rights standards) and through its Common Foreign and Security Policy (CFSP).[47] Regular human rights dialogues have been introduced in the EU's relations with some third countries, such as China, and the CFSP mechanism seek to promote a common standpoint of EU Member States in the United Nations human rights bodies.[48] The EU has taken a particularly active role in combating the death penalty world wide, on the basis of EU Guidelines on the Death Penalty adopted in 1998.[49]

The commitment of the EU to the promotion of the respect for human rights by means of its foreign policy is genuine and distinguishes its foreign policy from that of the traditional powers. Yet this self-proclaimed commitment also opens the door to criticism when the Union occasionally (and not so rarely)

[43] Rosas, above n 4, at 467.

[44] In the context of relations with ACP countries, suspensions of EU commitments are always partial and always temporary (but they can be continued or even strengthened upon their expiry). See, eg, in respect of Fiji, Council Decision 2007/641of 5 October 2007, [2007] OJ L260/15, as last amended by Council Decision 2010/208 of 29 March 2010, [2010] OJ L89/7.

[45] Council Common Position 2007/750 of 19 November 2007, [2007] OJ L308/1.

[46] See RJ Howse and JM Genser, 'Are EU Trade Sanctions on Burma Compatible with WTO Law?' (2007–8) *Michigan Journal of International Law* 165.

[47] See Rosas, above n 4, at 470–74.

[48] K Smith, 'Speaking with One Voice? European Union Coordination on Human Rights Issues at the United Nations' (2006) 44 *Journal of Common Market Studies* 113; K Smith, 'The European Union at the Human Rights Council: Speaking with One Voice but Having Little Influence' (2010) 17 *Journal of European Public Policy* 224.

[49] See F Hoffmeister, 'The Contribution of EU Practice to International Law' in M Cremona (ed), *Developments in EU External Relations Law* (Oxford, Oxford University Press, 2008) 115–16.

appears to act inconsistently,[50] by insisting on human rights standards in some circumstances, whilst giving priority to other foreign policy interests, such as economic benefits, conflict resolution[51] or international security,[52] in others.

D. The EU Charter as a Barrier to the Domestic Impact of International Human Rights Instruments?

Moving now from the domain of foreign policy to that of the EU's internal policies, we can observe that international human rights are much less prominently displayed here.

As long as fundamental rights had the status of unwritten general principles of Community law, they were prominent in the judicial discourse of the European Courts but remained relatively invisible in the law-making and executive activities of the EC and the EU. This has changed quite noticeably after the adoption of the EU Charter of Rights and Freedoms, and is likely to change even more now that the Charter has acquired binding force as primary EU law, after the entry into force of the Lisbon Treaty. By adopting the Charter in their solemn proclamation made in Nice in December 2000, the three institutions (Commission, Council and European Parliament) assumed the task of respecting and promoting the rights contained in the Charter. This was reflected in the frequent references, usually in the Preambles to EU legislative acts, to provisions of the Charter which those legislative acts were declared either to respect or to implement. Logically speaking, the Charter should exercise a much stronger influence on the content of the EU's legislation now that it has acquired full binding force.

It is true that the Charter, according to its Article 51(2), does not 'establish any new power or task for the Union, or modify powers and tasks as defined in the Treaties'. The intention of the drafters of the Charter was clearly to avoid that the mere enumeration of a fundamental right would create a competence for the European institutions to act for the protection of that right. The scope of the rights follows existing EU competences rather than the other way round. However, even though this intention is clear, the actual wording of the clause is misleading in its use of the word 'tasks'. Whereas it makes legal sense to affirm

[50] For an overall discussion of these issues, see U Khaliq, *Ethical Dimensions of the Foreign Policy of the European Union—A Legal Appraisal* (Cambridge, Cambridge University Press, 2008), and P Leino, 'The Journey Towards All that is Good and Beautiful: Human Rights and "Common Values" as Guiding Principles of EU Foreign Relations Law' in M Cremona and B De Witte (eds), *EU Foreign Relations Law—Constitutional Fundamentals* (Oxford, Oxford University Press, 2008) 259–89.

[51] There is both overlap and tension between human rights and conflict resolution as foreign policy goals of the EU; see discussion by N Tocci, 'Comparing the EU's Role in Neigbourhood Conflicts' in Cremona (ed), above n 49, at 216.

[52] On the role of the EU in the UN's anti-terrorism policy, and the questions of human rights protection arising in that context, see E Spaventa, 'Fundamental What? The Difficult Relationship between Foreign Policy and Fundamental Rights' in Cremona and De Witte (eds), above n 50, at 233.

that the Charter does not extend the powers of the EU, if one takes 'powers' as meaning 'legal competences', it does not make sense to state that the Charter will not extend the tasks of the EU. Indeed, the very purpose of adopting a Charter of Rights was to make it a task for the European institutions to apply the Charter rights in their various activities. So, whereas Article 51(2) can meaningfully be interpreted as a barrier to the extension of EU competences by the indirect means of promoting a Charter right, it cannot mean that the policies of the Union remain unaffected by the Charter. That would make a charade of the Charter. Moreover, the first paragraph of the same Article 51 of the Charter imposes an obligation on the Member States and the Union to 'promote the application' of the rights contained within it. Many Charter rights require positive action for 'the progressive achievement of their full realization' (to use the words of the UN Social Covenant), so that the right only becomes meaningful when seen in conjunction with the legislative and executive measures taken for its effective enjoyment.

Thus, the question is not so much whether the EU might gain *extra* legislative powers under the Charter for the promotion of human rights (it does not), but whether the *existing* legislative and other powers of the EU will be re-oriented and infused with a range of different values and policy considerations after the enactment of the Charter. Among the non-legislative activities that could be displayed by the EU institutions, one could mention the use of social rights as substantive indicators within the context of the open method of coordination (OMC) as used in social and educational policy. It has even been suggested recently that, beyond the incorporation of human rights concerns in existing OMC processes, one could also set up a separate open method of coordination wholly devoted to the progressive realisation of the Charter rights.[53]

For all those reasons, one can expect the Charter to occupy a central place in the legislative activity of the EU in the coming years, and this could perhaps be to the detriment of international human rights instruments. The text of the Charter is, of course, itself inspired by international human rights law. Whereas the influence of the ECHR was far stronger than the impact of the universal human rights treaties,[54] the European Social Charter has also been remarkably influential in the drafting of the Charter chapter on Solidarity which contains

[53] This idea is developed, among others, by O De Schutter, 'The Implementation of Fundamental Rights through the Open Method of Coordination' in O De Schutter and S Deakin (eds), *Social Rights and Market Forces: Is the Open Coordination of Employment and Social Policies the Future of Social Europe?* (Oxford, Hart Publishing, 2005) 279–343.

[54] For a survey of the content of the Charter from the perspective of the inclusion and exclusion of the international human rights 'acquis', see D McGoldrick, 'The Charter and United Nations Human Rights Treaties' in S Peers and A Ward (eds), *The European Union Charter of Fundamental Rights* (Oxford, Hart Publishing 2004) 83, at 109 ff; and S Parmar, 'International Human Rights and the EU Charter' (2001) 8 *Maastricht Journal of European and Comparative Law* 351.

a set of rights that is absent from the ECHR.[55] But now that the Charter has been enacted, its very existence could possibly act as a barrier against the future percolation of international human rights standards into EU law and policy.

On the other hand, the entry into force of the Charter as primary EU law could thus extend a phenomenon which we have seen at work in the last decade, especially but not only in the field of anti-discrimination law, namely that the EU is not only a 'taker' but also a 'giver': the Union may contribute, through its application of the Charter, to the progressive development of international human rights law, and provide, in turn, inspiration for the interpretation of international instruments by their respective judicial or monitoring bodies.

There is one particular area of human rights law, though, which is not covered by the Charter of Rights and in which international instruments could continue to play an inspirational role for the EU institutions, and that is the area of minority rights. The Lisbon Treaty introduced a prominent reference to the rights of minorities into the text of the Treaty on European Union. The text of Article 2 TEU, as amended by the Treaty of Lisbon, states that

> The Union is founded on the values of respect for human dignity, freedom, democracy, equality, the rule of law and respect for human rights, *including the rights of persons belonging to minorities.*

The words in italics had not been included in the Draft Constitutional Treaty of July 2003, which was the (remote) basis for the Lisbon Treaty. Despite repeated attempts and proposals by individual members of the Convention on the Future of Europe and by some non-governmental organisations, no reference to minority protection had been included in the text adopted by the Convention. However, a surprising development occurred during the Intergovernmental Conference that followed the Convention. The Hungarian Government strongly insisted on the inclusion of minority rights in the introductory articles of the Constitution, and despite the initial opposition of some delegations, an agreement emerged among the 25 governments to amend Article 2 of the draft Constitution (which listed the fundamental values of the Union), so as to add a reference to the rights of persons belonging to minorities. The text of Article 2 Constitutional Treaty was carried over, without any further changes, into the Lisbon Treaty, and has now become the new version of Article 2 TEU. The wording of this reference to minority rights is highly ambiguous: it could be read either as stating that the (general) human rights of members of minorities must be respected like those of everyone else, or as stating that minority members should be protected in special ways which reach

[55] For a 'nutshell' view of the major influence of the European Social Charter (and the lesser influence of other international human rights), see the official Explanations Relating to the Charter ([2007] OJ C303/17), which, though not offering a rigorous account of human rights cross-fertilisation, are nevertheless important due to the fact that the Charter itself, in its Art 52(7), states that the Explanations give guidance for its interpretation that 'shall be given due regard by the courts of the Union and of the Member States'.

beyond the generally applicable human rights. In view of the redundant nature of the former interpretation, the latter interpretation seems preferable. But then the question arises: which are those 'rights of persons belonging to minorities'? Unlike the other human rights that are spelled out elsewhere in primary law (namely in the Charter of Rights and, through the reference in Article 6, in the ECHR), minority rights are not listed anywhere else in the founding Treaties, neither are they included in the Charter of Rights (except to the extent that its Article 21, following the wording of Article 14 ECHR, prohibits discrimination on grounds of membership of a national minority). Once more, therefore, the Treaty text points to the existence of rights *outside* the EU legal order which are incorporated into the EU legal order, although only through their inclusion in the generic basic values clause of Article 2. One may wonder, though, whether the Court of Justice might be encouraged by this provision to insert minority protection rights into the general principles of Union law, finding inspiration, for example, in the Framework Convention on the Protection of National Minorities adopted within the Council of Europe. The Framework Convention has, so far, been ratified by most but not all EU Member States (France, Belgium and Greece have refused to do so) but, in the light of *Laval* and *Viking*, this might not be an obstacle to the Framework Convention's rights being transformed into general principles of EU law. Similarly, one might see international minority instruments being cited in Preambles to EU legislative acts. One recent example (still under the pre-Lisbon rules, though) is a reference to the UN Declaration on the Rights of Indigenous Peoples in the Preamble to the Regulation on the marketing of seal products.[56]

IV. CONCLUSION

On an overall view of the legal evolution in the last decade, it is clear that the EU has become more of an international human rights actor than it used to be. This is reflected in the evolution of the founding Treaties, and in particular in the incorporation of the EU's own Charter of Rights (which itself is heavily inspired by international human rights law) as binding primary EU law, as well as in the constitutional duty for the EU to seek accession to the ECHR. In day-to-day practice, one can observe the frequent, though irregular, use by the Court of Justice of the ECHR and the case law of the Strasbourg Court, combined with

[56] Regulation of the European Parliament and of the Council of 16 September 2009 on trade in seal products, [2009] OJ L286/36. This is an internal market measure 'harmonising the rules across the Community as regards commercial activities concerning seal products, and thereby prevent the disturbance of the internal market in the products concerned'. The main objective of this measure, though, is the protection of the welfare of animals in conjunction with the protection of cultural diversity: a general ban on the marketing of all products made from seals is accompanied by a derogation for products resulting from hunts traditionally conducted by Inuit and other indigenous communities, and in this connection the Preamble (in its recital 14) refers to the UN Declaration on the Rights of Indigenous Peoples.

occasional recourse to other international human rights instruments where the facts of the case call for it. It remains to be seen whether the upgrading of the Charter's legal status through the Treaty of Lisbon will reduce the Court's references to international human rights. In the activity of the political institutions of the EU, international human rights are, quite naturally, most visible in the field of external relations where the Union presents itself as an actor seeking to promote respect for human rights, although it is occasionally inconsistent in its action. It has now also become an active participant in the adoption of new international human rights standards. The main challenge, from a legal policy perspective, will be to link the EU's own human rights norms—which have now, with the Treaty of Lisbon, become much more central to the operation of the Union—with a continued attention to the development of international human rights norms outside the EU, and to the monitoring activities of international bodies. The EU should beware of moving to a splendid isolation in the human rights field; it should rather encourage and embrace the evolution of human rights at the broader regional and universal level.[57]

[57] This outward-looking human rights policy agenda is strongly advocated by I de Jesus Butler and O De Schutter, 'Binding the EU to International Human Rights Law' (2008) 27 *Yearbook of European Law* 277.

6

The European Union and the Rest of the World: Criminal Law and Policy Interconnections

VALSAMIS MITSILEGAS

I. INTRODUCTION

THE PAST TWO decades witnessed the emergence of the European Union (EU) as an active participant in international *fora* developing global multilateral standards in criminal matters. Attempts by the EU to influence the content of international law instruments in the field have evolved in parallel with constitutional and substantive law developments taking place within the Union. Taking these 'internal' developments into account, the aim of this chapter is to assess the role of the EU in the development of global multilateral criminal law standards and to examine the influence of these standards on internal Union law. In this context, the analysis will focus on the interconnections between the EU and the three international organisations/bodies which have been the primary contributors towards the globalisation of criminal law in recent years: the United Nations (the main organisation producing binding global criminal law standards in the form of treaties); the Council of Europe (another organisation active in the production of treaties in the field of criminal law, this time at the regional level); and the Financial Action Task Force (a prime example of 'soft' criminal law produced by an *ad hoc* body in the specific field of anti-money laundering law and policy). The chapter will aim to highlight the symbiotic relationship between the Union and these international *fora* as regards the globalisation of criminal law.

II. THE EUROPEAN UNION AND THE UNITED NATIONS

The EU has been an active participant in the negotiation of three major United Nations conventions in the field of criminal law: the 1988 Convention against drug trafficking; the 2000 Convention on transnational organised crime (also known as the 'Palermo Convention'); and the 2003 Convention against corruption.

These Conventions were negotiated and concluded in various stages of European integration, and in this light the institutional aspect of EU participation varies accordingly: the 1988 Convention was concluded in the pre-Maastricht era, in the days of the single Community pillar, whereas the Conventions on organised crime and corruption were concluded in the days of the three-pillar Union structure. The state of play of relevant internal Community/Union law at the time of their adoption also varies: while the 1988 Convention was concluded at a time when no relevant legislation in the field of money laundering was in place at Community level, the other two Conventions post-dated the adoption of internal Community/Union law in the respective fields. These differences are significant for the position of the EC/EU in the negotiation of the UN Conventions, but also in order to assess the subsequent impact of the UN standards on the Community/Union legal order.[1]

A. Interconnections in the Field of Money Laundering Law—the 1988 Vienna Convention and Community Law

A major step towards the globalisation of criminal law was undertaken by the United Nations in the 1980s in the form of the conclusion of the 1988 Vienna Convention against Illicit Trafficking in Narcotic Drugs and Psychotropic Substances. To a great extent prompted by the so-called US 'war on drugs', the Convention introduced a number of detailed provisions on drug trafficking, as well as—for the first time—the criminalisation of money laundering at the global level.[2] Negotiations on the Convention coincided with a growing interest by Community institutions to fight drug abuse and trafficking.[3] Although no express Community competence in criminal matters existed under the Treaties at the time, the Community did conclude the Vienna Convention on the basis of its common commercial policy competence.[4] According to the Declaration of Competence annexed to the above Decision (which was adopted under Article 113 of the EEC Treaty), the European Economic Community was at the time competent for questions of commercial policy relating to the substances frequently used in the illicit

[1] In examining the latter, account should be taken on the impact on EC/EU law of UN Conventions in the negotiation of which the Union was not as active, such as the 1999 Convention for the suppression of the financing of terrorism.

[2] For an analysis of the Vienna Convention, see WC Gilmore, *Dirty Money. The Evolution of International Measures to Counter Money Laundering and the Financing of Terrorism*, 3rd edn (Strasbourg, Council of Europe Press, 2004) ch 3; see also DP Stewart, 'Internationalizing the War on Drugs: the UN Convention Against Illicit Traffic in Narcotic Drugs and Psychotropic Substances' (1990) 18 *Denver Journal of International Law and Policy* 387.

[3] See in this context V Mitsilegas, *Money Laundering Counter-Measures in the European Union: A New Paradigm of Security Governance versus Fundamental Legal Principles* (The Hague, Kluwer Law International, 2003) 52–54.

[4] Council Decision of 22 October 1990 concerning the conclusion, on behalf of the European Economic Community, of the UN Convention against Illicit Trafficking in Narcotic Drugs and Psychotropic Substances, [1990] OJ L326/56.

manufacture of narcotic drugs and psychotropic substances, questions which are dealt with in Article 12 of the Convention.

Leaving aside the question of its conclusion by the Community, the impact of the substantive standards of the Vienna Convention for the development of internal Community law has been significant. Evading questions of Community competence in criminal matters (still in the pre-Maastricht era), the Council adopted in 1991 the first Money Laundering Directive.[5] The Directive was adopted on a dual internal market/free movement legal basis,[6] and was justified *inter alia* on the grounds of protecting the stability of financial institutions and confidence in the financial system as a whole.[7] It introduced a number of provisions addressing the preventive aspect of money laundering counter-measures.[8] It also introduced a definition of money laundering, and obliged Member States to 'prohibit' conduct defined as such.[9] The definition of money laundering (a concept for the first time introduced in the Community legal order) was copied almost *verbatim* from the Vienna Convention.[10] A similar choice was made as regards the definition of property constituting proceeds of crime and as regards the *mens rea* requirement for money laundering.[11] These definitions, which are considerably broad and have raised concerns with regard to over-criminalisation in the field,[12] have remained virtually unchanged in the subsequent revisions of the 1991 Directive, all the way to the adoption of the third Money Laundering Directive in 2005.[13]

The main area where Community law diverged from the Vienna Convention as regards the criminalisation of money laundering involves the criminal offences considered predicate money laundering offences. While predicate money laundering offences in the Vienna Convention were limited (perhaps unsurprisingly, given the focus of that Convention) to drug trafficking, by 1991 the Community legislator had adopted a more expansive approach, allowing Member States to

[5] Council Directive 91/308/EEC of 10 June 1991 on prevention of the use of the financial system for the purpose of money laundering, [1991] OJ L166/77.

[6] Arts 57(2), first and third sentences, and 100a of the EEC Treaty.

[7] For a discussion, see Mitsilegas, above n 3, ch 3.

[8] See section IV. below.

[9] The reference to 'prohibition' was introduced in order to circumvent the questionable Community competence to define criminal offences and impose criminal sanctions. However, Member States annexed to the text of the Directive a statement undertaking *de facto* to criminalise money laundering by the end of 1992.

[10] Art 1 of the Directive. See also Preamble, recital 9.

[11] Art 1 of the Directive.

[12] For an analysis, see Mitsilegas, above n 3, chs 3 and 4.

[13] Directive 2005/60/EC of the European Parliament and of the Council on the prevention of the use of the financial system for the purpose of money laundering and terrorist financing, [2005] OJ L309/15. The third Money Laundering Directive calls on Member States also to prohibit terrorist financing. The definition of the latter largely follows the wording of the 1999 UN Convention on the Suppression of the Financing of Terrorism (Art 1(4) of the 2005 Directive). See V Mitsilegas and B Gilmore, 'The EU legislative framework against money laundering and terrorist finance: A critical analysis in the light of evolving global standards' (2007) 56 *International and Comparative Law Quarterly* 119.

include in the list 'any other criminal activity'.[14] The list of predicate offences was subsequently extended—partly via references to another international law instrument, the 1990 Council of Europe Convention on money laundering—in money laundering directives.[15] Indicative of the synergy present in the development of Community and international instruments in the field, and reflecting a move from focusing on the proceeds of drug trafficking to targeting the proceeds of organised and serious crime more generally, the list of predicate offences (which was also mandated by the Financial Action Task Force on money laundering in the 1990s) was also extended at UN level in the criminalisation of money laundering by the 2000 Convention on Transnational Organised Crime.[16]

B. Interconnections in the Field of the Law on Transnational Organised Crime—the 2000 Palermo Convention and Community/Union Law

Perhaps the most impressive contribution of a United Nations multilateral treaty towards the globalisation of criminal law has been that of the Convention on Transnational Organised Crime and its Protocols, symbolically signed in Palermo in 2000. Negotiated throughout the 1990s, and reflecting the growing securitisation of organised crime at the time, the Convention is an ambitious and comprehensive multilateral instrument aiming at combating and preventing organised crime. It contains provisions ranging from the criminalisation of participation in an organised crime group, money laundering and corruption, to provisions on judicial cooperation with regard to organised crime, police cooperation and the law of criminal procedure. The Convention is complemented by three Protocols, on human trafficking, human smuggling, and the illicit manufacturing of and trafficking in firearms.[17]

[14] Art 1, indent 5 of the 1991 Directive. See also Preamble, recital 5, stating that 'Whereas for the purposes of this Directive the definition of money laundering is taken from that adopted in the Vienna Convention; whereas, however, since money laundering occurs not only in relation to the proceeds of drug-related offences but also in relation to the proceeds of other criminal activities (such as organised crime and terrorism), the Member States should, within the meaning of their legislation, extend the effects of the Directive to include the proceeds of such activities, to the extent that they are likely to result in laundering operations justifying sanctions on that basis'.

[15] The second Money Laundering Directive called upon Member States to bring the definition of 'serious crime' in line with the definition in the then Joint Action on Confiscation ([1998] OJ L333/1). Art 1 of the Joint Action (which was formally repealed by but in substance largely retained in the 2001 Framework Decision on confiscation ([2001] OJ L182/1) in turn called upon Member States not to make or uphold reservations with regard to Arts 2 and 6 of the 1990 Council of Europe Money Laundering Convention, as regards offences punishable under certain thresholds. The third Money Laundering Directive consolidated the position by including under 'serious crimes' all offences punishable by a minimum custodial sentence of one year or, as regards Member States which have a minimum threshold for offences in their legal system, all offences punishable by a minimum custodial sentence of at least six months (Art 3(5)(f)).

[16] See Art 6(2) of the Convention. Art 6(2)(a) calls upon State Parties to apply the criminalisation of money laundering 'to the widest range of predicate offences'.

[17] See D McClean, *Transnational Organized Crime. A Commentary on the UN Convention and its Protocols* (Oxford, Oxford University Press, 2007). For an overview of the background to and

Participation of the EU in the negotiations to the Convention was marked by legal complexity. The Convention was negotiated post-Maastricht (with negotiations continuing and the final conclusion taking place after the entry into force of the Amsterdam Treaty), at a time where the Union was granted competence in criminal matters under the third pillar. However, the wide range of provisions included in the Convention and its Protocols meant that there were also matters deemed to fall within Community competence. The result was that the those parts of the Convention where Community competence could be established were negotiated by the Commission, whereas matters falling under the third pillar were negotiated primarily by the Member States. It has been pointed out that the European Commission had joined the negotiations with observer status but during the negotiation process requested the Council to adopt recommendations allowing it to negotiate on behalf of the Community.[18] Ironically, transparency in terms of the negotiating mandate was greater in terms of the 'third pillar' aspects of the Convention as compared with those aspects related to Community law. Whereas a Joint Position (adopted before the entry into force of the Amsterdam Treaty) outlined the EU negotiating position,[19] subsequent negotiating mandates to the Commission can be found in an *ad hoc* manner in various Council Conclusions.[20] An exception to this trend has been the publication of a Common Position on the negotiation of the firearms Protocol; however, this Common Position was adopted on a third pillar legal basis,[21] with the Commission participating in negotiations (on the basis of Community competence) only subsequently.[22] Greater transparency at third pillar level may be explained by the

negotiating history of the Convention, see also D Vlassis, 'Drafting the United Nations Convention against Transnational Organized Crime', in P Williams and D Vlassis (eds), *Combating Transnational Crime. Concepts, Activities and Responses* (London and Portland, Oregon, Frank Cass, 2001) 356.

[18] C Rijken and V Kronenberger, 'The United Nations Convention against Transnational Organised Crime and the European Union' in V Kronenberger (ed), *The European Union and the International Legal Order: Discord or Harmony?* (The Hague, TMC Asser Press, 2001) 481, at 493–94. The authors argue that on the other hand, during the negotiation process, the Member States never gave full competence to the Presidency to negotiate the UN Convention on their behalf (at 493).

[19] Joint Position of 29 March 1999 defined by the Council on the basis of Article K.3 of the Treaty on European Union, on the proposed United Nations convention against organised crime, [1999] OJ L87/1.

[20] See, eg, the conclusions of the Telecommunications Council of 2 May 2000 (Council Doc 8058/00, Presse 127-G), according to which 'the Council authorised the Commission to negotiate on behalf of the Community the draft UNTOC with regard to measures against money laundering, one of the main strands of the Convention, which fall within the scope of the Community's powers, taking the provisions of the 1991 money laundering Directive as a basis.'

[21] Council Common Position of 31 January 2000 on the proposed protocol against the illicit manufacturing of and trafficking in firearms, their parts and components and ammunition, [2000] OJ L37/1, adopted on the basis of the TEU, and in particular Art 34(2)(a).

[22] See the conclusions of the ECOFIN Council of 31 January 2000 (Council Doc 5565/00, Presse 19-G), according to which 'the Council adopted a decision authorising the Commission to participate, on behalf of the European Union—in the negotiation of the draft protocol to the UNTOC to combat the illegal trafficking in and the manufacture of firearms, their parts, components and ammunition'. The reference to the Commission negotiating on behalf of the *European Union*—rather than the European Community—is noteworthy in this context.

combination of the relative lack of experience in international negotiations in the field, but also by the ambition to establish visible precedents confirming the emergence of the Union as a global actor in the field of criminal law.

The 1999 Joint Position provides important insights into both the constitutional aspects of negotiating international agreements with content related to the third pillar, and the content of the EU goals in these negotiations. Adopted under a combination of Maastricht third pillar legal bases (Articles K.3(2) and K.5 TEU), the Joint Position was justified as necessary in order to

> contribute as fully as possible to the negotiation of the proposed convention and to avoid incompatibility between the proposed convention and instruments drawn up in the Union.[23]

In this light, the Joint Position called for account to be taken of measures already adopted, or in the course of preparation or adoption in accordance with the 1997 EU Action Plan on Organised Crime.[24] Particular emphasis in this context was placed on the need for Member States to ensure consistency between the UN Convention and the 1998 EU Joint Action on the criminalisation of participation in a criminal organisation[25] as regards the definition of such participation and its criminalisation.[26] The Joint Position then went on to provide detailed guidelines on the negotiating position with regard to the scope of the Convention and the definition of organised crime, which mirrors the definition adopted at EU level.[27] Calls for consistency (and coordination) were primarily addressed to Member States (leaving a limited role for the Presidency).[28] The wording of the Joint Position has led commentators to argue that the Presidency was in fact not

[23] Joint Position, above n 19, Preamble, recital 8.

[24] *Ibid*, Preamble, recital 5. For an overview of the Action Plan, see WC Gilmore, 'The EU Action Plan to Combat Organised Crime: The Scope and Implementation of Legal Instruments' in *The Boundaries of Understanding. Essays in Honour of Malcolm Anderson* (Edinburgh, University of Edinburgh International Social Sciences Institute, 1999) 97–106.

[25] [1998] OJ L351/1. For an analysis, see V Mitsilegas, 'Defining Organised Crime in the European Union: The Limits of European Criminal Law in an Area of Freedom, Security and Justice' (2001) 26 *European Law Review* 565.

[26] Joint Position, above n 19, Art 1(2). The Joint Position also called for consistency between the Convention and the 1998 EU Joint Action on confiscation—see Art 1(6).

[27] Art 1(3) of the Joint Position (above n 19) states that 'insofar as the other provisions of the draft convention are concerned, it should apply as broadly as possible to the activities of criminal organisations and to international cooperation for combating such organisations. In principle, the relevant provisions of the draft convention should encompass the activities of persons, acting in concert with a view to committing serious crime, involved in any criminal organisation which has a structure and is, or has been, established for a certain period of time. They should not be limited to groups with a highly developed structure or enduring nature, such as mafia type organisations; and the organisations need not necessarily have formally defined roles for their participants or continuity of membership.'

[28] See *ibid*, Art 2, according to which 'in the negotiations on the proposed United Nations convention and any possible protocols, Member States shall, as far as is practicable, coordinate their positions, at the Presidency's initiative, and seek to arrive at common standpoints on all issues which have significant implications for the interests of the Union'. See also Art 3, calling upon Member States to ensure that the provisions of the proposed United Nations convention and any possible protocols are not inconsistent with instruments drawn up between them.

authorised by the Member States to negotiate on their behalf, and therefore that the UN Convention and its Protocols could not be considered as agreements in the sense of Articles 24 and 38 TEU.[29]

Instruments of signature and conclusion of the Palermo Convention and its Protocols were adopted only at Community level. As regards signature by the Community, two Decisions were adopted: one concerning the Convention itself and the Smuggling and Trafficking Protocols[30]; and another concerning the Firearms Protocol.[31] A clearer insight into the extent of Community competence is provided by the subsequent instruments on the conclusion of the Palermo Convention and its Protocols by the Community. Separate Decisions with regard to the Convention itself and the two Protocols on trafficking and smuggling have been adopted in this context. The Decision on the conclusion of the Convention[32] was adopted under Articles 47 (free movement/right of establishment), 55 (free movement of services), 95 (internal market) and 179 (development cooperation) TEC. It is worth quoting at length here the Declaration of Community Competence annexed thereto[33]:

> The Community points out that it has competence with regard to progressively establishing the internal market, comprising an area without internal frontiers in which the free movement of goods and services is ensured in accordance with the provisions of the Treaty establishing the European Community. For this purpose, the Community has adopted measures to combat money laundering. They do, however, at present not include measures concerning cooperation between Financial Intelligence Units, detection and monitoring the movement of cash across the borders between the Member States or cooperation among judicial and law enforcement authorities. The Community also has adopted measures to ensure transparency and the equal access of all candidates for the public contracts and services markets which contributes to preventing corruption. Where the Community has adopted measures, it is for the Community alone to enter into external undertakings with third States or competent international organisations which affect those measures or alter their scope. This competence relates to

[29] Rijken and Kronenberger, above n 18, at 494.

[30] Council Decision of 8 December 2000 on the signing, on behalf of the European Community, of the United Nations Convention against transnational organised crime and its Protocols, [2001] OJ L30/44. The legal bases for the Decision were Arts 47 (free movement /right of establishment), 62(2)(a) (border controls), 63(3)(b) (illegal immigration and illegal residence), and 95 (internal market) TEC (in conjunction with Art 300(2)). The Decision confirms that 'the elements of the Convention and the two Protocols thereto which are subject to Community competence were negotiated by the Commission, with the approval of the Council, on behalf of the Community' (Preamble, recital 1).

[31] Council Decision of 16 October 2001 on the signing, on behalf of the European Community, of the United Nations Protocol on the illicit manufacturing of and trafficking in firearms, [2001] OJ L280/5. The legal bases for the Decision were Arts 95 (internal market) and 133 (common commercial policy) TEC (in conjunction with Art 300(2)). As with the Decision on the signature of the Convention (above n 30), this Decision confirms the negotiation by the Commission of matters of the Protocol falling within Community competence (Preamble, recital 1).

[32] Council Decision of 29 April 2004 on the conclusion, on behalf of the European Community, of the United Nations Convention Against Transnational Organised Crime, [2004] OJ L261/69.

[33] *Ibid*, Annex II—Declaration of competence in accordance to Art 36(3) of the Convention.

> Articles 7,[34] 9[35]and 31(2)(c)[36] of the Convention. Moreover, Community policy in the sphere of development cooperation complements policies pursued by Member States and includes provisions to combat corruption. This competency relates to Article 30[37] of the Convention. Moreover, the Community considers itself bound by other provisions of the Convention to the extent that they are related to the application of Articles 7, 9, 30 and 31(2)(c), in particular the articles concerning its purpose and definitions and its final provisions.

Three points are noteworthy in the Decision and the Declaration of Competence. The first is that legal bases used to adopt the Decision concluding the Palermo Convention have been extended in relation to the signature Decision to include Articles 55 (free movement of services) and 179 (development cooperation) TEC. This 'extension' of competence is also reflected in the Declaration of Competence. The second point is that, contrary to the wording of the Declaration, there was now Community law on matters such as cooperation between Financial Intelligence Units and detection and monitoring the movement of cash across the borders between the Member States. While the Declaration recognises the potential development of Community law in this context,[38] it had not been amended at the time of writing to reflect these developments. The third point involves the scope of some of the provisions of the Palermo Convention included in the Declaration of Competence. According to the latter, Community competence relates to Articles 7 and 9 of the Convention (on money laundering and corruption respectively). While these provisions refer mostly to the preventive and not the criminal law aspects of money laundering and corruption law (these are dealt with in Articles 6 and 8 of the Convention respectively), they can still be seen as containing certain criminal law elements (not falling expressly within Community competence at the time).[39]

A two-pronged strategy was followed with regard to the conclusion of the Smuggling and Trafficking Protocols.[40] Two Decisions were adopted for the

[34] Money laundering.

[35] Corruption.

[36] Prevention of the misuse by organised criminal groups of tender procedures conducted by public authorities and of subsidies and licences granted by public authorities for commercial activity.

[37] Implementation of the Convention through Economic Development and Technical Assistance.

[38] 'The scope and the exercise of Community competence are, by their nature, subject to continuous development and the Community will complete or amend this declaration, if necessary, in accordance with Article 36(3) of the Convention.' (Declaration, above n 33, Annex II).

[39] Art 9(1) of the Palermo Convention calls upon State Parties to 'adopt legislative, administrative or other effective measures to promote integrity and to prevent, detect and punish the corruption of public officials'. Art 7(4) of the Convention calls for 'global, regional, subregional and bilateral cooperation among judicial, law enforcement and financial regulatory authorities in order to combat money laundering'. To the extent that this provision refers to Financial Intelligence Units, it must be noted that relevant provisions have since appeared in the (first pillar) 2005 third Money Laundering Directive (for an analysis of the constitutional implications of this inclusion, see Mitsilegas and Gilmore, above n 15).

[40] The EU had not yet concluded the Firearms Protocol at the time of writing (above n 31). This is due to the need to wait for the implementation of relevant Unionlegislation by Member States, see

conclusion of each of the Protocols, reflecting the wide range of fields in which Community competence did arise: one set of Decisions was adopted on legal bases related to development cooperation and economic, financial and technical cooperation with third countries[41]; and another set of Decisions was adopted on a Title IV legal basis (related to Community immigration and borders law).[42] The Declaration of Community Competence (found in Annex II and similar to all Decisions, with differences in terminology mainly as regards the titles of the respective Protocols, ie trafficking/smuggling) aimed at translating the *à la carte* participation of Denmark, Ireland and the United Kingdom in Title IV measures, and refers to exclusive Community competence with regard to border controls and visas, immigration policy regarding conditions of entry and residence and measures to counter illegal immigration and illegal residence, including repatriation of illegal residents and cooperation between the relevant departments of the administrations of the Member States, as well as between those departments and the Commission, in the aforementioned areas.[43] It was added that Community policy in the sphere of development cooperation complemented policies pursued by Member States and includes provisions to prevent and combat trafficking in persons. It is noteworthy that, unlike the Decision concluding the Palermo Convention, this was a rather general Declaration of Competence in that there was no reference to specific provisions of the Protocols with regard to Community competence.[44] This is notwithstanding the fact that a number of provisions in both Protocols relate to the adoption of criminal law, an area where the powers of the Community to legislate were contested at the time.[45]

the Commission's *Report on Implementation of the Hague Programme for 2007*, COM(2008) 373 final, Brussels, 2 July 2008.

[41] Arts 179 and 181a TEC respectively. See Council Decision of 24 July 2006 on the conclusion, on behalf of the European Community, of the Protocol to prevent, Suppress and Punish Trafficking in Persons ... in so far as the provisions of this Protocol fall within the scope of Articles 179 and 181a of the EC Treaty, [2006] OJ L262/44; and Council Decision of 24 July 2006 on the conclusion, on behalf of the European Community, of the Protocol Against the Smuggling of Migrants ... in so far as the provisions of this Protocol fall within the scope of Articles 179 and 181a of the EC Treaty, [2006] OJ L262/24.

[42] Council Decision of 24 July 2006 on the conclusion, on behalf of the European Community, of the Protocol to prevent, Suppress and Punish Trafficking in Persons ... in so far as the provisions of this Protocol fall within the scope of Part III, Title IV of the EC Treaty, [2006] OJ L262/51; and Council Decision of 24 July 2006 on the conclusion, on behalf of the European Community, of the Protocol Against the Smuggling of Migrants ... in so far as the provisions of this Protocol fall within the scope of Part III, Title IV of the EC Treaty, [2006] OJ L262/34.

[43] According to the Declaration, in these fields the Community has adopted rules and regulations and, where it has done so, it is hence solely for the Community to enter into external undertakings with third States or competent international organisations.

[44] A general clause common to all four Decisions states that they will apply in so far as the provisions of the Protocols fall within the scope of their respective legal bases (see, eg, Art 2 of the Decision on the conclusion of the trafficking Protocol on a Title IV legal basis, above n 42).

[45] The Community later adopted (still in the pre-Lisbon era), a first pillar Directive including criminal law provisions in the field of Title IV (on illegal work), [2009] OJ L168/24. Union competence to adopt criminal offences and sanctions is established in Art 83(1) and (2) TFEU post-Lisbon.

The substantive provisions of the Palermo Convention as regards the criminalisation of organised crime demonstrate that the 'consistency' objective outlined in the 1999 EU Joint Position has been largely achieved. The definition of an organised crime group and the criminalisation of participation in a criminal organisation in the Convention[46] largely mirror the provisions of the EU 1998 Joint Action making it a criminal offence to participate in a criminal organisation in a Member State of the EU.[47] The Joint Action, which constituted the first major attempt at international level to provide for harmonisation of the criminal law on organised crime, contained a broad definition of an organised crime group and a 'dual' model of criminalisation, with Member States given the choice to criminalise either participation in a criminal organisation as defined in the Joint Action, or conspiracy.[48] The Convention's criminalisation of participation in a criminal organisation largely follows this approach,[49] with the Convention text adding the criminalisation of 'organising, directing, aiding, abetting, facilitating or counselling the commission of serious crime involving an organised crime group'.[50]

The Palermo Convention was in turn a benchmark for the development of subsequent EU law on organised crime. In 2005, the Commission tabled a proposal for a Framework Decision 'on the fight against organised crime', aimed at replacing the 1998 Joint Action.[51] According to the Commission, the new proposal took into account developments since 1998, including the introduction of Framework Decisions as a form of third pillar law in Amsterdam and the need to take into account of subsequent legislative developments, such as the Palermo Convention and the EU Framework Decision on terrorism.[52] Negotiations have resulted in the recent adoption of a third pillar Framework Decision 'on the fight against organised crime'.[53] The Framework Decision claims to build upon the Palermo Convention[54] and repeals the 1998 Joint Action. The wording of the provisions on the definition of criminal organisation and the criminalisation of offences relating to participation therein are broadly similar to the provisions of the Palermo Convention. This is in particular the case as regards the definition of an organised crime group and the maintenance of the option for Member States to criminalise either participation in a criminal organisation or conspiracy. Unlike the Palermo

[46] Arts 2 and 5 respectively.

[47] Above n 25.

[48] For a discussion, see Mitsilegas, above n 25, 571–72.

[49] See McClean, above n 17, 67. Commenting on the implementation of Art 5, he notes that 'the statute books of the common law countries which have ratified the Convention will be searched in vain for crimes defined as set out in this Article. As has been clear from the beginning, the offences of conspiracy, soliciting, and other forms of participation in criminal conduct more than adequately cover the field described in the text of the Article'.

[50] Art 5(1)(b).

[51] COM(2005) 6, *Proposal for a Framework Decision on the fight against organised crime.*

[52] See V Mitsilegas, 'The Third Wave of Third Pillar Law: Which Direction for EU Criminal Justice?' (2009) 34 *European Law Review* 523.

[53] Framework Decision 2008/841/JHA on the fight against organised crime, [2008] OJ L300/42.

[54] *Ibid*, Preamble, recital 6.

Convention, however, the Framework Decision refrained from criminalising the *direction* of an organised criminal group. On the other hand, the EU instrument goes further than the Convention by including provisions of greater detail than the latter which are common to EU third pillar law, in particular detailed provisions on penalties. In this case, the Union legislator has used international law to update the internal *acquis*, while at the same time adding Union-specific elements in the internal instrument. Here, taking into account international standards was also used to enhance the effectiveness of Union law in the field of organised crime, by justifying the transition from a Union instrument of uncertain legal force (a Joint Action) to a clearly legally-binding Framework Decision.[55]

As regards the criminalisation of human trafficking and human smuggling, the Palermo Convention came at a time when no detailed EU legislation existed in the field.[56] A number of EU measures followed the adoption of the Convention. The Council adopted in 2002 a third pillar Framework Decision defining and criminalising trafficking in human beings.[57] It was designed not to implement, but rather to complement the work of the UN in the field.[58] Having said that, the definition—and criminalisation—of human trafficking in the Framework Decision follows very closely the definition adopted in the Palermo Protocol.[59] Unlike the Protocol, the Framework Decision introduces penalty levels (including a minimum custodial sentence of eight years) when a series of aggravating circumstances applies. The year 2002 also saw the adoption of EU measures on human smuggling (or, according to EU terminology, the facilitation of unauthorised entry, transit and residence): a first pillar Directive

[55] See V Mitsilegas, 'The EU and the Implementation of International Norms in Criminal Matters' in M Cremona, J Monar and S Poli (eds), *The External Dimension of the Area of Freedom, Security and Justice* (Bern, Peter Lang, forthcoming).

[56] Note in this context the Maastricht Joint Action 97/154/JHA concerning action to combat trafficking in human beings and sexual exploitation of children, [1997] OJ L63/2. However, the scope of the Joint Action was rather limited, with the focus being largely on trafficking for the purposes of sexual exploitation.

[57] Council Framework Decision of 19 July 2002 on combating trafficking in human beings, [2002] OJ L203/1.

[58] See Preamble, recitals 4 (referring to the Palermo Protocol as 'a decisive step towards international cooperation in the field) and 6 (referring to the need for the EU to complement work done in international *fora*, in particular the UN). A similar reference, indicating awareness of, but not overt deference to, the relevant UN standards can be found in the Preamble of a 2004 first pillar Directive on residence permits for victims of trafficking who cooperate with essentially law enforcement authorities ([2004] OJ L261/19, recital 3). The Directive (adopted on a Title IV legal basis) is largely drafted from the perspective of the efficiency of State action against traffickers, with the protective spirit permeating the Palermo Trafficking Protocol (in particular Art 6 thereof) as regards victims being scarcely discernible in the EU instrument.

[59] The offence includes trafficking for the purpose of labour exploitation. A notable omission from the EU text is trafficking for the purpose of removal of organs. A proposal tabled in 2003 by the then Greek EU Presidency to criminalise the trade in human organs has been blocked in the Council. See V Mitsilegas, *The Coherence of the Adopted Measures During the Last Years by the EU with Regard to Organised Crime and the UN Convention on Organised Crime*, Briefing Paper for the European Parliament LIBE Committee, 2006. Reproduced in A Baldaccini *et al*, *Controlling Security* (Paris, L'Harmattan, 2008) 65.

defining 'facilitation', accompanied by a third pillar Framework Decision criminalising it.[60] Neither of these instruments contains references to the Palermo Convention. The Directive defines 'facilitation' as assisting intentionally a third country national to enter or transit an EU Member State in breach of its aliens' laws, and assisting intentionally 'for financial gain' a third country national to reside in an EU Member State irregularly. The definition goes beyond the UN Smuggling Protocol, which requires 'a financial or other material benefit' as a condition for the criminalisation of procuring of illegal entry.[61] The Framework Decision introduces a series of criminal sanctions, including heavier penalties if the offences are committed for financial gain, or if they are committed within the framework of an organised crime group or they endanger the lives of the smuggled persons. The last two elements are also mentioned in the UN Smuggling Protocol, but the Protocol includes a further aggravating circumstance when smuggling entails inhuman or degrading treatment, including exploitation.[62]

C. Interconnections in the Field of the Law of Corruption: the 2003 Convention on Corruption and the EC/EU

The most recent major UN multilateral treaty in criminal matters is the 2003 UN Convention against corruption. It aims to establish a comprehensive anti-corruption framework, by focusing on both prevention and control.[63] The breadth of the Convention's scope meant that some areas covered were deemed to be related to Community competence, whereas other areas were deemed to be related to Union, third pillar powers. The approach taken with regard to the negotiations was thus broadly similar to the approach followed in the negotiations

[60] Council Directive 2002/90/EC of 8 November 2002 defining the facilitation of unauthorised entry, transit and residence, OJ L328, 5 December 2002, p4, and corresponding Framework Decision, same OJ, p1. This 'dual' approach was adopted in order to address Member States' concerns with regard to the extent of Community competence to adopt criminal law in the field; for an overview of the constitutional debate in this context, see V Mitsilegas, *EU Criminal Law* (Oxford and Portland, Oregon, Hart Publishing, 2009) ch 2.

[61] The disassociation of the financial gain element from the facilitation offence for the purposes of entry and transit raised concerns among humanitarian NGOs, which felt that they would be prosecuted for assisting third country nationals, including asylum seekers, to enter the EU. For that reason, and after protracted negotiations, a clause was added in the Directive granting Member States the discretion not to impose sanctions where the aim of the behaviour is to provide humanitarian assistance to the person concerned. See V Mitsilegas, J Monar and W Rees, *The European Union and Internal Security* (Basingstoke, Palgrave Macmillan, 2003) 106–08.

[62] Protocol Against the Smuggling of Migrants by Land, Sea and Air, supplementing the United Nations Convention Against Transnational Organized Crime, Article 6. The UN Smuggling Protocol also contains provisions on ensuring the safety and humane treatment of smuggled persons who are intercepted at sea, and a series of detailed provisions on prevention, elements which are absent from the EC/EU documents; see Mitsilegas, above n 59.

[63] For an overview, see P Webb, 'The United Nations Convention against Corruption. Global Achievement or Missed Opportunity?' (2005) 8 *Journal of International Economic Law* 191.

of the Palermo Convention. Transparency with regard to the various negotiating positions was limited. The eventual Council Decision on the conclusion, on behalf of the European Community, of the United Nations Convention against Corruption[64] confirmed that the elements of the Convention which were subject to Community competence were negotiated by the Commission.[65] The Community concluded the Convention on the basis of a plethora of legal bases, ranging from provisions on free movement and the internal market to development cooperation and provisions related to the functioning of the EU institutions.[66] Similarly, the Declaration annexed to the Decision established Community competence for a range of issues, starting with the prevention of corruption (including the adoption of codes of conduct and action within EU institutions), continuing with the proper functioning of the internal market (emphasising that the Community had adopted measures regarding transparency and equal access to public contracts and markets of Community relevance, appropriate accounting and auditing standards, and the prevention of money laundering) and concluding with development cooperation. This is a wide range of quite disparate fields, where Community action had not necessarily taken the form of legally-binding instruments. It reflects the many areas potentially affected by anti-corruption law, and extends both to addressing corruption at an internal, institutional level and to addressing corruption externally, as conduct which is detrimental to markets, the economy and beyond.

As regards the negotiations of the third pillar/criminal law aspects of the Convention, a series of draft negotiating common positions have now been declassified. The first of these documents refers to a draft Common Position at the initiative of the Belgian EU Presidency.[67] The draft Common Position contained detailed guidelines on the criminal law aspects of corruption to be included in the UN Convention.[68] It contained a 'red line', stating that the criminal offences

[64] [2008] OJ L287/1.

[65] *Ibid*, Preamble, recital 1.

[66] The legal bases of the Decision were: Arts 47(2) (free movement/right of establishment), 57(2) (free movement of capital), 95 (internal market), 107(5) (monetary policy, ESCB), 179 (development cooperation), 181a (economic, financial and technical cooperation with third countries), 190(5) (European Parliament), 195(4) (Ombudsman), 199 (European Parliament rules of procedure), 207(3) (Council rules of procedure), 218(2) (Commission rules of procedure), 279 (Council financial regulations), 280 (fraud against EC financial interests) and 283 (staff regulations of officials) TEC.

[67] Initiative of the Kingdom of Belgium for the adoption by the Council of a draft Common Position defined by the Council on negotiations within the United Nations to draw up a United Nations Convention against Corruption, Council Doc 12837/2/01 REV 2, Brussels, 30 October 2003. The draft Common Position was approved by the Article 36 Committee at its meeting of 12 and 13 November 2001, and Coreper was invited to recommend to the Council its adoption—Council Doc 14114/01, Brussels, 19 November 2001.

[68] According to Art 2 of the draft Common Position, the Convention should cover *inter alia* active and passive corruption in the private sector, and apply to corruption both of national officials and of foreign officials, and include corruption of international officials; it should also cover the criminalisation of the laundering of proceeds of corruption and seizure/confiscation matters; active and passive corruption in the private sector, trading in influence and accounting offences should also form part of the negotiations.

and penalties shall not call into question the fundamental principles underlying Member States' legal systems, and that

> in particular, in the negotiations on 'illicit enrichment', the Union should oppose any inclusion in the Convention of criminal offences so defined as to undermine those fundamental principles.[69]

The draft Common Position called for the Palermo Convention to be taken as the basis for a number of provisions in the new Convention.[70] Reflecting the growing importance of the fight against corruption in the context of the accession negotiations leading to the 2004 enlargement, candidate countries were invited to support the Common Position.[71] Member States were called upon to ensure that the provisions of the Convention did not call into question the instruments drawn up between them, 'in particular with regard to judicial assistance, extradition, combating corruption and the protection of the Community's financial interests.'[72] Last, but not least, the draft Common Position called upon Member States to 'coordinate their positions at the Presidency's initiative and seek to arrive at common standpoints on all issues which have significant implications for the interests of the European Union'.[73]

This three-fold approach, of mandating substantive negotiating guidelines (including 'red lines' in particular as regards provisions which would be deemed as threatening fundamental legal principles in Member States), safeguarding the internal *acquis* and calling for coordination in negotiations, was repeated in two subsequent draft Common Positions now publicly available. The draft second Common Position[74] expressed support in principle for the inclusion of anti-money laundering measures in the Convention. However, Member States were asked to ensure that the provisions of the Convention

> do not call into question either the instruments drawn up between them, in particular the Council Decision concerning arrangements for cooperation between financial intelligence units of the Member States in respect of exchanging information and other

[69] Draft Common Position, Art 2(3).

[70] Particularly for the provisions on laundering, seizure and confiscation of the proceeds of corruption, for the provisions on sanctions, the protection of witnesses, assistance and protection of victims, the liability of legal persons and jurisdiction, and for the provisions designed to improve international cooperation in criminal matters (draft Common Position, Art 2(5)). See also the EU Presidency Statement of 21 January 2002 on the UN Convention against corruption, in particular paras 9–12, at <http://www.europa-eu.un.org/articles/en/article_1081_en.htm>.

[71] Draft Common Position, Art 4.

[72] *Ibid*, Art 5.

[73] *Ibid*, Art 7.

[74] Draft second Common Position defined by the Council on the basis of Article 34(2)(a) of the Treaty on European Union on negotiations within the United Nations to draw up a United Nations Convention against Corruption, Council Doc 8897/4/02 REV 4, Brussels, 30 October 2003. The draft second Common Position was approved by the Article 36 Committee at its meeting of 20 and 21 May 2002, and Coreper was invited to recommend to the Council its adoption—Council Doc 9375/02, Brussels, 29 May 2002.

> measures taken in the field of money laundering, or other international instruments to which they are party.[75]

Moreover, as regards provisions on the identification, tracing, seizing, freezing and confiscation of funds, Member States were called to

> ensure that the provisions of the Convention concerning compliance with such measures do not call into question their fundamental principles, in particular as regards evidence, or their provisions on data protection.[76]

The draft third Common Position[77] focused primarily on substantive guidelines on the criminalisation of corruption by public officials, and advocated consistency with standards adopted in the Palermo Convention and the relevant Council of Europe Convention in the field.[78] The red line here involved the inclusion of offences such as abuse of functions, unlawful enrichment, use of classified or confidential information, and improper benefits, which Member States should not support. In the event of criminalisation of such offences, Member States were called upon to ensure that these crimes did not call into question the fundamental principles underlying their legal systems.[79]

An examination of the finally adopted text of the UN Convention against Corruption in the light of the aforementioned documents demonstrates that the EU negotiating objectives with regard to criminal law have been largely met. The Convention requires State Parties to criminalise three types of conduct: bribery of national public officials,[80] bribery of foreign public officials and officials of public international organisations,[81] and embezzlement, misappropriation or other diversion of property by a public official.[82] The last type of conduct is not currently covered by EU criminal law, while the EU has legislated on the criminalisation of corruption of national and Community officials.[83] The criminalisation of bribery of national public officials in the UN

[75] Draft second Common Position, Art 5.

[76] *Ibid*, Art 6.

[77] Initiative of the Kingdom of Denmark concerning the adoption by the Council of a draft third Common Position defined by the Council on the basis of Article 34(2)(a) of the Treaty on European Union on negotiations within the United Nations to draw up a United Nations Convention against Corruption, Council Doc 12215/2/02 REV 2, Brussels, 30 October 2003. The draft third Common Position was approved after some amendments by Coreper at its meeting of 25 September 2002, and the Council was invited to adopt it—Council Doc 12329/02, Brussels, 25 September 2002.

[78] See draft third Common Position, Arts 2 and 3 respectively. The same approach was followed with regard to criminalisation of money laundering (which, according to Art 8, should be compatible with Art 6 of the Palermo Convention) and corruption in the private sector (which should be compatible with Arts 7 and 8 of the Council of Europe Convention). It is noteworthy that compatibility is here requested with international—and not EU—standards in the field.

[79] Draft third Common Position, Art 6.

[80] UN Convention against Corruption, Art 15.

[81] *Ibid*, Art 16.

[82] *Ibid*, Art 17.

[83] See the Protocol to the EU Fraud Convention, [1996] OJ C313/2; and the EU Convention against corruption involving officials of the European Communities or officials of the Member States of the European Union, [1997] OJ C195/2.

Convention is worded in very similar terms to the relevant EU instruments on corruption.[84] The UN Convention also criminalises a series of further corruption-related offences (trading in influence,[85] abuse of functions,[86] illicit enrichment,[87] bribery in the private sector,[88] embezzlement of property[89]), but criminalisation here is not compulsory for State Parties, which need only *consider* going down that route. This wording seems to address EU concerns with regard to the criminalisation of illicit enrichment, which in any case would occur subject to the State Parties' constitutions and the fundamental principles of their legal system.[90] The inclusion in the Convention of the criminalisation of bribery in the private sector represents a partial victory for the EU. It has been reported that extending the Convention to cover the private sector was one of the most contentious issues during the negotiations, with the EU calling for criminalisation but the US resisting such a move.[91] The result has been a compromise, whereby the Convention includes the criminalisation of private sector corruption in very similar terms to the EU 2003 Framework Decision in the field,[92] but such criminalisation falls within the discretion of State Parties to the Convention.

The UN Convention against Corruption has introduced a number of corruption-related offences for State Parties to criminalise or to consider criminalising. The framework it puts forward is much more comprehensive when compared with the EU criminal law on corruption. The EU criminal law framework on corruption is both limited and fragmented, with Member States appearing reluctant to agree to a comprehensive anti-corruption law with teeth. Criminalisation has been introduced in the form of the quite 'intergovernmental' Maastricht Conventions (which have not been replaced post-Amsterdam by Framework Decisions). Where a Framework Decision has eventually been adopted (on corruption in the private sector), its implementation by Member States leaves much to be desired.[93] Unlike the fields of money laundering and organised crime, there has been no EU legislative action in the field following the adoption of the 2003 UN Convention. This may signal the fact that, in the field of the criminal law of

[84] The EU instruments refer to 'corruption', whereas the UN Convention refers to 'bribery'. The terms will be used interchangeably for the purposes of this chapter.

[85] UN Convention against Corruption, Art 18.

[86] *Ibid*, Art 19.

[87] *Ibid*, Art 20.

[88] *Ibid*, Art 21.

[89] *Ibid*, Art 22.

[90] Similarly, the Convention provisions on judicial cooperation in criminal matters appear to address EU concerns, as they are drafted in very general terms.

[91] Webb, above n 64, 213–14.

[92] Council Framework Decision 2003/568/JHA of 22 July 2003 on combating corruption in the private sector, [2003] OJ L192/54.

[93] See the Commission Report on the implementation of the Framework Decision on corruption in the private sector, COM(2007) 328 final, Brussels, 18 June 2007.

corruption, the Union has opted for pursuing its agenda via promoting standards at the global level instead of developing a comprehensive framework in internal EU law.[94]

III. THE EUROPEAN UNION AND THE COUNCIL OF EUROPE

Council of Europe multilateral Conventions have traditionally and for a number of decades provided the backbone for judicial cooperation in criminal matters in Europe, including cooperation between EU Member States. More recently, and in particular after the fall of the Berlin Wall, Council of Europe activities in the field of criminal law proliferated, with the adoption of a number of multilateral Conventions introducing substantive and procedural criminal law standards in the fight against serious and transnational crime. At the level of protection in the criminal law sphere, of course the Council of Europe has played a pivotal role via the adoption and enforcement of the European Convention on Human Rights.[95] In the light of these factors, the existence of a number of interconnections in the production of substantive criminal law between the Council of Europe and the European Union comes as no surprise. However, these interconnections have evolved in the light of the expansion of the membership of both organisations in criminal matters and the expansion of their role in criminal matters. On the one hand, membership of the Council of Europe has expanded eastwards and output in terms of multilateral Conventions in criminal matters has increased. On the other hand, the 2004 and 2007 enlargements of the Union have meant that now a great number of Council of Europe members are also now members of the EU. This is at a time when the work of the EU in criminal matters has increased dramatically. Taking into account these developments, this section of the chapter will cast light on the interconnections between the Council of Europe and the EU as regards the production of criminal law norms.[96]

[94] For the emphasis on action in international *fora*, see eg the Commission Communication *On a Comprehensive EU Policy Against Corruption*, COM(2003) 317 final, Brussels, 28 May 2003.

[95] For an overview of the activities of the Council of Europe in criminal matters, see P Csonka, 'Organised and Economic Crime (an overview of the Relevant Council of Europe Activities)' in PJ Cullen and WC Gilmore, *Crime sans Frontières: International and European Legal Approaches* (Edinburgh, Edinburgh University Press, 1998) 93–99. On the evolution of the relationship between the Council of Europe and the European Union more generally, see T Joris and J Vandenberghe, 'The Council of Europe and the European Union: Natural Partners or Uneasy Bedfellows?' (2008–2009) 15 *Columbia Journal of European Law* 1.

[96] Interconnections also exist in the field of compliance, with Council of Europe standards and compliance mechanisms in criminal matters playing a pivotal role in the external relations of the EU, both as regards enlargement and the relationship with its neighbours; for an analysis, see Mitsilegas, above n 55.

A. Interconnections in the Field of Judicial Cooperation in Criminal Matters

A key component of the Council of Europe's legislative work in criminal matters has traditionally been the adoption of a number of conventions dealing with judicial cooperation in criminal matters. In the years prior to the development of EU integration in the field, these instruments played a central role in the organisation of judicial cooperation in criminal matters between Member States of the EU. However, advancements in EU law post-Maastricht (and in particular post-Amsterdam)—most notably the introduction of mutual recognition as a principle underpinning judicial cooperation in criminal matters at EU level—have led to a radical rethinking of the relationship between Union law and Council of Europe law in the field. The proliferation of EU mutual recognition legislation in criminal matters has been accompanied by the gradual repeal (or partial replacement) of Council of Europe Conventions as regards the relationship between EU Member States. A prime example of the growing autonomy of the Union legal order in this context has been the 2002 Framework Decision on the European Arrest Warrant,[97] which replaced the provisions of a number of conventions, including the 1957 European Convention on Extradition, in relations between the Member States.[98]

The trend to replace Council of Europe law with Union law has recently been confirmed by the adoption of a number of further measures extending the principle of mutual recognition to various stages of the criminal process. The Framework Decision on the transfer of sentenced persons will replace the corresponding provisions of a number of Council of Europe Conventions (including the 1983 European Convention on the transfer of sentenced persons and its Additional Protocol of 1997) applicable in relations between the Member States.[99] A similar structure and logic to the transfer of sentenced persons instrument has been followed by the related Framework Decision on probation. In relations between the Member States, the latter will replace the corresponding provisions of the 1964 Council of Europe Convention on the Supervision of Conditionally Sentenced or Conditionally Released Offenders.[100] Last, but not least, the Framework Decision on the European Evidence Warrant does not replace but co-exists with existing

[97] Council Framework Decision of 13 June 2002 on the European arrest warrant and the surrender procedures between Member States, [2002] OJ L190/1.

[98] *Ibid*, Art 31(1). Along with its significance for the development of European integration in criminal matters, the European Arrest Warrant mechanism, based on mutual recognition, was deemed to provide a number of advantages to existing international law mechanisms, including greater automaticity and speed in the execution of requests. For an overview, see Mitsilegas, above n 61, ch 3.

[99] Framework Decision on the transfer of sentenced persons, [2008] OJ L327/27, Art 26(1). The added value of the Union instrument to the 1983 Convention and the 1997 Protocol is deemed to be twofold: it goes further in dispensing with the requirement of consent for the transfer; and it imposes a duty to take charge of sentenced persons for the enforcement of a sentence or an order—see Preamble, recital 4.

[100] Framework Decision on probation, [2008] OJ L337/102, Art 23(1).

mutual legal assistance provisions[101]; however, the ultimate aim, in particular post-Lisbon, is to adopt a more comprehensive EU instrument in the field which will replace traditional mutual legal assistance requirements.[102]

These developments point towards a future in which the legal order of the EU as an 'area of freedom, security and justice' becomes increasingly integrated, and at the same time distinct from international law instruments in the field.

B. Interconnections in the Field of Substantive Criminal Law

Interconnections between Council of Europe and EU criminal law can also be found in the development of substantive criminal law standards. As mentioned earlier in this chapter, Council of Europe standards have been used—via express references to Community law instruments—to extend criminalisation in the field of money laundering law.[103] However, it is in the past decade that the relationship between the two organisations in the field of the production of substantive criminal law standards has been mostly tested. Two factors have led to this development: the growing focus of Council of Europe legislative activity in the field of criminal law, in particular to tackle new, emerging or developing perceived security threats (cybercrime, money laundering, terrorism, trafficking in human beings are all subjects of recent Council of Europe criminal law Conventions); and the parallel boost in the production of EU legislation in substantive criminal law, in particular after the entry into force of the Amsterdam Treaty. In this light, the evolution of Council of Europe standards in the field saw the active participation of the Community and Member States in negotiations. Council of Europe standards have then been used to justify the adoption of internal Union legislation in the field. However, substantive EU law is not necessarily identical to the Council of Europe instruments, which in any case are not applicable in this context between EU Member States (which are bound by Union law).

An example of this EU strategy with regard to the adoption and subsequent use of Council of Europe criminal law instruments involves recent developments in the law of terrorism. At EU level, a new Framework Decision was adopted in

[101] [2008] OJ L350/72, Art 21.

[102] See in this context recital 25 of the Preamble to the European Evidence Warrant Framework Decision (*ibid*), which states that the Warrant 'should coexist with existing mutual assistance procedures, but such coexistence should be considered transitional until, in accordance with the Hague Programme, the types of evidence-gathering excluded from the scope of this Framework Decision are also the subject of a mutual recognition instrument, the adoption of which would provide a complete mutual recognition regime to replace mutual assistance procedures'. In the Stockholm Programme (the successor to the Hague Programme endorsed by the European Council in December 2009), the European Council invited the Commission to propose a comprehensive system to replace all the existing instruments in the area, including the European Evidence Warrant Framework Decision, covering as far as possible all types of evidence ([2010] OJ C115/1, point 3.1.1).

[103] See section II.A. above.

2008 to amend an earlier Framework Decision on combating terrorism.[104] The Framework Decision expands the scope of the 2002 instrument to introduce into the EU legal order offences related to the prevention of terrorism. The basis for the elaboration of these offences was the Council of Europe Convention on the Prevention of Terrorism.[105] The 2008 Framework Decision does not repeal but rather amends the 2002 Framework Decision on combating terrorism.[106] The 2008 instrument introduces three new offences: public provocation to commit a terrorist offence; recruitment for terrorism; and training for terrorism. These acts are treated as offences linked to terrorist acts when intentional. However, for any of these acts to be punishable it is not necessary that a terrorist offence is actually committed. This clause, which has been copied *verbatim* from the Council of Europe Convention, did not exist in the 2002 EU instrument and signals a move towards the adoption of 'preventive' criminal law by the EU. However, criminalisation in the Framework Decision has its limits. In particular, it is noteworthy that for conduct to be treated as a criminal offence, a 'terrorist motivation' must exist.[107] This condition, which does not exist in the main body of the Council of Europe Convention,[108] may serve to limit criminalisation when the Framework Decision is implemented.[109]

The EU strategy with regard to the use of the Council of Europe Convention on the Prevention of Terrorism demonstrates the increasing assertiveness of the Union as a global actor in criminal matters, especially in fields where there is already a developed Union *acquis*. The Union played an active part in the negotiations of the Council of Europe Convention, by opposing the negotiation of a comprehensive Council of Europe counter-terrorism convention and arguing in favour of narrowing down the scope of the latter to cover only areas where there are gaps in pre-existing international law.[110] This lack of consensus with regard to the adoption of a comprehensive approach[111] resulted in an instrument covering specific aspects of counter-terrorism action, in particular the criminalisation of 'glorification-type' conduct, and not covering aspects of the criminalisation of terrorism which had already been addressed in the 2002 EU Framework Decision.

[104] Framework Decision 2008/919/JHA amending the 2002 Framework Decision on combating terrorism, [2008] OJ L330/21.

[105] Council of Europe Convention on the Prevention of Terrorism, CETS No 196.

[106] Framework Decision 2002/475/JHA on combating terrorism, [2002] OJ L164/3.

[107] Art 1(1) of the 2002 Framework Decision criminalises as 'terrorist' offences which, given their nature or context, may seriously damage a country or an international organisation where committed with the aim of seriously intimidating a population, or unduly compelling a government or international organisation to perform or abstain from performing any act, or seriously destabilising or destroying the fundamental political, constitutional, economic or social structures of a country or an international organisation.

[108] For a discussion, see A Hunt, 'The Council of Europe Convention on the Prevention of Terrorism' (2006) 12 *European Public Law* 613.

[109] For further discussion of this Framework Decision, see Mitsilegas, above n 52.

[110] Hunt, above n 109, 606–07.

[111] See also para 11 of the Explanatory Memorandum to the Convention.

The Union then used the Convention to justify the extension of criminalisation internally, while justifying Union action externally by stressing the 'added value' of the Union legal order in terms of integration and enforcement.[112] According to the EU Justice and Home Affairs Ministers, the inclusion of the Convention offences in the Framework Decision is important,

> because it provides the advantages of the more integrated institutional framework of the EU and also because the legal regime of the Framework Decision in respect of the type and level of criminal penalties and compulsory rules on jurisdiction will be applicable to these offences.[113]

The references to the special nature and features of Union law echo the arguments developing the concept of primacy of Community law in the context of EU constitutional law. The following two points are noteworthy in this regard: that the specificity of the internal legal order—and the link with primacy—is established here with regard not to *Community* but to *Union* law (a significant assertion, in particular in the pre-Lisbon days); and that specificity and primacy come into play not only in relation to *national* but also in relation to *international* law. The other side of the coin to these considerations (justifying the adoption of Union law notwithstanding the existence of a comprehensive Council of Europe Convention in the very same field) is the insertion of a disconnection clause by the EU in the body of the Council of Europe instrument.[114] Article 26(3) of the Council of Europe Convention states that parties which are members of the European Union shall, in their mutual relations, apply Community and European Union rules in so far as there are Community or European Union rules governing the particular subject concerned and applicable to the specific case, without prejudice to the object and purpose of the present Convention and without prejudice to its full application with other parties.[115]

[112] The Commission provided a similar justification when tabling recently a proposal to amend the EU Framework Decision on trafficking in human beings: the advantages of an EU approach were deemed to be related to the stronger bond created by the EU legal order, namely the immediate entering into force, and the monitoring and implementation; see COM(2009) 136 final, 7.

[113] Justice and Home Affairs Council Conclusions of December 6–7, 2007, Council Doc 15966/07, Presse 275, 21. The integration of the Convention standards in the Union legal order has also been justified on the ground that the Framework Decision would 'trigger' the implementation of cooperation mechanisms under Union law, in particular as regards the exchange of information on terrorist offences between Member States and the transfer of such information to Europol and Eurojust. See comment by Tony McNulty, then a Home Office Minister, to the House of Commons European Scrutiny Committee, *26th Report* (session 2007–08), para 26.3.

[114] The inclusion of disconnection clauses has been standard practice with regard to Council of Europe Conventions, in particular as regards recent Conventions in criminal matters. For an overview and typology of disconnection clauses used by the European Community/Union in Council of Europe Conventions, see International Law Commission, *Fragmentation of International Law: Difficulties arising from the Diversification and Expansion of International Law*, Report of the Study Group of the International Law Commission (finalised by Martti Koskenniemi), UN General Assembly Doc A/CN.4/L.682, 13 April 2006, paras 289–94.

[115] See also the Declaration of Community Competence annexed to the Convention on Preventing Terrorism, which reads as follows: 'The European Community/European Union and its Member States

The wording of this clause tries to achieve a delicate balance between safeguarding the Community and Union *acquis*[116] (in particular as regards *the future*[117]) and preserving the autonomy and primacy of Community (and now Union) law[118] on the one hand, and alleviating concerns that such move will not undermine the very regime established by the Council of Europe Convention on the other.[119] Such concerns reflect fears with regard to the growing power of the EU, whose Member States constitute now the majority of Council of Europe members, and the impact of such power on the reach of Council of Europe rules.[120] From the point of view of an international lawyer, the inclusion of such disconnection clauses in Council of Europe instruments is a matter of concern, as it may lead to the fragmentation of international law.[121] However, from an EU law point of view, such concerns

reaffirm that their objective in requesting the inclusion of a "disconnection clause" is to take account of the institutional structure of the Union when acceding to international conventions, in particular in case of transfer of sovereign powers from the Member States to the Community. This clause is not aimed at reducing the rights or increasing the obligations of a non-European Union Party vis-à-vis the European Community/European Union and its Member States, inasmuch as the latter are also parties to this Convention. The disconnection clause is necessary for those parts of the Convention which fall within the competence of the Community/Union, in order to indicate that European Union Member States cannot invoke and apply the rights and obligations deriving from the Convention directly among themselves (or between themselves and the European Community/Union). This does not detract from the fact that the Convention applies fully between the European Community/European Union and its Member States on the one hand, and the other Parties to the Convention on the other; the Community and the European Union Member States will be bound by the Convention and will apply it like any Party to the Convention, if necessary, through Community/Union legislation. They will thus guarantee the full respect of the Convention's provisions vis-à-vis non-European Union Parties.'

[116] For a categorisation of disconnection clauses as '*acquis*-saving clauses', see J Klabbers, 'Safeguarding the Organizational *Acquis*: The EU's External Practice' (2007) 4 *International Organizations Law Review* 57, at 70–71.

[117] See in this context the criticism that disconnection clauses are quite 'open' and subject to change: International Law Commission, above n 115, para 293. In this context, they are, however, similar to the Declarations of Community Competence attached to the UN Conventions discussed in section II. of this chapter. However, the latter are also relevant for the determination of competence at Union level.

[118] For a discussion of disconnection clauses in the context of primacy in the first pillar, see M Cremona, 'Defending the Community Interest: the Duties of Cooperation and Compliance' in M Cremona and B De Witte (eds), *EU Foreign Relations Law. Constitutional Fundamentals* (Oxford and Portland, Oregon, Hart Publishing, 2008) 142–43.

[119] See International Law Commission, above n 115, para 294.

[120] According to the Deputy Secretary General of the Council of Europe, speaking in the context of the new EU proposals on trafficking in human beings and their relationship with the relevant Council of Europe Convention in the field (which also contains a disconnection clause): 'If EU legislation does not go as far as our Convention, for instance, as regards the 30 days recovery and reflection period, and if one applies the disconnection clause, we will find ourselves in a paradoxical situation of having two regimes applicable under the same Convention and a lower standard as compared to other parts of Europe.' Speech by Maud de Boer-Buquicchio, Hearing on Human Trafficking, 'Who is fighting trafficking—who is not?', European Parliament, Brussels, 8 October 2008.

[121] See in this context the aforementioned Report by the International Law Commission (above n 115), which examined disconnection clauses in the context of the fragmentation of international law. But see also the view of Klabbers, who notes that 'it is, indeed, no coincidence that the most ardent critics of the disconnection clause have to resort to systemic arguments (risk of increased fragmentation,

seem somewhat exaggerated: as regards *internal* Union law, efforts to safeguard the autonomy and primacy of the Community legal order are not something new[122]; as regards *EU external relations*, it is in the interests of the Union for Council of Europe standards to be enforced, as a key tool for EU policies with regard to candidate countries and its Council of Europe member neighbours.

C. Interconnections in the Field of the Protection of Fundamental Rights in the Criminal Justice Process

A third area with significant interconnections between the Union and the Council of Europe legal orders has to do with the protection of fundamental rights in the criminal justice process. Of course the major Council of Europe instrument in the field is the European Convention on Human Rights (ECHR). This has obtained an increasingly central role in discussions over whether EU criminal law measures (in particular measures such as the European Arrest Warrant) are compatible with fundamental rights.[123] Related to its role as a benchmark for EU action in criminal matters, the ECHR has also served as a source of inspiration and legitimacy for proposals for EU criminal law. This has been the case in particular in the context of proposals to establish EU legislation in the field of the rights of the defendant in criminal proceedings. In the light of concerns with regard to consistency between Union and ECHR standards, and the perceived risk of duplication, the Commission proposals went to great lengths to explain compatibility with the ECHR, while the Council of Europe was invited at various stages to comment on the Commission proposals. This remarkable synergy has served to provide legitimacy and support for EU proposals which have been met with strong resistance by Member States.[124] A first set of proposals on defence rights (on interpretation and translation) has now been agreed.[125] This move (especially in the post-Lisbon era, when the TFEU contains a specific legal basis enabling under certain conditions the adoption of minimum standards on the rights of individuals in criminal procedure[126]) will lead to further Commission proposals on other aspects of defence rights, where further synergies with the Council of Europe are likely to be developed.

undermining legal equality) rather than any concrete and enforceable legal norm': J Klabbers, *Treaty Conflict and the European Union* (Cambridge, Cambridge University Press, 2009) 222.

[122] Although it is significant that disconnection clauses in Council of Europe instruments dealing with criminal law have perhaps been the closest we have come to safeguarding the primacy of *Union* (and not Community) law in the pre-Lisbon era.

[123] For one of the first ECHR audits of the European Arrest Warrant, see S Alegre and M Leaf, 'Mutual Recognition in European Judicial Co-operation: A Step Too Far Too Soon? Case Study—The European Arrest Warrant' (2004) 10 *European Law Journal* 200.

[124] For further details, see Mitsilegas, above n 55.

[125] For the text see Directive 2010/64/EU, [2010] OJ L280/1.

[126] Art 82(2)(b) TFEU.

Another 'protective' Council of Europe instrument which appears repeatedly in EU criminal law is the 1981 Convention on Data Protection (and a related 1987 Recommendation on data protection in the police sector). The 1981 Convention has constituted—along with a series of instrument-specific data protection provisions relating to data processing, retention, access, etc—the main safeguard to the operation of EU databases since Maastricht. References to the 1981 Convention remain in recent laws revising the operation of existing, or introducing new, EU databases. References to the 1981 Convention can be found in the original Decision establishing Eurojust[127]; the recent Europol Decision[128]; the Decision on the second-generation Schengen Information System (SIS II)[129]; and the Decision incorporating the majority of the provisions of the Prüm Treaty into the Union legal order (calling for the intensification of the cooperation between national law enforcement authorities, including *inter alia* the exchange of a wide range of personal data including DNA data).[130]

The emphasis on the use of international norms on data protection in these instruments reflects the intergovernmental heritage of a number of EU instruments establishing databases (including in particular the Europol Convention and the Prüm Decision), and has been long justified by the absence of specific third pillar legislation on data protection. In this context, it is noteworthy that, when such a measure was finally agreed by Member States, the latter made sure that the

[127] [2002] OJ L63/1. According to Art 14(2) of the Decision: 'Eurojust shall take the necessary measures to guarantee a level of protection for personal data at least equivalent to that resulting from the application of the principles of the Council of Europe Convention of 28 January 1981 and subsequent amendments thereto where they are in force in the Member States'. Although the Eurojust Decision was recently amended (enhancing data exchange and extending at the same time the specific data protection provisions), Art 14(2) remained unchanged (Council Decision 2009/426/JHA, [2009] OJ L138/14).

[128] [2009] OJ L121/37. According to Art 27 of the Europol Decision: 'Without prejudice to specific provisions of this Decision, Europol shall take into account of the principles of the Council of Europe Convention for the Protection of individuals with regard to Automatic Processing of Personal Data of 28 January 1981 and of Recommendation No R (87) 15 of the Committee of Ministers of the Council of Europe of 17 September 1987'.

[129] [2007] OJ L205/63. According to Art 57 of the SIS II Decision: 'Personal data processed in application of this Decision shall be protected in accordance with the Council of Europe Convention of 28 January 1981 for the protection of individuals with regard to automatic processing of personal data, and subsequent amendments thereto'. Note also that the Decision envisages access to SIS II data by Europol (Art 41) and Eurojust (Art 42).

[130] Council Decision 2008/615/JHA of 23 June 2008 on the stepping up of cross-border cooperation, particularly in combating terrorism and cross-border crime, [2008] OJ L210/1. According to Art 25(1) of the Decision: 'As regards the processing of personal data which are or have been supplied pursuant to this Decision, each Member State shall guarantee a level of protection of personal data in its national law at least equal to that resulting from the Council of Europe Convention for the Protection of Individuals with regard to Automatic Processing of Personal Data of 28 January 1981 and the Additional Protocol of 8 November 2001 and in doing so, shall take into account of Recommendation No R (87) 15 of 17 September 1987 of the Committee of Ministers of the Council of Europe to the Member States regulating the use of personal data in the police sector, also where data are not processed automatically'.

Framework Decision will not affect the data-protection provisions in a number of specific sectoral third pillar instruments,

> in particular those governing the functioning of Europol, Eurojust, the Schengen Information System (SIS) and the Customs Information System (CIS), as well as those introducing direct access for the authorities of Member States to certain data systems of other Member States[131]

and the provisions in the Decision incorporating Prüm into EU law.[132] In an era marked by the proliferation of EU databases in criminal matters, by efforts to boost the powers of EU bodies in the field and by steps to use new laws and technologies to maximise enforcement agencies' collection of and access to an ever-growing range of personal (including sensitive) data, it is striking that the main legal safeguard at EU level remains a 1981 international law instrument.

IV. THE EUROPEAN UNION AND THE FINANCIAL ACTION TASK FORCE

The examination of interconnections between EU law and international law in criminal matters cannot be complete without an overview of the interconnections between Union law and global 'soft' law in the field. Nowhere else are such interconnections better illustrated than by looking at the relationship between the European Community/Union and the Financial Action Task Force on money laundering (and now terrorist finance) (FATF). The FATF is an *ad hoc* body, established by the G7 in 1989 within the auspices of the OECD.[133] It began with a specialised mandate to prevent money laundering,[134] and its mandate has been renewed regularly since.[135] As regards its membership, the FATF can be justifiably characterised a rich countries club. This was particularly the case at its inception (it must be recalled that it was established by the G7 under the auspices of the OECD[136]), with its membership

[131] Framework Decision on data protection, [2008] OJ L350/60, Preamble, recital 39. See also recital 12 to the Europol Decision (above n 129), stating that the data protection provisions therein will not be affected by the Framework Decision on data protection, as the Europol Decision 'should contain specific provisions on the protection of personal data regulating these matters in greater detail because of the particular nature, functions and competences of Europol'.

[132] Decision 2008/615/JHA on the stepping up of cross-border co-operation, particularly in combating terrorism and cross-border crime, [2008] OJ L210/1; and Decision 2008/616/JHA on the implementation of Decision 2008/615/JHA, [2008] OJ L210/12.

[133] For a detailed analysis of the role and work of the FATF, see Gilmore, above n 2, chs 4–6. Gilmore characterises the FATF as an 'ad hoc grouping of governments and others with a complex but highly focused agenda' (*ibid*, at 92).

[134] The original mandate was 'to assess the results of cooperation already undertaken in order to prevent the utilisation of the banking system and financial institutions for the purpose of money laundering, and to consider additional preventive efforts in this field, including the adaptation of the legal and regulatory systems so as to enhance multilateral judicial assistance' (Gilmore, *ibid*, at 89).

[135] For the latest mandate at the time of writing, see FATF, *FATF Revised Mandate 2008–2012*, 12 April 2008, downloaded from the FATF website at <http://www.fatf-gafi.org>.

[136] Gilmore notes that in addition to the participants in the G7 summit establishing the FATF (Canada, France, Germany, Italy, Japan, United Kingdom, United States and the Commission)

expanded since to include 'strategically important' countries and largely to reflect financial globalisation.[137] When looking at FATF membership today, it is striking that all 15 'old' EU Member States, along with the Commission, are now full FATF members. However, none of the 12 States which joined the EU in 2004 and 2007 is a FATF member (they are all members of MONEYVAL—the Committee of Experts on the Evaluation of Anti-Money Laundering Measures, established in 1997 under the auspices of the Council of Europe).[138]

The main output by the FATF in terms of normative production has been the 40 Recommendations, geared mainly towards the prevention of money laundering and first published in 1990. The Recommendations were revised in 1996 and 2003, and were complemented post-9/11 by a set of eight Special Recommendations on Terrorist Finance. Although these Recommendations are not strictly instruments of 'hard' international law, their influence on the development of EC/EU anti-money laundering law has been tremendous. Both the second and the third EC Directives in the field, adopted in 2001 and 2005 respectively, have been justified as reactions to international developments in the field. The second Money Laundering Directive[139] was justified by the Commission as necessary to implement (and go beyond) the revised FATF Recommendations of 1996.[140] Both main changes introduced by the Directive (namely the extension of the money laundering predicate offences and the extension of preventive duties to non-financial professions) were justified by reference to FATF findings and requirements: the Preamble to the Directive stated that

> there has been a trend in recent years towards a much wider definition of money laundering based on a broader range of predicate underlying offences, as reflected for example in the 1996 revision of the 40 Recommendations of the Financial Action Task Force, the leading international body devoted to the fight against money laundering.[141]

eight other States (Australia, Austria, Belgium, Luxembourg, The Netherlands, Spain, Sweden and Switzerland) were invited to take part: above n 2, at 89.

[137] The current membership criteria include, along with compliance with FATF standards, 'strategic importance': see FATF, *FATF Membership Policy*, 29 February 2008, downloaded from the FATF website, above n 136.

[138] See FATF, *FATF Members and Observers*, available at <http://www.fatfgafi.org/document/52/0,3343,en_32250379_32237295_34027188_1_1_1_1,00.html>.

[139] Directive 2001/97/EC of the European Parliament and of the Council of 4 December 2001 amending Council Directive 91/308/EEC on prevention of the use of the financial system for the purpose of money laundering, [2001] OJ L344/76.

[140] 'Just as the 1991 Directive moved ahead of the original FATF 40 Recommendations in requiring obligatory suspicious transaction reporting, the European Union should continue to impose a high standard on its Member States, giving effect to or even going beyond the 1996 update of the FATF 40 Recommendations. In particular the EU can show the way in seeking to involve certain professions more actively in the fight against money laundering alongside the financial sector': COM(1999) 352 final, Brussels, 14 July 1999, 3.

[141] Directive 2001/97/EC, above n 140, Preamble, recital 7.

It also accepted that

> there is a trend towards the increased use by money launderers of non-financial businesses as confirmed by the work of the FATF on money laundering techniques and typologies.[142]

On the basis of these findings, the Directive extended the list of predicate offences and the list of professions to be covered by the Directive obligations, to include *inter alia* lawyers.[143]

The third Money Laundering Directive was adopted in 2005.[144] Its aim was twofold: to extend the scope of the legislation also to cover the fight against terrorist finance, a key political priority in the post-9/11 world; and to update existing legislation in the light of international regulatory developments in the field, most notably as regards customer identification.[145] The Directive presents a major overhaul of the provisions on prevention—in particular those provisions on customer identification—in the light of the revised FATF Recommendations in the field, introducing a number of FATF-inspired concepts such as the so-called 'risk-based approach' to customer identification and more detailed provisions on beneficial ownership and 'politically exposed persons'.[146]

The influence of the FATF on the Community legal order is not limited to the successive Money Laundering Directives. The emphasis on terrorist finance this decade led to the adoption by the FATF of a series of 'Special Recommendations' on terrorist financing, reflecting the extension of the FATF mandate to cover the field. A number of Special Recommendations—which deal primarily with the surveillance of money flows—have now been implemented (quite swiftly) by the Union. These include a Regulation on controls of cash, which implements FATF Special Recommendation IX of 22 October 2004 and imposes *inter alia*

[142] *Ibid*, recital 14.

[143] Human rights concerns with regard to fair trial rights by the European Parliament have led to negotiations on the Directive being extended to the Conciliation stage—agreement was reached after the Directive was packaged as an emergency counter-terrorism measure in the weeks after 9/11. For an overview, see Mitsilegas, above n 3.

[144] Directive 2005/60/EC of the European Parliament and the Council of 26 October 2005 on the prevention of the use of the financial system for the purpose of money laundering and terrorist financing, [2005] OJ L309/15.

[145] According to the Preamble, recital 5: 'Money laundering and terrorist financing are frequently carried out in an international context. Measures adopted solely at national or even Community level, without taking account of international coordination and cooperation, would have very limited effects. The measures adopted by the Community in this field should therefore be consistent with other action undertaken in other international fora. The Community action should continue to take particular account of the Recommendations of the Financial Action Task Force ... which constitutes the foremost international body active in the fight against money laundering and terrorist financing. Since the FATF Recommendations were substantially revised and expanded in 2003, this Directive should be in line with the new international standard.'

[146] For further details and an overview of the third Money Laundering Directive, see Mitsilegas and Gilmore, above n 15.

requirements to declare cash over a certain threshold at the Union border[147]; a Regulation on information on the payer accompanying wire transfers,[148] implementing FATF Special Recommendation VII on wire transfers (SR VII)[149]; and a Directive on payment services in the internal market,[150] implementing FATF Special Recommendation VI on alternative remittance systems.[151] With the exception of the Special Recommendation on non-profit organisations (which has been dealt with by non legally-binding means at EU level), it can thus be seen that the 'preventive' FATF Special Recommendations have been implemented swiftly by the Union, and primarily in the form of Regulations (which are directly applicable across the EU).[152] This swift adoption is noteworthy in view of the potential conflict of some of these provisions with EU law. Along with the question of the existence of Community competence as regards the Cash Controls Regulation at the time,[153] there are also questions with regard to the compatibility of these measures with the development of the Union as an area without internal frontiers. A number of these provisions are essentially about the surveillance of money flows, which arguably constitutes an obstacle to the free movement of capital—with the Union already having to convince the FATF about the impossibility of imposing controls of cash within the internal borders of Member States.[154]

[147] Regulation (EC) No 1889/2005 of the European Parliament and of the Council of 26 October 2005 on controls of cash entering the Community, [2005] OJ L309/9. See recitals 4 and 5 of the Preamble to the Regulation. Recital 4 states that 'Account should also be taken of complementary activities carried out in international *fora*, in particular those of the Financial Action task Force on Money Laundering … Special Recommendation IX of 22 October 2004 of the FATF calls on governments to take measures to detect physical cash movements, including a declaration system or other disclosure obligation.'

[148] Regulation (EC) No 1781/2006 of the European Parliament and of the Council of 15 November 2006 on information on the payer accompanying transfers of funds, [2006] OJ L345/1.

[149] According to the Preamble, recital 2, to the Regulation: 'In order to facilitate their criminal activities, money launderers and terrorist financiers could try to take advantage of the freedom of capital movements entailed by the integrated financial area, unless certain coordinating measures are adopted at Community level. By its scale, Community action should ensure that Special Recommendation VII on wire transfers (SR VII) of the Financial Action Task Force … is transposed uniformly throughout the European Union, and, in particular, that there is no discrimination between national payments within a Member State and cross-border payments between Member States …'

[150] [2007] OJ L319/1.

[151] See Council Doc 8864/1/09 REV 1, Brussels, 5 May 2009.

[152] For further details and an evaluation in the light of the FATF standards, see Mitsilegas and Gilmore, above n 15, at 130.

[153] *Ibid.*

[154] According to the Report on the implementation of the revised Strategy on Terrorist Financing (Council Doc 8864/1/09 REV 1, Brussels, 5 May 2009, at 2): 'After almost 2 years of discussion, a global agreement on an amended FATF methodology on FATF Special Recommendation IX on cash controls at the borders was reached at the February 2009 meeting in Paris. This agreement acknowledges the specificity of the EU as one jurisdiction and the possibility for it to be compliant with SR IX without (re)introducing controls at Member States' internal borders.'

The influence of FATF standards on the EU legal order is noteworthy. These standards have been developed by a single agenda, *ad hoc* body, with selective membership and a minimum of transparency and accountability in its operations.[155] In turn, the FATF depoliticised expert orthodoxy in terms of both money laundering typologies and the necessary measures to counter the phenomenon[156] has constantly been renewed,[157] and every time uncritically adopted by the European Commission (itself an FATF member) in its proposals for Community law in the field and subsequently by Member States in the Council. In this manner, a specific agenda developed with limited scrutiny at the global level has been legitimised, via the EC decision-making process, and adopted at Community level to bind both FATF and non-FATF members. The growing assertiveness of the EU in the production of multilateral standards in criminal matters in more traditional international *fora* such as the United Nations or the Council of Europe cannot be confirmed in the context of the FATF, a great part owing to the lack of transparency in the production of 'soft law' in the field. In this manner, 'soft law' has perhaps proved to have harder teeth than the multilateral conventions in the field.

[155] For an approach including FATF within the so-called 'Global Administrative Law' model, see B Kingsbury, N Krisch and RB Stewart, 'The Emergence of Global Administrative Law' (2004–2005) 68 *Law and Contemporary Problems* 15. For thoughts on the issues of transparency and accountability, which are relevant in the context of the FATF, see also J Cohen and Ch F Sabel, 'Global Democracy?'(2004–2005) 37 *NYU Journal of International Law and Policy* 763, who note that 'to a substantial and growing extent, then, rulemaking directly affecting the freedom of action of individuals, firms, and nation states (and the making of the rules to regulate this rulemaking) is taking place, undemocratically but not entirely unaccountably, in global settings created by the world's nations but no longer under their effective control' (at 764).

[156] On various aspects of what I call the 'depoliticisation' in the development of global standards, see: A Somek, *Administration without Sovereignty*, University of Iowa Legal Studies Research Paper 09-04, January 2009 (noting that 'where "problem-solving" serves as the preferred descriptor of an activity, ideological conflict does not enter the picture. Problem-solving is the antithesis of political struggle'—at 17); J Klabbers, 'Institutional Ambivalence by Design: Soft Organizations in International Law' (2001) 70 *Nordic Journal of International Law* 403 (noting that 'the facility of doing business without being side-tracked or controlled, dovetails neatly with our late-modern (or post-modern) infatuation for management and technocracy as viable substitutes for politics'—at 417); and D Kennedy, 'Challenging Expert Rule: The Politics of Global Governance' (2005) 27 *Sydney Law Review* 5 (talking *inter alia* about 'the expert consensus'). For a more positive view, see A-M Slaughter, *A New World Order* (Princeton, Princeton University Press, 2004). Slaughter views the FATF typologies as 'important opportunities for operational experts to identify and describe current money laundering trends and effective countermeasures' and stresses the benefits of professional socialisation (at 54). Slaughter promotes the advantages of what she calls 'government networks', marrying hard and soft power and using information, persuasion and socialisation (at 168 *et seq*).

[157] Kennedy notes in this context that progress narratives become policy programs, 'both by solidifying a professional consensus and by defining what counts as progress for the international governance system as a whole' (above n 157, at 25). In the context of the FATF, the regular revision of both mandate and standards has been easier when compared to a more formal international organisation—see in this context A Boyle, 'Some Reflections on the Relationship of Treaties and Soft Law' (1999) 48 *International and Comparative Law Quarterly* 901, who notes that soft law instruments are easier to amend or replace than treaties (at 903).

V. CONCLUSION

The EU has been both actively involved in and influenced by the globalisation of criminal law which has been taking place for the last two decades. Notwithstanding internal constitutional and institutional complexities, the Union has emerged in one way or another as a global actor in the field. Along with attempts to influence global (and regional) standards in criminal matters, the EU has proved itself ready to advance the globalisation of criminal law via its internal *acquis*. Union institutions have not hesitated to internalise international law and use the text of international 'hard' and 'soft' law instruments as a basis to justify, establish and develop Community/Union criminal law. This has been particularly the case in the context of the development of money laundering counter-measures, where interconnections between the EU, the regional European and the global level have resulted in the development of a brand new regime of criminalisation, prevention and enforcement. In this and other fields (most notably organised crime and terrorism), in terms of substance, convergence between EU and international law has largely led to the extension of criminalisation and the proliferation of the powers of the State. In terms of the protection of fundamental rights on the other hand, EU Member States have been using international law largely to shield enforcement action from Union law.

This is a reminder that the Union's stance in international *fora* must be viewed in the light of internal developments in both constitutional and substantive law. The furthering of European integration in criminal matters the past decade has been coupled with a growing assertiveness by the Union in international negotiations. The EU has been actively involved in trying to shape the content of multilateral treaties in criminal matters (both at UN and Council of Europe levels), with not inconsiderable success thus far. At the same time—and in particular in relation to the Council of Europe, but also as regards the UN—it has not hesitated to stress the autonomy of the Union legal order and to reserve the freedom to legislate in similar matters at Union level in the future. For those viewing the glass half empty in terms of coherence and consistency, this may lead to the fragmentation of international law in the field. Those more optimistic would point out the growing interconnections between the EU and other international organisations and bodies in the production of criminal law (albeit in certain cases with minimal debate or transparency), and the striking similarities between global and EU standards in combating serious and transnational crime. It remains to be seen how the relationship between Union and international law in criminal matters will develop in the post-Lisbon era, an era when dramatic developments may occur in the EU *acquis* in the field.

7

*The Principle of Legality, Human Rights and the Management of Risks: Post-*Kadi *Reflections*

TAKIS TRIDIMAS

I. INTRODUCTION

THE JUDGMENT OF the European Court of Justice (ECJ; now the Court of Justice) in *Kadi*[1] is of defining constitutional importance. The Court understood the EC Treaty as establishing its own constitutional space, asserted the autonomy of EC law *vis-à-vis* international law, and held that responses to emergencies should be handled through, rather than outside, the bounds of the EU Treaties. The judgment is predicated on liberal democratic ideals and views respect for legality as a *sine qua non* in times of emergency.

This chapter seeks to discuss selected case law developments after *Kadi*. It focuses on issues pertaining to the validity and interpretation of Council Regulation No 881/2002,[2] economic sanctions against nuclear proliferation and corresponding developments in the case law of the UK Supreme Court. It does not deal exhaustively with post-*Kadi* case law.[3] Section II. provides a brief introduction to the judgment in *Kadi*. Section III. discusses selectively recent case law of the ECJ and the Court of First Instance (CFI; now the General Court), and section IV. explores in

[1] Joined Cases C-402/05 P and C-415/05 P *Kadi & Al Barakaat International Foundation v Council and Commission* [2008] ECR I-6351.

[2] Council Regulation (EC) No 881/2002 of 27 May 2002 imposing certain specific restrictive measures directed against certain persons and entities associated with Usama bin Laden, the Al-Qaeda network and the Taliban, [2002] OJ L139/9.

[3] The chapter discusses selected judgments pertaining to Regulation No 881/2002. It does not deal with the case law of the CFI generated by sanctions lists introduced by the European Community and not by the Sanctions Committee of the UN. For these cases, see Case T-284/08 *People's Mojahedin Organization of Iran v Council (OMPI III)* [2008] ECR II-3487; Case T- 256/07 *People's Mojahedin Organisation of Iran v Council (OMPI II)* [2008] ECR II-3019, Case T-228/02 *Organisation des Modjahedines du peuple d'Iran v Council (OMPI I)* [2006] ECR II-4655.

some detail the judgment of the UK Supreme Court in *HM Treasury v Mohammed Jabar Ahmed*.[4]

II. THE JUDGMENT IN *KADI*

In *Kadi* the ECJ was concerned with the validity of Regulation No 881/2002, by which the Council implemented United Nations Security Council (UNSC) Resolution 1390(2000) imposing economic sanctions on non-State actors associated with Osama Bin Laden and the Al Qaeda network. The names of the persons included in the sanctions list were determined by the UN Sanctions Committee which had been set up under UNSC Resolution 1267(1999).

The basic findings of the Court may be summarised as follows. First, the Court held that the European Community (now European Union (EU)) has competence to adopt economic sanctions against individuals on the basis of Articles 301, 60(1) and 308 of the EC Treaty.[5] Secondly, it held that measures adopted by the Community institutions to give effect to UNSC resolutions are subject to review on grounds of respect for fundamental rights as protected by EU law. The Court adopted a dualist approach, holding that, whilst it does not have power to review the lawfulness of a UNSC resolution, it does have jurisdiction to review the compatibility of measures adopted by the Community institutions with the Treaty. Such review of an EC regulation implementing a UNSC resolution does not entail any challenge to the primacy of that resolution in international law.[6] The Court upheld the paramountcy of fundamental rights, recalling its judgment in *les Verts* and reiterating that neither the Member States nor the EU institutions can avoid review of the conformity of their acts with the EC Treaty.[7] Thus, in the Court's rationale, the primacy of the UN Charter takes place only in the sphere of international law. It does not penetrate the constitutional space of the EU and, within that space, it cannot take precedence over the general principles of law of which fundamental rights form part.[8] On that basis, the Court proceeded to annul Regulation No 881/2002 by which the assets of the applicants had been frozen, on the ground that the applicants' right to a hearing, the right to judicial protection and the right to property had been infringed. The applicants had not been informed of the evidence against them, no reasons had been given for the inclusion of their names in the sanctions list and they had not been afforded any opportunity to put their case.[9]

[4] [2010] UKSC 2.

[5] Arts 60(1) and 301 EC have now been replaced by Arts 75 and 215 TFEU respectively, which provide expressly for the imposition of sanctions against non-State actors. Art 308 EC has been replaced by Art 352 TFEU.

[6] *Kadi*, above n 1, paras 287–88.

[7] Case 294/83 *Les Verts v Parliament* [1986] ECR 1339, para 23; *Kadi*, above n 1, para 281.

[8] *Kadi*, above n 1, para 308.

[9] *Ibid*, paras 345 *et seq*.

The judgment in *Kadi* has been the subject of extensive commentary.[10] It suffices to make some brief points here.

It may be said that the judgment carries a 'disobedience value'. If the ECJ trumps the UNSC, what is there to prevent the courts of another country—perhaps one which shows much less respect for the values of human rights—trumping UNSC resolutions for being incompatible with its own constitutional principles? Seen in that context, the judgment appears to contribute to the fragmentation of international law and undermine the authority of the Security Council.

It is correct that, if the Security Council is to fulfil its role as the ultimate guarantor of world peace and security, UNSC resolutions must be complied with and enforced effectively at national level. Full and effective enforcement requires the support not only of the executive but all branches of government. The judiciary should play its role by according due weight to decisions emanating from the Security Council. Respect for the Security Council, however, does not equate to government without law. It will be noted that, under Article 103 of the UN Charter, the primacy of the Charter and obligations arising under it applies in the sphere of international law. It does not interfere with the domestic law of the UN Member States, neither does it require those States to abrogate their own constitutional requirements. The classic argument of limited constitutional delegation applies here in full as it applies in the context of the EU: a national government cannot transfer to the UN more powers than it itself possesses under its national constitution. The ruling of the ECJ can therefore

[10] The judgment has generated a huge bibliography. See, among others, G De Búrca, 'The EU, the European Court of Justice and the International Legal Order after *Kadi*' (2010) 51 *Harvard International Law Journal* 1; D Halberstam and E Stein, 'The United Nations, the European Union, and the King of Sweden: Economic Sanctions and Individual Rights in a Plural World Order' (2009) 46 *CML Rev* 13; S Poli and M Tzanou, 'The *Kadi* Ruling: A Survey of the Literature' (2009) 28 *Oxford Yearbook of European Law* 531; M Cremona, 'EC Competence, "Smart Sanctions" and the *Kadi* case' (2009) 28 *Oxford Yearbook of European Law* 559; E Cannizzaro, 'Security Council Resolutions and EC Fundamental Rights: Some Remarks on the ECJ Decision in the *Kadi* case' (2009) 28 *Oxford Yearbook of European Law* 593; A Ciampi, 'The Potentially Competing Jurisdiction of the European Court of Human Rights and the European Court of Justice' (2009) 28 *Oxford Yearbook of European Law* 601; G Gaja, 'Are the Effects of the UN Charter under EC Law Governed by Article 307 of the EC Treaty?' (2009) 28 *Oxford Yearbook of European Law* 610; N Lavranos, 'The impact of the *Kadi* Judgment on the International Obligations of the EC Member States and the EC' (2009) 28 *Oxford Yearbook of European Law* 616; R Pavoni, 'Freedom to Choose the Legal Means for Implementing UN Security Council Resolutions and the ECJ *Kadi* Judgment: A Misplaced Argument Hindering the Enforcement of International Law in the EC' (2009) 28 *Oxford Yearbook of European Law* 626; M Scheinin, 'Is the ECJ Ruling in *Kadi* Incompatible with International Law?' (2009) 28 *Oxford Yearbook of European Law* 637; C Tomuschat, 'The *Kadi* Case: What Relationship is there between the Universal Legal Order under the Auspices of the United Nations and the EU Legal Order?' (2009) 28 *Oxford Yearbook of European Law* 654; F Fabbrini, 'The Role of the Judiciary in Times of Emergency: Judicial Review of Counter-Terrorism Measures in the United States Supreme Court and the European Court of Justice' (2009) 28 *Oxford Yearbook of European Law* 664; T Tridimas and JA Gutierrez-Fons, 'EU Law, International Law and Economic Sanctions against Terrorism: The Judiciary in Distress?' (2009) 32 *Fordham Journal of International Law* 901; T Tridimas, 'Terrorism and the ECJ: Empowerment and Democracy in the EC Legal Order' (2009) 34 *European Law Review* 103.

be viewed as a procedural one: Member States may not use the European Community to pursue political ends unless they observe the limitations imposed by the rule of law as they are articulated by the substantive rules and institutional arrangements established by the Treaty. The risk of disobedience identified above is inherent in Article 103 which operates only in the sphere of international law and does not interfere with the internal legal systems of UN Member States. There is no evidence to suggest that the courts of third countries will disrespect the UNSC because of the ECJ's judgment. The risk of fragmentation is also inevitable given the growing presence and significance of international law. It is the *quid quo* for the transfer of more powers to international organisations. By demanding higher standards of human rights, the ECJ in fact contributes to the democratisation and legitimacy of international law. The judgment marks the initiation of a constitutional conversation with the UN. In this respect, the ECJ should respond positively to the establishment of higher standards of justice by UN agencies. The higher the protection of human rights offered by them, the greater the deference that the ECJ should accord them.

It has been argued that, by asserting the primacy of EU human rights over the UN, the ECJ is behaving towards the Security Council in the way that the German and Italian Constitutional Courts behaved towards it in the aftermath of *Internationale Handelsgesellschaft*.[11] There is some truth in this observation. It is correct to say that judicial bodies feel very protective of their own jurisdiction. Just as national constitutional courts consider themselves the guardians of their constitutions, the ECJ sees as its task to safeguard what it perceives to be the integrity and the values of the EU legal order. However, there does not appear to be any inconsistency on the part of the ECJ. In its case law, it offered a set of endogenous standards for the protection of fundamental rights as a *quid pro quo* for asserting the primacy of EU law. No such set of standards appears to exist as yet at UN level.

Kadi must be viewed, first and foremost, as a statement of principle. It marks the beginning and not the end of the enquiry. Three points may perhaps be noted in relation to the case. First, the ECJ annulled the contested regulation on grounds of procedure and not on grounds of substance. Secondly, it preserved the effects of the regulation for a limited time, thus giving the opportunity to the Council to comply with process rights. Thirdly, the judgment tells us little about the way the ECJ would balance the need for public security and the prevention of terrorism, on the one hand, and the protection of the rights of the individual, on the other hand. In the circumstances of the case, there was no statement of reasons and a complete absence of the rights of defence. *Kadi* confirms that the

[11] Case 11/70 *Internationale Handelsgesellschaft v Einfuhr- und Vorratsstelle Getreide* [1970] ECR 1125.

executive enjoys no immunity, but does not tell us by what standards it will be held accountable.[12]

III. VALIDITY AND INTERPRETATION OF REGULATION NO 881/2002

A. Issues of Validity

The judgment in *Kadi* was followed by the CFI in *Othman*[13] and by the ECJ itself in *Hassan and Ayadi*.[14] Both cases related to sanctions lists prescribed by the UN Sanctions Committee and implemented by Regulation No 881/2002.[15]

In *Othman*,[16] the applicant had initiated proceedings in 2001 but they were suspended pending the outcome of the judgment in *Kadi*. Upon resumption of the proceedings, the CFI found for the applicant. Given the judgment of the ECJ in *Kadi*, it is not possible to see how the CFI could have reached any other conclusion. The judgment of the CFI was different, however, in one respect. The CFI denied the Council's request to maintain temporarily the effects of the contested regulation. It did so on two grounds.[17] It held that the period that had already elapsed since the delivery of the ECJ's judgment in *Kadi* far exceeded the maximum period of three months allowed by the ECJ in that case to enable the Council to remedy the breach of process rights. Since the applicant's situation was comparable to those of the appellants in *Kadi*, the Council could not have been unaware that it should have taken the same steps in relation to the applicant as those required in *Kadi*. This is an interesting pronouncement.

The CFI gave a second reason which made it inappropriate to preserve the effects of the contested regulation. It pointed out a difference between an ECJ judgment and a CFI judgment. Under Article 60 of the Statute of the ECJ, CFI rulings declaring a regulation to be void take effect only from the date of expiry of the two-month period allowed for appeal to the ECJ or, if an appeal has been brought, as from the date of dismissal of the appeal. Thus, in any event, in addition to the time elapsed since the delivery of the ECJ's judgment in *Kadi*, the

[12] For a more detailed discussion of process rights, see the judgments of the CFI in the *OMPI* cases referred to in n 3 above. Note also that, following the judgment in *Kadi*, the Commission by a new regulation re-included Mr Kadi's name in the sanctions list. The new regulation was challenged before the CFI, *inter alia*, on the ground that it suffered from the same procedural irregularities as Regulation No 881/2002. See Case T-85/09 *Kadi v Commission* (*Kadi II*) (introduced on 26 February 2009 . The General Court delivered its judgment on 30 September 2010. It accepted the arguments of the applicant and annulled the new regulation on grounds of breach of the rights of defence, the right to judicial protection and the right to property. Appeals have now been lodged aginst the judgment in *Kadi II* by the Commission (C-584/10), the Council (C-593/10 P), and the UK (C-595/10 P).

[13] Case T-318/01 *Othman v Council* [2009] ECR II-1627.

[14] Joined Cases C-399 and C-403/06 P *Hassan and Ayadi v Council and Commission*, judgment of 3 December 2009, *nyr*.

[15] Above n 2.

[16] Case T-318/01 *Othman*, above n 13.

[17] *Ibid*, paras 97–98.

Council had an additional period of at least two months in order to remedy the infringements found.

The CFI's approach suggests that the power to maintain in force the effects of a measure vitiated by illegality is to be used sparingly. It is, after all, an exceptional power which allows an illegal measure to produce effects on a temporary basis in order to satisfy a higher interest of justice. One may have some sympathy with the Council's position in *Kadi* since the sanctions lists originated from the UN, and it would not be possible for the Council to adduce any evidence or provide a statement of reasons to the applicant without first referring the matter to the Sanctions Committee, which the Council appears to have done.[18] Nevertheless, the obligation to comply with process rights cannot be viewed merely as a 'best efforts' obligation. It is an absolute one. Otherwise, one would run the risk of nullifying the substantive findings of the judgment by delaying compliance with the ruling for an indefinite period of time. Compliance with the judgments of the ECJ cannot be at the discretion of a third party—in this case, the UN Sanctions Committee.

In *Hassan and Ayadi*,[19] the applicants' assets had been frozen by Regulation No 881/2002. Their actions for annulment pre-dated the ECJ's judgment in *Kadi* and, at first instance,[20] the CFI rejected their actions on the basis of a reasoning similar to that in its judgment in *Kadi*.[21] When the applicants appealed against the CFI judgment, the case raised an interesting issue of procedure. Following the judgment of the ECJ in *Kadi*, the Commission by Regulation No 954/2009[22] amended Regulation No 881/2002 and decided, after hearing the applicants, to include them again in the sanctions list with retroactive effect. The question therefore arose whether, in view of the withdrawal of Regulation No 881/2002 and its retroactive replacement by Regulation No 954/2009, it was still necessary to rule on the appeal.

The ECJ answered in the affirmative. It held that the adoption of Regulation No 954/2009 could not be regarded as equivalent to annulment 'pure and simple' of Regulation No 881/2002.[23] Regulation No 954/2009 had kept the names of the appellants in the sanctions list with retroactive force, so that their assets continued to be frozen for the period for which Regulation No 881/22002 was applicable, although the purpose of their actions was precisely to have their names removed from the sanctions list. The adoption of Regulation No 954/2009 could not, therefore, be considered to be a fact occurring after the judgments under appeal and

[18] See paras 72 and 73 of the judgment.

[19] Above n 14.

[20] Case T-40/04 *Hassan v Council and Commission* [2006] ECR II-52; Case T-253/02 *Ayadi v Council* [2006] ECR II-2139.

[21] The CFI held that, since the sanctions list originated in UNSC resolutions, the CFI did not have jurisdiction to examine the compatibility of Regulation No 881/2002 with fundamental rights as they are protected in the EU legal order but only as they are recognised under *jus cogens*, and that, in the circumstances, the requirements of *jus cogens* had been met.

[22] [2009] OJ L269/20.

[23] *Hassan*, above n 14, para 61.

capable of rendering the appeals devoid of purpose.[24] The Court further observed that Regulation No 954/2009 was not yet definitive in that it could be the subject of an action for annulment. It therefore remained possible that Regulation No 881/2002 might come back into force in relation to the appellants in the event that Regulation No 954/2009 was challenged successfully.[25]

On substance, the ECJ allowed the appeal on the ground that the CFI's reasoning was marred by the same errors in law as those in its judgment in *Kadi*, and proceeded to annul Regulation No 881/2002 in so far as it applied to the appellants. In this case, the ECJ did not need to maintain the effects of the regulation in force since it had already been replaced by Regulation No 954/2009.

B. Issues of Interpretation

While *Kadi*, *Othman* and *Hassan* questioned the validity of Regulation No 881/2002, *M and Others v HM Treasury* gave rise to issues pertaining to its interpretation.[26] The Court was called upon to interpret Article 2(2) of the Regulation, which states as follows:

> No funds shall be made available, directly or indirectly, to or for the benefit of, a natural or legal person, group or entity designated by the Sanctions Committee and listed in Annex I.

Article 2a of the Regulation, which was added to give effect to UNSC Resolution 1452(2002), provides for an exception to the effect that the prohibition in Article 2(2) does not apply to funds which the competent authorities of the Member States have determined to be, with the approval of the Sanctions Committee, necessary to cover basic expenses, such as payments for food, rent and medical treatment. The UK Treasury decided that various social security benefits, including income support and housing benefit, payable to spouses of listed persons were caught by the prohibition in Article 2(2). The rationale of the Treasury was that, because the above benefits might be used to cover the basic needs of households to which listed persons belong, they are made indirectly available for their benefit within the meaning of Article 2(2). Consequently, the Treasury decided that such benefits could be paid only if they were covered by an exception under Article 2a which took the form of a licence. Such licences were issued to various public authorities, permitting them to continue to pay social benefits to spouses of listed persons, subject to certain conditions. The House of Lords considered that the Treasury's licensing system made for an intrusive regime that was not required by Article 2(2), and sought a preliminary

[24] *Ibid*, para 62.

[25] *Ibid*, para 63. On that ground the Court distinguished the contested regulation from the measure at issue in its earlier order in Case C-123/92 *Lezzi Pietro* v *Commission* [1993] ECR I-809.

[26] Case C-340/08 *The Queen on the application of M and Others v HM Treasury*, judgment of 29 April 2010, *nyr*. For a previous case pertaining to the interpretation of the sanctions regime, see Case C-117/06 *Möllendorf-Niehuus* [2007] ECR I-8361.

reference on whether the payment of social security benefits to the spouses of listed persons was caught by the prohibition in Article 2(2).

The ECJ answered this question in the negative. It identified differences in the various language versions of the regulation and held that a literal interpretation of Article 2(2) was not by itself capable of establishing its meaning. It noted that, in the English version, the prohibition in Article 2(2) included making funds available indirectly for the benefit of a listed person, and would thus cover the payment of a social security benefit to the spouse of a listed person. Whilst that interpretation was also supported by the Hungarian, Dutch, Finnish and Swedish versions, other groups of languages did not countenance it.[27] The ECJ also identified differences in the language versions of the UNSC resolutions to which the regulation was intended to give effect. In view of such divergences, it held that Article 2(2) must be interpreted in the light of the purpose and the general scheme of the legislation of which it forms part, and account must also be taken of the substance of Resolution 1390(2002) to which it intended to give effect.[28]

The Court held that, in the light of the objectives of the regulation, the sanctions applied only to those assets that could be turned into funds, goods or services capable of being used to support terrorist activities.[29] Essentially, in the circumstances of the case, the Treasury had followed an erroneous interpretation of Article 2(2). Its construction was not based on any danger whatsoever that the social security benefits might be diverted in order to support terrorist activities. It had not been argued that the spouses concerned handed over those funds to a listed person instead of allocating them to their basic household expenses. Such a misappropriation of funds would, in any event, be covered by Article 2(2) and constitute an offence punishable under national criminal law. It was also hard to imagine how those funds could support terrorist activities, since the benefits were fixed at a level intended to meet only strictly vital needs.[30]

Thus, in *M v HM Treasury* the Court was led to a narrow interpretation of Article 2(2) on the basis of a teleological interpretation. It is notable, however, that it did not look at the objectives of the regulation before establishing textual ambiguity in the light of the linguistic variations in Article 2(2). Its greater reliance on the text is attributable to the fact that the measure in issue was a regulation which needs to be applied uniformly throughout the EU.

Although human rights considerations are present in the judgment, they are less prominent than in the *Kadi* line of cases. The Court gave an additional reason

[27] The Court held that in the Spanish, French, Portuguese and Romanian texts, the prohibition referred to the 'use' of funds for the benefit of a listed person. These versions did not support the argument that, by making social security benefits available to the spouses of listed persons, the authorities used those funds for the benefit of the latter. A third group of language versions, such as those in German and Italian, did not fall within either of the above categories and used their own terminology. See *M v HM* Treasury, above n 26, para 43.

[28] *Ibid*, para 49.

[29] *Ibid*, paras 54–58.

[30] *Ibid*, paras 59–61.

in favour of a narrow interpretation of Article 2(2). Applying the presumption of constitutional interpretation, it held that, in construing EU legislation, preference should be given, as far as possible, to the interpretation which renders the provision consistent with the general principles of EU law and, more specifically, the principle of legal certainty.[31] That principle requires legislation which imposes economic sanctions and involves the imposition of penalties for their infringement to be clear and precise, so that the persons concerned, including third parties such as the social security bodies involved in the main proceedings, might know unambiguously their rights and duties. A construction which would bring the payment of social security benefits within the scope of Article 2(2) would engender legal uncertainty, in particular in triangular situations where funds are made available not to a listed person but someone close to him.[32]

What are the implications of the judgment? Since the payment of a social security benefit is not covered by the prohibition in Article 2(2), it follows that it cannot be made subject to a licence under UK implementing measures. It must be paid to the spouse freely without the need to be covered by the exception in Article 2a.[33] If, however, instead of being allocated to meeting basic household or other permissible expenses, the benefit was diverted in order to support terrorist activities, that would be a violation of the prohibition in Article 2(2) and carry criminal penalties under the UK implementing legislation.[34]

An interesting question which arises here is this: Can the Treasury introduce a licensing system not on the basis that the payment of a social security benefit to a spouse is prohibited under Article 2(2), but in order to enforce the prohibition in that article, ie as a mechanism to ensure that such payments cannot be diverted to terrorist activities? The answer appears to be in the affirmative. It would then be a matter of examining the conditions to which payment of the benefit was made subject. The judgment in *M v HM Treasury* should not be read as prohibiting a licensing system but as allowing one in so far as it is necessary to ensure compliance with the prohibition in Article 2(2), and subject to respect for human rights and the principle of proportionality. The unspoken principles underlying the reasoning of the Court are respect for human dignity and the right to family life. The conditions to which payment of the social security benefit was subject

[31] *Ibid*, para 64.

[32] *Ibid*, paras 64–66.

[33] The Court also stated that the narrow interpretation of Art 2(2) did not render the exception in Art 2a superfluous. That exception applies in cases where funds are made available directly or indirectly to a listed person and not to a third party, since, in such cases, the listed person can decide how to use those funds, and this in turn involves a danger of their being diverted for terrorist purposes. *Ibid*, para 71.

[34] *Ibid*, paras 58–59.

appeared too harsh and in breach of the right to dignity and the right to family life, although the Court did not expressly state so. [35]

C. Sanctions Against Nuclear Proliferation

Othman and *Hassan* contrast with *Melli Bank*,[36] where the CFI upheld the freezing of assets in a UK bank in implementation of a sanctions regime seeking to avoid the proliferation of nuclear weapons.[37] The case raised interesting issues pertaining, *inter alia*, to the vigour of judicial review, the Council's discretionary powers and the risk assessment carried out by the CFI.

The origins of the case lie in sanctions imposed by the UNSC on Iran. Melli Bank plc was a UK subsidiary of BMI, an Iranian bank controlled by the Iranian State. The assets of both banks were frozen by Council Decision 2008/475,[38] adopted on the basis of Council Regulation No 423/2007[39] which, in turn, gave effect to UNSC Resolution 1737(2006). Article 7(1) of Regulation No 423/2007 provides for the freezing of funds of the persons and entities designated by the Security Council. Article 7(2) extends the sanctions to persons and entities associated with Iran's nuclear program. More specifically, Articles 7(2)(a) and 7(2)(b) provide for the freezing of funds of entities which have been identified as being engaged in, directly associated with or providing support for, Iran's nuclear activities. Furthermore, Article 7(2)(d) provides for the freezing of funds of a legal person owned or controlled by an entity referred to under Article 7(2)(a) or 7(2)(b). The assets of BMI were frozen under Article 7(2). The freezing order was extended to Melli Bank's assets on the basis of Article 7(2)(d), as an entity owned or controlled by BMI.

Melli Bank argued that Article 7(2)(d) did not require the Council to freeze automatically the assets of all legal persons owned or controlled by entities whose funds had been frozen by virtue of Article 7(2)(a) or (b); and that if Article 7(2)(d) was interpreted to remove all discretion from the Council, it would run counter to the principle of proportionality. The CFI rejected this argument based on a textual argument and a teleological interpretation founded on a cautious assessment of risk. It held that Article 7(2)(d) uses peremptory language stating that all

[35] These conditions were the following: (a) the benefits had to be paid into a bank account from which the spouse concerned could draw only £10 in cash for each member of the household; other payments had to be made by debit card; (b) the spouse concerned had to send a monthly account to the Treasury detailing all her expenditure, and enclosing receipts for the goods purchased and a bank statement; (c) the licence included a warning to the spouse that it was a criminal offence to make funds available to her husband since he was a listed person. See the Al-Qa'eda and Taliban (United Nations Measures) Order 2002 (SI 2002/111) Art 7.

[36] Joined Cases T-246 and T-332/08 *Melli Bank plc v Council*, judgment of 9 July 2009, *nyr*.

[37] On the substantive policies on non-proliferation pursued by the EU, see ch 10 in this volume.

[38] [2008] OJ L163/29.

[39] [2007] OJ L103/1.

funds belonging to an entity owned or controlled by a person engaged in nuclear proliferation 'shall be frozen'. It followed that the freezing of funds was obligatory. The Council was under an obligation to undertake an evaluation in order to determine whether an entity is 'owned or controlled' by a person identified as engaged in nuclear proliferation, but once such ownership or control was ascertained, the Council enjoyed no discretion.[40] The CFI held that this interpretation was also in line with the objectives of the regulation, which was to prevent nuclear proliferation and, more generally, maintain international peace and security.[41]

The CFI further held that, in determining whether an entity was owned or controlled by another body, the Council had to take into account all the relevant aspects of the specific case, such as the degree of operational independence of the entity or the possible effect of the supervision to which it was subject by public regulators. In contrast, the nature of that entity's activities and the possible lack of any link between those activities and nuclear proliferation were not relevant criteria. Applying a risk-averse approach, the CFI held[42]:

> When the funds of an entity identified as being engaged in nuclear proliferation are frozen, there is a not insignificant danger that that entity may exert pressure on the entities it owns or controls in order to circumvent the effect of the measures applying to it, by encouraging them either to transfer their funds to it, directly or indirectly, or to carry out transactions which it cannot itself perform by reason of the freezing of its funds. That being so, it must be considered that the freezing of the funds of entities owned or controlled by an entity identified as being engaged in nuclear proliferation is necessary and appropriate in order to ensure the effectiveness of the measures adopted vis-à-vis that entity and to ensure that those measures are not circumvented.

The CFI also found that other less restrictive mechanisms might not guarantee fulfilment of the objectives of the regulation. Thus, the existence of rules prohibiting the carrying out of transactions with entities identified as being engaged in terrorism was not in itself a guarantee that such transactions would not take place. Nor could the reinforcement of supervision or financial transparency fill the risk gap.[43]

There are apparent similarities between *M v HM Treasury* and *Melli Bank*. Both cases involved the imposition of sanctions on persons associated with the primary targets of the sanctions regime. These similarities are superficial, however, whilst the differences are striking. In *M v HM Treasury*, the funds in question were insignificant. In *Melli*, human dignity, personal freedom and the right to life were not an issue. *Melli* involved a banking group controlled by the State which was the subject of sanctions. The CFI was correct to apply a high standard of scrutiny

[40] *Melli Bank*, above n 36, paras 63–65.
[41] *Ibid*, para 66.
[42] *Ibid*, para 103.
[43] *Ibid*, paras 71, 17, 108.

on the existence of ownership or control but a lower standard on the legislature's assessment of risk.

The CFI opted for a substantive rather than formal interpretation of the concept of control. It held that ownership of a company by another is not in itself a determining criterion. It had to be examined whether, because the applicant was owned by BMI, there was a considerable likelihood that it might be prompted to circumvent the sanctions adopted against its parent company.[44] The CFI sought guidance from competition law as to when the conduct of a subsidiary may be imputed to a parent undertaking,[45] and placed particular emphasis on the powers of the parent to appoint the directors of the subsidiary. It held that the fact that one entity is wholly owned by another generally means that the latter is entitled to appoint the directors of the former and may therefore exercise actual control over its management and its staff.[46] Whilst the CFI left the door open for the possibility that the freezing of funds of a company which is owned by a listed person might not be justified, this would occur only in 'extraordinary circumstances'.[47] The fact that the applicant was wholly-owned by BMI created a presumption which was very difficult to discharge, and which the applicant failed to discharge in the circumstances. Thus, the fact that BMI did not intervene in the day-to-day running of the applicant was of no relevance, since it did not affect the influence exerted by BMI, directly or indirectly, over the applicant's staff.[48] The fact that the applicant had complied with all the restrictive measures and the applicable sanctions was also irrelevant. Likewise, the dissuasive nature of the penalties to which the members of the applicant's staff would be exposed was insufficient, since there was a risk that the violation of the sanctions could be disguised by the use of intermediaries. In short, the CFI considered that *ex posto facto* means of intervention were no substitute for a strict preventative regime.

The CFI also upheld the autonomy of the Council's power to impose economic sanctions under Article 7(2). It will be remembered that Article 7(1) of the regulation provides for the freezing of funds of persons designated by the Security Council. The CFI held that Article 7(2) was independent of the adoption of economic sanctions by the UNSC, its purpose being to enable the Council to adopt sanctions against entities that were not the subject of similar measures decided by the Security Council. This had two implications. First, it meant that the compatibility of Article 7(2)(d) with the principle of subsidiarity could not be assessed by reference to the UNSC resolution. Secondly, the applicant could not claim that it had unjustifiably been equated with entities on which the Security

[44] *Ibid*, para 121.

[45] *Ibid*, para 121, referring to Case 48/69 *Imperial Chemical Industries* v *Commission* [1972] ECR 619, para 133, and Case C-73/95 P *Viho* v *Commission* [1996] ECR I-5457, para 16.

[46] *Melli Bank*, above n 36, para 123.

[47] *Ibid*, para 124.

[48] *Ibid*, para 125.

Council had imposed sanctions since the criteria for their imposition in each case were different.[49]

The CFI considered that the statement of reasons provided by the Council, although 'exceptionally concise', was sufficient to satisfy the requirement of reasoning. It also rejected claims that the right to property and the right to carry on an economic activity had been breached, recalling that they are not absolute prerogatives and that the importance of combating nuclear proliferation was such as to justify substantial negative consequences.[50]

Melli suggests a more nuanced approach to the assessment of risk than other cases on economic sanctions. However, the material differences from cases concerning the imposition of sanctions against suspected terrorists are the legislative background of the sanctions regime, the undisputed proximity of the applicant with the main target of sanctions and the lack of engagement of civil liberties. The case had to do more with substantive policies than with process rights, and the CFI was correct to defer to the choices of the Council.

IV. THE UK SUPREME COURT AND THE SEARCH FOR 'OLDER, NOBLER MORE ENDURING VALUES'

The UN sanctions regime also gave rise to important issues pertaining to the rule of law in English courts.[51] It is fitting that the first case heard by the new Supreme Court of the United Kingdom raised issues pertaining to constitutionalism, human rights and the separation of powers. In *HM Treasury v Mohammed Jabar Ahmed and others*,[52] the Treasury had frozen the funds of the appellants on the basis of delegated legislation passed to give effect to UNSC resolutions. The appellants fell into two groups. Those in the first group had been classified as designated persons under the Terrorism (United Nations Measures) Order 2006 ('the TO'), [53] which had been adopted to give effect to UNSC Resolution 1373(2001). Those in the second group had their resources frozen under the Al-Qaida and Taliban (United Nations Measures) Order 2006 ('the AQO')[54] as persons whose names appeared in

[49] *Ibid*, paras 103 and 138.

[50] *Ibid*, paras 111–12.

[51] The words quoted in the heading to this section come from Lord Bingham, 'The Case of *Liversidge v Anderson*: The Rule of Law Amid the Clash of Arms' (2009) 43 *The International Lawyer* 33, 38, where he stated: '[W]e are entitled to be proud that even in that extreme national emergency there was one voice—eloquent and courageous—which asserted older, nobler, more enduring values: the right of the individual against the State; the duty to govern in accordance with law; the role of the courts as guarantor of legality and individual right; the priceless gift, subject only to constraints by law established, of individual freedom.' They were cited with approval by Lord Hope in *HM Treasury v Mohammed Jabar Ahmed and others* [2010] EWCA Civ 1187, at [6].

[52] *HM Treasury v Mohammed Jabar Ahmed*, above n 51.

[53] The *Terrorism (United Nations Measures) Order 2006* (SI 2006/2657).

[54] The Al-Qaida and Taliban (United Nations Measures) Order 2006 (SI 2006/2952).

the UN Sanctions Committee List.[55] That list had been adopted by the Sanctions Committee under UNSC Resolution 1333(2000), which required UN Member States to freeze the funds of Osama bin Laden, the Al Qaida network and all other individuals or entities associated with them.

Both the TO and the AQO had been made by the Treasury under powers conferred by section 1 of the United Nations Act 1946 by which the UK gave effect to the UN Charter. Section 1 enables the Government to take, by Order in Council, any measures which are 'necessary or expedient' to implement UNSC resolutions adopted under Article 41 of the Charter. The fundamental issue in the case was whether the Treasury had power under section 1 to introduce economic sanctions by means of an Order in Council. The Supreme Court answered in the negative, applying a separation of powers rationale and relying on the principle of legality. At the heart of the Court's distrust lay the fact that orders made under section 1 of the 1946 Act are not subject to any parliamentary scrutiny. They are simply laid before Parliament for information, but the Parliament does not have any input as to their content. The judgment raised a number of issues, and the reasoning of the Supreme Court calls for detailed consideration. The two pieces of delegated legislation, the TO and the AQO, give rise to different issues and should be examined separately.

A. The TO

The TO was introduced to give effect to UNSC Resolution 1373(2001), paragraph (c) of which required States to freeze funds and other financial resources of persons who commit, or attempt to commit, terrorist acts, or participate in or facilitate the commission of terrorist acts. The TO empowered the Treasury to freeze the funds, *inter alia*, of any person where it had 'reasonable grounds for suspecting' that the person was involved in the commission of terrorist acts. The question was whether, by extending the sanctions to such suspects, the Treasury had exceeded the powers granted to it under section 1 of the 1946 Act.

The Supreme Court gave an affirmative reply. The starting point of its reasoning was the principle of legality. Under this principle, as articulated by Lord Hoffmann in *Simms*,[56] where Parliament intends to legislate contrary to human rights, it has to use clear and unambiguous language. In the absence of express language or necessary implication, the courts will presume that the general words of a statute are intended to be subject to the basic rights of the individual.[57] This

[55] One of the appellants, identified as appellant G, had been designated under both the TO and the AQO.

[56] *R v Secretary of State for the Home Department, ex p Simms* [2000] 2 AC 115, at 131; and see also *R v Secretary of State for the Home Department, ex p Pierson* [1998] AC 539, at 573 *per* Lord Browne-Wilkinson.

[57] *Ex p Simms*, above n 54, at 131.

dictated a narrow interpretation of the 1946 Act. Given the harsh effects of the freezing regime on human rights, the TO was found to be beyond the scope of the 1946 Act.

Lord Hope stated that since UNSC Resolution 1373(2001) was not phrased in terms of reasonable suspicion and left the standard of proof to the Member States to decide, it was not necessary to introduce the 'reasonable suspicion' test in order to comply with the resolution. Lord Phillips agreed that the TO was beyond the scope of the 1946 Act. After reviewing the wording of Resolution 1373 and other UNSC resolutions, he came to the view that Resolution 1373 did not require expressly or by implication the freezing of the assets of those who were merely suspected of criminal offences.[58] All their Lordships agreed that the consequences of the freezing of assets were dire, and therefore the expediency test of section 1 was not met. Lord Hope stated that the powers of the Treasury were draconian and struck 'at the very heart of the individual's basic rights to live his own life as he chooses'.[59] Notably, he endorsed Sedley LJ's dictum at the Court of Appeal that the sanctions regime interfered not only with the economic freedoms of the individuals involved, but also, ultimately, with their freedom of movement. Designated persons effectively became 'prisoners of the State'.[60] Lord Rodger stated that if measures which affect very basic rights of the individual are to be taken, it is for Parliament to deliberate and determine that the benefits of giving the Treasury such powers outweigh the potential disadvantages, and that it is therefore expedient to adopt such measures to fulfil the obligations arising from UNSC Resolution 1373(2001).[61] He considered, however, that section 1 of the 1946 Act would authorise the Government to make an Order in Council, even with these far-reaching effects, provided that it had only a limited life-span and was replaced, as soon as practically possible, by equivalent legislation passed by Parliament. In this way the United Kingdom could promptly fulfil its obligations under the United Nations Charter.[62]

Some aspects of the Supreme Court's reasoning are particularly instructive. Lord Hope took into account that other UN Member States had introduced measures to comply with UNSC resolutions through primary legislation providing for safeguards, and had not found it necessary to rely exclusively on unlimited delegation of powers to the Executive.[63] He also noted that the Anti-Terrorism, Crime and Security Act 2001, which had been enacted in the aftermath of the events of 9/11, made provision for freezing orders which were more precisely worded and contained various safeguards. The orders made under the 2001 Act were subject to the affirmative resolution procedure and ceased to have effect after two years.

[58] *Ibid*, 137.
[59] *Ibid*, para 60.
[60] *Ibid*, para 125.
[61] *Ibid*, para 174.
[62] *Ibid*, para 176.
[63] *Ibid*, para 50.

He stated that the powers given under that Act and orders passed to implement it would have enabled the Government to comply with the UNSC resolutions.

B. The AQO

The applicants whose resources had been frozen on the basis of the AQO were in a different position, in that they had been subject to freezing orders not on the basis of a reasonable suspicion but because their names had been included in the list maintained by the UN Sanctions Committee set up by UNSC Resolution 1267(1999). Here, the Treasury had not gone beyond what was strictly required to comply with the UN. The appellants argued that:

a) the AQO was unlawful because it breached Articles 6 and 8 of the European Convention on Human Rights (ECHR) and Article 1 of Protocol 1 to that Convention; and
b) that the AQO was *ultra vires* section 1 of the 1946 Act because there was no judicial remedy against the 1267 Committee.

The first claim was unanimously rejected, while the second was accepted.

The claim that the AQO was unlawful because it breached the ECHR was rejected essentially for two reasons. First, all their Lordships rejected the argument that the validity of the AQO could be tested by reference to the articles of the ECHR on the ground that, under Article 103 of the UN Charter, obligations under the Charter take precedence over any other obligations arising under international law. The Supreme Court thus fully endorsed the judgment of the House of Lords in *Al-Jedda*[64] and Lord Bingham's dictum to the effect that, if there was a conflict between the requirements of a UNSC resolution and the requirements of the ECHR, English courts would have no option but to give primacy to the former. Secondly, there was no conclusive proof that the European Court of Human Rights (ECtHR) would itself find a breach of the Convention. Lord Phillips, in particular, read the judgment in *Behrami*[65] as suggesting that the ECtHR was prepared to recognise the primacy of obligations under the UN Charter over Convention obligations.[66]

The appellants also argued that the AQO was contrary to rights emanating from the common law, namely the right to peaceful enjoyment of property and the right of unimpeded access to a court, neither of which could be interfered with except by clear legislative words. Those rights emanated from common law, and therefore their application remained unaffected by Article 103 of the UN

[64] *R (Al-Jedda) v Secretary of State for Defence* [2008] AC 332.

[65] Joined Cases *Behrami and Behrami v France;* Application no 71412/01 *Saramati v France, Germany and Norway* Application no 78166/01 (2007) 45 EHRR SE10.

[66] *HM Treasury v Mohammed Jabar Ahmed*, above n 51, paras 93–98.

Charter which provides for primacy only over international obligations. This argument proved successful.

Lord Hope accepted that the AQO was beyond the scope of section 1 because it exceeded the threshold of permissible interference with fundamental rights. The procedure for listing and de-listing persons before the UN Sanctions Committee did not meet the basic standards of natural justice and procedural fairness. Listed persons were not given reasons for their listing. It was not clear who the members of the Committee were, what rules of evidence they applied or what, if any, degree of independence they enjoyed. In adopting the 1946 Act, Parliament could not have intended to authorise such extensive interference with fundamental rights by a procedure which avoided parliamentary scrutiny.[67] Lord Phillips noted that the UN had gone some way towards addressing human rights concerns: UN guidelines made provision for notifying a listed individual of those parts of a Member State's statement of the case against him that the State considered could be publicly released; also, UNSC Resolution 1730 made express provision for de-listing. However, those provisions fell far short of satisfying the right of access to a court and of fulfilling the requirement of reasoning.[68]

Lord Brown's was the only partially dissenting voice, coming to the conclusion that the TO should be struck down but that the AQO should stand. In his view, the two orders could be distinguished. The TO, by extending the sanctions to persons reasonably suspected of association with terrorism, went beyond what was necessary to give effect to UNSC Resolution 1373(2001). The AQO, by contrast, implemented faithfully the UNSC resolutions to which it sought to give effect.[69] Lord Brown accepted that the AQO was contrary to fundamental principles of human rights, but he viewed this as the inevitable conclusion of UNSC Resolution 1267(1999). He argued that interference with human rights should be subject to parliamentary approval because, that way, it is made subject to political control and Parliament pays the 'political cost' due for interfering with the basic freedoms of the individual. But in this case the political cost rationale did not apply. Given the primacy of UN resolutions under Article 103 of the Charter and the unambiguous obligations flowing from UNSC Resolution 1267(1999), 'there could surely be no political cost in doing what, unless we were flagrantly to violate our UN Charter obligations, the UK had no alternative but to do'.[70] This somewhat functional approach to the principle of legality was rightly rejected by Lord Rodger, who stressed the value of transparency and political control. In his view, the essential issue was that severe restrictions on human rights should not pass unnoticed in the parliamentary process and should be decided by the legislature rather than the executive.[71]

[67] *Ibid*, paras 77–80.
[68] *Ibid*, para 149.
[69] *Ibid*, para 199
[70] *Ibid*, para 204.
[71] *Ibid*, para 186.

C. Assessment of the Judgment

The judgment in *HM Treasury v Mohammed Jabar Ahmed* raises a number of important issues, not all of which can be examined within the confines of this chapter. It suffices to explore here some aspects pertaining to the rule of law and some issues concerning the relevance of EU law.

The Supreme Court appeared to attribute particular importance to the lack of parliamentary scrutiny. Both the TO and the AQO were adopted without any parliamentary oversight. Lord Hope found it unacceptable to confer unlimited discretion on the Executive in deciding how to implement UNSC resolutions in the making of which the Executive itself had participated. That would conflict with 'the basic rules that lie at the heart of our democracy'.[72]

It will be remembered that the TO was found to be *ultra vires* because it exceeded what was necessary to implement Resolution 1373(2001) to which it sought to give effect; whilst the AQO was found to be *ultra vires* because it made severe inroads into basic human rights, which can be introduced by primary legislation alone. This gives rise to the following question in relation to the TO: What would be the response of the Supreme Court if Resolution 1373(2001) expressly cast the net wider and required the freezing of resources of those reasonably suspected of being associated with terrorism? Clearly, in such a case, the argument could be made that an Order in Council was necessary or expedient to implement the resolution. It would still be necessary, however, to examine whether the requirements of the principle of legality were satisfied. The question would be whether an Order in Council, adopted without parliamentary scrutiny, freezing the assets of individuals, would fall within the scope of the delegation of powers permitted by section 1 of the 1946 Act. The Supreme Court accepted that some interference with human rights is possible by Orders in Council in order to give effect to UNSC resolutions. The question is how much interference the Court would be prepared to tolerate under delegated legislation. It might be argued that the AQO imposed a more severe limitation to human rights than the TO since it foreclosed any possibility of judicial review. Still, it is an open question whether in our hypothetical example an Order in Council would survive scrutiny. First, the effects of the freezing of assets on the personal life of the individuals concerned attracted much criticism by the Supreme Court and were described as 'traumatic'.[73] Secondly, their permanent character exacerbated their restrictive effects, making the intrusion into personal freedom and the rights of the individual particularly onerous.[74]

The Supreme Court held in essence that UNSC resolutions which interfere severely with basic human rights may not be introduced by delegated legislation

[72] *Ibid*, para 45.
[73] *Ibid*, *per* Lord Brown, at para 203.
[74] *Ibid*, *per* Lord Mance, at para 230.

which is not subject to parliamentary scrutiny.[75] It is clear that both the TO and the AQO could be introduced by primary legislation. This raises the following question: To what human rights limitations, if any, would primary legislation, passed to comply with obligations arising from a UNSC resolution, be subject? This issue was not examined by the Supreme Court.

A possible source of limitations might be provided by the Human Rights Act 1998. So long as *Al Jedda* remains good law, however, the ECHR cannot trump obligations arising from the UN Charter. The Supreme Court might revisit its position in the event that in *Al Jedda* the Strasbourg Court takes the view that the UN Charter does not take precedence over the Convention. Even in such a case, it would be a matter for English law to decide whether to give priority to the Convention rather than the UN Charter, and how conflicting obligations arising under the two systems might be compromised.

A second source of limitation may be found in EU law. In so far as Member States act within the scope of EU law, they have an obligation to respect fundamental rights as guaranteed in the EU legal order.[76] Under Article 6 of the TEU, as amended by the Treaty of Lisbon, there are essentially three sources of such rights: the EU Charter on Fundamental Rights, the European Convention and the general principles of law articulated by the ECJ. This point is explored further below.[77] A third limitation is found in *jus cogens*. English courts will not give effect to a statute that violates the peremptory rules of international law, although those rules are not defined with clarity and, in general, are so basic that this safeguard will provide protection only in the most extreme of cases.

A fourth limitation can be found in common law and stems from the principle of legality. As Lord Hope put it, the more a measure comes close to affecting the basic rights of the individual, 'the more exacting this scrutiny must become'.[78] English courts will apply a presumption of constitutionality under which a statute will not be interpreted to deny a fundamental right unless the intention of Parliament to this effect is crystal clear. Within the UK constitutional system, which is based on the fundamental principle of parliamentary supremacy, the determining criterion is the intention of Parliament. It would thus be a question of what kind of language the Parliament must use to persuade the courts that it authorises the Executive to breach human rights. The judgment in *HM Treasury v Mohammed Jabar Ahmed* suggests that the Supreme Court is prepared to apply the principle of legality with an asphyxiating effect. Thus, where primary legislation seeks to implement a UNSC resolution that

[75] All their Lordships appeared to agree that a freezing of funds could be introduced by primary legislation. Whether it could also be introduced by delegated legislation which gave a greater role to Parliament, eg an Order in Council which was subject to the affirmative resolution procedure, remains an open question, although it is clear from the judgment that such a move would not be viewed favourably by the Supreme Court.

[76] See Case C-260/89 *ERT* [1991] ECR I-2925.

[77] See section IV.D. below.

[78] *HM Teasury v Mohammed Jabar Ahmed*, above n 51, para 45.

denies a fundamental right, the Court's inquiry is likely to focus on two aspects. First, it will look at the precise wording of the UNSC resolution to determine what effect it is intended to have on human rights and the scope of the restriction it aims to introduce. Given the UN's own commitment to human rights, the Court is likely to apply a strict construction to interferences with human rights and give the benefit of the doubt to an interpretation that provides for the least intrusion possible. Secondly, the Court will examine closely the domestic statute and will expect a high degree of precision. Any interference with human rights which is not absolutely necessary to comply with the UNSC resolution to which the statute intends to give effect, as that resolution is interpreted by the Court, will not be acceptable since Parliament will be presumed not to have intended to implement it.

The difference between English law and EU law is that the former, within the confines of the doctrine of parliamentary supremacy, understands the principle of legality as a rule of construction. English courts will not understand the intention of Parliament to be to violate fundamental rights unless Parliament expressly so states and uses the clearest and most specific language possible.[79] By contrast, this will not do for the EU legislature. Even if the Council makes it clear that it wishes to act in breach of fundamental rights as they are protected in the EU, the Court will strike the measure down, however clear the language used by the Council. In that respect, EU law ascribes to a substantive version of the rule of law, whilst English law follows a formal one. This is not to say, however, that the Court of Justice will necessarily apply a stricter level of scrutiny than that applied by English courts. Neither is it to say that the Court of Justice will necessarily exercise review of the merits rather than review of procedure. The difference of principle is fundamental, but the difference in results may be less so. As Lord Hoffmann put it in *ex p Simms*, by the principle of legality English courts manage to apply 'principles of constitutionality little different from those which exist in countries where the power of the legislature is expressly limited by a constitutional document'.[80] The procedural character of the principle of legality under English law provides a discipline for the accurate and specific drafting of legislation which is absent in EU law. The narrow interpretation given by the Supreme Court to the powers granted to the Executive by the 1946 Act contrasts sharply with the readiness of the ECJ in *Kadi* to accept that the EU had power to adopt economic

[79] Note, however, that the principle of legality may not go as far as the duty of consistent interpretation imposed on English courts by s 3(1) of the Human Rights Act 1998. That section requires that, so far as it is possible to do so, legislation must be read and given effect in a way which is compatible with the Convention rights. Lord Phillips stated that the principle of legality does not permit a court to disregard an unambiguous expression of Parliament intention, although in some cases s 3(1) has been understood as enabling courts to do precisely that: see *HM Treasury v Mohammed Jabar Ahmed*, above n 51, para 117.

[80] *Ex p Simms*, above n 54, at 131, cited with approval by Lord Phillips in *HM Treasury v Mohammed Jabar Ahmed*, above n 51 at para 111.

sanctions against individuals on the somewhat feeble basis of Articles 301, 60(1) and 308 EC.[81]

D. Influence of EU Law

The influence of EU law in *HM Treasury v Mohammed Jabar Ahmed* was only secondary and indirect. The appellants argued that the AQO ran counter to the right to a fair trial, the right to family life and the right to property as protected by the ECHR. They conceded that the judgment of the House of Lords in *Al Jedda* established the primacy of the UN Charter over obligations flowing from the Convention, but invited the Supreme Court to reconsider *Al Jedda* in the light of *Kadi*. The thrust of the argument was that, in the light of *Kadi*, the Strasbourg Court, before which *Al Jedda* was pending, could rule that Article 103 of the UN Charter did not trump the Convention. This argument was precarious. The Supreme Court rightly held that it could not speculate on how the ECtHR would decide in *Al Jedda*.[82] It placed emphasis on the ECtHR's judgment in *Behrami* and took a narrow view of *Kadi*.

Although the Supreme Court was correct to hold that it would be inappropriate to prejudge the decision that the Strasbourg Court might reach in *Al Jedda*, the existing authorities make it far from clear that the Strasbourg Court will accept unequivocally the primacy of UN obligations over the Convention. If that were not to be the case, English courts would be in the unenviable position of having to face a head-on clash between Convention rights and obligations emanating from the UN Charter. The solution offered by Lord Bingham in *Al Jedda* is that, in such a case, the Government must comply with the UN Charter whilst ensuring that the rights guaranteed by the Convention are not infringed to any greater extent than is inherent in the action necessary to comply with the respective UN resolution.[83] It seems that this would entail a balancing exercise performed by reference to a principle of proportionality applied not as a matter of the Convention but as a matter of English law.

Although the relevance of *Kadi* in *HM Treasury v Mohammed Jabar Ahmed* was only indirect, the reading of the ECJ judgment by the Supreme Court was somewhat narrow. Lord Phillips stated that the judgment concerned 'the legitimacy of a Council Regulation judged against the rules of the autonomous and self contained regime instituted under the EC Treaty'.[84] This was echoed by Lord Brown[85] and supported by Lord Hope, who pointed out that the ECJ did not have to face the problem of primacy of UN obligations which Article 103 of the Charter raises

[81] See section I. above.
[82] See eg *HM Treasury v Mohammed Jabar Ahmed*, above n 51, para 74, *per* Lord Hope.
[83] *Al Jedda*, above n 62, para 39, *per* Lord Bingham.
[84] *HM Treasury v Mohammed Jabar Ahmed*, above n 51, para 104, *per* Lord Phillips.
[85] *Ibid*, para 203.

for the Member States of the UN, since the institutions of the EU are not party to the Charter.[86] In *Kadi*, however, the ECJ did not base its reasoning on the fact that the European Community or the EU was not a contracting party to the UN. It rather stated that review of the contested Council regulation which implemented the sanctions list resolution, 'would not entail any challenge to the primacy of that resolution in international law'.[87] Thus, the ECJ based its reasoning on the fact that Article 103 of the UN Charter binds the Member States of the UN in international law only and does not interfere with their internal constitutional arrangements. For the Member States of the EU, part of those arrangements is the principle of primacy of EU law and the other obligations which flow from membership. Thus, if one were to follow the ECJ's federalist rationale as it can be derived from the existing case law, obligations arising from EU law will take precedence over obligations arising from the UN Charter since, for the purposes of Article 103 of the UN Charter, EU law has to be seen as an integral part of national law. The EU, in other words, establishes an internal constitutional space for all EU Member States, which forms part of the domestic law of each Member State and which is not penetrated by the sharp end of Article 103 of the Charter.

Thus, whilst the implication from *HM Treasury v Mohammed Jabar Ahmed* is that the judgment in *Kadi* does not impact on national measures adopted to give effect to UNSC resolutions, this is by no means clear from the reasoning of the ECJ. In *Jabar Ahmed* the Court was not faced with the argument that the AQO might fall within the scope of EU law and that human rights as protected by the EU legal order must therefore be respected. It is worth examining this scenario in more detail.

Suppose that the name of an EU national resident in the UK, who carries on economic activities in other EU States and regularly moves funds from the UK to other States, is included in the UN sanctions list. The freezing of his assets is clearly a restriction on his right to free movement. The precise freedom which may be engaged is less relevant and it depend on the facts: it could be the free movement of capital, his freedom of establishment or his freedom to provide services. The justification for this restriction is to be found in the need to safeguard public security, to combat terrorism and ensure international peace and security, and to comply with the UNSC resolutions which dictate the inclusion of his name in the sanctions list. Under established case law of the ECJ, however, a restriction on free movement can be justified only if it respects fundamental rights as protected in EU law.[88] Does that mean that a national measure implementing the sanctions list must observe EU fundamental rights? The Government could counter-argue that, under Article 351(1) TFEU (ex Article 307(1) EC), obligations arising from

[86] *Ibid*, para 71.

[87] *Kadi*, above n 1, para 288.

[88] See Case C-260/89 *ERT*, above n 74; Case C-368/95 *Vereinigte Familiapress Zeitungsverlags- und Vertreibs GmbH v Bauer Verlag* [1997] ECR I-3689; Case C-71/02 *Herbert Karner Industrie-Auktionen GmbH v Troostwijk GmbH* [2004] ECR I-3025.

pre-existing international agreements concluded by the Member States are not to be affected by the provisions of the EU Treaties. On this basis, EU human rights would not be applicable, since membership of the UN by the individual EU States pre-dates their membership of the European Community and the EU.

This argument, however, encounters an important objection. Article 351(1) TFEU (ex Article 307(1) EC) does not give the complete picture. Article 351(2) TFEU (ex Article 307(2) EC) states that, to the extent that pre-existing international agreements are not compatible with the EU Treaties, Member States must take all appropriate steps to eliminate the incompatibilities established. This is a 'best efforts' clause which has received a strict interpretation favourable to the EU. It follows that, in so far as a UNSC resolution breaches fundamental rights as guaranteed by EU law, Member States, including national courts, are under an obligation to eliminate that breach. The precise obligations which flow from this are not clear and will need to be decided on a case-by-case basis. It is important to note, however, that in *Kadi* the ECJ expressly held that Article 307 (now Article 351 TFEU) could not 'be understood to authorise any derogation from the principles of liberty, democracy and respect for human rights and fundamental freedoms enshrined in Article 6(1) EU'[89] and 'may in no circumstances permit any challenge to the principles that form part of the very foundations of the Community legal order, one of which is the protection of fundamental rights'.[90] The peremptory language used by the ECJ suggests that Article Article 351 TFEU (ex Article 307 EC) does not preclude judicial review on grounds of compatibility with EU rights of a national measure which has been adopted to give effect to a UNSC resolution but which falls within the scope of EU law. A number of consequential issues arise in this context. Could it be said, for example, that the standard of scrutiny of such a national measure would be lower than that applicable to determine the compatibility of a measure adopted by the EU institutions? It is not clear why the answer to this question should be in the affirmative.

V. CONCLUSION

There is a striking degree of convergence among courts in the EU, the UK and beyond that responses to emergencies which make for serious intrusions on fundamental rights should be channeled through constitutional procedures and institutional practices which are most respectful of democracy, accountability and the rights of the individual. The EU legal system is committed to a substantive version of the rule of law, while English law, bred in the doctrine of parliamentary supremacy, subscribes to a formal version. Despite the fact that the two systems

[89] *Kadi*, above n 1, para 303.
[90] *Ibid*, para 304.

commence from different points of principle, the difference in judicial outcomes is less clear. English courts have proved skilful in applying the principle of legality, with an asphyxiating effect for the Executive.

Neither *Kadi* nor the judgment in *HM Treasury v Mohammed Jabar Ahmed* addresses some fundamental problems which may result from the interaction between national law, UN obligations and EU law. In particular, it is not clear whether, in the event of a conflict between obligations flowing from EU law and obligations flowing from the UN Charter, national courts will give precedence to the former or to the latter. As a matter of EU law, the answer appears clear, although the ECJ did not have to confront the issue directly in *Kadi*: national courts should give effect to EU law obligations. This solution is dictated by the principle of primacy and the fact that the ECJ treats EU and national law as two tiers of the same legal system which can be viewed as part of domestic law for the purposes of Article 103 of the UN Charter. Any other solution would contradict the solutions reached by the ECJ. If, under the principle of primacy of EU law, the latter takes precedence over the national constitutions, why should it not take precedence over obligations emanating from membership of the UN? After all, those obligations can be given effect only in accordance with the national constitutions and, from the point of view of EU law, are part of them and thus subordinate to EU law. Whether such strict EU law orthodoxy would be accepted by the national courts remains to be seen. Too strict an orthodoxy carries with it a higher risk of rebellion. The bottom line is that we are faced again with the problem of *competenz competenz* to which there is no conclusive answer. Is it national courts or the ECJ which have ultimate authority to determine the scope of application of EU law? In English law, the parameters are firmly set by the doctrine of parliamentary supremacy. It will thus be a question of ascertaining what the judiciary perceives to be the true wishes of Parliament as to the priority between EU and UN obligations in a given context.

Part Three

Security Governance

8

Europe's Counter-terrorism Law(s): Outlines of a Critical Approach

JAN KLABBERS

I. INTRODUCTION

FINDING MY WAY in Greenwich Village in the rain in September 2009, I walk past a station of the New York Fire Department. Inside, something of an event seems to be going on: people are gathered together, others hasten to make their way inside, and the atmosphere seems to be a bit eerie; no lighthearted laughter but solemn faces, people staring into the distance with a vacant look in their eyes, or talking together but not really engaging with one another. Many are seemingly having a quiet moment for themselves, but are doing so together. And then I remember: the date is 11 September 2009, and it is exactly eight years ago that the Twin Towers went down.

Ever since what has simply become known as 9/11, terrorism has occupied a prominent place on the global political agenda, and many a study has appeared outlining the emerging international legal regime on terrorism.[1] Somewhat surprisingly perhaps, it has been less well noticed that the EU too has been working hard on devising an anti-terrorism regime: there are EU anti-terrorism policies, there is an official EU anti-terrorism strategy and there is a handful of pertinent legal instruments as well.[2]

The purpose of this chapter is threefold. The first, and rather modest, aim is to provide a brief overview of the international legal regime, and explain why it is that this is, as yet, far from comprehensive. Then it looks at the EU's Counter-terrorism Strategy and, lastly, it provides an overview of the general approaches

[1] See, eg, T Becker, *Terrorism and the State: Rethinking the Rules of State Responsibility* (Oxford, Hart Publishing, 2006), and M Lehto, *International Responsibility for Terrorist Acts: A Shift Towards More Indirect Forms of Responsibility* (doctoral thesis, University of Lapland, 2008).

[2] These include a Council Common Position on Combating Terrorism 2001/930/CFSP, [2001] OJ L344/90; Council Framework Decision 2002/475/JHA, [2002] OJ L164/3, substantively amended by Council Framework Decision 2008/919/JHA, [2008] OJ L330/21, and Council Regulation (EC) 2580/2001, [2001] OJ L344/70. The European Union Counter-terrorism Strategy was adopted by the Justice and Home Affairs Council Meeting of 1 December 2005.

in the three pillars which comprised the EU prior to the entry into force of the Lisbon Treaty, picking up a few salient issues while by and large ignoring some of the technical details, and devoting a word or two to coherence.[3] Hence, the main, if modest, purpose of the present chapter is to provide an overview of the way the EU authorities aim to address terrorism.

Yet while the idea is to provide a brief overview of some of the more salient aspects of the nascent EU regime on counter-terrorism, it is to do so 'with a purpose'. The main proposition underlying this chapter is that, like the international legal regime, the EU's terrorism policy is neither very coherent nor comprehensive. It is riddled with many of the same tensions which hamper the emergence of a coherent regime under international law; and while some of the problems making a universal approach difficult on the international level are missing, their place is taken by other political problems, most notably the ever-competitive relationship between the Member States and the Union, and the division of competences amongst what used to be the three pillars of the EU. Given the constraints of space, the present chapter can only flesh out the outlines of a critical assessment of the EU's counter-terrorism policy; a fuller assessment will have to await another occasion.

The critical approach outlined in this chapter has two main sources. First, as an article of faith, one ought to have a natural inclination to be suspicious about pretty much anything done by pretty much anyone in pretty much any position of power. And those suspicions are hardly alleviated by the silly things one encounters when travelling abroad these days. If Michel Foucault were to write today (and without there having been a Foucault writing previously), it is not unlikely that he would develop his concept of governmentality in light of the fight against terrorism—indeed, some philosophers working in a Foucauldian vein come close enough.[4]

Secondly (and more to the point perhaps), terrorism is a highly ambivalent concept, filled with tensions and contradictions. Because of this, legal responses too can hardly be anything other than ambivalent. This also entails that not too much need be expected from big words in smooth strategies and other official documents—these may serve useful political purposes and provide some legal handles to the topic, but the likelihood is that the tensions and contradictions they contain can be suppressed only for so long.

II. THE INTERNATIONAL LAW ON TERRORISM

Terrorism and law have an uneasy relationship. This uneasiness applies to terrorism's connections to constitutional law, as recent developments in Guantanamo

[3] For a very useful earlier overview (with a focus on detail), see S Peers, 'EU Responses to Terrorism' (2003) 52 *International and Comparative Law Quarterly* 227.

[4] This applies most obviously to G Agamben, *State of Exception* (Chicago, University of Chicago Press, 2005, Attell trans).

Bay and elsewhere have made abundantly clear,[5] but it also applies to international law. International law has, for instance, been unable to come up with a definition of terrorism, despite many decades' worth of attempts. This stems, partly, from the old adage that my terrorist may be your freedom fighter: even Grotius might have been called a terrorist if only the word had existed when he was tried, in 1618, for advocating a liberal form of Protestantism.[6] Partly this may also stem, so some may add, from the circumstance that States and terrorists rely to some extent on each other: terrorists can profile themselves and derive legitimacy only by contrasting themselves with a State; whereas States can legitimise part of their statehood—and some of their less palatable policies—precisely by an appeal to be fighting terror. Hence, they feed off each other in decidedly uncomfortable ways; they both derive some of their *raison d'être* from each other.[7] While some of the worst effects of the absence of a definition may be mitigated by listing offences that are linked to terrorism (as will be discussed below), nonetheless the absence of an authoritative definition is not simply due to a lack of political agreement—its cause is more structural.

Possibly the main reason why law has a hard time dealing with terrorism is that terrorism does not neatly fit into the constructs and categories of law. In principle, there would seem to be two main techniques for fighting acts of terrorism.[8] One is through criminal law, on the working premise that terrorist acts are to be regarded as (more or less) common crimes. This makes some sense, of course: there are usually identifiable victims, for instance, and often enough, the perpetrators form a small group of identifiable individuals, or even work individually. On this view, then, terrorism is really murder writ large, or serial killing in one stroke. The nagging problem, however, is that to regard terrorism as a common crime tends to ignore precisely the one thing that makes terrorists tick: the politics behind their acts.[9] This has the serious implication, for example, that such staples of regular criminal law philosophy as, for instance, the deterrent effect of criminal law are bound to be of little use: the terrorist is not inspired by the same motives as regular criminals, and thus is unlikely to be deterred. He (or she) is not working out of greed or hatred of individuals, or even pathological disturbances; instead, he or

[5] See generally D Dyzenhaus, *The Constitution of Law: Legality in a Time of Emergency* (Cambridge, Cambridge University Press, 2006).

[6] A fine biography in Dutch is by H Nellen, *Hugo de Groot: Een leven in strijd om de vrede 1583–1645* (Amsterdam, Balans, 2006).

[7] The seminal piece is by I Porras, 'On Terrorism: Reflections on Violence and the Outlaw' (1994) 12 *Utah Law Review* 119.

[8] This follows J Klabbers, 'Rebel with a Cause? Terrorists and Humanitarian Law' (2003) 14 *European Journal of International Law* 299.

[9] Morgan puts it adroitly: terrorism 'is both crime and politics, and is culpable on both accounts'. See E Morgan, 'International Law's Literature of Terror' (2002) 15 *Canadian Journal of Law and Jurisprudence* 317, 324.

she is acting for political reasons (however unspecified, however perverse even). Hence, simply applying criminal law is bound to remain unsatisfactory.[10]

Moreover, from a governmental perspective, there might be some problems in taking the criminal law approach. Thus, at least in western-style democracies governed by the rule of law, every criminal typically has a right to a fair trial, has *habeas corpus* rights, has rights to representation in court, rights to be free from torture or ill-treatment, etc. Yet to uphold these rights may seem, to governments, less than fully attractive with respect to terrorists in particular. Terrorists, after all, are the people who represent the ultimate evil in ways that transcend our regular moral categories. We can understand, however dimly perhaps, when people kill for money, or because they can no longer stand their husbands or wives, or even out of sheer lust or pathology perhaps. But killing for some ideal, be it a well-defined ideal or a vague ideal? That is, quite literally, incomprehensible.

The alternative, then, is to focus on the body of law which is more in tune with political sentiments: the law of armed conflict, the body of law that addresses both the right to wage war and proper conduct during war. After all, many would agree, in Clausewitz's classic terms, that war is the continuation of politics by other means—there is thus an almost natural connection between politics and the law of armed conflict, in that armed conflict will typically be motivated by political reasons. But this too, from a governmental perspective, is problematic: it would—or could—amount to legitimising terrorism, for although the *jus in bello* is sceptical about methods of warfare, it is usually agnostic about the cause of war, and may even be said to assume that the cause of war may be just. While the law of armed conflict works on the basis of a rigid distinction between the *jus ad bellum* and the *jus in bello*, it is possible to claim that with respect to terrorism, such distinction cannot fruitfully be maintained, leading to the problematic proposition that an unjust war should nevertheless be fought justly—by all sides.[11] Applying the law of armed conflict therewith could be interpreted as a political gesture, telling terrorists (and the world at large) that the terrorists' struggle is a legitimate one. If we do not negotiate with terrorists (as our political leaders often insist) then surely we will also be reluctant to grant them the courtesy of treating their cause as respectable, and even as potentially just.[12]

Furthermore, there is a host of technical details which may render armed conflict law less than appropriate. Much of it is based on a chivalrous idea of warfare, not unlike yesteryear's duel between gentlemen. Thus, wars ought, ideally, to be declared; combatants ought, ideally, to be recognisable as such, eg by wearing

[10] For similar reasons the deterrent effect of international criminal law will prove disappointing. See J Klabbers, 'Just Revenge? The Deterrence Argument in International Criminal Law' (2002) 13 *Finnish Yearbook of International Law* 249.

[11] See J Klabbers, 'Off Limits? International Law and the Excessive Use of Force' (2006) 7 *Theoretical Inquiries in Law* 59.

[12] See the seminal work by M Walzer, *Just and Unjust Wars*, 3rd edn (New York, Basic Books, 2000).

uniforms or other insignia, and it is one of the 'intransgressible principles' of the law of armed conflict (as the International Court of Justice inimitably put it in the *Nuclear Weapons* opinion[13]) that a distinction shall at all times be maintained between combatants and civilians. All these desiderata are, typically, flouted by terrorist acts: these typically use the element of surprise, helped by being incognito, and often ignore the distinction between combatants and civilians.

So the law is caught between a rock and hard place: terrorism does not fit neatly into our criminal law categories; but it does not fit neatly into our armed conflict categories either. Small wonder, then, that States have tried to find some comfortable nesting place between that rock and that hard place. Sometimes this takes the form of simply ignoring both criminal law and the law of armed conflict, resulting in such phenomena as Guantanamo Bay or so-called 'extraordinary renditions': not quite extradition, not quite transfer of prisoners of war either. And some among the gloomier post-structuralist philosophers go so far as to predict that this sort of thing is rapidly becoming the norm: what were once thought of as provisional and exceptional measures become standard techniques of government.[14]

However this may be, at the very least the observation can be made that the law on terrorism is in a state of flux. International law has been unable to come up with a generally accepted definition of terrorism thus far, and this is unlikely to change any time soon, the perennial optimism of negotiators notwithstanding.[15] That is not to say that nothing ever happens: the UN Security Council, for instance, established a Counter Terrorism Committee in 2001[16]; its Executive Directorate provides technical assistance to States aiming to combat terrorism, and even engages in such activities as country visits. Sometimes, moreover, specific acts are, *ex post facto*, condemned as acts of terrorism by the international community, regardless of whether they fit any generally accepted definition, and may meet with multilateral sanctions.

Given the absence of a general definition (and thus also, importantly, a general and workable prohibition), two other avenues have been tried and tested over the years. One of these goes back to the 1970s and involves concentrating on specific acts. Thus, there is a host of conventions addressing specific issues which can be seen as linked to terrorism, including a convention outlawing the hijacking of civil aircraft, another one on crimes against internationally protected persons, including diplomatic agents, a convention on the safety of maritime navigation, a convention on terrorist bombings, one on nuclear terrorism, one on the marking of

[13] See *Legality of the Threat or Use of Nuclear Weapons* (Advisory Opinion) [1996] *ICJ Rep* 226.

[14] See Agamben, above n 4, at 2.

[15] An anecdotal reflection: whenever one speaks to negotiators trying to hammer out a definition of terrorism, they usually claim that a breakthrough is expected very soon, or that consensus is within reach. This would be excellent, but for the fact that they have been saying the same thing for many, many years!

[16] See UN Security Council Resolution 1373(2001).

explosives, conventions on protecting airports and oil platforms, etc.[17] Here, the main approach has been to ignore any abstract definitions of terrorism and focus on concrete acts of violence. Indeed, the word 'terrorism' is studiously avoided in these conventions, with the result that possible prosecutions can focus on the acts themselves without having to delve into complicated issues about whether or not the authors of the crime are to be considered terrorists.

The alternative approach, sometimes used in conjunction with the 'specific issues' approach, is of more recent origin and concentrates not so much on terrorism itself, but rather on ancillary activities. Most eye-catching is the convention on the financing of terrorism,[18] while a 2005 Council of Europe convention addresses prevention of terrorism by focusing on such things as recruitment and training, rather than on the actual commission of terrorist acts.[19] Here, definitional problems are avoided by referring back to the various specific activity-orientated conventions (aircraft hijacking, maritime safety, etc). Taken together, the two approaches present an almost seamless web of provisions.[20]

As the above discussion already suggests, much of the work on terrorism is centralised: in particular the UN Security Council has taken up the responsibility. Not only has it created its Counter-terrorism Committee and imposed and monitored sanctions,[21] but some of its resolutions have also been regarded as coming close to being of law-making character, none more so than Resolution 1373(2001). Given the circumstance that it is controversial whether the Security Council has been endowed with legislative powers, the propriety of these resolutions too has given rise to debate, with some arguing that such resolutions lack legitimacy, while others suggest that the Council might be an effective medium in the fight against terrorism.[22]

The only thing missing, in the end, is the definition of 'terrorism', and there remains a nagging sense that such a definition is required not only to present a general prohibition, but also because it is only such a definition that allows full concentration on issues of intent and *mens rea*. And in the western liberal tradition, these issues are of the utmost importance: there is a general reluctance to

[17] The UN Security Council's Counter-Terrorism Committee lists 16 relevant conventions: see <http://www.un.org/sc/ctc/laws.html#t11> (visited 1 March 2010).

[18] For a brief comment, see A Aust, 'Counter-terrorism—A New Approach: The International Convention for the Suppression of the Financing of Terrorism' (2001) 5 *Max Planck Yearbook of United Nations Law* 285.

[19] This is the Council of Europe Convention on the Prevention of Terrorism, concluded in Warsaw in 2005 with entry into force in 2007, to be found in European Treaty Series, no 196.

[20] The list mentioned in n 17 above covers the convention on the financing of terrorism as well as the various 'specific issue' conventions.

[21] A very useful study is JM Farrall, *United Nations Sanctions and the Rule of Law* (Cambridge, Cambridge University Press, 2007).

[22] For a nuanced general discussion, see J Alvarez, *International Organizations as Law-Makers* (Oxford, Oxford University Press, 2005). Fairly critical is M Happold, 'Security Council Resolution 1373 and the Constitution of the United Nations' (2003) 16 *Leiden Journal of International Law* 593; fairly sanguine, on the other hand, is E Rosand, 'The Security Council as "Global Legislator": Ultra Vires or Ultra Innovative?' (2004) 28 *Fordham International Law Journal* 542.

punish people without first establishing that they can be held responsible in some meaningful way.[23]

III. THE EUROPEAN STRATEGY

If the international legal regime on terrorism remains *in statu nascendi*, can the same be said about a possible EU regime on terrorism? One of the perennial problems with respect to the EU is the dispersion of legal powers. Anti-terrorism work took place in all the three pillars that comprised the Union prior to the entry into force of the Lisbon Treaty: EC measures were involved, but also measures relating to Europe's Common Foreign and Security Policy, as well as measures relating to the area that was known, for a short period of time, as Justice and Home Affairs, and briefly also known as Police and Judicial Cooperation in Criminal Matters.[24] In addition, there is the natural tension between international organisations and their Member States generally[25]: this too helps inform and explain the precise shape the law on terrorism in Europe takes—or does not take.

Either way, the dispersion among pillars and tensions between the EU and its Member States called, quite obviously, for an overall strategy, and such a strategy has been in place since 2005.[26] The EU Counter-terrorism Strategy, developed by an office of a similar name headed by a former member of the European Parliament, the Dutch conservative politician Gijs de Vries, works on the basis of four focal points.[27] The Strategy aims to prevent terrorism, protect citizens and infrastructure, pursue terrorists and respond properly once attacks have taken place. Hence, the Strategy has adopted four keywords (it actually, and rather ill-advisedly, refers to them using the term 'pillars'): Prevent, Protect, Pursue and Respond.[28]

While terrorism has been high on the global political agenda since 11 September 2001, the EU faced terrorist attacks on its own territory in 2004 (the Madrid train bombings) and 2005 (the London subway bombings), giving the fight against

[23] See generally HLA Hart, *Punishment and Responsibility: Essays in the Philosophy of Law* (Oxford, Oxford University Press, 1968).

[24] Indeed, somewhat incongruously perhaps, it is here that the Treaty provides a most explicit legal basis: Art 29 TEU specifies that Police and Judicial Cooperation in Criminal Matters shall serve the citizens of Europe and that this objective 'shall be achieved by preventing and combating crime, organised or otherwise, in particular terrorism'. Post-Lisbon, the Treaty aspires to create an area of Freedom, Security and Justice.

[25] For a general discussion, see J Klabbers, *An Introduction to International Institutional Law*, 2nd edn (Cambridge, Cambridge University Press, 2009).

[26] For an overall review, see O Bures, 'EU Counterterrorism Policy: A Paper Tiger?' (2006) 18 *Terrorism and Political Violence* 57.

[27] This makes no doubt for wonderfully coherent Powerpoint presentations, and indeed, the version prepared for the press starts off with nice boxes representing the four main focal points, and arrows between them. Available at <http://ue.eu.int/Newsroom>.

[28] One cannot help but wonder, given the bureaucratic tendency to use alliterations or acronyms, how much time was spent on trying to find a synonym for 'respond' that would start with the letter 'p'.

terror a distinctly fresh impetus. Through these attacks, global terrorism had turned from an abstract threat to Europe to something highly concrete. Europe's history may include its fair share of home-grown terrorism (think only of Northern Ireland, the Red Armies in Italy and Germany in the 1970s, and Basque separatism), but these examples were, by comparison, not nearly as indiscriminate as the threat posed by Al Qaeda and its sympathisers. The EU's Strategy must be read against the background of the London and Madrid attacks as well as 9/11.

This 2005 Counter-terrorism Strategy is informed by what is called a 'strategic commitment', printed in bold by way of headline to the entire document:

> **To combat terrorism globally while respecting human rights, and make Europe safer, allowing its citizens to live in an area of freedom, security and justice.**

Enthusiastic deconstructivists might notice that this single sentence contains at least three points of tension.

First, the strategic commitment betrays a tension between combating terrorism and respecting human rights. It is by no means self-evident that effectively combating terrorism goes hand in hand with respect for human rights, and I later suggest that human rights play but a marginal role in the Strategy. While it may eventually be the case that only a human rights-based approach will be considered legitimate enough to muster popular support, and to muster it on a long-term basis, in the short run there may always be the temptation to diminish the significance of human rights for the sake of security: the prison cells of Guantanamo Bay form a mortifying example. Moreover, it is not immediately clear which human rights are at issue: while the report no doubt pays homage to due process requirements and the absence of torture, some might argue that economic and social rights ought not to be forgotten: if poverty is a breeding ground for terrorism then a focus on economic and social rights may prove more effective as a means of combating terrorism than a focus on fair trial rights. And indeed, to some extent this is recognised when the Strategy advocates the promotion of economic prosperity.[29]

Secondly, there is the tension between fighting global terrorism and doing so with a view to creating a European (local) area of freedom, security and justice. Surely terrorism is a global phenomenon, and threats can come from anywhere. Similarly, Europe's first priority is—and should—be the defence of the realm. But having said this, a focus solely on European security, while neglecting security elsewhere, is problematic. This is problematic, pragmatically, due to the fact that many Europeans travel to, or reside in, other parts of the globe: bombs exploding

[29] It does so in para 11 of the Strategy, and repeats it in para 13 where it enumerates key priorities. Whether the Strategy thinks of economic prosperity in human rights terms is unclear, though; and what is downright curious is that while para 11 stipulates that the Union must promote human rights elsewhere (in addition to good governance, democracy, education and prosperity), the reference to human rights has gone missing from the 'key priorities' of para 13.

in Bali or Nairobi may not be directed at Europeans, but they will not avoid them either if they happen to be in the wrong place at the wrong time. But a focus solely on Europe is also philosophically hard to defend, as it makes a distinction between those worthy of being defended and those less worthy. Moreover, again, as with economic and social rights, it might be a lot more effective to ensure that places like Pakistan or Yemen are also left in security. This is not, to be sure, an admonition to intervene; but it is to suggest that concentrating on 'fortress Europe' alone might be insufficient. Interestingly, the 2003 European Security Strategy more clearly recognises the mutual dependence of security and prosperity, suggesting that security is a precondition for development but, likewise, that prosperity elsewhere will make Europe a safer place.[30]

Thirdly, there is a rather curious distinction made between Europe and its citizens which, again, draws on the distinction between Europeans and others.[31] Europe is to be made a safe place but apparently for the sole benefit of Europe's citizens, not for those without citizenship. Suspicious minds may wonder whether this entails an explicit exclusion of the millions of immigrant workers, mostly from Muslim countries, or whether the drafters of the Counter-terrorism Strategy merely tried to find a more or less elegant way to avoid saying 'Europe' twice in one sentence; but even then, the emphasis on citizenship (as opposed to residence, for instance) may not be the most fortunate. To respond that the language is simply taken directly from the Treaty establishing the EU would be correct,[32] but it also merely divert attention from the issue: why, then, does the EU Treaty make such a distinction?

And not surprisingly, there is a fourth, more general, tension running through the entire Strategy: the distinction between Europe and its Member States. Interestingly, the document oozes the idea that an EU role is secondary: prime responsibility for prevention, protection, pursuit and response rests with the Member States. In light of the usual eagerness of the EU and its institutions to usurp competences and claim responsibilities, this does come as something of a surprise, and is no doubt best understood as a tacit reminder of the complexities involved in the fight against terrorism and the political risks involved in engaging with terrorism. If terrorism is here to stay (and this seems to be the assumption underlying the Strategy), it is best for the EU to be involved—but not too closely. Hence, the EU's modesty regarding terrorism is perhaps an elaborate form of scape-goating: whenever things go wrong, the Member States will be the first to carry the blame. And when things go right, it is not too far-fetched to suppose that the EU will claim some of the credit. The surprise is not that the Member States

[30] See 'A Secure Europe in a Better World', European Security Strategy, adopted in Brussels, 12 December 2003, at 2, 10.

[31] I hesitate to capitalise 'The Other' since, though impressive, it does not seem to add much explanatory force.

[32] Art 29 TEU. It is probably no accident that the distinction is no longer present, post-Lisbon, in Art 67 TFEU.

remain involved—this is the logical consequence of the very structure of the EU. The surprise resides, instead, in the scope of the latitude left to the Member States. Either way, there is little truly novel to be observed in a struggle between the EU and its Member States: from the first hesitant efforts at setting up EU-wide anti-terrorism mechanisms and institutions, the whole and its parts have been striving for prominence.

The need to cooperate was recognised as early as the mid-1970s in the creation, under yet another of those acronyms and without any legal basis or document, of the Terrorism, Radicalism, Extremism and Political Violence Group (the TREVI Group); it would later find expression in such institutions as Europol. And yet most observers would agree that Member States would be more trusting of their own agencies and their traditional bilateral contacts than of these newly-created European institutions, and not only to avoid duplication of efforts.[33]

The tension between local and global runs across the entire Strategy, or in its own words is a 'horizontal feature'. In the UN and elsewhere, the EU will help to build consensus and promote standards to counter terrorism. It does so on the basis of some idea as to what a safe society looks like.[34] Terrorism, so paragraph 5 suggests, follows from radicalisation; hence, radicalisation must be stopped, and can be stopped by promoting good governance and democracy, and engaging in dialogue and alliances between cultures, between faiths and between civilisations.

The key to understanding the Strategy is to recognise its sequential approach. It follows an imaginary time-line, where terrorism first must be prevented, for instance by preventing radicalisation or by community policing. Secondly, protection will be needed, and ought to be achieved by raising standards in transport security, more effective border controls and more secure passports which include biometric information. Thirdly, should terrorist activities take place, the suspects[35] must be pursued: their networks must be disrupted, their funding cut off and they must be brought to justice. Fourthly, terrorist acts must be responded to and civilians must be protected. This, then, is general background.

A. Prevention

Under the heading 'Prevention', the Strategy focuses on radicalisation and recruitment, and on terrorist training, by use of such things as 'community policing' and monitoring travel. Any clashing of values is dismissed as 'propaganda', and a 'non-emotive lexicon' is required to prevent the deepening of divisions. The basic idea

[33] See, eg, O Bures, 'Europol's Fledgling Counterterrorism Role' (2008) 20 *Terrorism and Political Violence* 498.

[34] See para 5 of the Strategy.

[35] The word 'suspects' is not to be found in the Strategy, which consistently speaks of 'terrorists'.

seems to be that young and potentially radical Muslims should be educated (or re-educated) to become young and tolerant liberals. This demands intra-cultural dialogue; the promotion of good governance, democracy, education and prosperity; and, most tantalising perhaps, the development of 'a media and communication strategy to better explain EU policies'.[36]

B. Protection

The *protection* of Europe and its citizens is to take place by means of capture and exchange of passenger data, and by the use of biometric passports, leading to more effective border controls. A Visa Information System is mentioned, as is the second generation Schengen Information System. Airport, seaport and aircraft security must be improved, as well as road and rail security. In classic pragmatist fashion, the Strategy suggests that Europe's Research & Development policy should be geared towards this—one might as well turn the vice of terrorism into the virtue of innovative research. Note that human rights are not specifically mentioned here, despite all these things (especially the creation of information systems and the exchange of data) having a fairly large potential to put human rights at risk.

C. Pursue

Under the heading 'Pursue' the Strategy addresses the disruption of terrorist activities and pursuing the perpetrators across borders. The Strategy mentions such things as the European Arrest Warrant and the European Evidence Warrant, as well as further cooperation through Europol and Eurojust, and setting up Joint Investigation Teams. Here the global also makes an appearance: the EU 'will work to reinforce the international consensus through the United Nations and other international bodies' and 'will work for agreement of a UN Comprehensive Convention against Terrorism'.[37] In themselves, these phrases do not mean all that much: surely anyone could rally behind the reinforcement of the international consensus or 'work for agreement'. And yet, without them, the Strategy would have appeared vacuous.

The most concrete point mentioned under 'Pursue' is the necessity to retain telecommunications data, accompanied by the expressed desire to impede communication and the spreading of technical expertise among terrorists by means of the Internet. How the latter is supposed to take place is left unspecified, though, as are the potential human rights ramifications. Again, the human rights risks at stake

[36] See para 13 of the Strategy.
[37] See para 30 of the Strategy.

are quite serious, given that freedom of expression and freedom of information form the bedrock of liberal democracy.

D. Respond

Lastly, the Strategy envisages a way to *respond* to terrorism. This section deals partly with what to do when an attack occurs, and partly with the aftermath. The first part is obvious: it mentions such staples as information-sharing, media coordination, mutual support and the use of the Civil Protection Mechanism. The 'aftermath part' provides predominantly for compensation to victims and assistance to EU citizens in third countries.

E. Tensions within the Strategy

The Strategy cannot escape some of the tensions mentioned above. On the one hand, it posits terrorism as a crime (tapping into the criminal law paradigm outlined above), and does so unapologetically: 'Terrorism is criminal and unjustifiable', reads the opening paragraph, and a few paragraphs later the document reiterates that '[t]errorism can never be justified. There can be no excuse or impunity for terrorist acts.'[38] These are absolutes, but curiously, the next sentences soften the tone: having posited these absolutes, the Strategy continues by suggesting that the statements are a matter of majority opinion, rather than absolute values. It continues by stating that a majority of Europeans do not accept extremist ideologies, and that even amongst those who do, 'only a few turn to terrorism'.[39] Whether this is an admission that terrorism may sometimes be something of a 'lifestyle choice' is unclear (if unlikely), but it goes some way towards suggesting that few people respond automatically to sticks or carrots.

Yet despite generally applying the criminal paradigm and the recognition that sticks and carrots may have a limited effect only (or maybe because of this), some of the language used and some of the concrete proposals are reminiscent of a military paradigm or, more accurately perhaps, a decidedly non-liberal law-enforcement paradigm. This comes out, if by default perhaps, in the scant attention to human rights. The general theme of the Strategy (its 'strategic commitment'), it may be recalled, emphasised the need 'to combat terrorism globally while respecting human rights'. Yet in the entire document (some eight pages of text, 41 separate paragraphs), the term 'human rights' is mentioned only twice; and of those two occasions, only one relates to the EU policy itself. This is in paragraph 22, when under the heading 'Pursue' the objectives include impeding terrorist planning

[38] See para 7 of the Strategy.
[39] See para 7 of the Strategy.

and cutting off their funding, 'while continuing to respect human rights and international law'. The other mention is in paragraph 11, in which the Strategy proclaims that outside the Union such things as democracy, good governance and human rights must be promoted. Surprisingly, as noted above, this reference was not reiterated two paragraphs below, where the key priorities for prevention are enumerated.

At the very least this would seem to suggest that the terrorism strategists have not been working from a human rights mindset but rather a more military mindset, or law-enforcement mindset perhaps. Moreover, they arguably seem to think, still, that human rights are really something for the outside world—in Europe, the human rights situation is fine and, more importantly, not seriously at risk. Then again, this should perhaps not come as a surprise, as historically the EU has paid far more attention to human rights in its external relations than internally where, until the entry into force of the Lisbon Treaty, Europe's citizens had little more to rely on than a non-binding Charter of Fundamental Rights.

IV. THE LEGAL INSTRUMENTS

One interesting point about the Strategy is that it dates from 2005; it is pre-dated, actually, by most of the relevant legal instruments.[40] Therefore, in a sense, it largely codifies and rationalises the existing legal framework. In their turn, some of the relevant legal instruments have been said to have passed 'exceptionally swiftly'.[41] This may simply be an illustration of legislative effectiveness, but may also, as has been suggested, raise concerns about democracy and accountability within the EU.[42] As will be suggested below, on occasion Europe's leaders may give in to the temptation to use a crisis as an argument for quick and swift action—and sometimes the action is not all that closely related to the crisis.

A. The Foreign Policy Dimension

Much of the relevant law is traceable to two Common Positions. First, there is Common Position 2001/930/CFSP, adopted in December 2001.[43] Terrorism is defined as crime, triggering the application of criminal law (instead of the law of armed conflict), and it follows Security Council Resolution 1373 by focusing

[40] An early overview of some of the relevant instruments is provided by I Thomas, 'La mise en oeuvre en droit européen des dispositions internationals de lutte contre le terrorisme' (2004) 108 *Revue Générale de Droit International Public* 463.

[41] See M O'Neill, 'A Critical Analysis of the EU Legal Provisions on Terrorism' (2008) 20 *Terrorism and Political Violence* 26, 29, referring to Council Framework Decisions on Terrorism and the Arrest Warrant.

[42] *Ibid*.

[43] See above n 2.

on the funding of terrorism and other related activities, such as providing safe haven. Terrorism is not specifically defined; instead, the Common Position refers to a number of international conventions—typically those that were mentioned above on hijacking, the taking of hostages, terrorist bombings, and the financing of terrorism.

A second Common Position,[44] adopted on the same date, does, however, provide a lengthy definition of 'terrorism', consisting essentially of a list of prohibited activities (kidnapping, destroying infrastructure, seizing aircraft or other means of transportation, etc), if done intentionally, and with the aim of seriously intimidating a population, unduly compelling a government or international organisation to do (or not do) something, or destabilising or destroying the structures of a country or an international organisation. The threshold is a fairly high one, which is necessary, of course, to prevent the conflation of terrorism and common crimes. Hence the use of the adjective 'seriously'; hence also the insistence on terrorist intentions.

There are two surprising elements here. The first is that the list of offences also includes directing a terrorist group and participating in the activities of such a group. Terrorist groups themselves are further defined as 'structured'[45]: this means, on the one hand, that it must concern groups 'not randomly formed for the immediate commission of a terrorist act',[46] but, on the other hand, such a group need not have any formalised or developed structures. This was probably inserted so as to be able to capture networks such as Al Qaeda.

Secondly, there is the recurring reference to terrorism being directed against an international organisation. While probably meant as shorthand for the EU and its institutions, the interesting element resides in the sort of risk terrorism could pose to organisations to begin with. Since organisations have no territorial basis they can call their own, this can only refer to one of two things: either a direct attack on the organisation's headquarters, or a direct attack on its leadership or staff. Either way, while it would not have been strictly necessary perhaps to single out organisations as victims (in that staff typically have citizenship of at least one State, and Belgium surely could act upon an attack against the Commission buildings in Brussels), doing so singles out a conviction that the organisation is not reducible to its Member States, and reflects the scenario that gave rise to the *Reparation for Injuries* Advisory Opinion of the International Court of Justice in 1949. It will be recalled that the incident leading up to the Opinion was the killing of a UN mediator in Israel, which gave rise to heated discussions as to whether

[44] See Common Position 2001/931/CFSP on the Application of Specific Measures to Combat Terrorism, [2001] OJ L344/93.

[45] *Ibid*, Art 1, para 3.

[46] *Ibid*.

the UN could exercise diplomatic protection on behalf of its representative, or whether this would remain the sole province of his State of nationality.[47]

Intriguingly, Common Position 2001/931/CFSP, drawn up in the direct aftermath of 9/11, also contains an annex of names of individuals and groups suspected of terrorism. The list is to be regularly reviewed (at least every six months), and indeed Article 6 provides that the Common Position itself 'shall be kept under constant review'. The first annex, published in 2001, consisted of 29 names of individuals. An overwhelming majority—21—of those listed were ETA activists; the remaining eight had Arab names. And while the list of groups and entities also mentions the Real IRA, the Orange Volunteers, etc, none of the individuals mentioned can plausibly be considered as belonging to one of those groups: indeed, the annex does not make an effort, simply mentioning parenthetically that the 21 individuals with Basque names are ETA activists. Curiously then, and perhaps worryingly, if one brackets the 9/11 background, the document reads like an anti-ETA document more than anything else. This, in turn, gives rise to worries about governments using a crisis as an excuse to push through, almost unnoticed, measures dealing with something else. It is not implausible that political support to address ETA in this manner would have been lacking if it had not been for 9/11.[48]

B. The Union Dimension

Within Union law strictly speaking, the foundational document is Council Regulation 2580/2001, also of 27 December 2001.[49] This deals predominantly with the freezing of assets of those who are suspected of committing or attempting terrorism, or participating in or facilitating terrorist acts. The definition of 'terrorist acts' is the one contained in Common Position 2001/931/CFSP.

The Regulation is quite detailed. It determines, for instance, that not only funds themselves may be frozen, but also interest due to frozen accounts. It provides for humanitarian exceptions too (essential human needs: rent or mortgage, foodstuffs, medicines, but only, it seems, within the Union), and many will be pleased to know that payments of taxes and other, similar financial obligations (such as compulsory insurance and utility charges) will still be possible from frozen accounts: being suspected of collusion with terrorists does not provide a tax exemption.

[47] See *Reparation for Injuries Suffered in the Service of the United Nations* (Advisory Opinion) [1949] *ICJ Rep* 174. The Court took the view that the UN could exercise diplomatic protection on its own behalf.

[48] While initially some suspected that the 2004 Madrid train bombings were the work of ETA, later it transpired that the operation had been inspired by Al Qaeda. Either way, the Common Position predates the Madrid bombings by more than two years.

[49] See above n 2.

Perhaps the most interesting aspects are the links between the Regulation and existing law. These come in two guises, neither of which is addressed very satisfactorily perhaps. First, while the Regulation states that it is without prejudice to applicable rules concerning reporting, confidentiality and professional secrecy, nonetheless any relevant information should be 'provided immediately'. How this relates to, for instance, banking secrecy is anyone's guess, and may give rise to speculation: surely, if the Regulation prevails, it can be regarded as usurping yet another Member State prerogative.

The second aspect is, once again, the human rights aspect. It is the Council that shall decide which individuals and groups shall have their funds frozen, and it is the Council that shall review and amend this list. Judicial safeguards are absent; no review mechanism is envisaged, let alone something approximating a fair trial. Since the *Kadi* decision of the European Court of Justice (although this concerned the more specific Regulation 881/2002), the absence of sufficient human rights protection in the relevant legal instruments is common knowledge.[50]

C. The Justice Dimension

Within what was the third pillar, the leading instrument is Council Framework Decision 2002/475/JHA, of 13 June 2002.[51] It set a framework for the harmonisation of the substantive criminal codes of the Member States, typically instructing them to 'take the necessary measures to ensure' that certain acts are criminalised, certain penalties applied, certain entities are covered and criminal jurisdiction is established. Clearly, following what used to be Article 34 TEU, the text speaks to the Member States, and will thus not be directly applicable.[52]

On the level of substance, a few elements stand out. Thus, there is recognition of a special intent related to terrorism, so as to distinguish terrorist kidnappings from a kidnapping carried out by a father after divorce. This recurs in the definitions of 'terrorist acts', and also when discussing penalties: Article 5 of the Framework Decision suggests that custodial sentences shall be heavier if this special intent can be established.

The definition follows that found in the Common Position mentioned above,[53] but it separates terrorist acts as such from the crimes of directing a group or being a member of a group. Still, the definition of 'group' is identical to the one from

[50] See Case C-402/05 P, *Kadi* v *Council and Commission* [2008] ECR I-6351. For an analysis in much more detail, see ch 7 of this volume. For useful background, see W Vlcek, 'Acts to Combat the Financing of Terrorism: Common Foreign and Security Policy at the European Court of Justice' (2006) 11 *European Foreign Affairs Review* 491.

[51] See above n 2.

[52] Note, however, that national legislation must be interpreted to the fullest extent possible in conformity with Framework Decisions. See Case C-105/03, *Criminal Proceedings against Maria Pupino* [2005] ECR I-5285, para 43.

[53] See Common Position 2001/931/CFSP, above n 44.

the earlier Common Position. Article 3 casts the net fairly wide: it criminalises also aggravated theft, extortion and the drawing up of false instruments if done in relation to terrorist acts. Article 4, likewise, criminalises inciting, aiding and abetting, and attempting to commit terrorist crimes. Importantly, though, in light of the perennial problems of agreeing a definition under international law, the definition contained in the Framework Decision does not have to address the vexed issue of terrorism by armed forces: the Preamble specifies that actions by the armed forces of a State are not covered by the Framework Decision, at least not to the extent that such actions are governed by other rules of international law.

The penalties, as noted, should be heavier if special intent can be proven, and at any rate should be 'effective, proportionate and dissuasive'.[54] What is interesting, and going beyond harmonisation proper perhaps, is the call for certain minimum penalties (cast in negative terms). Thus, directing a terrorist group shall carry a maximum sentence of no less than 15 years, whereas participating in a group shall carry a maximum sentence of no less than eight years. Still, cooperation with authorities may help reduce sentences, and the same applies if suspects renounce terrorism.

Perhaps most challenging from the criminal law point of view is the idea that legal persons too shall be held liable. Here, punishment may include criminal and non-criminal fines, but also such things as judicial winding-up orders or exclusion from entitlement to public benefits.

The provisions on jurisdiction and prosecution follow standard international legal logic, embedding the principles of territoriality and nationality as well as the protective principle. In this connection, perhaps the most interesting thing is that 'the dog did not bark': there is no mention of the universality principle. Hence, in order to prosecute, there must be some connection to the EU; the Framework Decision provides no legal basis for prosecuting, say, Kuwaiti nationals engaged in 9/11 having prepared their acts in Canada. That said, Member States which do apply universal jurisdiction can continue to do so, in accordance with Article 9(5).[55]

The Framework Decision has two other highly salient elements. First, as mentioned above, the Preamble excludes the operations of armed forces from its scope. This is on the global level one of the pivotal points preventing consensus on a definition of terrorism: can public actors, such as States or international organisations, engage in terrorism? Many in the Arab world would answer in the affirmative (having Israel in mind, perhaps). Arab States tend to insist that State terrorism be included; others maintain that it should not be. Excluding it here renders the EU vulnerable to criticism, in that in doing so it lays down an authoritative definition which possibly pre-empts future global attempts at definition. On the other hand, it

[54] See Art 5, para 1 of Council Framework Decision 2002/475/JHA, above n 2.

[55] On universal jurisdiction generally, see L Reydams, *Universal Jurisdiction: International and Municipal Legal Perspectives* (Oxford, Oxford University Press, 2003).

can also be seen as a recognition of the applicability of international humanitarian law to acts which otherwise might be characterised as terrorist and fall within the remit of (national) criminal law.[56]

Secondly, Article 1 specifies, in curious language, that the Framework Decision

> shall not have the effect of altering the obligation to respect fundamental rights and fundamental legal principles as enshrined in Article 6 of the Treaty on European Union.

This is remarkable language, for two reasons. First, the Framework Decision is directed at the Member States, whereas the obligation of Article 6 TEU is an obligation resting on the EU ('the Union shall respect fundamental rights').[57] Logically, it is not easy to see how instructions to Member States could possibly alter an obligation resting on the EU to begin with. Still, it is useful to point out that the language recurs in the Arrest Warrant and Evidence Warrant Framework Decisions too, albeit that in those instruments 'altering' has been replaced by 'modifying'.[58] Secondly, the combination 'fundamental rights and fundamental legal principles' is unexpected, especially as Article 6(3) TEU holds that fundamental rights be treated 'as general principles of the Union's law'.[59] Again, this may not mean much, but the human rights activist may note that no mention is made here of fundamental freedoms. The question then is what exactly this provision is intended to protect, and the suspicion arises that it protects most of all the four freedoms, dressed up in the ill-fitting language of human rights.[60]

While the Arrest Warrant (Framework Decision 2002/584/JHA) was already in existence when the Strategy was developed, the Evidence Warrant (Framework Decision 2008/978/JHA) is a novel instrument, in force since mid-January 2009, and to be implemented before 19 January 2011. It deals with the production and exchange of evidence generally, and only on a few occasions does it touch upon terrorism. One of these, potentially at any rate, is that execution of the European Evidence Warrant may be refused in the name of national security interests (Article 13(g)).

56 For such a reading, see F Hoffmeister, 'The Contribution of EU Practice to International Law' in M Cremona (ed), *Developments in EU External Relations Law* (Oxford, Oxford University Press, 2008) 37, 104.

57 The Lisbon Treaty leaves this intact.

58 See Council Framework Decision 2002/584/JHA on the European Arrest Warrant and the Surrender Procedures between Member States, [2002] OJ L190/1, Art 1(3), and Council Framework Decision 2008/978/JHA on the European Evidence Warrant for the Purpose of Obtaining Objects, Documents and Data for Use in Proceedings in Criminal Matters, [2008] OJ L350/72, Art 1(3).

59 Pre-Lisbon Treaty, Art 6(2) TEU held that fundamental rights and fundamental legal principles should be treated as identical; it spoke of fundamental rights as 'general principles of Community law'.

60 This has often been seen—and sometimes applauded—as the prevailing approach of the EU to human rights: turning the market freedoms into human rights. One of the staunchest advocates of such an approach is Ernst-Ulrich Petersmann. See, eg, his 'Time for a United Nations "Global Compact" for Integrating Human Rights into the Law of Worldwide Organizations: Lessons from European Integration' (2002) 13 *European Journal of International Law* 621.

More to the point, though, is that terrorism, as well as certain terrorist acts such as hostage-taking and seizing aircraft, are excluded from the double criminality test. Indeed, the list of offences excluded 'under any circumstances' from double criminality verification is rather lengthy, covering no fewer than 32 different items. It is no coincidence perhaps that Germany, arguably the most human rights-conscious of all Member States, had reserved the right to depart from this with respect to some of the offences, including terrorism.[61]

V. COHERENCE

While the Counter-terrorism Strategy aims to bring the approaches of the former three pillars together on the political level, it does so (as noted) *ex post facto*. Instead of serving as a blueprint, therefore, the Strategy serves more as a justification. On the political level, this may be adequate, but this does not necessarily apply on the level of legal detail as well.

Indeed, the Strategy is not terribly good at positing legal coherence to begin with. Much remains unclear, for instance, about the human rights ramifications of the fight against terrorism. While the EU generally places much emphasis on human rights, in particular in its external policies,[62] the attention to human rights in the Strategy is scant at best. It also remains an open question how counter-terrorism would intersect with the EU's development policies, beyond the somewhat bland injunction that economic prosperity must be stimulated so as to prevent terrorism.[63]

Pre-Lisbon, the edifice of EU and EC law contained some mechanisms for ensuring coherence,[64] both between the pillars, and between the EU and EC and their Member States. Many of these were procedural in nature (duties to inform and consult), and could to some extent be deemed derivative of the *deus ex machina* of Community law that is the fidelity principle (*Gemeinschaftstreue*) laid down, since the entry into force of the Lisbon Treaty, in Article 4(3) TEU. It is this principle that can time and again be invoked in order to give effect to existing Member State obligations, or redraw the boundaries between Community competence and Member State competence.[65]

Still, this might not suffice: part of the notion of coherence also resides in the substance of what the various actors are expected to do. The substance of the matter

[61] See Declaration of the Federal Republic of Germany, [2008] OJ L350/92.

[62] See, eg, P Leino-Sandberg, *Particularity as Universality: The Politics of Human Rights in the European Union* (doctoral dissertation, University of Helsinki, 2005).

[63] The European Consensus on Development, adopted around the same time as the Counter-Terrorism Strategy, does not make the link explicit either, although it does discuss genocide and ethnic cleansing in para 37. See [2006] OJ C46/01.

[64] For an excellent overview, see C Hillion, 'Tous pour un, un pour tous! Coherence in the External Relations of the European Union' in Cremona (ed), above n 56, 10–36. Since the entry into force of the Lisbon Treaty, Art 7 TFEU aims to guarantee consistency between the various policies.

[65] This arguably happened, eg, in the 2002 *Open Skies* cases, such as Case C-471/98 *Commission v Belgium* [2002] ECR I-9681. See, for general discussion, J Klabbers, *Treaty Conflict and the European Union* (Cambridge, Cambridge University Press, 2008).

(to take or not to take human rights into consideration) trumps any formal attempt at reaching coherence—however commendable coherence itself would be, and however desirable the substance might be.

VI. CONCLUSION

This, then, effectively concludes this brief *tour d'horizon*. It would seem that a fairly elaborate system is already in place in the EU, and that the system at the very least can be seen to try to find a balance between effective action and human rights protection. Whether it actually achieves this balance to a satisfactory degree seems debatable: the Strategy and the relevant legal instruments tilt in favour of effective action, at the expense of human rights protection, unless one could charitably interpret general EU law as being so much infused with human rights protection that it compensates for the relative disregard for human rights in the fight against terror. On such a reading, it would be arguable to hold that all instruments must be read against the background of strong human rights protection, but realistically speaking there seems little reason to be overly optimistic and resort to such a reading. Moreover, it turns out that EU law too cannot escape from the tensions inherent in the very notion of terrorism—the same tensions which have coloured the creation of the international legal framework on terrorism.

Tantalisingly, though, the one area where EU law might, substantially, be capable of going beyond traditional international law frameworks and thereby strengthen international law, has been closed off by the European Court of Justice. Where international law is traditionally not known for the strength of its enforcement capabilities, some commentators suggested, and expected perhaps, that EU law might constitute 'a more robust legal framework'.[66] The decision of the Court in *Kadi*,[67] however, makes clear that this is not taking place: *Kadi* suggests that the strengthening of international law is subordinated to the strengthening of EU law. Instead of allowing the EU to function as the regional enforcement branch of the United Nations, thereby guaranteeing that at least within Europe international law would be enforceable in a meaningful way, the European Court of Justice decided that international law need not be respected unless it meets with European standards. While admittedly there are many things wrong about the Security Council's attempts to fight terror, isolating the EU from the workings of general international law is not the proper response, and sets an awkward precedent. It may be a truism, but it seems obvious that any counter-terrorism action needs to be global in reach and aspiration; it is to be regretted that both the drafters of the Strategy and the European Court of Justice have by and large ignored this.

[66] So, eg, O'Neill, above n 41, at 26.
[67] See Case C-402/05 P, above n 50.

9

Reflections on European Effective Multilateralism and the Use of Force

PER CRAMÉR

THE DEVELOPMENT OF a EU military capacity for international crisis management operations constitutes one of the most dynamic aspects of the process of European integration. In the following I shall reflect on a limited but crucial issue connected to this development that I believe deserves greater attention in the legal/political debate: How does the European doctrine of effective multilateralism relate to the regulation of the international use of force in the UN Charter? More specifically, this chapter is an attempt to analyse the potential political and legal effects of the conditional loyalty to the UN system that is encapsulated in the European doctrine of effective multilateralism.

I. NEW PERCEPTIONS OF THREAT AND DEFENCE

Since the end of the Cold War a rapid reformulation of threat perceptions has taken place in the Western hemisphere. This process had already started in the early 1990s, primarily within NATO and the Western European Union (WEU).[1] The perceived threat of territorial aggression was then replaced by a much more diffuse and complex set of threat perceptions that included terrorism, primarily by non-State actors, proliferation of weapons of mass destruction, State failure, regional conflicts, international organised crime and the disruption of the flow of vital resources.

These threat perceptions have since then been consolidated, and constitute today, with minor variations, a core for both American and European strategic thinking, as well as for the NATO strategic concept.[2]

[1] Concerning NATO, see *The Alliance's New Strategic Concept*, Rome, 7–8 November 1991, paras 7–14, available at <http://www.nato.int/cps/en/natolive/official_texts_23847.htm?selectedLocale=en>. Concerning the WEU, see *WEU Council of Ministers: European Security a Common Concept of the 27 WEU Countries*, Madrid, 14 November 1995, paras 31–64, 92–110, available at <http://www.bits.de/NRANEU/docs/WEU141195.pdf>.

[2] Concerning the EU, see *A Secure Europe in a Better World, European Security Strategy*, 12 December 2003, available at <http://www.consilium.europa.eu/uedocs/cmsUpload/78367.pdf>, and *Report on the*

In parallel with this development we have also experienced a shift in the balance between the traditional concept of State sovereignty and individual human rights. The exercise of State sovereignty has thus been perceived, to an increasing extent, as limited by the imperative interest to protect fundamental human rights.[3]

As a consequence of these changes in perceptions, the defence doctrines of the defence alliances NATO and the WEU were revised during the early 1990s. In addition to their traditional roles as defensive alliances, both organisations declared their willingness to conduct peacekeeping and peace-shaping operations based on mandates from the UN Security Council or the Organization for Security and Co-operation in Europe (OSCE).[4]

Primarily through the creation of the Partnership for Peace, NATO has expanded involvement in crisis management operations to a number of non-Member States too.[5] A present concrete example of this development is the International Security Assistance Force (ISAF) in Afghanistan, which under NATO command is operating on a mandate adopted by the Security Council.[6] NATO has furthermore established a permanent multinational response force that could be used for crisis management operations as well as collective self-defence.[7]

In Europe, the crisis management tasks of the WEU were integrated into the framework of the European Union through the Treaty of Amsterdam 1999. These so-called 'Petersberg tasks' include humanitarian and rescue tasks, peacekeeping

Implementation of the European Security Strategy, Providing Security in a Changing World, 11 December 2008, available at <http://www.consilium.europa.eu/ueDocs/cms_Data/docs/pressData/en/reports/104630.pdf>. Concerning the US, see *The National Security Strategy of the United States of America*, March 2006, available at <http://georgewbush-whitehouse.archives.gov/nsc/nss/2006/nss2006.pdf>. The present US administration has not yet published a comprehensive security strategy. However, on the basis of available public statements, it seems that the threat perceptions formulated in the strategy of 2006 are still valid. Concerning NATO, see *The Alliance's Strategic Concept*, Washington DC, 24 April 1999, paras 20–24, available at <http://www.nato.int/cps/en/natolive/official_texts_27433.htm?selectedLocale=en>. At the NATO summit in Strasbourg/Kehl on 4 April 2009, the Member States gave the Secretary General the task to develop a new NATO Strategic Concept. This exercise should be completed by the time of NATO's next Summit, which is expected to take place in autumn 2010.

[3] This shift can be illustrated by the development of a norm stipulating international responsibility to protect the population in any State from genocide, war crimes, ethnic cleansing and crimes against humanity if that State fails to protect its own population: *United Nations General Assembly 2005 World Summit Outcome*, UNGA A/60/L.1, para 139.

[4] Concerning NATO, see *Ministerial Meeting of the North Atlantic Council, Final Communiqué*, Oslo, 4 June 1992, available at <http://www.otan.nato.int/cps/en/SID-3062D50F-8C8FD300/natolive/official_texts_23983.htm> and *Ministerial Meeting of the North Atlantic Council, Final Communiqué*, Brussels, 17 December 1992, available at <http://www.nato.int/cps/en/SID-4A03621E-32FA52CC/natolive/official_texts_23972.htm>. Concerning the WEU, see *WEU Council of Ministers: Petersberg Declaration*, Bonn, 19 June 1992, available at <http://www.weu.int/documents/920619peten.pdf>.

[5] Partnership for Peace was established in 1994. See *Partnership for Peace: Framework Document*, 11 January 1994, available at <http://www.nato.int/cps/en/SID-59589987-9F143945/natolive/official_texts_24469.htm>. At present the cooperation includes 22 States that are not members of the alliance.

[6] Security Council Resolution (SC Res) 1386 (2001), SC Res 1510 (2004).

[7] NATO Response Force (NRF). The NRF has been operational since October 2004. For an official description of the NRF, see *The NATO Response Force—At the centre of NATO transformation*, available at <http://www.nato.int/cps/en/natolive/topics_49755.htm>.

tasks and tasks of combat forces in crisis management, including peace-making.[8] This in turn has, during the last decade, led to the development of a European crisis management capacity, named the European Security and Defence Policy (ESDP), including the setting up of military forces, answerable to the EU, with the objective of contributing to the execution of the Petersberg tasks. This globally deployable military capacity has been operational since 2003, and has been developed continuously ever since.[9]

From a general perspective, at the core of this development lies a widespread understanding that the use of military force is primarily no longer to be exercised along national territorial borders. Rather, in order to counteract the threats that now dominate our perceptions, it may be exercised anywhere on the globe. A partial decoupling of defence and territory has thus taken place.

Nevertheless, also in this new environment the exercise of military power is regulated by the UN Charter, which is based on an inter-State paradigm.

II. THE UN FRAMEWORK

The UN Charter establishes a general prohibition[10] on the threat or use of force against the territorial integrity or political independence of any State.[11] In order to enforce this prohibition the Charter establishes a centralised but imperfect system of collective security, for which the Security Council has been given primary responsibility and exclusive decision-making competence.[12]

To the prohibition against the international use of force there are only two exceptions. First, the use of force is legal when it has been mandated by the Security Council as a measure necessary to maintain or restore international peace

[8] This non-exhaustive listing of possible EU crisis management operations has been elaborated through the Lisbon Treaty. See Art 43(1) TEU (post-Lisbon): 'The tasks ... in the course of which the Union may use civilian and military means, shall include joint disarmament operations, humanitarian and rescue tasks, military advice and assistance tasks, conflict prevention and peace-keeping tasks, tasks of combat forces in crisis management, including peace-making and post-conflict stabilisation. All these tasks may contribute to the fight against terrorism, including by supporting third countries in combating terrorism in their territories.'

[9] For a comprehensive official account of the development of the ESDP, see *Development of European Military Capabilities*, available at <http://www.consilium.europa.eu/uedocs/cmsUpload/090720%20Factsheet%20capacites%20militaires%20EN.pdf>. Concerning the present stage of development, see Council declaration of 8 December 2008 on the enhancement of the capabilities of the European Security and Defence Policy, available at <http://www.consilium.europa.eu/ueDocs/cms_Data/docs/pressData/en/esdp/104676.pdf>.

[10] Charter of the United Nations, Art 2(4).

[11] There is an abundance of international law literature on the regulation of the use of force. As general references, see B Simma, *The Charter of the United Nations: A Commentary*, 2nd edn (Oxford, Oxford University Press, 2002); T Franck, *Recourse to Force* (Cambridge, Cambridge University Press, 2002); C Gray, *International Law and the Use of Force*, 3rd edn (Oxford, Oxford University Press, 2008); D Sarooshi, *The United Nations Charter and the Development of Collective Security* (Oxford, Clarendon Press, 1999). For a historical account of the development of the law on the use of force, see I Brownlie, *International Law and the Use of Force by States* (Oxford, Oxford University Press, 1963).

[12] Charter of the United Nations, Art 24.

and security. Such a decision could be taken by the Council in accordance with the rules laid down in Chapter VII of the UN Charter. The decision-making process in the Council has a political rather than a judicial character. The Council has considerable freedom when determining whether a given action, or situation, constitutes a threat to, or breach of, the peace. Furthermore, it has a discretionary choice between adopting recommendations or decisions on legally-binding sanctions that might include a mandate for the use of military force. The decisions are taken through a process of diplomatic negotiations under the shadow of a potential veto from any one of the five permanent Member States.[13] The veto power could be described as a consciously created imperfection in the system, which was necessary in order to gain acceptance of the Charter by the five most powerful States participating at the San Francisco Conference 1945. It could also be seen as a guarantee that small States could not be dragged into a great power conflict through the application of the collective security system.

The primary importance of the veto power is that a decision on sanctions cannot be adopted when one (or more) of the permanent Members has a special interest with reference to the question that has been brought up, and it deems that this interest is worth safeguarding by using the veto. Thus, the system is highly dynamic and reflects, albeit imperfectly, the present global political situation. In a situation of manifest polarisation of the permanent Members of the Council, decisions on sanctions can be adopted only in rare cases. In order to function, the system requires that there exists a fundamental concordance in interests between the permanent five. When such a concordance is at hand, the veto power does not paralyse the system but rather creates a moment of inertia. This could be beneficial for the system, in that decisions on military operations that could lead to large-scale material destruction and human suffering are not adopted without full consideration. Nevertheless, the system still leaves open the possibility for individual permanent Member States to (ab)use the power of veto in order to further exclusive national interests, by blocking the adoption of decisions that are supported by all other Members of the Council. However, depending on the circumstances, such behaviour could incur high political costs, both for the State using the veto and for the Security Council as a whole.[14]

As a second exception to the general prohibition against the international use of force, the UN Charter reconfirms all States' inherent right of individual or collective self-defence until the Security Council has taken those measures necessary to maintain international peace and security.[15] This exception has no relevance for the following text.

During the bi-polar confrontation of the Cold War, the collective security system was never actualised in the great number of regional conflicts that were linked to the East–West struggle for power. However, the UN system managed to avoid

[13] *Ibid*, Art 27.

[14] On the use of the veto, see A Patil, *The UN Veto in World Affairs 1946–1992* (London, Mansell, 1992).

[15] Charter of the United Nations, Art 51.

being totally redundant with regard to its paramount objective, the maintenance of international peace and security. The clearest example of such a constructive development is the creation of peacekeeping operations, the so-called Blue Helmets.[16] This instrument has no explicit foundation in the Charter and should be seen as an outflow of the competence of the Council to call upon the parties concerned to comply with provisional measures, as it deems necessary.

According to principles that have been developed successively since 1956,[17] a peacekeeping operation is deployed with the consent of the host State, the operation is neutral to the parties of the conflict, and the use of force is limited to self-defence and defence of the mandate.[18] Thus, peacekeeping operations are not coercive measures that have the character of sanctions, and a mandate based on Chapter VII is not necessary. Traditionally, peacekeeping operations have been essentially military in character, primarily involving observation, monitoring, reporting, supervision of ceasefires and confidence-building measures.

III. UN CRISIS MANAGEMENT AFTER THE END OF THE COLD WAR

After the end of the Cold War, the possibility for Common Positions to be agreed by the permanent Members of the Security Council greatly improved. This new situation made it possible to activate the collective security system for the first time in an international conflict: the 1990 authorisation of the use of coercive military force against Iraq as a sanction for the Iraqi military aggression against Kuwait.[19] The UN system also faced the challenge of adapting itself to a new international political landscape including new perceptions of threat.[20] This adaptation has included a far more ambitious UN involvement in crisis management, most importantly through the development of the peacekeeping instrument.

The operations have evolved from a primarily military model of observing ceasefires and the separation of forces after inter-State wars, to incorporate a complex model of many elements—military, police and civilian—primarily answering to the need to establish political stability following intra-State conflicts. While maintaining

[16] Concerning the development of UN peacekeeping operations during the Cold War, see W Durch (ed), *The Evolution of Peacekeeping* (New York, St Martins Press, 1992).

[17] At which time UN Emergency Force I (UNEF I) was deployed with the mandate to supervise the Israel–Egypt truce in the Sinai. The decision to set up the operation was taken by the UN General Assembly in its first special emergency session, 5 November 1956, UNGA Res 1000 (ES-I), available at <http://www.un.org/ga/search/view_doc.asp?symbol=A/3354&Lang=E>.

[18] *United Nations Peacekeeping Operations—Principles and Guidelines* (United Nations Department of Peacekeeping Operations, New York, 2008) 31–35.

[19] SC Res 678 (1990).

[20] See the Common Statement by the Heads of State or Government of the members of the Security Council, published in UN Doc S/PV.3046, 31 January 1992, 141–47, available at <http://daccess-dds-ny.un.org/doc/UNDOC/PRO/N92/601/98/PDF/N9260198.pdf?OpenElement>. This Statement intitated a process whereby the UN Secretary-General took further initiative for reform in *An Agenda for Peace. Preventive diplomacy, peacemaking and peace-keeping. Report of the Secretary-General pursuant to the statement adopted by the Summit Meeting of the Security Council on 31 January 1992*, UN Doc A/47/277-S/24111, available at <http://www.un.org/Docs/SG/agpeace.html>.

the fundamental principles of consent, neutrality and limited use of force, the Security Council to an increasing extent has made use of Chapter VII of the UN Charter to mandate so-called *robust* peacekeeping operations, thereby blurring the distinction between peacekeeping and mandates for the coercive use of military force.[21] This modern type of peacekeeping operation could in most cases be referred to as a *peace-implementing operation.* It is deployed with the consent of the host State, and is mandated by the Security Council under Chapter VII of the UN Charter. Therefore the scope for the use of force is usually greater than in a traditional peacekeeping operation. Such operations often have the aim of implementing a ceasefire or armistice agreement, and constitute an instrument in a process of State building. An example illustrating this kind of operation is the United Nations Organization Mission in the Democratic Republic of Congo (MONUC), monitoring the implementation of the Lusaka Agreement on ceasefire in the Democratic Republic of Congo.[22]

In addition to their increasingly ambitious scope, it should also be noted that the number of UN-led peacekeeping operations has increased dramatically since the early 1990s.[23] As a consequence of these developments, the demand for resources to execute such operations has increased radically.

The Security Council has, furthermore, in addition to the expansion of UN-led peacekeeping, to an increasing extent, with reference to Chapter VII of the UN Charter, adopted mandates for regional arrangements or *ad hoc* coalitions to execute robust peacekeeping operations. Examples of such 'subcontracted' operations include the EU Military Force in Bosnia and Herzegovina (EUFOR-Althea) executed by the EU within the framework of the ESDP, monitoring the implementation of the Dayton Agreement,[24] and the ISAF in Afghanistan, executed under NATO command, furthering the implementation of the Bonn Agreement on the future of Afghanistan.[25] This model of subcontracting, through Security Council mandates, has also been used for operations with the aim of supporting ongoing UN-led operations, or as emergency actions of shorter duration, preparing for the arrival of a UN-led operation. As examples could be mentioned the EU military operation in the Democratic Republic of Congo 2006, which worked in close coordination with the UN MONUC operation, and the EU military

[21] Cf above n 18, 9–17.

[22] *Ceasefire agreement*, Lusaka July 1999, available at <http://www.iss.co.za/af/profiles/drcongo/cdreader/bin/2lusaka.pdf>. MONUC was established by SC Res 1291 (2000).

[23] From 1956 until 2009 the Security Council decided on the setting up of 63 peacekeeping operations. Of these, 45 were set up after 1990. A comprehensive list of past and present UN peacekeeping operations is available at <http://www.un.org/en/peacekeeping/list.shtml>.

[24] *The General Framework Agreement for Peace in Bosnia and Herzegovina*, Paris, 14 December 1995. Available at <http://www.ohr.int/dpa/default.asp?content_id=380>. EUFOR-Althea was mandated by SC Res 1575 (2004) and established by Council Joint Action 2004/570/CFSP, [2004] OJ L252/10.

[25] *Agreement on provisional arrangements in Afghanistan pending the re-establishment of permanent government institutions*, Bonn, 5 December 2001, available at <http://www.afghangovernment.com/AfghanAgreementBonn.htm>. ISAF was initially mandated by SC Res 1386 (2001). NATO took command of ISAF in August 2003 upon the request of the UN and the Government of the Islamic Republic of Afghanistan.

operation in Chad 2008, which had the objective of protecting refugees from Darfur and facilitating delivery of humanitarian assistance before the arrival of the UN MINURCAT operation.[26]

IV. THE QUESTION OF HUMANITARIAN INTERVENTION

When speaking of 'humanitarian intervention' we refer to a coercive military crisis management operation in the territory of another State with the aim of preventing or ending widespread and systematic violations of fundamental human rights in that State.

In accordance with practice established by the Security Council in the 1990s, such an operation could be mandated on the basis of Chapter VII of the UN Charter. In a number of cases the Security Council has established that grave and consistent violations of human rights within a State may constitute a 'threat to peace' as set out in Article 39 of the UN Charter. Based on this finding, the Council, in a limited number of cases, has authorised military interventions with the aim of addressing humanitarian crises. Thus, the potential importance of the UN system for safeguarding fundamental human rights has been demonstrated.[27] The central example of such a situation is the mandate authorising the use of force in Somalia adopted by the Security Council in 1992.[28] The primary objective of this operation was to establish a secure environment for humanitarian relief operations in Somalia.[29] The mandates for military operations safeguarding deliveries of humanitarian assistance to Sarajevo in 1992[30] and for the enforcement of the flight ban in the airspace of Bosnia[31] fall into the same category. So does the Security Council authorisation of the French military intervention in Rwanda 1994, with the aim of establishing safe havens for refugees.[32]

[26] EUFOR Democratic Republic of Congo, deployed April 2006 to November 2006, mandated by SC Res 1671 (2006) and established by Council Joint Action 2006/319/CFSP, [2006] OJ L116/98. EUFOR Tchad/RCA, deployed January 2008 to March 2009, mandated by SC Res 1778 (2007) and established by Council Joint Action 2007/677/CFSP, [2007] OJ L279/21.

[27] For a detailed account of this development, see D Amnéus, *Responsibility to Protect by Military Means—Emerging Norms on Humanitarian Intervention?* (Stockholm, Stockholm University Press, 2008) 342–82.

[28] Operation 'Restore Hope', mandated by SC Res 794 (1992). Forces from the USA and 24 other States under US command executed the operation.

[29] The operation was considered as successful, at least initially. However, the follow-up UN operation (UNOSOM II), established by SC Res 814 (1993), later became drawn into conflict with one of the parties to the ongoing civil war and could not carry out its mandate.

[30] SC Res 770 (1992). NATO and States participating in Partnership for Peace executed the operation (IFOR)

[31] SC Res 816 (1993). NATO executed the operation.

[32] Operation 'Turquoise', mandated by SC Res 929 (1994). The operation was led by France and included French and Senegalese troops. This limited operation could be seen as an imperfect measure of last resort in a situation when there were no willing contributors of resources for an expansion of the already established UN-led operation in Rwanda, UNAMIR. It was never in a position effectively

Since 1994, the Security Council has adopted no effective mandates for coercive humanitarian interventions,[33] and in the following years the question of humanitarian intervention primarily has been discussed with reference to the responsibility to take action against manifest violations of fundamental human rights. To which extent does the UN system have a duty to act, and to what extent has the international community a right to act in cases where the UN system fails to meet such a responsibility?

This debate should be seen as a reaction to the failure of the UN system to prevent mass killing and systematic ethnic cleansing in a number of shocking situations, such as Northern Iraq (1991), Rwanda (1993–94), Kosovo (1999) and Darfur (2003 to the present). This inability of the UN to address humanitarian catastrophes could be attributed both to the reluctance of the UN Member States to provide necessary resources for the effective execution of operations and to the use of the veto by permanent Members of the Security Council.

The debate was furthermore boosted by the NATO aerial operations against Serbia in 1999, in response to the Yugoslavian policy of repression, persecution and ethnic cleansing of the Kosovo Albanians in Kosovo. These coercive acts of military force were not authorised by the Security Council under Chapter VII.[34] Thus, the NATO operation constituted a principal infringement of the prohibitions on the international use of force laid down in the UN Charter. Nevertheless, it gained wide acceptance within the Member States of the EU and the NATO. This acceptance was not, however, based primarily on a legal line of argument but on a political one. The common formula became that the operation was *illegal but politically/morally legitimate*, with reference to the imperative to avoid a humanitarian catastrophe, a formula for justification that is also expressed in the Final Report of the Independent International Commission on Kosovo.[35]

to halt the ongoing genocide. For an analysis of operation 'Turquoise', see L Melvern, *A People betrayed: the role of the West in Rwanda's genocide* (London and Cape Town, Zed Books, 2000) 210–38.

[33] There are two later cases that could be viewed as falling within this category. The mandate for the International Force for East Timor, SC Res 1264 (1999), was adopted under Chapter VII with the objectives of restoring order and security, protecting the UN Mission in East Timor (UNAMET) and facilitating the delivery of humanitarian assistance. However, the operation was not of a formally coercive character when the Government of Indonesia consented to it. In 2006 the Security Council, referring to Chapter VII, authorised the use of all necessary means to protect UN personnel in Darfur and to prevent the disruption of the implementation of the Darfur Peace Agreement, SC Res 1706 (2006), para 12. This was a mandate for a UN-led coercive humanitarian intervention, not requiring the consent of the target State. However, due to the lack of consent by the Sudanese Government, no troop contributions were offered for the execution of this mandate. The risk of becoming involved in an armed conflict with the regular Sudanese army constituted a major deterring factor.

[34] The Security Council could not reach an agreement on authorising enforcement action in the resolutions preceding the aerial operations, because of resistance from Russia and China. Nevertheless the situation in Kosovo was determined by the Council to constitute a threat to peace and security in the region. See SC Res 1203 (1998).

[35] Independent International Commission on Kosovo, *The Kosovo Report: International Responses, Lessons Learned* (Oxford, Oxford University Press, 2000) 163–96.

This line of argument is certainly hard to defend from a legal theoretical perspective, as it constitutes an attempt to safeguard the general normativity of international law and simultaneously justify law-breaking behaviour in the particular case. Thus, according to this position, the legal prohibition on the use of international force is made relative to political preferences. It follows that such a stance contributes to the undermining of law's primacy over political decision making.

Recognising this problem, a number of proposals for establishing criteria for the legality of humanitarian intervention were presented in the international debate during the early 2000s.

In the 2001 Report by the Independent International Commission on Kosovo (above), an inconclusive attempt was made to close the gap between legality and legitimacy. The Report recommended in this connection that a framework of principles for humanitarian intervention should be developed and formally adopted by the UN General Assembly in the form of a 'Declaration on the Right and Responsibility of Humanitarian Intervention'. The UN Charter should thereafter be adapted to this Declaration, either by amendments or by a case-by-case approach in the Security Council.[36]

The proposal with the greatest impact in this field is undoubtedly the Report of the International Commission on Intervention and State Sovereignty (ICISS), *The Responsibility to Protect*, which was published in 2001.[37] The Report can be seen as an attempt to reconcile State sovereignty with the concept of humanitarian intervention. At the core of the argument lies the principle that State sovereignty implies responsibility, and that the primary responsibility for the protection of its people lies with the State. However, where a population is suffering serious harm due to the failure of the State to meet this responsibility, the principle of non-intervention yields to the international responsibility to protect. The ICISS Report develops criteria for military intervention in terms of just cause thresholds and right authority. In this connection the Report reconfirms the primary responsibility of Security Council and calls on the permanent Member States to act on their special responsibility by limiting their use of the veto.[38] In a case where the Council fails to meet the responsibility to protect, the Report identifies two alternative options to gain authority: the referral of the matter to the General Assembly under the 'Uniting for Peace' procedure; or relying on action by regional organisations *within* the organisation's defining borders, under Chapter VIII of the UN Charter.[39] Such an internal

[36] *Ibid*, 187.

[37] *The Responsibility to Protect*, Report of the International Commission on Intervention and State Sovereignty (Ottawa, International Development Research Center, 2001) available at <http://www.idrc.ca/openbooks/960-7/>.

[38] *Ibid*, paras 6.13–6.21. The Report proposes the development of a principle of constructive abstention in cases where no vital national interests are at stake, through an informal mutual agreement between the five permanent Member States. The risk of an abusive use of the veto could thereby be decreased.

[39] This approach has been made concrete within the African Union, where the Member States, by acceding to the organisation's constitutive act, have accepted the right of the Union to intervene *in*

regional action should be clearly differentiated from an external action by a regional organisation against a non-Member State, which is rightly perceived as much more controversial.[40] It is, however, recognised that neither of these alternative options can establish a formal legality for an intervention. The General Assembly can act only through recommendations, not legally-binding decisions, and actions decided upon by regional organisations under Chapter VIII are formally subject to prior authorisation by the Security Council. Rather, the use of the above-mentioned alternative options could strengthen the political legitimacy of the action taken, and generate pressure on the Security Council to give approval *ex post facto*.[41] The ICISS Report thus identifies the central dilemma and formulates it clearly:

> As a matter of political reality, it would be impossible to find consensus, in the Commission's view, around any set of proposals for military intervention, which acknowledges the validity of any intervention not authorised by the Security Council or the General Assembly. But that may still leave circumstances when the Security Council fails to discharge what this Commission would regard as its responsibility to protect, in a conscience-shocking situation crying out for action. It is a real question in these circumstances where lies the most harm: in the damage to international order if the Security Council is bypassed or in the damage to that order if human beings are slaughtered while the Security Council stands by.[42]

Hence, the bottom line of the Report could be summarised as a call on the Security Council to shoulder its responsibility. Otherwise the legitimacy of the UN system will be at risk.

As predicted in the ICISS Report, no international consensus on alternative bases for rendering legality to a humanitarian intervention, in a situation where the Security Council has failed to act, has been attained.[43] Nevertheless, the

a Member State pursuant to a decision of the Assembly in respect of grave circumstances, namely: war crimes, genocide and crimes against humanity, as well as serious threat to the Member State of the Union upon the recommendation of the Peace and Security Council: the Constitutive Act of the African Union, Art 4(h), as amended by the Protocol on Amendments to the Constitutive Act of the African Union, Maputo, July 2003 (emphasis added), available at <http://www.africa-union.org/root/au/AboutAU/Constitutive_Act_en.htm>. It should be noted in this connection that there are no signs that the EU aspires to be perceived as a regional arrangement for collective security in the meaning of the UN Charter, Chapter VIII. In order to control the internal situation in the Member States, the EU primarily relies on the ability to suspend a Member State that seriously and persistently has acted in breach of the Union's founding values: Art 7 TEU (post-Lisbon).

40 Above n 37, para 6.34.

41 *Ibid*, paras 6.30 and 6.35. The opening up for *ex post facto* authorisation could be seen as inconsistent with the proposition that the Security Council is the only proper authority for a humanitarian intervention. For a critical analysis of the issue of *ex post facto* authorisation by the Security Council, see E De Wet, 'The relationship between the Security Council and Regional Organizations during Enforcement Action under Chapter VII of the United Nations Charter' (2002) 71 *Nordic Journal of International Law* 1.

42 Above n 37, para 6.37.

43 In spite of the lack of an international consensus, it is frequently maintained in doctrine that there exist criteria for legal unilateral humanitarian intervention in cases where the Security Council has been unable to authorise intervention to address a compelling and urgent situation of extreme humanitarian distress. See, eg, A Aust, *Handbook of International Law* (Cambridge, Cambridge University Press, 2005) 231.

responsibility to protect was addressed in the 2005 World Summit Outcome.[44] In this authoritative statement by the UN General Assembly, the primary responsibility of each State to protect its population from genocide, war crimes, ethnic cleansing and crimes against humanity is reaffirmed, and the subsidiary external responsibility of the international community is acknowledged and specified.[45] Accordingly, all States have a responsibility to make available resources necessary to prevent or halt a humanitarian catastrophe taking place elsewhere. Concerning legal authority, the Security Council is acknowledged as the exclusive source.[46] However, it should be noted that, in contrast to the ICISS Report, the World Summit Outcome does not call on the permanent Members of the Security Council to refrain from using their veto in cases of genocide, war crimes, ethnic cleansing and crimes against humanity.[47] Neither does it address explicitly a situation where the Security Council has failed to meet its responsibility.

V. EFFECTIVE MULTILATERALISM—A CONDITIONAL EUROPEAN LOYALTY TO THE UN SYSTEM

As a collective, the Member States of the EU constitute a central actor within the UN system. They provide financing for approximately 40 per cent of the regular UN budget as well as of the budget for UN-led crisis management operations.[48] Furthermore, several of the Member States have a tradition of active UN support, including the provision of military and diplomatic resources for peacekeeping operations. In this connection, the Member States that conducted a Cold War policy of active neutrality stand out. It should be noted, however, that since the 1990s, in parallel with the development of the ESDP, there has been a clear shift in this pattern, as the Member States have been increasingly reluctant to provide personnel to UN-led operations. The majority of manpower for such operations is today provided by South-Asian or African States.[49]

[44] UNGA Res 2005 World Summit Outcome, UN Doc A/RES/60/1, available at <http://daccess-dds-ny.un.org/doc/UNDOC/GEN/N05/487/60/PDF/N0548760.pdf?OpenElement>.

[45] *Ibid*, paras 138–39.

[46] *Ibid*, para 79.

[47] See further on this issue AL Bannon, 'The Responsibility To Protect: The UN World Summit and the Question of Unilateralism' (2006) 115 *Yale Law Journal* 1157, 1160. Bannon holds that it was largely due to US opposition that the World Summit Outcome did not include a proposed call on the permanent members of the Security Council to refrain from using their veto power in a situation of grave humanitarian suffering. According to Bannon, this leaves the permanent members with a powerful negotiating tool, permitting bad faith vetoes in the face of clear atrocities.

[48] *Assessment of Member States' contributions to the United Nations regular budget for the year 2009*, UN Doc ST/ADM/SER.B/755, available at <http://www.un.org/ga/search/view_doc.asp?symbol=ST/ADM/SER.B/755>.

[49] Cf *Monthly Summary of Contributors of Military and Civilian Police Personnel*, available at <http://www.un.org/en/peacekeeping/contributors/>. This reluctance to participate in UN operations has been attributed to experiences from the failed UN-led operation in Srebrenica in 1995. See A Novosseloff, *EU–UN Partnership in Crisis Management: Developments and Prospects* (New York,

The Member States' history of loyalty to the UN and the hope of making the UN an effective structure for furthering international peace and security are nevertheless mirrored in the development of the ESDP. The introduction of the Petersberg tasks into the EU framework, and the design of military capacities answerable to the EU, clearly reflect the needs of the UN in the execution of crisis management operations mandated by the Security Council.

On a political, strategic level, the European loyalty to the UN is encapsulated in the doctrine of effective multilateralism, which constitutes a cornerstone of the European Security Strategy (ESS), adopted in 2003 and reviewed in 2008.[50] In the ESS, which is officially referred to as a key framework for policy formulation,[51] the Union confirms its commitment to multilateral solutions and the position that the

> fundamental framework for international relations is the United Nations Charter. The United Nations Security Council has the primary responsibility for the maintenance of international peace and security. Strengthening the United Nations, equipping it to fulfil its responsibilities and to act effectively, is a European priority.[52]

This statement echoes a European credo regarding rule-based governance, and it does in this respect *prima facie* differ from the corresponding principles expressed in the US National Security Strategies adopted during the Bush era.[53]

Through the Lisbon Treaty amendments, the commitment to multilateralism has become codified in an explicit provision reconfirming that the Union shall promote multilateral solutions to common problems, in particular in the framework of the United Nations.[54]

However, at the same time as the Union declares its loyalty to the UN system, and its willingness to equip this system with resources in order to make it more effective, the Union seems to reserve to itself a non-defined scope for unilateral military action in exceptional situations.

International Peace Academy, 2004) 8. Concerning the experiences drawn from the inability to prevent genocide in Srebrenica, see *Report of the Secretary-General pursuant to General Assembly resolution 53/35 The fall of Srebrenica*, UN Doc A /54/549, available at <http://www.un.org/peace/srebrenica.pdf>. For a general analysis of this development, see J Wouters and T Ruys, 'UN–EU cooperation on crisis management' in J Wouters, F Hoffmeister and T Ruys (eds), *The United Nations and the European Union: An Even Stronger Partnership* (The Hague, TMC Asser Press, 2006) 229, 248–50.

[50] *A Secure Europe in a Better World, European Security Strategy*, 12 December 2003, available at <http://www.consilium.europa.eu/uedocs/cmsUpload/78367.pdf>. *Report on the Implementation of the European Security Strategy, Providing Security in a Changing World*, 11 December 2008, available at <http://www.consilium.europa.eu/ueDocs/cms_Data/docs/pressData/en/reports/104630.pdf>.

[51] See, eg, *Brussels European Council 17 and 18 June 2004 Presidency Conclusions*, p 11, available at <http://www.consilium.europa.eu/uedocs/cmsUpload/81742.pdf>.

[52] *A Secure Europe in a Better World*, above n 50, at 9.

[53] *The National Security Strategy of the United States of America*, September 2002, available at <http://www.globalsecurity.org/military/library/policy/national/nss-020920.pdf>. *The National Security Strategy of the United States of America*, March 2006, available at <http://georgewbush-whitehouse.archives.gov/nsc/nss/2006/nss2006.pdf>.

[54] Art 21(1) TEU (post-Lisbon).

Neither in the Treaty on European Union, nor in the Security Strategy are there any references to the fact that coercive military operations require a mandate from the Security Council under Chapter VII of the UN Charter. In Article 21(2) TEU (post-Lisbon), defining the objectives of the Common Foreign and Security Policy (CFSP), we find a general reference to the UN Charter: Union policy, with the objectives of preserving peace, preventing conflicts and strengthening international security, shall be conducted *in accordance with the purposes and principles of the United Nations Charter*. Moreover, the TEU (post-Lisbon) includes a specific provision stating that ESDP missions may be used outside the Union for peacekeeping, conflict prevention and strengthening international security *in accordance with the principles of the United Nations Charter*.[55]

The normative meaning of these general references can be discussed. However, it is clear that there is a wide scope for interpretation of the purposes and principles of the UN Charter, and there exists no consensus among the Member States on such an interpretation.

This principled loyalty to the UN system is echoed in the doctrine of effective multilateralism as spelled out in the ESS. In addition to a preparedness to support the UN, this doctrine also includes a demand that international organisations, regimes and treaties are to be effective *in confronting threats to international peace and security,* and that the EU *must therefore be ready to act when their rules are broken.*[56] Thus, effective multilateralism seems to mean enforceable multilateralism.

The ESS is silent on the issue how the Union should act when a multilateral organisation is perceived as not being capable of acting in order to safeguard compliance with the rules it is set to uphold. A concrete situation of this kind would be when the Security Council is not capable of adopting mandates for coercive measures under Chapter VII of the UN Charter against a State that, according to the EU, constitutes a threat to international peace and security. Thus, the doctrine of effective multilateralism opens up alternative ways of action in cases of perceived multilateral inefficiency.

Through the absence of more precise references to the UN Charter, and the doctrine of effective multilateralism, a conscious ambiguity has been established which could be interpreted differently by different Member States. This ambiguity is due to the absence of agreement among the Member States on whether a Security Council mandate is a *necessary* precondition for executing a coercive military operation that, in exceptional circumstances, could be justified as politically/morally legitimate with reference to the principles of the UN Charter. Evidently this does not contradict that there exists unanimity

[55] Art 42(1) TEU (post-Lisbon).

[56] *A Secure Europe in a Better World*, above n 50, at 9.

among the Member States that a Security Council mandate is a *desirable* precondition.[57]

Hence, the EU has reserved to itself room for unilateral action in situations when multilateralism within the UN sphere is not considered to be effective with reference to the principles of the UN Charter. The more precise scope of this reserved room for unilateral action has to be defined through negotiations between the Member States in each specific case.[58]

VI. CONCRETE COOPERATION BETWEEN THE EU AND THE UN

Before analysing the possible structural effects of the doctrine of effective multilateralism, a brief account is required of the development of concrete cooperation between the EU and the UN on crisis management since 2003. That year constitutes the watershed for the rapid process of intensified EU–UN cooperation. In May 2003, the first military ESDP units were declared to be ready for deployment across the full range of Petersberg tasks,[59] largely in accordance with the 1999 Helsinki Headline Goal.[60] Two military ESDP crisis management operations, based on mandates adopted by the Security Council and acceptance by the host States, were put into action the same year.[61] These operations were soon recognised as providing a

[57] Cf General Affairs and External Relations Council, *Paper for the submission to the High-Level Panel on Threats, Challenges and Change*, 18 May 2004, p 12, available at <http://www.consilium.europa.eu/uedocs/cmsUpload/EU%20written%20contribution2.pdf, para 38>: 'The EU holds the view that massive violations of human rights and genocide represent a threat to international peace and security and that the use of force may be needed to prevent or to halt them. The Security Council should assume its responsibility in this regard. The EU believes that there is a need to clarify the international principles that would authorise, in exceptional circumstances outside intervention in the territory of a sovereign country to prevent a humanitarian catastrophe.'

[58] Strangely enough, it is possible to find a more precise definition in the literature according to which the EU has granted itself the option to intervene without a UN mandate in Europe and only with a UN mandate elsewhere. See, eg, Novosseloff, above n 49, at 8, available at <http://www.ipacademy.org/media/pdf/publications/eu_un_partnership.pdf>.

[59] General Affairs and External Relations Council, 19 May 2003, *Declaration on EU Military Capabilities*, available at <http://www.consilium.europa.eu/uedocs/cmsUpload/Declaration%20on%20EU%20Military%20Capabilities%20-%20May%202003.pdf>. Already in 2001 the European Council had stated that 'the Union is now capable to conduct some crisis-management operations'. See *Presidency Conclusions, European Council in Laeken, 14 and 15 December 2001*, 27, available at <http://www.consilium.europa.eu/uedocs/cms_data/docs/pressdata/en/ec/68827.pdf>.

[60] *Helsinki European Council, 10 and 11 December 1999, Presidency Conclusions*, Annex 1 to Annex IV, available at <http://www.consilium.europa.eu/uedocs/cms_data/docs/pressdata/en/ec/ACFA4C.htm>.

[61] Operation 'Concordia', deployed January to December 2003, was a successor of the NATO operation 'Allied Harmony', with the objective to facilitate the implementation of the Ohrid Framework Agreement in the Former Yugoslav Republic of Macedonia. Council Joint Action 2003/92/CFSP, [2003] OJ L34/26; SC Res 1317 (2000). Operation 'Artemis', deployed June to September 2003, had the objective to further stability in the eastern parts of the Democratic Republic of Congo before the arrival of the UN-led operation MONUC. Council Joint Action 2003/423/CFSP, [2003] OJ L143/50; SC Res 1484 (2003).

strong impetus to cooperation between the EU and the UN.[62] From an institutional perspective, formalisation of the relationship between the EU and the UN took place through a Joint Declaration, issued in September 2003, concerning crisis management, communication, capacity building and experience sharing on completed operations.[63] Subsequently a Joint Consultative Mechanism was created.[64]

Building on the success of the then deployed operations, and in order to contribute to the implementation of the Joint Declaration, the European Council subsequently decided to develop the ESDP military capacity further by setting up flexible rapid reaction capabilities—so-called Battle Groups, primarily designed for operations following UN requests, ready for deployment in 2007[65]—and establishing a new Headline Goal to be attained in 2010.[66] As a final element of the intensive development of the ESDP during 2003, the ESS was adopted in December, underlining the EU's willingness to strengthen the UN system.

It should be noted that this development took place in the aftermath of the Iraq crisis, when the Member States of the Union were fundamentally split on the issues of the legality and legitimacy of the US-led intervention in Iraq, and trust in the UN system was at a very low point. Hence, the European actions strengthening the ESDP could be seen as a conscious move to further the rehabilitation of the UN system.

Since 2003 the EU has deployed 22 ESDP operations, mainly in the Balkans and Sub-Saharan Africa. Sixteen of these have had a civilian character, and thus are not relevant as regards the regulation of the international use of force. All six military operations were based on a mandate from the Security Council and consent from

[62] *Thessaloniki European Council, 19 and 20 June 2003, Presidency Conclusions*, 18, available at <http://www.consilium.europa.eu/ueDocs/cms_Data/docs/pressData/en/ec/76279.pdf>.

[63] *Joint Declaration on UN–EU Cooperation in Crisis Management*, New York, 24 September 2003, available at <http://www.consilium.europa.eu/uedocs/cmsUpload/st12730.en03.pdf>. See also *EU–UN Co-operation in Military Crisis Management Operations Elements of Implementation of the EU–UN Joint Declaration*, adopted by the European Council 17–18 June 2004, available at <http://www.consilium.europa.eu/uedocs/cmsUpload/EUUN_cooperation_in_Military_Crisis_Management_Operations.pdf>. A subsequent *Joint Statement on UN–EU Cooperation in Crisis Management* was issued 7 June 2007, available at <http://www.consilium.europa.eu/uedocs/cmsUpload/EU-UNstatmntoncrsmngmnt.pdf>.

[64] The Joint Consultative Mechanism became operational in January 2004. See: *EU–UN Co-operation in Military Crisis Management Operations Elements of Implementation of the EU–UN Joint Declaration*, adopted by the European Council, 17–18 June 2004, para 2, available at <http://www.consilium.europa.eu/uedocs/cmsUpload/EU-UN%20co-operation%20in%20Military%20Crisis%20Management%20Operations.pdf>.

[65] On the setting up of the EU battlegroups, see G Lindstrom, 'Enter the EU Battlegroups' (Paris, Institute for Security Studies, 2007) 9–26, available at <http://www.iss.europa.eu/uploads/media/cp097.pdf>.

[66] The Headline Goal 2010 was approved by General Affairs and External Relations Council on 17 May 2004. See *Headline Goal 2010*, available at <http://www.consilium.europa.eu/uedocs/cmsUpload/2010%20Headline%20Goal.pdf>. It was subsequently endorsed by the European Council, *Brussels European Council, 17 and 18 June 2004, Presidency Conclusions*, p 13, available at <http://www.consilium.europa.eu/uedocs/cmsUpload/81742.pdf>.

the host State.[67] When appropriate, the ESDP operations were coordinated with UN-led operations.

Even if the number of ESDP operations so far has been limited, it is possible to differentiate between three different categories of operations:

a) *stand-alone operations* that are mandated by the Security Council with no simultaneous UN-led deployment[68];
b) *stand-by operations* with the objective of supporting a pre-existing UN-led operation[69]; and
c) *rapidly deployed bridging operations* of relatively short duration, preparing for the arrival of an UN-led operation.[70]

It may be concluded that the deployed ESDP operations have been executed in concordance with the UN system. Within the Union there seems to have developed a presumption of the existence of mutually beneficial relationship where the UN and the EU are 'natural partners'.[71] The willingness of the EU to develop military capabilities for the execution of robust peacekeeping operations has been recognised and commended by the UN.[72] Thus, it cannot be doubted that the EU, so far, through concrete ESDP operations, has contributed to the strengthening of the UN system, making multilateralism somewhat more effective.

It should be noted, however, that the military ESDP operations, with no exceptions, have been of an independent character. In no case has the Union accepted subordination to UN command. Rather, autonomy of action has been stressed as a core concept.[73] In combination with the increased reluctance of EU Member

[67] In addition to the two operations deployed in 2003 and mentioned above in n 60, the EU has deployed the following military ESDP crisis management operations: EUFOR Althea, Bosnia-Herzegovina, deployed in December 2004 and still in operation, with the objective to contribute to the consolidation of peace in accordance with the Dayton Agreement, Council Joint Action 2004/570/CFSP, [2004] OJ L252/10, SC Res 1575 (2004); EUFOR Democratic Republic of Congo, deployed April to November 2006, with the objective to support the UN operation MONUC, Council Joint Action 2006/319/CFSP, [2006] OJ L116/98, SC Res 1671 (2006); EUFOR Chad/RCA, deployed January 2008 to March 2009, with the objective to protect refugees from Darfur and facilitating delivery of humanitarian assistance before the arrival of the UN operation MINURCAT, Joint Action 2007/677/CFSP, [2007] OJ L279/21, SC Res 1778 (2007); EU NAVFOR Somalia, deployed since December 2008, with the objective to protect vessels of the World Food Programme delivering food aid to Somalia as well as other vessels cruising off the Somali coast, Joint Actions 2008/749/CFSP, [2008] OJ L252/39 and 2008/851/CFSP, [2008] OJ L 301/33, SC Res 1814 (2008), 1816 (2008) and 1846 (2008).

[68] Operation 'Concordia', Former Yugoslav Republic of Macedonia, deployed January to December 2003; EUFOR Althea, Bosnia-Herzegovina, deployed since December 2004; EU NAVFOR Somalia, deployed since December 2008.

[69] EUFOR Democratic Republic of Congo, deployed April to November 2006.

[70] Operation Artemis, eastern parts of the Democratic Republic of Congo, deployed June to September 2003; EUFOR Chad/RCA, deployed January 2008 to March 2009.

[71] See, eg, statement of Commissioner Ferrero-Waldner on the UN Summit press conference, 12 September 2005, available at <http://www.europa-eu-un.org/articles/en/article_5011_en.htm>.

[72] *UNGA 2005 World Summit Outcome*, A/60/L.1, para 93.

[73] Cf T Tardy, *UN–EU Relations in Crisis Management, Taking Stock and Looking Ahead* (Geneva, Geneva Centre for Security Policy, 2008) 16, available at <http://www.gcsp.ch/e/publications/Issues_Institutions/Int_Organisations/policy_papers/tardy_eu_un.pdf>.

States to provide troops for UN-led operations, it might accordingly be argued that the development of the ESDP has meant that the Member States have shifted their focus from direct involvement in multilateral action to regional action, in coordination with the multilateral structure. This situation could be criticised as leading to the risk of crisis management segregation, where better-trained and better-equipped EU troops seldom operate alongside troops from the relatively poorer States that provide the bulk of personnel for UN-led operations.[74] Taking a longer-term view, there is a risk that this situation will lead to tensions along the North–South divide, thereby undermining the mutual multilateral trust that is necessary for the effective functioning of the UN. Consequently, it seems appropriate to hoist a flag of warning that the future development of the ESDP could lead to a 'peacekeeping apartheid' that would counteract the objective of attaining an effective multilateralism.[75]

VII. POTENTIAL STRUCTURAL EFFECTS OF THE UNION'S CONDITIONAL LOYALTY TO THE UNITED NATIONS

A legal infringement of the prohibition on the international use of force can occur only with regard to the use of military force of a coercive character. With regard to military peacekeeping and peace-implementing operations, which are conducted with the consent of the host State, a mandate from the Security Council does not constitute a legal prerequisite for them to be carried out. Hence, a legal tension or conflict with reference to the doctrine of effective multilateralism cannot develop concerning this type of operation. However, from a political perspective, it should be underlined that a mandate adopted at the multilateral UN level does strengthen the legitimacy of such operations. The multilateral character of the UN system leads to the situation that a mandate adopted by the Security Council conveys an air of impartiality to the operation, which furthers the chances of its successful completion. This legitimacy-strengthening effect is probably most important with regard to operations relating to intra-State conflicts. In such a case, an invitation to foreign military forces issued by the host State's government would hardly be a legitimising factor in the eyes of the opposition to that government. In a situation where the internal legitimacy of the government in power is weak, the need for legitimacy through a mandate from the Security Council is even greater. It should of course be underlined that a mandate through a resolution from the Security Council adds to the transparency of the operation, which furthers predictability concerning its execution. The resolution is a public, easily accessible document that sets down the objectives and the scope of the operation, and establishes limits to the level of force to be used.

[74] See above n 49.

[75] See further in WPS Sidhu, 'Regional Groups and Alliances' in TG Weiss and S Daws (eds), *Oxford Handbook on the United Nations* (Oxford, Oxford University Press, 2007).

All military ESDP operations deployed by the EU have had a non-coercive character, fulfilling the considerations mentioned above; and a kind of symbiosis seems to have been developed, whereby the UN gains efficiency and the EU legally-based legitimacy for its crisis management policy.

VIII. POTENTIAL REPERCUSSIONS ON THE MULTILATERAL LEGAL ORDER

As mentioned in the previous section, so far the EU has not executed any coercive military operations mandated by the Security Council; moreover, the EU has not yet been faced with the situation where an operation strongly favoured by its Member States as a collective, has been hindered due to the inability of the Security Council to decide upon a mandate for the use of force. Hence, the doctrine of effective multilateralism has not been fully tested yet.

However, the deliberate vagueness of the European stance regarding the possibility of exercising *coercive* military force without authorisation from the Security Council constitutes a reserved scope of action, primarily in cases where strong moral/ethical considerations call for the use of military force in accordance with the principles of the UN Charter and where the Security Council is not able to issue a mandate for such action—a situation of perceived ineffective multilateralism.

The position of the Union may be viewed as a consequence of the developing doctrine of an international responsibility to protect human beings from gross violations of human rights. Against this backdrop, the Union's position may be buttressed with strong, morally-based humanistic arguments. Nevertheless, it brings with it the risk of contributing to the erosion of the regulation of the international use force laid down in the UN Charter. The position taken may therefore counteract the EU objective of strengthening the UN system.

It should be noted in this connection that the conditionality expressed by the Union in the ESS is of a general character. It does not explicitly refer to a particular type of situation, such as a manifest humanitarian crisis. Thus, it seems that the Union, through the doctrine of effective multilateralism, touches upon a tension between a principled interest to strengthen international law by its own compliance, and a political interest to assert Union power effectively in the international arena. In certain situations these two interests may not be congruent.

The conditional loyalty to the UN system seems primarily to be based on an understanding that the power of veto of the five permanent Member States of the Security Council may be abused. In the European debate it is not uncommon to put forward as unsatisfactory a situation in which China has the ability to prevent the EU from intervening with military means in order to prevent a humanitarian catastrophe. The core of this line of argument is thus that certain permanent Member States of the Security Council are not seen as fully capable of taking responsibility for international peace and security in accordance with the principles of the UN Charter, and accordingly their power of veto cannot be accepted without reservations. The position of the Union further means that a consensus between the Member States concerning the execution of a military operation outside Union territory could be given priority over the UN Charter's prohibition on the international use of military force. The Member States of the Union have reserved to themselves a right to review the multilateral order in the light of a self-defined efficiency criterion with ethical/moral characteristics.

A mandate adopted by the Security Council is a legally-defined prerequisite for justifying the use of coercive military force. The argument that an operation may be illegal but still justified with reference to its political and moral legitimacy is, as stated above, an argument that from a legal and theoretical perspective effectively undermines the normativity of international law in general and the regulation of the use of force in particular. Moreover, international law is based on the principle of reciprocity of rights and duties between States. Accordingly, we have to ask ourselves the following question: Can it be accepted, from an EU perspective, that other States, or regional organisations, reserve to themselves a right to review the position taken by the UN Security Council with reference to a self-defined efficiency criterion, related to an unilateral interpretation of the principles of the UN Charter?

The conditional loyalty to the UN Charter's prohibition on the use of force expressed by the EU may accordingly lead to negative structural effects for the international legal system. Already the mere expression of a political doctrine of conditional loyalty may be used, or abused, by other States or regional organisations as a basis for arguments defending coercive interventions without a Security Council authorisation.[76]

In a situation where the Union decided to go ahead with a coercive international military operation without a prior mandate adopted by the Security Council, the negative effects for the international legal system could be acute. Moreover, if such an operation were perceived as an instrument to further the Union's interests, rather than as a necessary measure of last resort in order to stop a humanitarian catastrophe, the detrimental effects would be very serious indeed. This would further lead to an erosion of the general trust in the Union as a responsible international actor, as its actions could be condemned with reference to arguments of law. Nevertheless, the risks that such a situation would occur are certainly limited. The decision to conduct an ESDP operation requires unanimity among the Member States. As long as there exists a dominating belief in the importance of the normativity of the multilateral legal system among the Member States, such a decision could come about only in extreme, exceptional situations.

[76] See, eg, the argument presented by the Russian Minister of Foreign Affairs, Sergei Lavrov, in defence of the Russian intervention in Georgia 2008 with reference to the doctrine of the international responsibility to protect: Council of Foreign Relations, *A Conversation with Foreign Minister Sergei Lavrov, September 28, 2008*, available at <http://www.cfr.org/publication/17384/conversation_with_sergey_lavrov.html?breadcrumb=%2Fregion%2F324%2Fcaucasus>.

IX. CONDITIONAL LOYALTY AS A POLITICAL ARGUMENT

As has been shown above, the doctrine of effective multilateralism may lead to negative structural effects for the international legal order. Nevertheless, the EU position could also be viewed as a statement in an ongoing legal/political debate concerning the responsibilities of the Security Council. The conditional loyalty of the EU might generate pressure on the Security Council, resulting in a more effective multilateralism since it contributes to an increase in the political price for permanent Member States of the Council to hinder the adoption of a mandate for the use of force in a situation where a military operation is motivated by the need to counteract a serious humanitarian crisis. In its 2001 Report, *The Responsibility to Protect*, the ICISS also observed this type of dynamic effect, as an outflow of the involved actors' conditional loyalty:

> The Security Council should take into account in all its deliberations that, if it fails to discharge its responsibility to protect in conscience-shocking situations crying out for action, concerned states may not rule out other means to meet the gravity and urgency of that situation—and that the stature and credibility of the United Nations may suffer thereby.[77]

The conditional loyalty, encapsulated in the doctrine of effective multilateralism, might thereby further the effectiveness of the UN system, but only as long as the reserved scope for unilateral action is a reservation not perceived as a deviation from its basic loyalty to the UN system.

X. CONDITIONAL LOYALTY FORMULATED IN THE JUDICIAL ARENA

The political conditionality expressed by the Union which has been accounted for above, bears functional similarities with the judicial conditionality expressed by the European Court of Justice (ECJ) in its ruling in the *Kadi* case.[78] In its reasoning the ECJ found that an individual, identified as a target for sanctions by a sanctions committee set up by the UN Security Council, had no access to an efficient review procedure at the UN level.[79] Subsequently the Court asserted its competence to review the lawfulness of all Community acts in the light of the fundamental rights protected by Community law, including acts explicitly designed to give effect to a resolution adopted by the Security Council under Chapter VII of the UN Charter.[80]

[77] ICISS, above n 37, Core Principles; Principles for Military Intervention; (3) Right authority, para F.

[78] Joined Cases C-402/05 P and C-415/05 P *Yassin Abdullah Kadi and Al Barakaat International Foundation* v *Council of the European Union and Commission of the European Communities* [2008] ECR I-6351. An in-depth commentary on the *Kadi* case is to be found in ch 7 of this volume.

[79] *Ibid*, paras 320–25.

[80] *Ibid*, para 326.

By finding that a Community act implementing such sanctions infringed fundamental rights of the targeted individual under Community law, while not questioning the binding character of international law,[81] the ECJ expressed a conditional loyalty to the UN system. Thus, the ruling created pressure on the Security Council that may further reforms leading to more transparent and fair procedures at the UN level for review of decisions on individually-targeted sanctions. It could thereby contribute to a development that would increase the legitimacy of the UN system in general and the use of targeted sanctions in particular, thus improving the long-term efficiency of multilateralism.[82] This effect was probably not unintended by the Court. It responded to a widespread criticism of the Security Council's use of sanctions targeted at individuals while denying those individuals the right of access to a fair and efficient procedure for review.[83] It could also be argued, however, that the ruling brings with it negative repercussions for the general normativity of international law. Thus, this judicial conditionality includes a dilemma, similar to that which exists in the political doctrine of effective multilateralism. This dilemma was hinted at in the opinion by Advocate General Maduro, who came to the conclusion that the repercussions of the position taken by the ECJ on the international stage 'need not necessarily be negative'.[84]

It should also be noted that the ECJ judgment in the *Kadi* case to some extent might have been implicitly motivated by considerations internal to the Union. It is not unlikely that the long-established conditional acceptance of the supremacy of the Community legal order by the constitutional courts of the Member States created pressure on the ECJ. At least in theory, there existed a risk that a national

[81] *Ibid*, para 291.

[82] This effect of the conditional loyalty implicitly expressed by the ECJ in the *Kadi* case has been noted in several commentaries. See, eg: D Halberstam and E Stern 'The United Nations, the European Union, and the King of Sweden: Economic Sanctions and Individual Rights in a Plural World Order' (2009) 46 *CML Rev* 13; A Posch, 'The *Kadi* Case: Rethinking the Relationship Between EU Law and International Law' (2009) 15 *Columbia Journal of European Law Online*, available at <http://www.cjel.net/online/15_2-posch/>; M Heupel, 'Multilateral Sanctions Against Terror suspects and the Violation of Due Process Standards' (2009) 85 *International Affairs* 307.

[83] See, as examples of this critique: I Cameron, 'UN Targeted Sanctions, Legal Safeguards, and the ECHR' (2003) 72 *Nordic Journal of International Law* 1; P Cramér, 'Recent Swedish Experiences of with Targeted UN Sanctions: The Erosion of Trust in the Security Council' in E de Wet and A Nollenkaemper (eds), *Review of the Security Council by Member States* (Antwerp, Oxford, New York, Intersentia, 2003); JE Alvarez, 'Hegemonic International Law Revisited' (2003) 97 *American Journal of International Law* 873. See also the report *Strengthening Targeted Sanctions Through Fair and Clear Procedures*, White Paper prepared by the Watson Institute Targeted Sanctions Project, Brown University (Providence RI, Watson Institute for International Studies, 2006), available at <http://www.watsoninstitute.org/pub/Strengthening_Targeted_Sanctions.pdf>.

[84] Opinion of AG Poires Maduro, Case C-402/05, available at <http://curia.europa.eu/jurisp/cgi-bin/form.pl?lang=EN&Submit=rechercher&numaff=C-402/05>, para 38: 'Of course, if the Court were to find that the contested resolution cannot be applied in the Community legal order, this is likely to have certain repercussions on the international stage. It should be noted, however, that these repercussions need not necessarily be negative. They are the immediate consequence of the fact that, as the system governing the functioning of the United Nations now stands, the only option available to individuals who wish to have access to an independent tribunal in order to obtain adequate protection of their fundamental rights is to challenge domestic implementing measures before a domestic court.'

court in a Member State would have conducted a review in the light of national constitutional safeguards for fundamental rights, even if the ECJ had declined to review the contested act. Such an open revolt against the autonomy of the Community legal order would certainly have brought with it long-lasting detrimental effects for the Community legal system.[85]

In sum, the judgment in the *Kadi* case is a good illustration of the functioning of a multi-layered, polycentric legal system, where the conditional acceptance of the formally-established hierarchy by a lower level exerts pressure for reform at higher levels. This conditional loyalty voiced in the judicial arena should not, however, be seen as a deliberately wielded instrument to implement the political doctrine of effective multilateralism. Rather, in this specific case, European political and judicial conditionality ended up in concordance. Nevertheless, from an external perspective, the ruling in *Kadi* could be perceived as reinforcing a general European position of conditional loyalty to the UN system.

XI. FINAL REFLECTIONS

Conditional loyalty constitutes an expression of lack of trust in the Security Council's ability effectively to meet the responsibilities it has been given. Following the arguments above, there is a clear risk that such a position could contribute to an erosion of the normativity, and thereby the trustworthiness, of the international legal system. At the same time it could be viewed as a legal/political argument that contributes to the efficiency of the UN system. It seems clear that the position of the Union, based on a conditional loyalty to the UN system, contains an internal dilemma that could be translated into a number of concrete questions which have to be handled responsibly, in an open manner, by both the Union and its Member States. Might it be that inclusion of an express reference to Security Council authorisation in the ESS would strengthen the system of collective security, and thereby make multilateralism more effective? Of course this would lead to a decrease in the pressure on the Security Council that is generated by the doctrine of effective multilateralism as a legal/political argument. Could that loss of perceived political leverage be offset by gains in the authority of the collective security system that would follow from a declaration of unconditional Union loyalty?

Would a less radical way to decrease the potential negative structural effects emanating from the doctrine of effective multilateralism be to limit the scope for possible unilateral EU action by the express inclusion of thresholds referring

[85] Cf I Govaere, *The Importance of International Developments in the Case-law of the European Court of Justice:* Kadi *and the autonomy of the EC legal order* (Brugge, College of Europe Research Papers in Law, 1/2009); B Kunoy and A Dawes, 'Plate Tectonics in Luxembourg: The *Ménage à trois* between EC Law, International Law and the European Convention on Human Rights following the UN Sanctions Case' (2009) 26 *CML Rev* 73.

to the responsibility to prevent or halt large-scale loss of life or large-scale ethnic cleansing, along the lines presented in the ICISS Report? This would preserve the value of the doctrine of effective multilateralism as a political/legal argument generating pressure on the Security Council. However, such an explicit reference could easily be construed as a European commitment to act, a commitment which could hardly be met in all situations that meet the threshold.

Lastly, it has to be underlined that the development of the Union's external identity, of which the ESDP constitutes a central component, is the outcome of an intergovernmental decision-making process based on unanimity, with a possibility for constructive abstention.[86] Furthermore, individual Member States cannot be forced to participate in military operations against their nationally-defined political will. From this it follows that the political arena in each Member State needs to be activated for a wide debate concerning the future development of the ESDP.

[86] Art 31 TEU (post-Lisbon).

10

The Non-proliferation Policy of the European Union

PANOS KOUTRAKOS

I. INTRODUCTION

THE PROFILE OF the European Union (EU) in non-proliferation has become higher in the light of its involvement with Iran.[1] However, the Union became interested in pursuing non-proliferation policies as soon as it started shaping its international role. After all, the Common Foreign and Security Policy (CFSP) covers 'all areas of foreign and security policy' (Article 24 (1) TEU), and its objectives include 'to strengthen international security' (Article 21(2)(c) TEU). This became clearer by the Thessaloniki European Council of June 2003, which adopted a Declaration on Non-proliferation of Weapons of Mass Destruction where non-proliferation is identified as 'a central element in the EU external action, including the common foreign and security policy'.[2]

It was the events of 11 September 2001 which gave the EU non-proliferation policy a sense of urgency and momentum. Meeting 10 days later at an extraordinary meeting, the European Council set out a plan of action for the fight against terrorism, the latter defined as 'a priority objective for the European Union'.[3] Shortly afterwards, the Council elaborated on the implications of the terrorist threat on the non-proliferation, disarmament and arms control policy of the Union.[4] This document became the starting point for the gradual development of the EU's non-proliferation policy. In the host of documents and initiatives shaping this policy (European Council Declarations, Council Conclusions, Presidency Reports, Reports endorsed by the Council, and a number of measures adopted and proposed under the then Community legal order as well as the second and

[1] See Council Conclusions on Iran's nuclear programme of 26 July 2010 (12560/10, 10). For an account of earlier developments, see E Denza, 'Non-Proliferation of Nuclear Weapons: The European Union and Iran' (2005) 10 *European Foreign Affairs Review* 289.

[2] Thessaloniki European Council, 19 and 20 June 2003, Presidency Conclusions, Annex II, 37.

[3] Conclusions and Plan of Action of the Extraordinary European Council Meeting on 21 September 2001, 1.

[4] Council Conclusions, Brussels, 29 November 2001, 14732/01.

third pillars), two have been central: the 2003 Strategy against proliferation of weapons of mass destruction (WMD Strategy),[5] and the Strategy to combat illicit accumulation and trafficking of Small Arms and Light Weapons (SALW) and their ammunition (SALW Strategy).[6]

An exhaustive analysis of this landscape is beyond the confines of this chapter, as is a detailed analysis of the various measures taken against Iran. Instead, it aims to identify the threads which bring these initiatives together, the ways in which they relate to international legal developments, and the light they shed on the role of the EU as an international actor.

II. HORIZONTAL PRINCIPLES GOVERNING EU NON-PROLIFERATION POLICY

The Union's various non-proliferation initiatives are characterised by a number of principles.

A. Commitment to Effective Multilateralism

This is a constant theme in the EU initiatives. The WMD Strategy states the Union's

> conviction that a multilateralist approach to security, including disarmament and non-proliferation, provides the best way to maintain international order and hence our commitment to uphold, implement and strengthen the multilateral disarmament and non-proliferation treaties and agreements[.][7]

Indeed, effective multilateralism is viewed as 'the cornerstone of the European strategy for combating proliferations of WMD'.[8] Similarly, the starting point for the SALW Strategy is the United Nations Programme of Action to prevent, combat and eradicate the illicit trade in small arms and light weapons in all its aspects, which stresses the need for complementarity at global, regional and national levels in its implementation.[9]

This commitment is consistent with the clear focus on effective multilateralism that underpins the EU external relations and which has been expressed more

[5] Doc 15708/03, EU Strategy Against Proliferation of Weapons of Mass Destruction (Brussels, 10 December 2003).

[6] Doc 5319/06 (Brussels, 13 January 2006). Its provisions supplement the existing framework as set out in CFSP measures: Joint Action 1999/34/CFSP on the European Union's contribution to combating the destabilising accumulation and spread of small arms and light weapons [1999] OJ L9/1, repealed by Joint Action 2002/589/CFSP [2002] OJ L191/1.

[7] Above n 5, 5.

[8] *Ibid*, 6.

[9] UN Document A/CONF.192/15 (20 July 2001).

distinctly in recent years,[10] not least in the Lisbon Treaty which refers to it as an objective to be pursued by the entire range of EU external action.[11]

In relation to non-proliferation in particular, the commitment to effective multilateralism takes various forms, some of which are outlined below.

1. Universalisation of relevant international treaties

Political efforts to ensure universal adherence to international instruments relating to WMD and their means of delivery are central to the Union's policy. This has become apparent by the adoption of Common Position 2003/805/CFSP specifically dealing with the universalisation and reinforcement of multilateral agreements in the area.[12] Drawing on previous commitments to this effect,[13] its aim is to 'serve as a yardstick in the negotiations of EU positions in international forums'.[14]

This instrument refers to five specific international sets of rules: the Non-proliferation Treaty and Safeguards Agreements (NPT), the Additional Protocols with the International Atomic Energy Agency (IAEA Additional Protocols), the Chemical Weapons Convention (CWC), the Biological and Toxin Weapons Convention (BTWC) and the Hague Code of Conduct against Ballistic Missile Proliferation. It sets out two objectives: to promote the universal ratification of and adherence to these instruments, and to reinforce their provisions, including by ensuring compliance. In addition, the Common Position aims to promote the early entry into force of the Comprehensive Nuclear Test Ban Treaty (CTBT). This commitment of the Union and its Member States has been articulated and set out in detail in relation to specific Treaties individually.[15]

2. Reinforcement of the role of the United Nations

This has been central to the EU's policy since its inception. The Thessaloniki Declaration states that the EU 'will focus in particular on [amongst other things] fostering the role of the UN Security Council (UNSC), and enhancing its expertise in meeting the challenge of proliferation'.[16] In this vein, the WMD Strategy states that, once political and diplomatic preventative measures have failed and coercive measures under Chapter VII of the UN Charter are envisaged, 'the role of the UN Security Council, as the final arbiter on the consequences of non-compliance—as

[10] See COM (2003) 526 fin, 'The European Union and the United Nations: The choice of multilateralism and European Security Strategy', 9 *et seq*.

[11] Art 21(2)(h) TEU.

[12] Common Position 2003/805/CFSP, [2003] OJ L302/34.

[13] See, eg, the WMD Strategy, above n 5, 9, as well as the Declaration on Non-proliferation of Weapons of Mass Destruction (Thessaloniki European Council, Presidency Conclusions, Annex II, 37).

[14] Above n 12, recital (3) of Preamble.

[15] See Common Position 2005/329/CFSP on 2005 NPT Review Conference [2005] OJ L106/32; Common Position 2006/242/CFSP on the 2006 BTWC Review Conference [2006] OJ L88/65; Common Position 2007/469/CFSP on the 2008 CWC Review Conference [2007] OJ L176/39.

[16] Above n 2, 38.

foreseen in multilateral regimes—needs to be effectively strengthened'.[17] This also underpins Common Position 2003/805/CFSP, which refers to the need to strengthen the role of the UNSC as it has primary responsibility for the maintenance of international peace and security,[18] as well as the SALW Strategy.

A specific illustration of the UN–EU interaction is provided by UNSC Resolution 1540 (2004). Adopted in April 2004 under Chapter VII of the UN Charter, it deals with non-proliferation of WMD and, in effect, requires that States prevent WMD materials or technology falling into the hands of terrorists. It forbids States from supporting non-State actors involved in terrorism, obliges them to enact and enforce the necessary laws to prevent proliferation activities on their territories, and requires them to monitor and control sensitive technologies, materials and equipment that exist in, are manufactured by or transit their territories.[19]

The European Council welcomed the adoption of the Resolution and invited the Council

> to review the appropriate political and legal instruments, including possible actions within the framework of Justice and Home Affairs, that would further the adoption of concrete steps towards this objective.[20]

In the Union's initiatives in this area, grand policy statements coexist with practical, bottom-up, specific measures. An example is provided by the Union's efforts to support compliance with UNSC Resolution 1540 (2004). The latter requires that the States submit a report on a Security Council Committee on steps they have taken in order to comply with its provisions. In addition to individual reports submitted by its Member States, the EU presented a Report drawn up by the Netherlands Presidency assisted by the High Representative for the CFSP, and in full association with the Commission.[21] Furthermore, it has relied upon its legal panoply in order actively to encourage third States to comply with their duties and submit reports: it has carried out *démarches* and organised and funded programmes in three areas identified by Committee 1540 (Africa, Latin America and Caribbean, Asia-Pacific), which aimed to raise awareness of requirements and obligations under the Resolution, to strengthen national capacities in drafting national reports on its implementation and to share experience from the adoption of national measures required for the implementation of the Resolution.[22]

Later on, when Committee 1540 suggested that the focus should shift to implementation of the Resolution and the practical steps which some States in

[17] Above n 5, para 17. To that effect, there is provision for enabling it 'to benefit from independent expertise and a pool of readily available competence, on order to carry out the verification of proliferating activities that are a potential threat to international peace and security'.

[18] Above n 12, Art 2. See also Art 8, which mentions the need to strengthen the links between the Hague Code against Ballistic Missile Proliferation and the EU system.

[19] UNSC Resolution 1540 (2004), Art 3.

[20] Doc 10774/04, Declaration by the European Council on Criminal Sanctions (Brussels, 13 June 2004) 2.

[21] Brussels, October 2004.

[22] Joint Action 2006/419/CFSP [2006] OJ L165/30.

certain areas find it difficult to take, the EU responded by drawing road maps, tied in with the provision of technical assistance. It targeted border, customs and regulatory officials within six regions (Africa, Central America, Mercosur, the Middle East and Gulf Regions, Pacific Islands and South-East Asia). It then organised six workshops covering the main elements of an export control process, including applicable laws (including national and international legal aspects), regulatory controls (including licensing provisions, end-user verification and awareness-raising programmes) and enforcement (including commodity identification, risk-assessment and detection methods).[23]

3. *Provision of financial and technical support for specific projects carried out in the context of international non-proliferation treaties aiming to enhance compliance*

The universalisation of international non-proliferation treaty mechanisms has been supported by the EU pursuant to a range of specific measures. For instance, the Union has provided financial support for activities of the Organisation for the Prohibition of Chemical Weapons (OPCW)—these include measures promoting the universalisation of the Chemical Weapons Convention (by the organisation of workshops for States which are not parties in areas such as the Caribbean, Africa and the Middle East), its effective implementation (by the organisation of assistance meetings and seminars) and international cooperation in the field of chemical activities (by providing equipment support and laboratory assistance).[24] Similar measures were also funded in support of the BTWC,[25] in relation to which the EU also introduced projects in support of activities carried out by World Health Organisation in the area of laboratory bio-safety and biosecurity.[26]

Financial support is also provided to the Preparatory Commission of the Comprehensive Nuclear Test Ban Treaty Organisation (CTBTO), provisionally responsible for the effective implementation of the CTBT, to support its activities in the area of training and capacity building for verification (in particular the development of a computer-based training programme).[27]

[23] Joint Action 2008/368/CFSP [2008] OJ L127/78.

[24] Joint Action 2004/797/CFSP [2004] OJL349/63. This was followed up by Joint Action 2005/913/CFSP [2005] OJ L331/34 and Joint Action 2007/185/CFSP [2007] OJ L85/10 (the latter points out that 'since the beginning of the implementation of the EU Joint Actions in support of the OPCW in 2005, 14 countries have signed and ratified the CWC, bringing the number of OPCW Member States up to 181' (recital 4).

[25] Joint Action 2006/184/CFSP [2006] OJ L65/51, followed up by Joint Action 2008/858/CFSP [2008] OJ L302/29.

[26] Joint Action 2008/307/CFSP [2008] OJ L106/17.

[27] Joint Action 2006/243/CFSP [2006] OJ L88/68. This was followed up by financial assistance on other matters under Joint Action 2007/468/CFSP [2007] OJ L176/31, and Joint Action 2008/588/CFSP [2008] OJ L189/28.

Lastly, the EU has funded International Atomic Energy Agency (IAEA) activities under its Nuclear Security Programme.[28]

4. *Export controls*

The regulation and management of export controls are central to the non-proliferation policy of the EU. The WMD Strategy outlines the objective of 'making the EU a leading cooperative player in the export control regimes'.[29] The means to achieve this vary, and include coordination of EU positions within the different regimes, support of the membership of acceding countries, promotion of a catch-all clause in export controls regimes and strengthening information exchange. Similarly, the SALW Strategy, in its Action Plan, commits to supporting the strengthening of export controls and assisting third countries in the process of drafting relevant legislation.

There are various such regimes, and the link of the EU with them varies. The European Commission is an observer in the Zangger Committee (dealing with the interpretation of the Nuclear Non-proliferation Treaty, the 37 members of which include all the nuclear weapon States) and the Nuclear Suppliers Group (a group of nuclear supplier countries with 45 members). It participates in the Australia Group (a group of 41 suppliers and/or trans-shippers of chemicals, biological agents and/or production equipment which could be used in chemical and/or biological weapons programmes). It does not participate in the Missile Technology Control Regime (aiming to non-proliferation of unmanned delivery systems for weapons of mass destruction) and the Wassenaar Arrangement on export controls for conventional arms and dual-use goods and technologies.

In terms of their regulation and management, export controls of military equipment and dual-use goods have given rise to different issues: regulation of the former has been viewed as falling beyond the scope of the Union legal order; whereas regulation of the latter, covering products which may be of both civil and military application, has given rise to considerable controversy between the EU institutions and the Member States.

(i) Armaments

The EU rules on exports of military technology and equipment are laid down in Common Position 2008/944/CFSP.[30] Formalising an earlier Code of Conduct[31] the scope of which was defined in 2000[32] and the provisions of which are updated

[28] Joint Action 2004/495/CFSP [2004] OJ L182/46, followed up by Joint Action 2005/574/CFSP [2005] OJ L193/44, Joint Action 2006/418/CFSP [2006] OJ L165/20, Joint Action 2007/185/CFSP [2007] OJ L85/10.

[29] Above n 5, 10.

[30] Common Position 2008/944/CFSP [2008] OJ L335/99.

[31] Doc 8675/2/98 (Brussels, 5 June 1998).

[32] Common Military List of the European Union [2000] OJ C191/1.

regularly[33] and assessed by the Council annually,[34] this set of rules puts forward eight criteria on the basis of which national authorities are to assess the export licence applications they receive for items included in the EU Common Military List. These criteria include the following: respect for the international obligations and commitments of Member States; respect for human rights in the country of final destination, as well as respect by that country of international humanitarian law; the internal situation in the country of final destination; preservation of regional peace, security and stability; the national security of the Member States, as well as that of friendly and allied countries; the behaviour of the buyer country with regard to the international community, as regards in particular its attitude to terrorism, the nature of its alliances and respect for international law; the existence of a risk that the military technology or equipment will be diverted within the buyer country or re-exported under undesirable conditions; compatibility of the exports of the military technology or equipment with the technical and economic capacity of the recipient country.

As for its material scope, the Common Position applies to exports, brokering, transit or transhipment, as well as any intangible transfer of software and technology. It also provides for a consultation procedure (following circulation of details of exports denied) in confidence.[35]

The Union's commitment to effective multilateralism and the role of the UN is illustrated clearly by the content of the criteria set out in the Common Position. Compliance with sanctions regimes adopted by the UN Security Council is expressly mentioned in the context of the criteria which national authorities must observe, along with the commitments of Member States to enforce UN and Organisation for Security and Cooperation in Europe (OSCE) arms embargoes. Similarly, reference is made to the rules and guidelines of the various international export control regimes. In this vein, national authorities are required to exercise special caution and vigilance in issuing licences to countries where serious violations of human rights have been established by the competent bodies of the UN.

The Union has taken steps to promote respect for the criteria set out in the Code of Conduct (and, one would presume, the Common Position too) beyond its own borders. It has funded and organised workshops aiming to provide technical assistance to targeted third countries (in South Eastern Europe, North African and Mediterranean partners, and Eastern European Caucasian partners of ENP, Turkey and Ukraine).[36] These are organised by the Presidency and run by the Council Secretariat.

[33] For the most recent amendment, see [2010] OJ C69/3.

[34] For the most recent report, see [2009] OJ C265/1.

[35] The Council Working Party on Conventional Arms Exports produced a *User's Guide to the EU Code of Conduct on Arms Exports* (last updated on 29 April 2009: available at < http://register.consilium.europa.eu/pdf/en/09/st09/st09241.en09.pdf >). Under Art 13 of Common Position 2008/944/CFSP, this serves as guidance for its implementation.

[36] See Joint Action 2008/230/CFSP [2008] OJ L75/81.

In relation to arms brokering in particular, the EU adopted a specific measure, requiring that Member States apply a licence or written authorisation system for arms-brokering Member States and establish a system for exchange of information on brokering activities among themselves as well as with third countries.[37] Again, this measure is underpinned by the Union's commitment to effective multilateralism, as its objective is to control arms brokering in order to avoid circumvention of, amongst other things, UN and OSCE embargoes on arms exports.

(ii) Dual-use goods

The legal regulation of exports of dual-use goods provides some quite interesting insight into both the interaction between the international legal order and the Union legal order, and the various forces which shape the development of the latter. Exports of dual-use goods have been a central part of any export controls regime. The Thessaloniki Action Plan provided for a process of peer review of the export control rules of all Member States (as well as those of the acceding countries). In December 2004, the Council endorsed the recommendations which formed the outcome of this process (as formulated by a Task Force which assisted the EU institution in the conduct of the process).[38] One of the recommendations was to reach agreement on best practices for the enforcement of controls. This process gave rise to work in the Council bodies[39] and then a proposal by the Commission on the review of the EC rules in December 2006.[40] This was accompanied by a legislative proposal[41] which led to the adoption of the current rules, laid down in Council Regulation 428/2009.[42]

The starting point of this instrument is the international framework:

> An effective common system of export controls on dual-use items is necessary to ensure that the international commitments and responsibilities of the Member States, especially regarding non-proliferation, and of the European Union … are complied with.[43]

[37] Common Position 2003/468/CFSP [2003] OJ L156/79.

[38] Council Statement of 13 December 2004 further to the first stage of the Peer Review of Member States' Export Control Systems for Dual Use Goods conducted in the framework of the EU Strategy against Proliferation of Weapons of Mass Destruction (Doc 16069/04, Brussels, 13 December 2004).

[39] The Council Working Group on Dual-Use Goods worked on these: see Report on progress made during 2005 to implement the recommendations of the Peer Review of Member States' export control systems for dual use goods (Council Doc 15826/05, Brussels, 15 December 2005) and Implementation of the recommendations of the Peer Review of Member States' export control systems for dual use goods—Report on progress made in 2006 noted by Council on 11 December 2006 (Council Doc 16507/06, Brussels, 12 December 2006).

[40] COM(2006) 828 fin (Brussels, 18 December 2006).

[41] COM(2006) 829 fin (Brussels, 18 December 2006).

[42] [2009] OJ L134/1, third recital.

[43] *Ibid*. This is also stressed in relation to the material scope of the measure, that is the common list of items subject to export controls and the process of their update: see *ibid*, sixth recital.

Council Regulation 428/2009 establishes a system of authorisations for exports which are granted by national authorities and are recognised as valid throughout the Union.

Detailed discussion of this system is beyond the scope of this chapter.[44] For the purposes of this analysis, it suffices to point out the constitutionally charged and politically sensitive background against which EU rules on exports of dual-use items are adopted: in the light of the dual-use nature of such products and technologies, the Union first adopted a set of rules which was based on both the EC legal framework and the CFSP,[45] and it was only following the case law of the Court of Justice that this approach was viewed as unsustainable and was duly amended by a single EC instrument.[46] This context is significant, for it suggests that the process of the transposition of the international commitments of the Member States and the Union into EU law is subject to the constitutional idiosyncrasies of the Union legal order, which may well have an impact on the intensity of the ensuing legal framework.

The issue of sanctions illustrates the above. According to the precursor to the current regime, it is for the Member States to provide for sanctions for infringements of its rules, provided that these are effective, proportionate and dissuasive.[47] In its proposal, the Commission suggested that the Member States be required to introduce criminal penalties at least for serious infringements.[48]

This proposal was noteworthy for a number of reasons. First, as criminal law is an area widely viewed as traditionally falling within the powers of the Member States, the proposal entered politically sensitive territory. Secondly, there was a clear international context within which the Commission justified its proposal. It should be recalled that UNSC Resolution 1540, a reference point for EU initiatives in the area, refers to criminal sanctions expressly.[49] It is also to be recalled that the establishment of criminal sanctions for violations of export control rules is also mentioned in a number of EU policy documents, such as the WMD and SALW Strategies. In a Declaration on Criminal Sanctions, the European Council welcomed the adoption of Resolution 1540

[44] For an overview of its precursor, see P Koutrakos, *EU International Relations Law* (Oxford, Hart Publishing, 2006) 419 *et seq*. See also A Wetter, *Enforcing European Union Law on Exports of Dual-Use Goods* (SIPRI Research Report 24) (Oxford, Oxford University Press, 2009).

[45] Council Regulation 3381/94 [1994] OJ L367/1 and Decision 94/942/CFSP [1994] OJ L367/8.

[46] This was the precursor to Regulation 429/2009, namely Council Regulation 1334/2000 [2000] L159/1, last amended by Council Regulation 1167/2008 [2008] OJ L325/1. For an analysis, see P Koutrakos, *Trade, Foreign Policy and Defence in EU Constitutional Law* (Oxford, Hart Publishing, 2001) chs 5 and 6.

[47] Art 19 of Regulation 1334/2000, above n 46.

[48] These would include an intentional export intended for use in a programme for the development or manufacture of chemical, biological, nuclear weapons or of missiles capable of their delivery without the authorisation required under this Regulation, or the falsification or omission of information with a view to obtaining an authorisation that would otherwise have been denied.

[49] At para 3(d).

and invited the Council to take concrete measures in order to achieve its objectives.[50]

Thirdly, in 2005, that is 15 months prior to the Commission's proposal, the Court of Justice rendered its judgment in the *Environmental Crimes* case, where it held that Member States may be required to impose effective, proportionate and dissuasive criminal penalties for serious environmental offences when this is necessary in order to ensure the full effectiveness of the relevant rules.[51] This judgment was followed up by the *Maritime Pollution* judgment, where the Court confirmed the broad application of the principle, albeit whilst tampering with its scope.[52] It is interesting that neither the Commission's Communication on the review of the relevant rules, nor its proposal for a re-cast Regulation included a reference to this case law; what makes this even more curious is the fact that the current legal regime, as the Preamble to Regulation 1334/2000 indicated, largely owes its existence to the case law of the Court.[53]

The proposal regarding criminal penalties has not been taken up by the Council and, in Article 24, Regulation 428/2009 merely duplicates the general provision about effective, proportionate and dissuasive measures laid down in Article 19 of Regulation 1334/2000. Instead, there is now an express reference to UNSC Resolution 1540 (albeit in order to substantiate the application of the new rules to related materials), and a long recital in the Preamble about the benefits of greater convergence and harmonisation of the application of the relevant rules by the competent authorities.[54]

This episode illustrates how the interactions between the EU legal order and the international community, whilst dynamic and direct, are subject to the legal and political constraints which surround the Union's idiosyncratic constitutional landscape; these inform the practical manifestations of these interactions, and determine both their pace and direction. This is a point which will be made further, in a different context, below.

5. *Other measures*

A recent example of promotion of effective multilateralism is the initiative to support a legally-binding International Arms Trade Treaty. Originating in United Nations General Assembly Resolution 61/89,[55] a process was initiated where a

[50] Annex to Council Doc 1077/04 (Brussels, 23 June 2004), where reference is made 'in particular [to] the measures to be taken in order to more effectively prevent the spread of sensitive goods and technologies' (at 2).

[51] Case C-176/03 *Commission v Council* [2005] ECR I-7879, para 48.

[52] Case C-440/05 *Commission v Council* [2007] ECR I-9097. See S Peers, 'The European Community's criminal law competence: the plot thickens' (2008) 33 *EL Rev* 399.

[53] For a different view, see A Dashwood, 'Dual-use Goods: (Mis)Understanding *Werner* and *Leifer*' in A Arnull, P Eeckhout, and T Tridimas (eds), *Continuity and Change in EU Law—Essays in Honour of Sir Francis Jacobs* (Oxford, Oxford University Press, 2008) 354.

[54] Above n 42, eighteenth recital.

[55] Entitled 'Towards an arms trade treaty: establishing common international standards for the import, export and transfer of conventional arms' and adopted in December 2006.

Group of Governmental Experts suggested step-by-step work within the UN context, and which culminated in the adoption by the UN General Assembly of a Resolution entitled 'Towards an arms trade treaty: establishing common international standards for the import, export and transfer of conventional arms'.[56]

All EU Member States support this process. The EU is organising a number of activities aiming to increase awareness amongst national and regional actors, UN Members, civil society and industry of the discussions about the Treaty, and to promote an exchange of views between these actors.[57]

B. Broad Construction of Security

The Union's approach is based on a broad understanding of security. Both the WMD and SALW Strategies use the European Security Strategy (ESS) as a point of reference.[58] Adopted by the European Council in December 2003, this document set out the global challenges facing the EU (terrorism, proliferation of weapons of mass destruction, regional conflicts, State failure, organised crime) and the ways in which the EU must meet them. An analysis of the ESS falls beyond the scope of this chapter,[59] but its broad definition of 'security' is relevant to our discussion. The document stresses the link between security and development, as well as energy, and points out that:

> [i]n contrast to the massive visible threat in the Cold War, none of the new threats is purely military; nor can any be tackled by purely military means. Each requires a mixture of instruments.[60]

The SALW Strategy refers to the ESS time and again. It starts off by mentioning a point made in the latter, namely that the post-Cold War environment is one of increasingly open borders in which the internal and external aspects of security are indissolubly linked.

This close relationship between the ESS, on the one hand, and the WMD and SALW Strategies, on the other hand, is also illustrated by the common principles which govern their understanding of the prevailing international environment. The commitment to an international order based on effective multilateralism, for instance, is also drawn upon in the ESS. Therefore, the adoption of the WMD and SALW initiatives against the background of the ESS suggests a tangible impact of the ESS on, potentially, the entire range of EU policies.

[56] 63/240, adopted in December 2008.

[57] Council Decision 2009/42/CFSP [2009] OJ L17/39.

[58] *A secure Europe in a better world—European Security Strategy* (ESS) (Brussels, 12 December 2003).

[59] See, amongst others, S Biscop and JJ Andersson (eds), *The EU and the European Security Strategy* (London, Routledge, 2008).

[60] ESS, above n 58, 7.

C. Cross-pillar

Following from the above, the initiatives adopted by the EU in the areas both of WMD and SALW are comprehensive in scope, covering, under the pre-Lisbon constitutional arrangements, the Community legal order, as well as the second (CFSP) and third (Area of Freedom, Security and Justice) pillars. Following the entry into force of the Lisbon Treaty on 1 December 2009, it is not correct, strictly speaking, to refer to pillars, as this complex arrangement which had chartacterised the constitutional configuration of power since the Maastricht Treaty was abolished. However, while, in substantive terms, the third pillar has now been integrated fully in the Union legal order, the new Treaty has maintained fully the distinct legal characteristcs of the second pillar (CFSP) in relation to instruments, decision-making, institutional involvement and judicial supervision. Therefore, in essence, the Lisbon Treaty has abolished the pillars in all but name.[61] Viewed from this angle, the term 'cross-pillar' is less problematic in the current constitutional arrangements than it may appear originally.

The WMD Strategy points out in its introduction that the 'EU must act with resolve, using all instruments and policies at its disposal', and then sets out 'a broad approach covering a wide spectrum of actions' whereby 'non-proliferation should be mainstreamed in our overall policies drawing upon all resources and instruments available to the Union'.[62] To that effect, it provides for multilateral treaties and verification mechanisms, political initiatives, export controls, regulations on dual-use good, common policies related to criminal sanctions, and integration of WMD non-proliferation concerns into the EU's political, diplomatic and economic activities.

Similarly, and in addition to the existing CFSP measures, the SALW Strategy sets out to

> develop a comprehensive and coherent approach which harnesses all forms of leverage at the European Union's disposal and is based on the recognition, formulated in the ESS, that human security and human development are interdependent [and to] develop new facets of the Union's action to cover all the dimensions of the phenomenon, preventive and reactive.[63]

Its objectives are achieved through a cross-pillar approach too, including CFSP and security and defence instruments, partnership and cooperation agreements on political, development and trade areas, and coordination mechanisms, such as Europol and Eurojust. In fact, the SALW Strategy identifies three levels of means of cooperation: the EU resources, both economic and political; the resources of

[61] See P Koutrakos, 'Primary law and policy in EU external relations-moving away from the big picture' (2008) 33 *EL Rev* 666 at 668–70.

[62] Above n 5, 2 and 5 respectively.

[63] Above n 6, 7.

the Member States; and the resources of the various multilateral players with which the EU has forged cooperation ties.

This broad approach becomes apparent in the Action Plan under the SALW Strategy. Consistent with the theme of effective multilateralism, its sets out a range of initiatives at international, regional and EU levels. Of these, the regional and EU initiatives are particularly interesting. In relation to the former, the Action Plan suggests the provision of financial and technical support for regional and national organisations such as the Economic Community of West African States (ECOWAS) Moratorium, and for transforming them into legally-binding regional Conventions. It also mentions the provision of support to the African Union and African regional organisations with the means to ensure the effective application of UN embargoes, as well as support for the OSCE action. On the EU level, the Action Plan provides for the inclusion of brokering and illicit transfers of SALW on the agenda for all the EU's structured political dialogues with countries which export them, and raises this matter in the political dialogue with third countries and international, regional or sub-regional organisations. It also suggests an integrated approach to agreements with third countries, in particular envisaging the possibility of inserting a clause or an undertaking to cooperate in combating the illicit trade in SALW and their ammunitions in all agreements with third countries.[64]

There is clear merit in the emphasis on the interconnections between the different facets of the Union's external relations policies. On the one hand, it reflects the increasingly interdependent relations between security, development, foreign policy and economic progress—this is recognised on the international plane and is illustrated by the work undertaken under the aegis of the United Nations. On the other hand, it reflects the very genesis of European integration: the establishment of a common market and the various developments which stemmed from it gave the impetus for a gradual expansion of the activities covered by European integration, albeit at a different pace and pursuant to varied institutional and procedural arrangements. It is only appropriate that, in construing its international role, the Union integrates the very core of its development into the wider framework of its external relations.

However, this raises a number of questions, which will be addressed below: How is this ambitious construction of security (in general) and non-proliferation (in particular) accommodated within the Union's idiosyncratic constitutional framework? How are the different functions of the Union's institutions to be managed

[64] In terms of tackling the problems raised by the availability of existing stocks, the Strategy also covers measures as diverse as the promotion of a commitment by all countries only to import and retain small arms to meet their legitimate security needs, financial assistance under older programmes such as Disarmament, Demobilisation and Reintegration operations, financial and technical assistance for measures such as the keeping of regional small arms registers and the regular exchange of available information on exports, imports, the production and holding of small arms legislation, and appropriate measures to deal with the causes and consequences for human development of the illicit spread of SALW.

in a way which would ensure the effectiveness of the Union's policy? And to what extent would that be in compliance with the distinct normative characteristics of the different sets of rules involved?

D. The Union's Understanding of its own Role

The principles outlined so far illustrate how the EU understands its overall role in the world. This appears to be based on two interrelated notions. The first is about 'responsibility' in international affairs, which the Union is convinced it must assume. The WMD Strategy, for instance, states that 'all the States of the Union and the EU institutions have a collective responsibility for preventing these risks by actively contributing to the fight against proliferation'.[65] And the SALW Strategy refers to the EU's 'compelling obligation to act'.[66]

This understanding of the EU's international responsibility draws upon the thread which brings together different strands of the EU's external relations. For instance, the ESS is based on the idea that 'Europe should be ready to share in the responsibility for global security and in building a better world'.[67] And in the Laeken Declaration on the Future of European Union, the European Council wondered:

> Does Europe not, now that it is finally unified, have a leading role to play in a new world order, that of a stabilising role worldwide and to point the way ahead for many countries and peoples?[68]

And the then President of the Commission, Romano Prodi, stated on the day of signing that Treaty that

> today, Europe is reaffirming the unique nature of its political organisation in order to respond to the challenges of globalisation, and to promote its values and play its rightful role on the international scene.[69]

The second tenet of the Union's understanding of its international role in the area is its unique nature. The WMD Strategy states that the 'European Union has special strengths and experience to bring to this collective effort'.[70] This follows from the cross-pillar approach and the range of instruments into which the EU may tap, which is set out as the Union's distinct advantage: the SALW Strategy points out that the

[65] Above n 5, para 12.
[66] Above n 6, 6.
[67] Above n 58, 2.
[68] Laeken Declaration on the Future of European Union, 14–15 December 2001.
[69] Speech delivered in Rome at the ceremony on the signing of the Constitutional Treaty, available at <http://www.europa.eu.int/constitution/speaches_en.htm>.
[70] Above n 5, para 29.

> European Union has unique assets for responding to this threat. With its capacity to use a full spectrum of civilian and military instruments for managing crises and post-conflict situations and to contribute to reconstruction, the Union is well placed to provide a comprehensive response.[71]

Again, this is a notion which is apparent in other areas of EU external relations too. The ESS points out that the 'European Union is particularly well equipped to respond to such multi-faceted situations'.[72] And in relation to the civilian aspects of crisis management, the Report of the Portuguese Presidency, adopted by the Feira European Council in June 2000, pointed out that

> particular attention could be paid to those areas where the international community so far has demonstrated weaknesses. It would provide 'added value' as it would improve the Union's capacity to react as well as the Union's capability to meet the requests of the other lead organisations … This would … increase the Union's visibility.[73]

III. VERTICAL PRINCIPLES GOVERNING EU NON-PROLIFERATION POLICY

In addition to the above, there are some principles which characterise the specific measures which flesh out the WMD and SALW Strategies.

A. Mainstreaming and the Case of Non-proliferation Clauses

The WMD Strategy provides for the mainstreaming of non-proliferation policies in the EU's international relations, and refers, in particular, to the introduction of a non-proliferation clause in agreements with third countries. Similarly, the SALW Strategy refers to the need to include the brokering and illicit transfer of SALW on the agenda of all the EU's structured political dialogue with third countries; it refers in particular to countries in Eastern Europe and South-Eastern Europe (which hold surplus stocks of SALW left over from the Cold War), as well as Ukraine and Moldova in the context of the European Neighbourhood Policy (ENP). It also refers to the possibility of including a clause or an undertaking to cooperate in combating the illicit trade in SALW and their ammunition in all agreements with third countries.

In an agreement reached in November 2003 as to the content and the scope of its application,[74] the Council decided that the WMD clause should have two elements. The first provides for full compliance with and national implementation of the parties' existing obligations under international disarmament and

[71] Above n 6, para 18.
[72] Above n 58, 7.
[73] Feira European Council, 18–20 June 2000, Presidency Conclusions, Annex I, Appendix 3, Part A.
[74] Council Conclusions 17 December 2003, Doc 14997/03, Brussels, 19 November 2003.

non-proliferation treaties and agreements, and other relevant international obligations. This provision constitutes an essential part of the agreement. It is noteworthy that it does not commit a State to sign, ratify and implement any agreements which it has not already signed.[75] The second part of the WMD clause provides for cooperation between the parties by fully implementing all other relevant international instruments and by establishing an effective system of national export controls—this provision may be considered as an essential element on an *ad hoc* basis.[76]

In 2009, five years after the introduction of this practice, the Council revisited the issue.[77] Its Note provides a positive assessment of the EU's practice. It refers to agreements with almost 100 countries in which non-proliferation clauses have been inserted (in new or renewed mixed agreements and agreements concluded under ex Article 24 TEU). It also refers to additional text occasionally included in Preambles or other relevant provisions of treaties in order to respond to specific concerns of the EU's partners, in particular regarding conventional weapons and SALW. Lastly, it refers to a non legally-binding non-proliferation section, inserted in several political documents adopted in the context of the ENP.

So far, such a clause has been inserted in the agreement with the ACP countries,[78] the Stabilisation and Association Agreement with Albania,[79] the Partnership and Cooperation Agreement with Tajikistan,[80] and agreements with the Gulf Cooperation Council and with Syria. This covers nearly 100 States.[81] It is interesting, though, that the EU should not feel bound to follow the wording of the standard clause to the letter. Instead, it 'ensur[ed] that respective WMD clauses were compatible with the spirit and the content of the WMD standard clause'.[82]

[75] Note, for instance, that India, Pakistan and Israel have not signed the Nuclear Non-proliferation Treaty.

[76] As for its scope of application, the WMD clause was envisaged as being inserted in future mixed agreements, existing mixed agreements (on any occasion of renewal or revision, or even at the suggestion of the EU for an amendment, or, if the above fails, by the negotiation of a separate legally-binding instrument between the Parties which may include a link to the overall agreement) and under the pre-Lisbon constitutional arrangements, pure Community agreements (through the conclusion of a parallel instrument establishing a link with the EC agreement).

[77] See Doc 5503/09, Note on the implementation of the WMD Clause (Brussels, 19 January 2009).

[78] See also, separately, the Agreement between the EC and its Member States, of the one part, and South Africa, of the other part, amending the Agreement on Trade, Development and Cooperation: COM(2010) 220 fin (Brussels, 7 May 2010).

[79] Art 8(3); see Council Doc 8164/06 (Brussels, 22 May 2006)—this includes the two additional provisions mentioned in relation to the Agreement with Tajikistan.

[80] Art 4(2) and (3); see COM(2004) 521 fin (Brussels, 26 July 2004). This duplicates the model WMD clause save for two additions: (i) a reference to the first part of the clause as part of the political dialogue that will accompany and consolidate the elements referred to therein, (ii) and a statement in relation to export controls that such dialogue may take place on a regional basis.

[81] See Six-monthly Progress Report on the implementation of the EU Strategy against the Proliferation of Weapons of Mass Destruction (2010/II), Council Doc 17080/10 (Brussels, 16 December 2010) 47. Furthemore, agreement on the WMD clause was reached with Vietnam in 2010 (the Partnership and Cooperation Agreement between the EU and Vietnam was initialled in October 2010), while negotiations with Armenia, Azerbaijan, Georgia, Malaysia, Russia, Singapore and Thailand on this matter continue (*ibid*).

[82] *Ibid.*

In practical terms, the EU's record in the area has not been uncontroversial.[83] In the case of India, there was only a vague reference to non-proliferation in the EU–India Joint Action Plan,[84] which became even briefer in its 2008 reviewed version.[85] The Commission also decided to propose the negotiation of a trade and investment agreement without a non-proliferation clause. The EU envisages an upgrading of the current 1994 EU–India Framework Agreement, or the negotiation of a new EU–India partnership and cooperation agreement which would include a non-proliferation clause.[86] There is a Free Trade Agreement currently negotiated with India which is limited to trade and investment issues, and which is envisaged by the Commission to be linked clearly in legal and institutional terms with the Framework Agreement.

The inclusion of a WMD clause in the Association Agreement with Syria (finalised in December 2004, but initialled only in December 2008) was also controversial, as its wording was changed a number of times in order to make it acceptable to the Syrian Government whilst satisfying the demands of the Member States. The negotiation of the clause threatened to derail the negotiation of the Agreement.

B. Proceduralisation and Institutionalisation

The implementation of the initiatives undertaken by the EU in the area of non-proliferation relies upon an intricate web of subsidiary bodies and considerable interaction (both formal and informal) amongst them and between them and the EU institutions. A number of layers of institutional interaction may be identified.

The first layer involves the main actors in the area, namely the Council, the Commission and Javier Solana.[87] Javier Solana appointed a Personal Representative on non-proliferation and WMD, who is also responsible for the SALW Strategy.[88] Her appointment was envisaged as bringing these issues into sharper focus in the dialogue with third countries. She assists EU Member States in their efforts to coordinate policies in the area of conventional arms exports controls.

There is also a Council CFSP Working Group on global arms control and disarmament (CODUN), and one on non-proliferation (CONOP), the latter dealing mainly with the Nuclear Non-proliferation Treaty, other non-proliferation and export control regimes, and assistance to Russia for chemical weapons destruction. Both Groups consist of senior disarmament and non-proliferation officials from

[83] See the account in L Grip, *The EU Non-Proliferation Clause: A Preliminary Assessment* (SIPRI Background Paper, November 2009).

[84] EU Strategic Plan—Joint Action Plan (New Delhi, 7 September 2005).

[85] 'Global partners for global challenges: The EU–India Joint Action Plan (JAP)' (Marseille, 29 September 2008).

[86] See Written Question E-3607/2007 by A Beer to the Commission.

[87] For the role of the European Parliament, see EP Resolution on non-proliferation of weapons of mass destruction: A role for the European Parliament [2006] OJ C280E/453, at 462.

[88] Annalisa Giannella, who was appointed in October 2003.

Member States, as well as personnel from the non-proliferation and disarmament section of the Council's General Secretariat, and an official from the Commission's security policy unit; they meet once a month in Brussels. There is also a Working Group on export of arms (COARM) which reviews the application of the Code of Conduct, provides support for the negotiation of an International Arms Trade Treaty, oversees the implementation of the Common Position of 2003 on brokering, and deals with the issue of end-use controls, as well as the organisation of outreach activities with third countries (in particular Ukraine and Norway).

There is another layer, consisting of the WMD Monitoring Centre (WMD-MC), which is envisaged as overseeing the implementation and development of the WMD Strategy, creating synergy between efforts by the various EU actors involved, and supporting the EU's contacts with third countries and organisations.[89] The same applies to the SALW Policy, where practical measures are envisaged to strengthen the synergy between the various actors.[90]

Lastly, other external relations bodies are involved, such as the Political and Security Committee whose role is set out in Article 38 TEU. Made up of the political directors of the Member States' foreign ministries, it is responsible for monitoring the international situation in the CFSP area, contributing to the definition of policies and monitoring the implementation of the Council's decisions.

Against this background of intense institutional activity, the policies provide for their regular monitoring. For instance, the SALW Policy is reviewed regularly and updated every six months by means of an interim report by the Presidency on its implementation.[91] This heavily structured and proceduralised framework, with its multiple institutional layers, needs to be understood in the light of the broad range of activities which the Union carries out within the different sets of rules accommodated in its constitutional configuration, and the ensuing quest for coherence.

C. The Quest for Coherence

The broad understanding of security, the consolidation of the various legal instruments available within the Union's panoply, the cross-pillar dimension of the relevant activities, all suggest that the coherence of the EU's action is of paramount importance. This is entirely consistent with the central role the requirement of coherence has assumed in the conduct of EU external relations.[92] In normative

[89] Council Doc 6694/06 EU Strategy against the proliferation of WMD: Monitoring and enhancing consistent implementation (Brussels, 12 December 2006), 4 *et seq*.

[90] The EU Strategy refers to the Council Secretariat, which is to work closely with the Situation Centre to promote the collection and circulation of information and intelligence from the Member States, *ibid*, 15.

[91] Above n 6, 9.

[92] See M Cremona, 'Coherence in EU Foreign Relations Law' in P Koutrakos (ed), *European Foreign Policy—Legal and Political Perspectives* (Cheltenham, E Elgar, 2011) 55.

terms, Article 3 TEU refers to the 'consistency and the continuity of the activities carried out [by the Union] in order to achieve its objectives', as well as to the requirement of 'consistency of its external activities as a whole in the context of its external relations, security, economic and development policies'.

Furthermore, the coherence of EU external action has been at the very heart of the 'group therapy process' which the EU underwent since the drafting of the Constitutional Treaty, and which went on, rather intensely, through the process of its ratification, as well as the drafting and ratification of the Lisbon Treaty. This is illustrated by the mandate of the 2007 Intergovernmental Conference, which mentions it in the very first paragraph.[93]

In terms of policy, the increasing emphasis on the requirement of coherence is also illustrated by the concerted effort of EU institutions and the Member States to address it, at least as a matter of principle, in the EU external relations activities where it seems to matter the most, such as development[94] and humanitarian aid, where the Council, the Representatives of the Governments of the Member States meeting within the Council, the European Parliament and the Commission have adopted policy documents where they stress the multifarious dimensions of development and humanitarian aid policies, set out common principles and good practice, and underline the need for coherence, complementarity and effectiveness as a matter of policy.[95]

Non-proliferation features prominently in these efforts. *The European Consensus on Development*, for instance, having acknowledged the complementarity between security and development policies within the context of the EU, goes on to state as follows[96]:

> The EU, within the respective competences of the Community and the Member States, will strengthen the control of its arms exports, with the aim of avoiding that EU-manufactured weaponry be used against civilian populations or aggravate existing tensions or conflicts in developing countries, and take concrete steps to limit the uncontrolled proliferation of small arms and light weapons, in line with the European strategy against the illicit traffic of small arms and light weapons and their ammunitions.

In practical terms, the quest for coherence renders the issue of management of the EU's activities of vital importance. The SALW Strategy notes the need to

[93] See IGC 2007 Mandate, Council SG/11218/07, POLGEN74, para 1: 'The IGC is asked to draw up a Treaty (hereinafter called the "Reform Treaty") amending the existing Treaties with a view to enhancing the efficiency and democratic legitimacy of the enlarged Union, as well as the coherence of its external action.'

[94] See, for instance, the Council's Resolution on Coherence Between the Community Development Cooperation and its Other Policies (Annex to Development Council meeting of June 5, 1997), the Parliament's Resolution on the coherence of the various policies with development policy (Doc B5-0117/2000 [2000] OJ C339/208), and the Commission's COM(2005) 134 fin, *Policy Coherence for Development*.

[95] See *The European Consensus on Development* [2006] OJ C46/1, and *The European Consensus on Humanitarian Aid* [2008] OJ C25/1.

[96] *The European Consensus on Development*, above n 95, para 37.

> ensure consistency and complementarity between Council decisions in the CFSP framework and actions implemented by the Commission in the field of development aid in order to promote a consistent approach for all EU activities in the SALW area.[97]

The Union's approach to ensuring coordination appears to have certain common features. First, it targets specific areas in relation to which it develops a structured and integrated policy approach. This is illustrated by the EU's approach to Africa. In 2005, the EU adopted the *EU Strategy for Africa*,[98] in which non-proliferation of WMD features as a specific area as regards which the EU is to step up its efforts to promote peace and security, by improving overall coordination and cooperation to ensure full compliance with relevant international obligations and export control regimes. In addition, special emphasis is laid on the promotion of an integrated approach to address the proliferation of SALW and landmines.[99] The EU then, along with the African Union, adopted the Joint Africa–EU Strategy.[100] One of the four objectives of this long-term partnership is to address global challenges and common concerns, amongst which feature the proliferation of WMD and the illicit trafficking of SALW.[101]

Secondly, the Union focuses on the development of a distinct procedural dimension, aiming to enhance the management and coordination of the relevant actors and their output. For instance, the Joint Progress Report on the implementation of the Africa–EU Joint Strategy, drawn up following the Africa–EU Ministerial Troika Meeting in Addis Ababa in November 2008, refers to

> the holding of the first ever meeting between the AU Peace and Security Council and the EU Political and Security Committee, the regular consultations and exchange of information between the AU Commission, on the one hand, the European Commission and the Council's General Secretariat, on the other.[102]

Thirdly, there is a distinct focus on enhancing capacity-building, networking, cooperation and the exchange of information. For instance, in relation to SALW, explosive remnants of war (ERW), anti-personnel landmines and the fight against illicit trafficking, the specific measures envisaged include work towards the development of an African Small Arms and Light Weapons Strategy by December 2009, the development of modalities to engage African experts in the implementation of the EC-funded project in support of activities in the field of SALW by the end of June 2009 and the organisation of a joint workshop on the eradication of ERW in 2009.[103]

[97] Above n 6, 15.

[98] COM(2005) 489 fin, *EU Strategy for Africa—Towards a Euro-African pact to accelerate Africa's Development* (Brussels, 12 October 2005).

[99] *Ibid*, 22.

[100] Lisbon Summit, December 2007.

[101] *Ibid*, 2–3.

[102] Para 9.

[103] *Ibid*, 5. On the progress so far, see Ninth Annual Report on the implementation of the Council Joint Action of 12 July 2002 on the European Union's contribution to combating the destabilising accumulation and spread of small arms and light weapons (2002/589/CFSP) [2010] C 198/1.

Fourthly, there is the multiplicity of administrative layers and institutional actors mentioned above. In relation to the Union's policy towards Africa, for instance, Javier Solana appointed a Special Representative to the area ('the EUSR').[104] The Joint Action setting out his mandate makes it clear that he is responsible for the CFSP/ESDP aspects of the policy objectives laid down in the EU–Africa Strategy. However, as these objectives are intrinsically linked, his coexistence with other relevant EU actors becomes of paramount significance. Article 12 of Joint Action 2008/898/CFSP is entitled 'Coordination' and reads as follows:

> The EUSR shall promote overall EU political coordination. He shall help to ensure that all EU instruments in the field are engaged coherently to attain the EU's policy objectives. The activities of the EUSR shall be coordinated with those of the Presidency and the Commission, as well as those of other EUSRs active in the region as appropriate. The EUSR shall provide Member States' missions and Commission's delegations with regular briefings.
>
> In the field, close liaison shall be maintained with the Presidency, Commission and Member States' Heads of Mission who shall make best efforts to assist the EUSR in the implementation of the mandate. The EUSR shall also liaise with other international and regional actors in the field.

What is interesting is that the EUSR was also appointed as the European Commission Head of Delegation. This 'double-hatting' is seen as improving the coherence of the EU's approach.[105] However, this 'managerial', inward-looking and structure-focused approach risks making the effectiveness of the Union's policies hostage to the complex internal dymamics of the relationship between the various Union bodies and institutions involved.

IV. INTER-INSTITUTIONAL TENSIONS AND JUDICIALISATION

The broad understanding of security by the EU actors, the ever-wider range of activities which non-proliferation policies underpin, and the multiplicity of legal rules and procedures governing them, have created a significant degree of inter-institutional tension. Whilst by no means unique in this area,[106] this phenomenon has manifested itself in a controversial manner in the process of the Union's efforts to combat SALW proliferation. In *ECOWAS*,[107] the Commission challenged the

[104] Joint Action 2007/805/CFSP [2007] OJ L323/45, extended by Joint Action 2008/898/CFSP [2008] OJ L322/50.

[105] In a statement, Javier Solana, the then Union's High Representative for Common Foreign and Security Policy, stated that 'The joint appointment of Mr Vervaeke is a reflection of our common will to combine all the instruments of the European Union and thereby ensure a coherent approach towards Africa at all levels' (6 December 2007, S355/07).

[106] In the area of EU external relations generally, see P Koutrakos, 'Legal Basis and Delimitation of Competence in EU External Relations' in M Cremona and B de Witte (eds), *EU Foreign Relations Law* (Oxford, Hart Publishing, 2008) 171.

[107] Case C-91/05 *Commission v Council* [2008] ECR I-3651.

adoption by the Council of Decision 2004/833/CFSP implementing Joint Action 2002/589/CFSP on an EU contribution to the Economic Community of West African States (ECOWAS).[108] This measure had been adopted in order to provide for a financial contribution and technical assistance in order to set up the Light Weapons Unit within the ECOWAS structure, and to convert the Moratorium on SALW into a Convention between the ECOWAS Member States. The Commission argued that such action fell within the scope of development policy and, as such, ought to have been adopted under EC law. The Court annulled the Council Decision and held that

> a measure having legal effects adopted under Title V of the EU Treaty affects the provisions of the EC Treaty within the meaning of ex Article 47 TEU whenever it could have been adopted on the basis of the EC Treaty, it being unnecessary to examine whether the measure prevents or limits the exercise by the Community of its competences.[109]

The judgment was rendered under the constitutional arrangements which preceded the entry into force of the Lisbon Treaty. The current rules have amended the main point of reference of the judgment, namely ex Article 47 TEU: whilst the latter gave precedence to preserving the integrity of the Community legal order, the new provision of Article 40 TEU adds another dimension: 'Similarly, the implementation of the policies listed in [Articles 3-6 TFEU] shall not affect the implication of the procedures and the extent of the powers of the institutions laid down by the Treaties for the exercise of the Union competences under [Chapter 2 TEU which deals with CFSP and CSDP]'.

However, for the purposes of this Chapter, suffice it to focus on the implications of the ruling for the substantive interactions between non-proliferation and other EU external policies and, in particular, the clear inter-institutional tension which underpins their conduct. This sets the background against which substantive policy choices are made. It becomes very clear that the rhetoric of coherence, when assessed in the light of the inter-institutional interactions, tells us a story distinctly more nuanced than that emerging from the Union's policy documents. This, in turn, brings the Court of Justice to the very centre of the external relations arena.

In *ECOWAS*, the Court concluded that a dual-legal basis involving both EC and CFSP rules is 'impossible' where a measure carries out both security and development cooperation functions.[110] It further suggested that a CFSP measure might also contribute to EC objectives if it had the implementation of the CFSP as its main

[108] [2004] OJ L359/65.

[109] Above n 107, para 60. See the annotation by C Hillion and R Wessel, 'Competence distribution in EU external relations after *Ecowas*: Clarification or continued fuzziness?' (2009) 46 *CML Rev* 551 and the criticism in Editorial, 'Development and foreign policy: where to draw the line between the pillars' (2008) 33 *EL Rev* 289. For another recent judgment on the relationship between EC and CFSP rules, see Case C-403/05 *Parliament v Commission (re: Philippines borders)* [2007] ECR I-19045, and the annotation by M Cremona in (2008) 45 *CML Rev* 1727.

[110] Above n 107, para 76.

purpose. However, this is precisely what the problem is: this assessment is heavily dependent upon finely-balanced views as to the proper objective of a measure and its content. Such an assessment is extremely difficult to make, and the willingness of the EU institutions to question each other's assessment before the Court, as well as the latter's controversial approach, is bound to fuel inter-institutional tensions and challenge the application of the legal rules aiming to bring coherence in the everyday conduct of the Union's external action. In this respect, the impact of the formal abolition of the pillar structure by the Lisbon Treaty is questionable, given the distinct legal characteristics of the set of rules and procedures governing CFSP.

In the context of non-proliferation, for instance, Regulation 1717/2006 establishing an Instrument for Stability deals with assistance in response to situations of crisis or emerging crisis. Its aim is

> to contribute to stability by providing an effective response to help preserve, establish or re-establish the conditions essential to the proper implementation of the Community's development and cooperation policies.[111]

In this context, it refers to technical and financial assistance regarding the impact on the civilian population of the illicit use of and access to firearms, and covers survey activities, victim assistance, raising public awareness and the development of legal and administrative expertise and good practice. In terms of principle, assistance is purported to 'be provided only to the extent necessary to re-establish the conditions for social and economic development of the populations concerned, in a situation of crisis or emerging crisis' and is intended 'not [to] include support for measures to combat the proliferation of arms'.[112]

In practical terms, the intense interdependence between different activities and the multiplicity of actors and administrative bodies involved in the conduct of the overall policy would entail a difficult balancing exercise, with unclear repercussions for the effectiveness and timing of the specific policy initiatives. All this makes the role of the Court increasingly prominent and important. This, in itself, is not surprising—after all, the genesis of the Union's external relations policies and their development owe a considerable debt to its contribution.[113] However, viewed against the background of the increasingly interdependent policies pronounced by the Union and the bitter inter-institutional disputes to which these give rise, it is regrettable that the Court has neither produced principles clear and consistent in their application, nor avoided the danger of rendering its role increasingly politicised.[114]

[111] [2006] OJ L327/1, Art 1(2)(a). The Commission has proposed its amendment to reflect the *ECOWAS* judgment: see COM(2009) 195 fin.

[112] *Ibid*, Art 3(2)(i).

[113] This is illustrated by the introduction of the principle of implied competence, the construction of the Community's exclusive competence in the area of CCP as well as the broad construction of the scope of the latter in the 1970s: see Koutrakos, above n 44, chs 1–3.

[114] See M Cremona, *External Relations of the EU and the Member States: Competence, Mixed Agreements, International Responsibility, and Effects of International Law* (EUI Working Papers, Law No 206/22) fn 51, and Koutrakos, above n 106, 176–85.

Against this background, the Court's approach to ex Article 47 TEU in *ECOWAS* may have various implications. First, it may encourage further inter-institutional disputes, and therefore is likely to hinder the already difficult exercise of achieving coherence in the EU's external relations policy. Secondly, it may make the Member States more reluctant to establish express links between different sets of rules in instruments adopted in related areas but within different legal frameworks. Thirdly, it does not contribute to addressing the difficulties of achieving coherence. This last point may be seen as the other side of the coin: to stress the interdependence between the Union's security, non-proliferation, development and economic policies is a commendable political imperative, but its corollary is that standards of coherence are set which are extremely difficult to achieve in the Union's multidimensional, idiosyncratic constitutional order. And the Union's way of dealing with this problem is by thinking both broadly and narrowly: that is, by introducing instruments which straddle legal frameworks, and by creating layers of administrative structures entrusted with the coordination of the various activities and the management of their implications. The practice of these gives rise to disputes which gives rise to legal proceedings, creating, therefore, a vicious circle which appears to govern the Union's international role.

V. CONCLUSION

This chapter set out to examine the interactions between the EU and the rest of the world in the area of non-proliferation. It has suggested that the Union not only acknowledges the significance of non-proliferation in the current geopolitical environment, but that it also engages actively and directly with the international community in ways which have an impact across the range of the activities it pursues. However, the picture of the actor which it emerges is one of considerable ambidexterity: grand statements coexist with small-scale projects aimed to produce tangible effects; direct interactions with third countries and international organisations multiply, and yet they are subject to administrative and institutional layers of considerable density; the politically-sensitive implications of the policy are addressed whilst Europe's judges are gradually dragged into the regulation and management of the ensuing initiatives. As it is linked to the constitutionally idiosyncratic nature of the EU's legal order, this characteristic—and the complex web of actors, policies and interests in which it originates—would be difficult to remove. The challenge for the Union is to manage it—and this is a challenge which law cannot meet on its own...[115]

[115] For the limited effects that the Lisbon amendments of the EU primary rules may have, see Koutrakos, n 61 above.

Part Four

European and Global Integration Process

11

Values in EU Foreign Policy

MARISE CREMONA

I. INTRODUCTION

THE FOCUS OF this contribution is on the role played in the EU's foreign policy by those values which the EU claims as (in some sense) 'its own', and the legal instruments and processes through which values are both imported into, and exported from, the EU legal order. The aim is not to discuss the nature and content, or the 'European' or universal character, of specific values. Indeed, we shall start from the position that in order to lead to concrete outcomes, the 'values' which have a symbolic significance for the EU must find practical expression in legal norms. These norms, whether derived from the Treaties or imported into the EU legal order, may take on a foundational or constitutional character and thus become constitutive of the Union's identity and its self-perception (and self-projection) as an international actor. Basing itself on this identity the EU commits itself to 'uphold and promote its values in its relations with the wider world'.[1] Further, the EU participates increasingly actively in the process of developing norms at the international level, norms which it then integrates into its own legal order and which it also promotes in its relations with third States.

The idea of the EU as a union of values is reflected in the Laeken Declaration which launched the Convention on the Future of Europe, specifically in the context of the Union's external policy:

> What is Europe's role in this changed world? Does Europe not, now that is finally unified, have a leading role to play in a new world order, that of a power able both to play a stabilizing role worldwide and to point the way ahead for many countries and peoples? Europe as the continent of humane values, the Magna Carta, the Bill of Rights, the French Revolution and the fall of the Berlin Wall; the continent of liberty, solidarity and

[1] Arts 2 and 3(5) of the Treaty on European Union as amended by the Treaty of Lisbon. Throughout this chapter references to the Treaties as amended by the Treaty of Lisbon will be to the Treaty on European Union (TEU) and the Treaty on the Functioning of the European Union (TFEU); references to the Treaties prior to the Treaty of Lisbon will be to the Treaty on European Union (EU) and the EC Treaty (EC).

> above all diversity, meaning respect for others' languages, cultures and traditions. The European Union's one boundary is democracy and human rights. …[2]

As this passage demonstrates, values may be presented both as characteristic of the Union's identity, and as the key to achieving specific Union objectives, especially security and stability within Europe and its neighbourhood. The external dimension of the EU's values, which is the subject of this chapter, reflects both these constitutive and instrumentalist aspects. It is unsurprising that as the Union develops a sense of its identity as being somehow defined in terms of its values, this should be reflected in its external projection of itself and in its external as well as internal policies.[3] However, we can go further and see that very process of identification as a result as well as a cause of the Union's foreign policy. There are certainly other factors—the process of drawing up the Charter of Fundamental Rights being just one—which have contributed to this development; but the need to justify and to conceptualise the increasingly important role played in particular by human rights, the rule of law and democracy in the Union's external policy has led the Union to define itself in terms of values to its citizens as well as to the world.[4]

Fundamental to any examination of the role of values in EU external policy is the interaction between the EU legal order and international norms, and at its heart is the connection made by the Union between multilateralism and 'a rule-based international order'. The Treaty of Lisbon makes explicit the importance of international law and multilateralism to the EU's external policy:

> In its relations with the wider world, the Union shall uphold and promote its values and contribute to … the strict observance and the development of international law, including respect for the principles of the United Nations Charter.[5]

> The Union's action on the international scene shall be guided by the principles which have inspired its own creation, development and enlargement, and which it seeks to advance in the wider world: … [including] respect for the principles of the United Nations Charter and international law. The Union shall … promote multilateral solutions to common problems, in particular in the framework of the United Nations.[6]

These commitments are also expressed in policy documents, and in particular in the European Security Strategy, adopted by the European Council in December 2003 and reviewed in 2008, which places 'an international order based on effective multilateralism' as one of the Union's three key strategic objectives.

[2] Laeken Declaration on the Future of the Union, European Council, 14–15 December 2001.

[3] I Manners, 'Normative Power Europe: A Contradiction in Terms?' (2002) 40 *Journal of Common Market Studies* 235; H Sjursen, 'The EU as a 'Normative' Power: How Can This Be?' (2006) 13 *Journal of European Public Policy* 235.

[4] S Lucarelli and I Manners (eds), *Values and Principles in European Union Foreign Policy* (London; New York, Routledge, 2006); A Williams, *EU Human Rights Policies: A Study in Irony* (Oxford, Oxford University Press, 2004).

[5] Art 3(5) TEU.

[6] Art 21(1) TEU.

> The development of a stronger international society, well functioning international institutions and a rule-based international order is our objective. We are committed to upholding and developing International Law. ... It is a condition of a rule-based international order that law evolves in response to developments such as proliferation, terrorism and global warming.[7]

High Representative Solana's Report on the European Security Strategy in December 2008 reaffirms this commitment:

> At a global level, Europe must lead a renewal of the multilateral order. The UN stands at the apex of the international system. Everything the EU has done in the field of security has been linked to UN objectives. We have a unique moment to renew multilateralism, working with the United States and with our partners around the world.[8]

These Treaty provisions and policy statements illustrate the double nature of the EU's commitment to international law and more specifically to multilateralism. On the one hand it is in itself declared to be one of the values upheld and promoted by the Union; on the other, the development of a rule-based international order will—in the Union's view—contribute to the defence and promotion of the Union's values more generally, including democracy, human rights and the rule of law. In this way the oft-proclaimed commitment to multilateralism can co-exist with the frequently observed tendency of the Union to export its own values and norms.

In what follows we shall examine the ways in which values are connected with EU foreign policy from three perspectives. In each case, if we want to identify specific examples we need to look not only at the generalised provisions on 'values' in the EU (and formerly in the EC) Treaties and other legal instruments, but also at their translation into specific norms, within the Union legal system and at international level.

The first perspective is that of values as *identity-defining* and constitutive. This may include:

- values as a condition of EU membership;
- the definition of values and derivative norms within the EU, in the Treaties and the Charter of Fundamental Rights, and also by the Court of Justice in the form of general principles of law;
- the import and integration into the EU legal order of international values and norms, including their defence in the EU's own legal order;
- the application of international values and norms, via the Union, in the legal order of the Member States;
- the EU as a 'model' for certain values, including in particular peace and respect for international law and peaceful settlement of disputes.

[7] European Security Strategy, 9–10.

[8] Secretary General/High Representative Report on the Implementation of the European Security Strategy— Providing Security in a Changing World, 10 December 2008, Doc 17104/08, p 4.

The second perspective is the *promotion* of values. This may include:

— exporting values via forms of unilateral action, such as trade policy;
— exporting values via technical assistance;
— exporting values via bilateral 'soft' instruments, such as human rights dialogues, or the European Neighbourhood Policy (ENP) and its Action Plans;
— shared values as a basis for developing a relationship, bilateral or multilateral, such as the Stabilisation and Association Process (SAP) and the ENP;
— shared values as an essential element of a contractual relationship.

The third perspective is the EU's contribution to *building* values, spear-heading or influencing the production of new norms, their adoption, interpretation and enforcement through diplomacy and participation in international organisations and agencies, including the UN. This may involve:

— consensus-building among Member States, candidates and potential candidates and neighbours, the formation of EU strategies and Common Positions;
— negotiation, decision-making and treaty-making, including within international organisations.

This chapter will explore the ways in which the EU interacts with multilateral norms by taking these three perspectives: values and identity; promoting values; building values. Its aim is two-fold: first, to illustrate the wide range of instruments and methodologies available to and used by the Union in adopting, integrating, promoting and developing international (multilateral) norms; and, secondly, to begin to explore the reiterative processes whereby international norms are imported into, and exported from, the Union's legal order, helping both to form and to instrumentalise its values.

II. VALUES, PRINCIPLES AND OBJECTIVES IN THE EU TREATIES

The three ways just outlined in which values interact with EU foreign policy find their basis in the EU Treaties not only in the form of explicit references to '*values*', but also in statements as to the *principles* governing the EU and the *objectives* of its policies. The Treaty of Lisbon is more explicit in its appeal to values than the earlier Treaties but an overlap in terminology between values, principles and objectives remains.

A. Foundation Values

In the pre-Lisbon Treaty structure, the Union's values appeared in two contexts.

First we have what we might call the 'foundation values' declared in Article 6 EU, albeit as 'principles': liberty, democracy, respect for human rights and fundamental freedoms, and the rule of law. These are said to be common to the Member States, the Union is 'founded' on them, respect for them is a condition of membership and a serious breach of them attracts sanctions. From the point of view of external policy, these principles are important in reflecting the general principles of law which emerged as a component of external policy in the late 1980s and early 1990s:

> This process emphasised the legal, political and moral values that make up the European identity, particularly the principles of representative democracy, the rule of law and respect for human rights.[9]

Thus, not only are they conditions of membership (via the link between Articles 6 and 49 EU), but they also form the basis of the 'essential elements' clauses introduced into Union agreements as a matter of practice from 1990.[10]

Secondly, since the Maastricht Treaty two external policy areas have specifically included among their objectives the promotion of these foundation values. The EU's development cooperation policy (introduced formally into the EC Treaty by the Treaty of Maastricht) provides that Community policy 'shall contribute to the general objective of developing and consolidating democracy and the rule of law, and to that of respecting human rights and fundamental freedoms.' (Article 177(2) EC). This general objective also appears in the same words among the objectives of the Common Foreign and Security Policy (CFSP) introduced by the Treaty of Maastricht (Article 11 EU).

Thus, in the Union's external policy the focus as far as Treaty-based objectives are concerned has been on the core values which it claims to be universal and indivisible (protection of human rights and fundamental freedoms), together with democracy and the rule of law. It has argued for the essential complementarity and interdependence of human rights and democracy, and between democracy and the rule of law.[11]

B. Common Values

In addition to these references to human rights, democracy and the rule of law, the original CFSP objectives included safeguarding the 'common values' of the Union. The common values are not defined, and thus are capable of evolutionary interpretation, but would clearly include the foundational values set out in Article

[9] Commission Communication, 'The External Dimension of the EU's Human Rights Policy: From Rome to Maastricht and Beyond', COM(1995) 567, p 1.

[10] Commission Communication of 23 May 1995 on The Inclusion of Respect for Democratic Principles and Human Rights in Agreements Between the Community and Third Countries, COM(1995) 216. These clauses all emphasise respect for democratic principles and fundamental human rights, although they differ in the specific international and regional instruments to which reference might be made (Universal Declaration of Human Rights, Helsinki Final Act, Charter of Paris, European Convention on Human Rights) and they may also include other essential elements, such as minority rights and the principles of a market economy. See further below.

[11] Commission Communication, above n 9, p 6.

6 EU. The phrase is also significant in introducing the concept of *values* as such, and in linking the idea of common values to the *principles* of Article 6 and the *objectives* of Union policy. These links, and indeed a degree of ambiguity between values, principles and objectives, are also found in the Treaties as amended by the Lisbon Treaty.

C. Values, Principles and Objectives in the Treaty of Lisbon

The Lisbon Treaty represents a further evolutionary stage. First, we have an articulation of the list of foundation values in Article 2 TEU ('the Union is *founded* on ...') and its extension to include, in addition to democracy, the rule of law and respect for human rights, respect for human dignity, freedom and equality, as well as a specific reference to the rights of those belonging to minorities. These values are also stated to be *common* to the Member States in a society of pluralism, non-discrimination, tolerance, justice, solidarity and equality between women and men. They are to be *upheld and promoted* by the Union 'in its relations with the wider world' (Article 3(5) TEU), and are thus directly linked to external policy. Other Union objectives in its external action are also linked to Union values, including peace, solidarity and mutual respect among peoples.

The Treaty then provides that the Union's action 'on the international scene shall be guided by the principles which have inspired its own creation, development and enlargement, and which it seeks to advance in the wider world' (Article 21(1) TEU). These principles reflect the values and objectives set out in Articles 2 and 3 TEU: democracy, the rule of law, universality and indivisibility of human rights and fundamental freedoms, respect for human dignity, the principles of equality and solidarity, respect for the principles of the UN Charter and international law.

The common set of objectives for the Union's external action, set out in the following paragraph (Article 21(2) TEU), includes those which previously governed the CFSP and development cooperation policy, *viz*, safeguarding the Union's common values, and consolidating and supporting democracy, the rule of law, human rights and the principles of international law. As well as expanding the list of Union values beyond those hitherto associated with external policy, the revised Treaty thus makes more explicit than was previously the case that the whole of the Union's external action (not just certain policy areas) is to be guided by its *common values*.

As we have seen, the Lisbon Treaty also represents a shift from the language of principles, found in the former Article 6 EU, to values, as defined in Article 2 TEU. This shift may represent a certain 'added value', as well as the identity-constitutive dimension of common values. However, even within the Lisbon Treaty itself there is a confusion or conflation of values and principles. The list of *values* in Article 2 is repeated in Article 21(1) as *principles*, and the Preamble to the Charter of Fundamental Rights distinguishes between the indivisible universal *values* ('human dignity, freedom, equality and solidarity') and the *principles* of democracy and the rule of law. Does this matter? A *value* may be defined as something which has intrinsic worth, which is esteemed for its own sake.[12] Values can be seen as part of the cultural patrimony or common heritage of Europe, and thus creative of a sense of belonging. A *principle* is defined as a fundamental truth, a fundamental motive or reason for action, in particular one that is consciously recognised and followed. Perhaps the shift from values in Article 2 to principles in Article 21 signifies the shift from defining the Union's identity to setting out its policies and the actions (this shift was perhaps was more obvious in the Constitutional Treaty, where Article 2 appeared in Part I and what is now Article 21 TEU was in Part III). More specifically, the reference to 'principles' in Article 21 is significant in terms of the potential of the provision in the hands of the Court of Justice. Principles, as we have seen from the Court's case law on general principles of law, are at least potentially justiciable, as well as offering a degree of flexibility and a recognition that different competing principles may need to be reconciled when engaging in concrete actions. In fact, both terms have been used within the EU in multiple senses: as a foundation for Union identity, as a basis for policy, as guiding practice or implementation of policy, and as a goal or objective for action.

III. VALUES AND IDENTITY

In 1995 the Commission argued that 'the European Union has gradually come to define itself in terms of the promotion of [human] rights and democratic freedoms'.[13] Over the last decade, the identification of the European Union with a set of common values—not always fully articulated but with human rights and democracy at their heart—has become an increasingly important part of EU policy-making, both internally and externally. Although it is right to see this espousal of values as in some sense replacing a more difficult debate as to the Union's identity, the idea of common values has emerged as part of the Union's constitutional development, underwriting its legitimacy[14] and representing that collective identity.[15]

A. A Condition of Membership

The perception of values as constitutive of a European identity is—not coincidentally—reflected in the Commission's highly influential paper on 'The

[12] *Oxford English Dictionary*.

[13] Commission Communication, above n 9, p 3.

[14] As Andrew Hurrell has pointed out, 'It is true that legitimacy is often not easy to divorce from the calculation of interests.' It does however have a normative content: 'In order for an institution or political arrangement to be legitimate, its core principles need to be justifiable on the basis of shared moral values.' See A Hurrell, *On Global Order: Power, Values and the Constitution of International Society* (Oxford, Oxford University Press, 2007) 77 and 83.

[15] JHH Weiler, 'A Constitution for Europe? Some Hard Choices' (2002) 40 *Journal of Common Market Studies* 563 at 569.

Challenge of Enlargement', prepared for the Lisbon European Council in 1992. The Commission reflects on what it means to be European, and develops its ideas on conditions for membership which were to evolve into the Copenhagen criteria of June 1993. Starting from the (then) simple statement in both the EEC and Maastricht Treaties that 'any European State' may apply for membership, the Commission recognises that the term 'European' has not been defined officially:

> It combines geographical, historical and cultural elements which all contribute to European identity. The shared experience of proximity, ideas, values, and historical interaction cannot be condensed into a simple formula, and is subject to review by each succeeding generation.[16]

The Commission turns to the references to democracy and respect for fundamental human rights in Article F of the Maastricht Treaty (now Article 6 TEU) as essential characteristics of the Union (although not at the time formally linked to Union membership) and comes up with a three-fold set of conditions for membership: European identity (encompassing shared values), democratic status and respect for human rights.[17]

Since then, of course, the 'Copenhagen criteria' of June 1992 have formalised these conditions (and added to them) and the membership clause (Article 49 TEU) has been revised to include an express cross-reference to the Union's values. As the European Council declared at Helsinki in December 1999, 'The candidate States ... must share the values and objectives of the European Union as set out in the Treaties.'[18] The provision on accession of new members in the Treaty of Lisbon (Article 49 TEU) preserves the link between Union membership and respect for its foundational values: prospective Members must not only respect the Union's values, but must also be committed to promoting them. In addition, as part of the accession process, 'the conditions of eligibility agreed upon by the European Council shall be taken into account'—a clear if implicit reference to the Copenhagen criteria, but worded so as to allow for subsequent evolution of accession conditionalities.[19]

Common values as constitutive of identity (both as a 'European' State and as the European Union) in this way enable accession criteria to be applied which can be characterised as open (the Union is not a closed club) and which do not foreclose

[16] European Commission, 'The Challenge of Enlargement', 1992, *Bulletin of the EC*, supplement 3/92, para 7.

[17] *Ibid*, para 8.

[18] Conclusions of the European Council, Helsinki, 10–11 December 1999, para 4. The Millennium Declaration adopted at Helsinki also claimed that 'The Union's citizens are bound together by common values such as freedom, tolerance, equality, solidarity and cultural diversity.'

[19] Cf the reference to 'the conditionality of the Stabilisation and Association Process' alongside the Copenhagen criteria in the context of the accession perspective of the Western Balkans, in European Council Conclusions of 14–15 December 2006, para 8.

membership or establish immutable frontiers.[20] As the European Council claimed in the Laeken Declaration:

> The European Union's one boundary is democracy and human rights. The Union is open only to countries which uphold basic values such as free elections, respect for minorities and respect for the rule of law.[21]

The aim is to create—or maybe rather to assert—a Union identity which is based on inclusion (sharing common values) rather than exclusion. It is in this sense that Article 21 TEU declares that the Union's foundational principles have inspired its enlargement as well as its creation.

B. Values as a Source of Union Law

As we have already seen, the EU Treaties define which values are regarded as foundational, or common. These have emerged not only out of the reiterative Treaty-amendment and drafting process, but also as a result of institutional deliberation and legislation as well as the broader normative process which led to the formulation of the Charter of Fundamental Rights.[22] As Bruno De Witte has pointed out,[23] the Court of Justice has built its concept of fundamental rights as general principles of Union law basing itself not only on the constitutional traditions common to the Member States and the European Convention for the Protection of Human Rights, but also on a range of other international human rights instruments.[24] In doing this, and in shaping these norms in the specific context of the Union's legal order, the Court has created a distinctive body of general principles *of EU law*. General principles initially functioned to ensure the cohesiveness of the system and its legal and ideological continuity with the laws of the Member States; however, 'as the Community legal order reached a stage of relative maturity, the general principles came to embody constitutional values attuned to the special needs of the Community polity.'[25] As such they affect both the Union institutions and the Member States. Compliance with fundamental human rights, as general

[20] On the problematic issue of the link between values and identity in the context of enlargement, see P Leino, 'Rights, Rules and Democracy in the EU Enlargement Process: Between Universalism and Identity' (2002) 7 *Austrian Review of International and European Law* 53.

[21] Laeken Declaration, above n 2.

[22] G de Búrca, 'The Drafting of the EU Charter of Fundamental Rights' (2001) 26 *EL Rev* 126.

[23] See ch 5 in this volume.

[24] To take one example, in Case C-438/05 *International Transport Workers' Federation and Finnish Seamen's Union v Viking Line ABP and OÜ Viking Line Eesti*, [2007] ECR I-10779, as well as referring to the Community Charter of the Fundamental Social Rights of Workers and to the Charter of Fundamental Rights, the Court relied on Convention No 87 adopted by the International Labour Organisation, concerning Freedom of Association and Protection of the Right to Organise, concluding on the basis of these instruments that 'the right to take collective action, including the right to strike, must therefore be recognised as a fundamental right which forms an integral part of the general principles of Community law the observance of which the Court ensures' (para 44).

[25] T Tridimas, *The General Principles of EU Law*, 2nd edn (Oxford, Oxford University Press, 2006) 553.

principles of law, is a condition of legality of Union secondary legislation,[26] and 'measures incompatible with respect for human rights are not acceptable in the Community'.[27] Member States too, when acting within the scope of Union law, must comply with fundamental human rights as general principles of law,[28] and may rely on the need to protect fundamental rights in order to justify a derogation from treaty-based free movement rights.[29]

The Charter of Fundamental Rights of the European Union, solemnly proclaimed by the European Parliament, the Council and the Commission, 'makes more visible', 'reaffirms' and 'recognises' the

> rights as they result, in particular, from the constitutional traditions and international obligations common to the Member States, the European Convention for the Protection of Human Rights and Fundamental Freedoms, the Social Charters adopted by the Union and by the Council of Europe and the case-law of the Court of Justice of the European Union and of the European Court of Human Rights.[30]

Together with a restatement of the freedoms, citizens' rights and other principles[31] derived from the EU Treaties, they are intended to preserve and develop the Union's common values.[32] In the words of Graínne de Búrca:

> In the broadest political sense, the drafting and proclamation of the Charter both heralds and concretizes a shift in the normative underpinning of the EU as a polity.[33]

Although when first proclaimed the Charter itself was not granted binding legal force, it was treated as an important form of legal guidance by both the Court of Justice and political institutions,[34] and under the Treaty of Lisbon it has 'the same legal value as the Treaties'.[35]

[26] Art 263 TFEU (ex Art 230 EC); *Opinion 2/94* [1996] ECR I-1759, paras 33–34.

[27] Joined Cases C-402/05P and C-415/05P *Yassin Abdullah Kadi and Al Barakaat International Foundation v Council and Commission* [2008] ECR I-06351, para 284.

[28] See, eg, Case C-260/89 *ERT* [1991] ECR I-2925, paras 41–43.

[29] Case C-112/00 *Schmidberger* [2003] ECR I-5659, para 74; Case C-36/02 *Omega* [2004] ECR I-9609, para 35; Case C-438/05 *International Transport Workers' Federation and Finnish Seamen's Union v Viking Line ABP and OÜ Viking Line Eesti*, [2007] ECR I-10779, para 45.

[30] Preamble, Charter of Fundamental Rights of the European Union, [2010] OJ C83/389. The 'explanations' of the individual Charter Articles offered by the Praesidium to the Convention which drew up the Charter refer to the external instruments, especially the European Convention on Human Rights (ECHR), from which its provisions are derived.

[31] Eg, non-discrimination, equality between men and women, cultural religious and linguistic diversity, sustainable development and consumer protection.

[32] Preamble, Charter of Fundamental Rights of the European Union, above n 30.

[33] G de Búrca, 'Human Rights: The Charter and Beyond' *Jean Monnet Working Paper* No 10/2001, p 6.

[34] P Craig and G de Búrca, *EU Law: Text, Cases and Materials*, 4th edn (Oxford, Oxford University Press, 2007) 413; B De Witte, 'The Legal Status of the Charter: Vital Question or Non-Issue' (2001) *Maastricht Journal of International and Comparative Law* 81.

[35] Art 6(1) TEU; see, however, Protocol on The Application of the Charter of Fundamental Rights of the European Union to Poland and to the United Kingdom. This solution raises questions as to the relationship between the Charter and the provisions of the Treaties, especially where there are inconsistencies and overlap: de Búrca, above n 33, p 6. For an example, since the coming into force of the Treaty of Lisbon, of a reference by the Court to the Charter, see Case C-555/07 *Seda Kücükdeveci v Swedex GmbH & Co KG*, judgment 19 January 2010, *nyr*.

In both the development of general principles of Community law, and in the Charter of Fundamental Rights (now being used as a source of those general principles) we can see how norms derived from external international instruments have inspired and helped to create a *Community* (or Union) set of norms and values. In some cases, as with equality and non-discrimination, they have found their way into the EU Treaties and thus have formed a basis for more detailed legislative provision.[36]

C. Importing Values and Norms

In addition to the way in which EU law has been fashioned, at least in part, from values and norms which derive their inspiration and ultimate source from international norms, the EU also imports international norms more directly and integrates them into its legal order. In the first place, the Treaties themselves in places make express reference to international norms. Article 6(3) TEU requires the Union to respect fundamental rights 'as guaranteed by the European Convention for the Protection of Human Rights and Fundamental Freedoms ... [which] shall constitute general principles of the Union's law', thus giving this Convention a special status in Union law.[37] Article 78(1) TFEU (ex-Article 63(1) EC) requires the Council, in adopting measures on asylum, to act 'in accordance with the Geneva Convention of 28 July 1951 and Protocol of 31 January 1967 relating to the status of refugees and other relevant treaties'. Article 208(2) TFEU (ex-Article 177(3) EC) requires the Union and Member States in their policy on development cooperation to 'comply with the commitments and take account of the objectives they have approved in the context of the United Nations and other competent international organisations.' We have already seen that the Treaties impose a more general obligation that in its external action the Union will be guided by respect for the principles of the UN Charter and international law.[38]

In the second place, international agreements concluded by the Union are binding on the Member States as well as the institutions,[39] and according to the Court of Justice they become an integral part of the Union legal order.[40] The fact that Union agreements are binding on the Union institutions means that 'those agreements prevail over provisions of secondary [Union] legislation',[41] and so

[36] Eg, Art 19 TFEU (ex Art 13 EC) and the equality directives: Directive 2000/43/EC on the principle of equal treatment between persons irrespective of racial or ethnic origin, [2000] OJ L180/22; Directive 2000/78/EC establishing a general framework for equal treatment in employment and occupation, [2000] OJ L303/16. See Tridimas, above n 25, 59–135.

[37] See further ch 5 in this volume.

[38] Art 21(1) TEU.

[39] Art 300(7) EC.

[40] Case 181/73 *Haegeman* [1974] ECR 449.

[41] Case C-344/04 *R v Department of Transport, ex p IATA* [2006] ECR I-00403, at para 35; see also Case C-61/94 *Commission v Germany* [1996] ECR I-3989, at para 52.

in judging the legality of Union secondary legislation the Court may assess its conformity with binding provisions in Union agreements.[42] So if, as proposed, the EU concludes the UN Convention of the Rights of Persons with Disabilities,[43] it will be binding on the Member States, it will take precedence over secondary legislation and some of its provisions may be held to create rights directly enforceable by individuals in national courts.

In the third place, legal instruments adopted or concluded by the EU may refer to international sources of law or statements of principle. Thus the 'essential elements' clauses in Union agreements, which we shall discuss below in the context of promoting values,[44] which may include references to (for example) the Universal Declaration of Human Rights, the Helsinki Final Act or 'existing obligations under international disarmament and non-proliferation treaties and agreements', are also declaratory of an EU commitment to those values. In a rather different context, the legal acts which provide the basis for Common Security and Defence Policy (CSDP) missions will normally refer to the international legal framework, including the international instruments which provide authorisation for the action.[45]

In the fourth place, the EU may engage itself, in a non-binding document or statement, to abide by specific values or international norms. Thus, in the Joint Statement of Development Policy (the 'European Consensus on Development') adopted in 2005, we find the following under the heading of 'Common Values':

> EU partnership and dialogue with third countries will promote common values of: respect for human rights, fundamental freedoms, peace, democracy, good governance, gender equality, the rule of law, solidarity and justice. The EU is strongly committed to effective multilateralism whereby all the world's nations share responsibility for development.[46]

[42] Case C-344/04, *ex p IATA*, above n 41, at para 35. For a fuller discussion of these points, see M Cremona, 'External Relations of the EU and the Member States: Competence, Mixed Agreements, International Responsibility, and Effects of International Law,' report of Community Rapporteur, FIDE 2006 National Reports, X Xenopoulos (ed); originally published as EUI Working Paper LAW No 2006/22.

[43] Proposal for a Council Decision concerning the conclusion, by the European Community, of the United Nations Convention on the Rights of Persons with Disabilities, Proposal for a Council Decision concerning the conclusion, by the European Community, of the Optional Protocol to the United Nations Convention on the Rights of Persons with Disabilities COM (2008)530 final.

[44] See text below at nn 128 ff.

[45] So, eg, the Joint Action which established Operation Atalanta in Somalia, as well as referring to the relevant UN Security Council Resolutions in its Preamble, provides that the mission shall carry out its mandate 'under the conditions set by the relevant international law and by UNSC Resolutions 1814 (2008), 1816 (2008) and 1838 (2008)': Council Joint Action 2008/851/CFSP on a European Union military operation to contribute to the deterrence, prevention and repression of acts of piracy and armed robbery off the Somali coast, [2008] OJ L301/33, Art 2.

[46] Joint Statement by the Council and the Representatives of the Governments of the Member States meeting within the Council, the European Parliament and the Commission on European Union Development Policy, 'The European Consensus', 22 November 2005, [2006] OJ C46/1.

Other documents may refer to more specific instruments. In 2008 the Council adopted an update of the EU's Guidelines on Children in Armed Conflict.[47] Recalling that the EU is founded on the principle of respect for human rights, and that this is a key objective of the CFSP and 'part of the Community's policies regarding trade and development cooperation and humanitarian assistance', the Guidelines go on to state that

> In its work to ensure the protection of children affected by armed conflict, the EU is guided by relevant international and regional norms and standards on human rights and humanitarian law[48]

The major relevant 'international norms, standards and principles' are listed in an Annex, including not only the Convention on the Rights of the Child and its Protocols and International Humanitarian Law, but also UN Security Council and General Assembly resolutions. These Guidelines and similar references elsewhere do not as such incorporate the norms referred to into the EU legal order, but they do something more than indicating the EU's willingness to frame its policies and action in terms of international legal norms; by expressly linking them to the EU's binding commitments to human rights they are helping to define that commitment in concrete terms and to shape its content.

Lastly and more generally, the Court of Justice has stated that the Community (and now the Union) 'must respect international law in the exercise of its powers'[49]; and in *Racke* it went further, holding that it had jurisdiction under Article 234 EC (now Article 267 TFEU) to review the legality of a Community act on grounds of breach of a rule of international law: the rules of customary international law were held to be not only binding on the institutions but also part of the Community legal order:

> [T]he European Community must respect international law in the exercise of its powers. ... It follows that the rules of customary international law concerning the termination and the suspension of treaty relations by reason of a fundamental change of circumstances are binding upon the Community institutions and form part of the Community legal order.[50]

Likewise, in *Opel Austria*, the CFI applied the international law principles of good faith and legitimate expectations as expressed in Article 18 of the Vienna Convention on the Law of Treaties, concerning the obligation to refrain from

[47] EU Guidelines on Children in Armed Conflict, adopted by the General Affairs Council 16 June 2008; Council Doc 10019/08. The Guidelines were originally adopted by the General Affairs Council of 8 December 2003. See also EU Guidelines for the Promotion and Protection of the Rights of the Child, Docs 16031/07 and 16457/07, and Conclusions of the Council and the Representatives of the Governments of the Member States meeting within the Council on the promotion and protection of the rights of the child in the European Union's external action—the development and humanitarian dimensions, 27 May 2008, Doc 9739/08.

[48] EU Guidelines on Children in Armed Conflict, above n 47, para 9.

[49] Case C-286/90 *Poulsen* [1992] ECR I-6048.

[50] Case C-162/96 *Racke GmbH & Co v Hauptzollamt Mainz* [1998] ECR I-3655, at paras 45–46.

acts which would defeat the object and purpose of a treaty before its entry into force.[51]

Somewhat more controversial than the binding force of international agreements and this general commitment to international law is the degree to which international law may prevail over primary Union law—that is, over the Treaties and general principles fundamental to the Union legal order, including fundamental human rights. As far as international treaty obligations of the Union are concerned, it may be argued that Article 218(11) TFEU (ex Article 300(6) EC)—by providing that a proposed treaty which is incompatible with the EU Treaties may not enter into force unless it is amended or the Treaties are revised—implies that, in the absence of such amendment, the institutional decision concluding an incompatible agreement is invalid.[52] The institutions may not validly, in terms of Union law, enter into international obligations which conflict with primary law, and thus such agreements, following Article 218(11) TFEU, would not become a part of the Union legal order. This would suggest that the EU Treaties should prevail over conflicting provisions of international agreements. The Court of Justice in *Kadi* agreed:

> [T]he obligations imposed by an international agreement cannot have the effect of prejudicing the constitutional principles of the EC Treaty, which include the principle that all Community acts must respect fundamental rights …
>
> Article 300(7) EC provides that agreements concluded under the conditions set out in that article are to be binding on the institutions of the Community and on Member States. … That primacy at the level of Community law would not, however, extend to primary law, in particular to the general principles of which fundamental rights form part.[53]

The Court is here adopting a delicate position. On the one hand international norms, while binding on the Union, cannot prevail over primary Union law and its 'basic constitutional charter'. On the other hand, that primary Union law includes 'the general principles of which fundamental rights form part', which have been formed by the Court of Justice in a process of integration drawing on international norms. International norms which have been transformed in this way into fundamental principles of the Union legal order are more than 'an integral part' of Union law[54]; they are constitutive of the Union's identity, 'the very foundations' of the Union legal order. Even Article 351 TFEU (ex Article 307 EC), which permits Member States under some circumstances to derogate from

[51] Case T-115/94 *Opel Austria GmbH v Council* [1997] ECR II-39.

[52] In Case C-122/95 Germany v Council [1998] ECR I973, for example, the Court declared the Council decision concluding the Framework Agreement on Bananas invalid in so far as certain aspects of the Agreement were contrary to the fundamental Community law principle of non-discrimination. See K Lenaerts and E De Smijter, 'The European Union as an Actor under International Law' (1999–2000)19 *Yearbook of European Law* 95 at 102. Note that it is the decision concluding the agreement that is declared invalid; the validity in international law of the agreement itself is not affected.

[53] Joined Cases C-402/05P and C-415/05P, above n 27, paras 285, 306 and 308. See further ch 7 in this volume.

[54] The phrase used of binding Union agreements: see above n 40.

primary Union law in order to fulfill a prior international obligation, cannot permit a derogation from these principles:

> Article 307 EC may in no circumstances permit any challenge to the principles that form part of the very foundations of the Community legal order, one of which is the protection of fundamental rights ...[55]

As the judgment in *Kadi* reminds us, Article 216(2) TFEU (ex Article 300(7) EC) provides that international agreements concluded by the Union are binding upon the Member States. Indeed, in so far as international values and norms become part of the Union legal order they may take effect and be enforced within the legal order of the Member States. Provisions in Union agreements may be capable of creating rights for individuals which are directly enforceable in national courts.[56] Obligations in Union agreements may be enforced against Member States as Union obligations by means of the normal enforcement procedures (ie Articles 258–260 TFEU, ex Articles 226–228 EC).[57]

The EU may act as a 'conduit' for the enforcement of international norms in the Member States in other ways. Commitments in an international instrument may be translated into Union legislation, with all that that implies in terms of enforceability in relation to the Member States. For example, the Protocol to Prevent, Suppress and Punish Trafficking in Persons, especially Women and Children, adopted in 2000 to supplement the UN Convention against Transnational Organized Crime (Palermo Convention) has been signed and/or ratified by all Member States and the EC.[58] Council Directive 2004/81/EC, which requires Member States to grant residence status and assistance to victims of trafficking who are third-country nationals, refers to these international instruments in its Preamble.[59] In a recent proposal to adopt a new Framework Decision on trafficking in human beings, the Commission refers to these initiatives as well as to a more recent Council of Europe Convention which creates an obligation to criminalise trafficking in human beings,[60] and argues, as

[55] Joined Cases C-402/05P and C-415/05P, above n 27, para 304.

[56] See, eg, Case 104/81 *Hauptzollampt Mainz v Kupferberg* [1982] ECR 3641; Case 12/86 *Demirel* [1987] ECR 3719; C-265/03 *Simutenkov* [2005] ECR I-2579.

[57] See, eg, Cases C-61/94 *Commission v Germany* [1996] ECR I-3989; C-13/00 *Commission v Ireland* [2002] ECR I-2943; C-239/03 *Commission v France* [2004] ECR I-9325.

[58] Council Decision 2006/618/EC on the conclusion, on behalf of the European Community, of the Protocol to Prevent, Suppress and Punish Trafficking in Persons, Especially Women And Children, in so far as the provisions of this Protocol fall within the scope of Articles 179 and 181a of the EC Treaty, [2006] OJ L262/44; Council Decision 2006/619/EC on the conclusion, on behalf of the European Community, of the Protocol to Prevent, Suppress and Punish Trafficking in Persons, Especially Women And Children, in so far as the provisions of the Protocol fall within the scope of Part III, Title IV of the EC Treaty, [2006] OJ L262/51. On the use of two concluding Decisions, see M Cremona, 'EU External Action in the JHA Domain: A Legal Perspective' *EUI Working Papers*, LAW 2008/24.

[59] Council Directive 2004/81/EC on the residence permit issued to third-country nationals who are victims of trafficking in human beings or who have been the subject of an action to facilitate illegal immigration, who cooperate with the competent authorities, [2004] OJ L261/19.

[60] Council of Europe Convention on Action against Trafficking in Human Beings 2005, CETS No 197.

a rationale for the new Framework Decision, that 'Implementing such measures would lead to significant improvements'.[61]

Less formally, the Union may undertake, as a matter of policy, to encourage Member States to improve their level of commitment and capacity to meet internationally agreed standards. As an example, let us take the EU's strategy on weapons of mass destruction. On 16 June 2003, in the context of discussion of the European Security Strategy prepared by SG/HR Solana, the GAER Council endorsed both a statement of 'Basic principles for an EU strategy against proliferation of Weapons of Mass Destruction'[62] and an Action Plan for the implementation of these Basic Principles.[63] It also adopted a Declaration on non-proliferation of weapons of mass destruction (WMD) which refers to both the Basic Principles and the Action Plan. The Declaration adopted by the GAER Council was endorsed by the Thessaloniki European Council of 19–20 June 2003 and an EU Strategy was adopted in December 2003.[64] Among the priorities in the Action Plan were a number directed at the Member States: the ratification by all EU Member States and Accession States of all IAEA Protocols, and the adoption of the necessary implementing legislation within the framework of Euratom; seeking a political commitment by the Member States to increase the IAEA's budget; supporting membership of Accession States in export control regimes and improving the efficiency of EU export controls in the light of enlargement, including a Peer Review scheme coordinated by the Commission; consideration of a common EU approach to the criminalisation of illegal export or brokering of WMD-related material[65]; and a new Directive to harmonise and strengthen Member State controls in relation to radioactive sources.[66] In such ways the EU's commitment to and promotion of 'the multilateral treaty regime, which provides the normative basis for all non-proliferation efforts'[67] is directed at its own Member States as well as at third countries.[68]

[61] Proposal for a Council Framework Decision on preventing and combating trafficking in human beings, and protecting victims, repealing Framework Decision 2002/629/JHA, COM/2009/0136 final, 25 March 2009.

[62] Basic Principles for an EU Strategy against Proliferation of Weapons of Mass Destruction, Council Doc 10352/03.

[63] Earlier conclusions were adopted in November 2001 on the link between terrorism and WMD: Council conclusions on implications of the terrorist threat on the non-proliferation, disarmament and arms control policy of the European Union, 29 Nov 2001, Doc 14732/01.

[64] EU Strategy against proliferation of Weapons of Mass Destruction, Doc 15708/03.

[65] According to the most recent Progress Report on the implementation of the EU Strategy against the Proliferation of Weapons of Mass Destruction, this issue is still being discussed in the Council Working Party on Substantive Criminal Law: Council Doc 11490/09, 26 June 2009.

[66] The Directive was adopted later the same year: Council Directive 2003/122/Euratom of 22 December 2003 on the control of high-activity sealed radioactive sources and orphan sources, [2003] OJ L346/57.

[67] Basic Principles, above n 62, para 6.

[68] For a full discussion of EU policy on non-proliferation, see ch 10 in this volume.

D. The EU as a Model for Values

'... how to develop the Union into a stabilizing factor and a model in the new, multipolar world.' (Laeken Declaration) If values are part of the Union's own identity, that characteristic is seen in the context of Union external policy as providing a model, particularly a model of stability and conflict resolution, but also a model of 'unity in diversity'. Thus, in addition to being a model for a certain kind of regional economic integration, a regulatory model, or a model of multi-level governance,[69] the Union models its values of respect for human rights, democracy, equality and the rule of law.

Certain values have a particular resonance in this context: peace, respect for international law and peaceful settlement of disputes, and the value of cultural diversity. Thus in 1999, launching the Stabilisation and Association Process (SAP) for the Western Balkans, the Commission claimed that

> The EU is itself a model for overcoming conflict and promoting reconciliation through close cooperation to achieve common goals, while respecting national sovereignty and territorial integrity.[70]

In implementing the SAP, the Commission said, the countries of the Western Balkans would be expect to align themselves towards 'European Union values and models of democracy, respect for human and minority rights, the rule of law and the market economy.'[71] Although the SAP is based on the stated 'vocation' of the Western Balkan States as potential candidates for EU membership (and Croatia and the former Yugoslav Republic of Macedonia are now candidate States), this promotion of the EU as a model of particular values is presented not only as part of the package of membership conditionality, but as a means to the end of securing peace, stability and prosperity in the region.

The presentation of the EU as a model for its common values is thus one mechanism whereby the Union seeks to achieve its external objectives of preserving peace, preventing conflict and strengthening international security.[72] The particularity of the EU as a model derives from its emphasis on what Manners characterises as sustainable peace,[73] developed out of its own history and incorporating sustainable economic and social development and the rule of law. Its emerging role in peace building and crisis management draws upon these aspects of the Union as a global

[69] M Cremona, 'The Union as a global actor: Roles, Models and Identity' (2004) 41 *CML Rev* 553.

[70] Commission Communication of 26 May 1999 on the Stabilisation and Association Process, COM(1999) 235.

[71] Proposal for a Council Regulation on assistance for Albania, Bosnia and Herzegovina, Croatia, the Federal Republic of Yugoslavia and the former Yugoslav Republic of Macedonia, COM(2000) 281 final. The Western Balkans is now covered by the financial instrument for pre-accession assistance (Council Regulation 1085/2006/EC establishing an Instrument for Pre-Accession Assistance (IPA), [2006] OJ L210/82) which itself links its conditionality to the 'principles on which the European Union is founded' (Preamble, para 21; see also Art 21).

[72] Art 21(2)(c) TEU.

[73] I Manners, 'The Normative Ethics of the European Union' (2008) 84 *International Affairs* 45.

civil power. But moving beyond this in writing on the EU as an 'ethical power', Aggestam argues that the notion of 'ethical power Europe' is underpinned by

> a conceptual shift in the EU's role and aspirations from what it 'is' to what it 'does': from simply representing a 'power of attraction' and a positive role model to proactively working to change the world in the direction of its vision of the 'global common good'[74]

a statement which encourages us to turn to the ways in which the EU promotes its values.

IV. PROMOTING VALUES

In addition to the ways in which the EU defines itself in terms of values, integrating them into its own legal order, it also engages in the promotion of values, both self-defined EU values and 'adopted' integrated international values. The promotion of Union values, which has now become an explicit objective of the Union in Article 3(5) TEU, has formed an important element of Union external policy for some time.[75] The European Security Strategy sets out the Union's strategic objectives against an overall aim: 'To defend its security and to promote its values'.[76] The Union engages in promoting its values in a variety of ways, through unilateral instruments, bilateral agreements, using positive and negative conditionality, and more recently by attempting to build reciprocal partnerships with third countries on the basis of 'shared values'.

What follows is an outline of some aspects of that policy, and the use of conditionality as a characteristic mechanism for the promotion of values and in particular fundamental human rights. In this context the concept of Union values has largely been focused on the core values of democracy, respect for fundamental human rights and the rule of law, promoted not only as Union values but as universal.[77] The claim of universality, and its use to justify conditionality, is itself contested at a number of levels, as are the actual inconsistencies between internal and external dimensions of the EU human rights policy,[78] but within the context of this chapter we can only note that the claim forms the basis for a wider promotion

[74] L Aggestam, 'Introduction: Ethical Power Europe?' (2008) 84 *International Affairs* 1.

[75] See generally, E Fierro, *The EU's Approach to Human Rights Conditionality in Practice* (The Hague; London, Martinus Nijhoff, 2003); R Brandtner and A Rosas, 'Human Rights and the External Relations of the European Community: An Analysis of Doctrine and Practice' (1998) 9 *EJIL* 468; A Clapham, 'Where is the EU's Human Rights Common Foreign Policy, and How is it Manifested in Multilateral Fora?' in P Alston (ed), *The EU and Human Rights* (Oxford, Oxford University Press, 1999), and other contributions to that volume; A Williams, *EU Human Rights Policies, A Study in Irony* (Oxford, Oxford University Press, 2004); K Smith, *European Union Foreign Policy in a Changing World*, 2nd edn (Cambridge, Polity Press, 2008), ch 5.

[76] European Security Strategy, above n 7, 6.

[77] See, eg, Commission Communication, 'The External Dimension of the EU's Human Rights Policy: From Rome to Maastricht and Beyond', COM(1995) 567, p 3.

[78] P Leino, 'European Universalism? The EU and Human Rights Conditionality' (2005) 24 *Yearbook of European Law* 329; Williams, above n 75.

of values beyond the Union's neighbours and candidate States and for the use of conditionality as a instrument of policy. More recently the EU has used the instruments and methods at its disposal, including conditionality, to promote those multilateral norms which reflect its foreign policy objectives, particularly the objectives of its Security Strategy; these include, for example, international norms relating to both counter-terrorism and non-proliferation of WMD.

A. Promoting Values via Technical Assistance

The EU's financial and technical assistance programmes address the promotion of values and norms in two ways. First, the programmes may themselves directly support the development of values or the implementation of international norms. Since 2007 the main instrument for the promotion of democracy and human rights has been Regulation 1889/2006/EC (EIDHR).[79] Union instruments may also be used with the objective of promoting compliance with international norms. Thus, the Union's Strategy and Action Plan on WMD includes support for the implementation of relevant UN Security Council Resolutions, and EU technical support is available under the Joint Actions adopted to support UNSC Resolution 1540,[80] for example regional workshops on export control systems including end-use control of dual-use technologies, as well as channelling assistance through the IAEA:

> In order to achieve the objective of strengthening the security of nuclear and radioactive materials, a series of assistance projects have been undertaken or are under preparation in countries in the Balkans, Caucasus, Central Asia, the Mediterranean region, Africa and in Southeast Asia. Through a financial contribution of more than 20 million EUR since 2004, the EU has now become the major donor to the IAEA nuclear security fund.[81]

Secondly, financial and technical assistance instruments have since 1990 increasingly developed an element of conditionality based on respect for human rights and democracy. Some form of explicit conditionality is now found in each of the financial instruments covering 2007–2013.

In November 1991, the EC Council of Ministers, together with the Member States, adopted an influential Resolution on Democracy and Development which stated that the Community and Member States would in their development policies give a high priority to a 'positive approach that stimulates respect for human

[79] Regulation 1886/2006/EC, [2006] OJ L386/1. This Regulation replaces Regulations 975/99/EC and 976/99/EC.

[80] Council Joint Action 2006/419/CFSP in support of the implementation of the United Nations Security Council Resolution 1540 (2004) and in the framework of the implementation of the EU Strategy against the Proliferation of Weapons of Mass Destruction, [2006] OJ L165/30; Council Joint Action 2008/368/CFSP in support of the implementation of United Nations Security Council Resolution 1540 (2004) and in the framework of the implementation of the EU strategy against the proliferation of weapons of mass destruction, [2008] OJ L127/78.

[81] Six-monthly Progress Report on the implementation of the EU Strategy against the Proliferation of Weapons of Mass Destruction, December 2008, Doc 17184/08.

rights and encourages democracy'.[82] The positive approach would include the possibility of increased assistance to countries in which positive changes had taken place; however the Resolution also envisaged 'appropriate responses' in cases of grave and persistent violations of human rights or serious interruption of democratic processes. These graduated responses include confidential or public *démarches*, changes in content of cooperation programmes, deferment of decisions, through to suspension of cooperation. The European Consensus for Development, adopted in December 2005, also maintains that 'progress in the protection of human rights, good governance and democratisation is fundamental for poverty reduction and sustainable development'.[83]

From 1992 this approach was underpinned by the express provision on development cooperation in the EC Treaty:

> Community policy in this area [development cooperation] shall contribute to the general objective of developing and consolidating democracy and the rule of law, and to that of respecting human rights and fundamental freedoms.[84]

What of cooperation with third countries more generally? The Treaty of Nice provided a basis in Article 181a EC for economic, financial and technical cooperation with third countries outside the development context, which referred in identical terms to the consolidation of democracy and the rule of law, and respect for human rights as a general policy objective. Thus there was an explicit Treaty legal base for the promotion of these core values in all technical assistance programmes,[85] and under the Treaty of Lisbon revision, this objective has now been generalised to all external action.[86]

In this context, then, the standards of political conditionality (based on respect for human rights and democratic principles) will inform the objectives and purposes of financial assistance programmes, and breaches of political conditionality may stimulate—rather than a complete withdrawal of assistance—positive measures such as the targeting of assistance to support democratic initiatives, the work of non-governmental organisations or the independent media. The November 1991 Resolution on Democracy and Development also makes it clear that humanitarian assistance and emergency aid will not be subject to conditionality, and this is reflected in both the Regulation on Humanitarian Assistance and the provision on humanitarian aid added to the Treaties by the Treaty of

[82] Resolution of the Council and of the Member States meeting in Council on human rights, democracy and development, *Bull EC* 11-1991 p 122.

[83] Above n 46.

[84] Art 177(2) EC Treaty.

[85] For discussion of the historically problematic legal basis for EU human rights policies, see JHH Weiler and S Fries, 'A Human Rights Policy for the European Community and Union: The Question of Competences' in P Alston (ed), *The EU and Human Rights* (Oxford, Oxford University Press, 1999).

[86] Art 21(2)(a) and (b) TEU; the corresponding specific references have been removed from the provisions on development and cooperation in the TFEU.

Lisbon.[87] In addition, the new financial instruments covering 2007–2013 all contain an element of conditionality linked to democracy, human rights and the rule of law. Thus, Article 3(1) of Regulation 1905/2006/EC, creating a financing instrument for development cooperation, establishes as the first of its general principles:

> The Community is founded on the values of democracy, the rule of law, respect for human rights and fundamental freedoms and seeks to develop and consolidate commitment to these values in partner countries and regions through dialogue and cooperation.

Article 37 of the same Regulation provides for the possibility of suspension of assistance where these principles are not observed[88]; similarly, Articles 1(3) and 28 of the European Neighbourhood and Partnership Instrument (ENPI),[89] Article 21 of the Instrument for Pre-Accession Assistance (IPA),[90] and Article 3(1) of Regulation 1934/2006/EC establishing a financing instrument for cooperation with industrialised and other high-income countries and territories.[91] Not surprisingly given the conditions in which it is applied, the Stability Instrument, like the Regulation on humanitarian aid, does not contain an equivalent conditionality clause.[92]

B. Promoting Values via Unilateral Trade Instruments

The current Regulation establishing the Union's Generalised System of Preferences (GSP), known as 'GSP-plus', incorporates incentives in the form of further preferences to those countries that can show that they have both ratified and effectively implement 27 key Conventions related to sustainable development, good governance, core labour standards and human rights, including the International Covenants on Civil and Political Rights and on Economic, Social and Cultural Rights, the International Convention on the Elimination of All Forms of Racial

[87] Council Regulation 1257/96/EC concerning humanitarian aid, [1996] OJ L163/1; Art 214(2) TFEU.

[88] Regulation 1905/2006/EC establishing a financing instrument for development cooperation, [2006] OJ L378/41, Art 37: 'Without prejudice to the provisions on suspension of aid in partnership and cooperation agreements with partner countries and regions, where a partner country fails to observe the principles referred to in Article 3(1), and where consultations with the partner country do not lead to a solution acceptable to both parties, or if consultations are refused or in cases of special urgency, the Council, acting by a qualified majority on a proposal from the Commission, may take appropriate measures in respect of any assistance granted to the partner country under this Regulation. Such measures may include full or partial suspension of assistance.'

[89] Regulation 1638/2006/EC establishing a European Neighbourhood and Partnership Instrument (ENPI), [2006] OJ L310/1.

[90] Regulation 1085/2006/EC establishing an Instrument for Pre-Accession Assistance (IPA), [2006] OJ L210/82.

[91] Regulation 1934/2006/EC establishing a financing instrument for cooperation with industrialised and other high-income countries and territories, [2006] OJ L405/41; note that this Regulation does not contain a suspension clause.

[92] See above n 87; Regulation 1717/2006/EC establishing an instrument for stability, [2006] OJ L327/1.

Discrimination, the Convention Against Torture, the Convention on the Rights of the Child, the Genocide Convention and a number of core ILO Conventions.[93] The rationale for these incentives is that developing countries classified by the EU as vulnerable,[94] which assume 'special burdens and responsibilities due to the ratification and effective implementation of core international conventions', will benefit from additional tariff preferences 'designed to promote further economic growth and thereby to respond positively to the need for sustainable development'.[95] Despite this rationale, the link between the international instruments being promoted by the EU and the additional trade preferences, except as a simple incentive, is questionable, raising doubts as to the compatibility of the system with WTO law.[96]

C. Promoting Values via Non-binding Instruments

In addition to formal legal instruments such as the GSP Regulation, the EU may use a variety of non-binding instruments to promote its values and the international norms that may embody them. Here we shall mention three: human rights dialogues; the use of Council conclusions, Guidelines and CFSP Common Positions to promote EU policy; and the Action Plans agreed within the framework of the European Neighbourhood Policy (ENP).

[93] Regulation 732/2008 applying a scheme of generalised tariff preferences for the period from 1 January 2009 to 31 December 2011, [2008] OJ L211/1, Arts 7–10 and Annex III.

[94] The concept of 'vulnerable' is defined *ibid*, Art 8(2).

[95] Regulation 732/2008, above n 93, recitals 8–9. For the period 1 January 2009 to 31 December 2011, 16 countries have qualified for the special incentive arrangement: Armenia, Azerbaijan, Bolivia, Colombia, Costa Rica, Ecuador, El Salvador, Georgia, Guatemala, Honduras, Mongolia, Nicaragua, Paraguay, Peru, Sri Lanka and Venezuela; see further Commission Decision 2008/938/EC, [2008] OJ L334/90. The special measures may be withdrawn if domestic legislation incorporating the international conventions is not effectively implemented: see for example Council Implementing Regulation 143/2010/EU temporarily withdrawing the special incentive arrangement for sustainable development and good governance provided for under Regulation (EC) No 732/2008 with respect to the Democratic Socialist Republic of Sri Lanka [2010] OJ L45/1.

[96] The WTO Appellate Body, in ruling against an earlier selective incentive scheme in the EU's GSP Regulation, held that differential treatment between developing countries on grounds of development, financial or trade needs is permissible under the Enabling Clause, provided that 'a sufficient nexus [exists] between, on the one hand, the preferential treatment provided … and, on the other hand, the likelihood of alleviating the relevant "development, financial [or] trade need"': *European Communities—Conditions for the Granting of Tariff Preferences to Developing Countries—Report of the Appellate Body*, WT/DS246/AB/R (7 April 2004), para 164. For further discussion, see L Bartels, 'The WTO Enabling Clause and Positive Conditionality in the European Community's GSP Program' (2003) 6 *Journal of International Economic Law* 507; R Howse, 'India's WTO Challenge to Drug Enforcement Conditions in the European Community Generalised System of Preferences: A Little Known Case with Major Repercussions for "Political" Conditionality in US Trade Policy' (2003) *Chicago Journal of International Law* 385; J Harrison, 'Incentives for Development: The EC's Generalised System of Preferences, India's WTO Challenge and Proposals for Reform' (2005) 42 *CML Rev* 1663; G Marín Durán and E Morgera, 'Case Note on the WTO India-EC GSP Dispute: The Future of Unilateral Trade Incentives Linked to Multilateral Environmental Agreements' (2005) 14 *Review of European Community and International Environmental Law* 173.

In December 2001 the Council adopted a set of Guidelines on Human Rights Dialogues, and they were reviewed and readopted in January 2009.[97] The Guidelines point out that although all human rights dialogues are initiated by Council decision, there exists a wide variety of types of dialogue and levels at which the dialogue takes place. Four broad types of dialogue are identified:

a) those taking place within a broader framework of political dialogue, often established through bilateral agreements or regional arrangements, such as those with candidate countries, the Western Balkans, ASEM and ASEAN, and the ACP States in the framework of the Cotonou Convention;
b) institutionalised dialogues devoted specifically to human rights, such as those existing with China, Russia and the African Union;
c) ad hoc dialogue carried out through the head of mission, as has happened with Sudan;
d) dialogues on matters of common interest and cooperation within multilateral human rights bodies with countries holding 'broadly converging views', including the United States, Canada, New Zealand and Japan.

A human rights-specific dialogue is a supplement to the 'mainstreaming' of human rights objectives into EU external policy as a whole. The Guidelines set out the procedure for initiation of a new dialogue, and priority issues to be included in discussion, emphasising consistency both with Member States' bilateral dialogues and with EU Resolutions submitted to the UN General Assembly and the Human Rights Council. As well as identifying a number of substantive human rights issues (for example, the death penalty, torture, children's rights, the rule of law), the Guidelines prioritise more generally the signing, ratification and implementation of international human rights instruments, and cooperation with international human rights procedures and mechanisms. Dialogues 'are held on a reciprocal basis, which enables the third country to raise the human rights situation in the European Union'.[98]

The EU also engages in more general diplomatic promotion of its policies, using CFSP Common Positions, Council Conclusions and Guidelines.[99] The Council has adopted Human Rights Guidelines on a number of specific issues which set out EU policy and can be used as a basis for dialogue and the submission of resolutions and other initiatives in multilateral fora; these include Guidelines on the death penalty, children in armed conflict, the rights of the child, and International Humanitarian Law. In 2005 the Council adopted the 'European Union Guidelines on promoting compliance with international humanitarian law', their purpose

[97] EU Guidelines on Human Rights Dialogues, adopted by Economic and Financial Affairs Council of 13 December 2001, updated Guidelines adopted 19 January 2009, Council Doc 16526/08.

[98] *Ibid*, 6.

[99] See F Hoffmeister, 'The Contribution of EU Practice to International Law' in M Cremona (ed), *Developments in EU External Relations Law* (Oxford, Oxford University Press, 2008).

being 'to set out operational tools for the European Union and its institutions and bodies to promote compliance with international humanitarian law (IHL)' by third States and non-State actors operating in third States.[100]

To take another example from outside the human rights context, we have already seen that in June 2003 the Council of Ministers endorsed both a statement of 'Basic principles for an EU strategy against proliferation of Weapons of Mass Destruction' and an Action Plan for the implementation of these Basic Principles.[101] The mechanisms envisaged in the Action Plan, and the EU Strategy on WMD adopted in December 2003, include diplomatic action including use of political dialogue and diplomatic pressure, *démarches* and 'defining and disseminating master messages', and the adoption of a Common Position to restate the EU's position on universalisation of a number of key international agreements. The Common Position, which was adopted in November 2003,[102] encourages accession to five key international agreements as well as ratification of the Comprehensive Nuclear Test Ban Treaty to ensure its entry into force: the Nuclear Non-proliferation Treaty and Safeguards Agreements (NPT),[103] the IAEA Additional Protocols,[104] the Chemical Weapons Convention,[105] the Biological and Toxin Weapons Convention,[106] the (non-binding) Hague Code of Conduct against Ballistic Missile Proliferation (Article 1)[107] and the Comprehensive Nuclear Test

[100] EU guidelines on promoting compliance with international humanitarian law, adopted by the General Affairs Council 12 December 2005, [2005] OJ C327/4, para 1.

[101] Basic Principles for an EU Strategy against Proliferation of Weapons of Mass Destruction, Council Doc 10352/03; see above n 62.

[102] Common Position 2003/805/CFSP on the universalisation and reinforcement of multilateral agreements in the field of non-proliferation of weapons of mass destruction and means of delivery, [2003] OJ L302/34.

[103] Council Common Position 2005/329/PESC relating to the 2005 Review Conference of the Parties to the Treaty on the Non-Proliferation of Nuclear Weapons, [2005] OJ L106/32.

[104] Council Joint Action 2008/314/CFSP on support for IAEA activities in the areas of nuclear security and verification and in the framework of the implementation of the EU Strategy against Proliferation of Weapons of Mass Destruction, [2008] OJ L107/62; see also Joint Action 2007/753/CFSP, [2007] OJ L304/38; Joint Action 2006/418/CFSP, [2006] OJ L165/20; Joint Action 2005/574/CFSP, [2005] OJ L193/44; Joint Action 2004/495/CFSP, [2004] OJ L182/46.

[105] Council Common Position 2007/469/CFSP relating to the 2008 Review Conference of the Convention on the Prohibition of the Development, Production, Stockpiling and Use of Chemical Weapons and on their Destruction (CWC), [2007] OJ L176/39; see also Council Joint Action 2007/185/CFSP, [2007] OJ L85/10; Council Joint Action 2005/913/CFSP, [2005] OJ L331/34; Council Joint Action 2004/797/CFSP, [2004] OJ L349/63.

[106] Council Joint Action 2008/858/CFSP in support of the Biological and Toxin Weapons Convention (BTWC), in the framework of the implementation of the EU Strategy against the Proliferation of Weapons of Mass Destruction, [2008] OJ L302/29; see also Council Common Position 2006/242/CFSP, [2006] OJ L88/65; EU Action Plan on biological and toxin weapons, complementary to the EU Joint Action in support of the BTWC, [2006] OJ C57/1; Council Joint Action 2006/184/CFSP, [2006] OJ L65/51.

[107] Council Decision 2008/974/CFSP in support of the Hague Code of Conduct against Ballistic Missile Proliferation in the framework of the implementation of the EU Strategy against Proliferation of Weapons of Mass Destruction [2008] OJ L345/91.

Ban Treaty.[108] The language is of diplomatic action: the EU and Member States are to 'urge', 'encourage', 'make efforts to convince' and 'call on' third States, 'support' and 'promote' initiatives within the framework of these conventions and 'work towards' their goals.

The Action Plans adopted within the ENP provide another example of non-binding instruments the objectives of which include the promotion of the Union's values. In its Conclusions of June 2004, in which the key elements of the new policy were set out, the Council stated:

> The Council confirmed that the privileged relationship with neighbours covered by the ENP will … build on commitments to common values, including democracy, the rule of law, good governance and respect for human rights, and to the principles of market economy, free trade and sustainable development, as well as poverty reduction. Consistent commitments will also be sought on certain essential concerns of the EU's external action including the fight against terrorism, non-proliferation of weapons of mass destruction and efforts towards the peaceful resolution of regional conflicts as well as cooperation in justice and home affairs matters.[109]

The common values and essential concerns then find expression in the bilateral Action Plans. To illustrate the point, let us again take the example of the EU's policy on WMD. The Action Plans are one vehicle for pursuing the objectives of the 2003 Common Position on WMD. They all contain references to non-proliferation and WMD, with a focus on cooperation and dialogue, implementation of international commitments and implementation of UNSC Resolution 1540 (2004). So for example, among the priorities of the EU–Egypt Action Plan appears:

> Enhance dialogue on security issues such as disarmament and arms control; nonproliferation of weapons of mass destruction and their delivery systems, including the objective of establishing a zone free of WMD and their delivery systems in the Middle East.

More detail is given within the section of the Action Plan dealing with cooperation on foreign and security policy:

> *Non-proliferation of weapons of mass destruction and their means of delivery*
>
> — Co-operate on non-proliferation of weapons of mass destruction as well as their means of delivery including through implementing UNSC Resolution 1540/04, ensuring full compliance with and national implementation of existing international obligations and consider promoting the accession to and implementation of other relevant international instruments.

[108] Council Joint Action 2008/588/ on support for activities of the Preparatory Commission of the Comprehensive Nuclear-Test-Ban Treaty Organisation (CTBTO) in order to strengthen its monitoring and verification capabilities and in the framework of the implementation of the EU Strategy against Proliferation of Weapons of Mass Destruction, [2008] OJ L189/28; see also Council Joint Action 2007/468/CFSP, [2007] OJ L176/31; Council Joint Action 2006/243/CFSP, [2006] OJ L88/68; Common Position 1999/533/CFSP and Council Decision 2003/567/CFSP, [2003] OJ L192/53.

[109] GAERC Council conclusions on European Neighbourhood Policy, 14 June 2004, para 4.

— Further develop cooperation in the prevention of and fight against the illicit trafficking of WMD-related materials.
— Cooperate on developing effective systems of national export control, controlling export and transit of WMD-related materials, including WMD end-use control on dual use of technologies, and effective sanctions for breaches of these export controls.
— Improve overall coordination in the non-proliferation area and examine specific threats related to WMD which undermine regional security and the scope of cooperation in addressing them.
— Promote the relevant provisions on the political and security partnership of the Barcelona Declaration with the objective to pursue a mutually and effectively verifiable Middle East zone free of weapons of mass destruction and their delivery systems in consonance both with President Mubarak's initiative in this regard and the principles of the EU Strategy against the proliferation of WMD.

The Commission's progress report on the Egyptian Action Plan of April 2008 interestingly indicates a reciprocal aspect to the ENP:

> Egypt actively pursued a regional policy of disarmament and non-proliferation of weapons of mass destruction, in particular, a Middle East free of nuclear weapons. The government criticised EU Member States who abstained from a vote in September 2007 on an IAEA resolution calling on Middle East countries to renounce nuclear weapons. Egypt supported international conventions on nuclear controls, and advocated the peaceful use of nuclear energy, under NPT conditions.[110]

Not all Action Plans contain this level of detail. The EU–Ukraine Action Plan, for example, refers to WMD but is less detailed:

> Cooperate on non-proliferation of weapons of mass destruction, including on aspects related to the accession to and implementation of relevant international instruments and export control regimes, in the light of the EU WMD Strategy adopted by the European Council in December 2003 and the GAERC conclusions of 17 November 2003; Further improve an effective system of national export control controlling export and transit of WMD related goods, including WMD end use control on dual use technologies.

Here again we find the EU establishing as part of its policy agenda the promotion of internationally-derived norms and institutional structures.

D. Shared Values as a Basis for Developing a Relationship

Shared values are not only a basis for Union membership. They also find expression as the basis for relations with non-Member countries. In Article 21(1) the TEU requires the Union to 'seek to develop relations and build partnerships with third countries and international, regional or global organisations which share

[110] Commission Staff Working Document accompanying the Communication from the Commission to the Council and the European Parliament 'Implementation of the European Neighbourhood Policy in 2007' Progress Report Egypt, 3 April 2008, SEC (2008) 395.

the principles' on which it is founded.[111] This includes, but is not limited to, neighbouring countries. The Joint Statement issued after the EU–India Summit held on 6 November 2009, to take just one recent example, starts with a declaration of shared values and links this to support for multilateralism:

> Recalling that their Strategic Partnership is rooted in shared values and principles—democracy, rule of law, respect for human rights and fundamental freedoms—both India and the EU agreed on the importance of an effective multilateral system, centred on a strong United Nations, as a key factor in tackling global challenges.[112]

But it is the EU's policy towards its neighbours which is perhaps most firmly associated with shared values. At Copenhagen in December 2002, the European Council stated that the 'new dynamic' created by enlargement 'presents an important opportunity to take forward relations with neighbouring countries based on shared political and economic values'. This was in the context of attempting to reassure the 'new neighbours' that enlargement should not become an instrument for creating new dividing lines within Europe. Shared values, then, may provide a starting point for bridging the divide between Members and non-Members, in the interest of promoting stability and prosperity within and beyond the new borders of the Union.[113] Since then we have seen the idea of shared values emerge as a cornerstone of two distinct policies towards the EU's new neighbours, the policy towards the Western Balkans, based on the Stabilisation Process and which has evolved into a pre-accession policy, and the ENP.

The Statement issued by the EU–Western Balkans Summit held in Thessaloniki in June 2003 starts with a declaration of commitment to shared values:

> We all share the values of democracy, the rule of law, respect for human and minority rights, solidarity and a market economy, fully aware that they constitute the very foundations of the European Union. Respect of [*sic*] international law, inviolability of international borders, peaceful resolution of conflicts and regional cooperation are principles of the highest importance, to which we are all committed.

Shared values are also said to be foundational to the ENP of the Union, directed not at the potential candidate States of the Western Balkans but at those neighbours without a current prospect of membership.[114] In their joint letter of 7 August 2002, Solana and Patten, in arguing for the need for flexibility and differentiation, take the view that '[t]he starting point should be that relations with all our neighbours should be based on a shared set on political and economic

[111] For the principles referred to here, and their link with the EU's values, see Section II.C above.

[112] EU–India Summit, New Delhi, 6 November 2009, Joint Statement, Doc 15582/09 (Presse 320), para 2.

[113] Conclusions of the European Council, Copenhagen, December 2002, para 22.

[114] Commission Communication, 'Wider Europe—Neighbourhood: A New Framework for Relations with our Eastern and Southern Neighbours', 11 March 2003, COM(2003) 104. The ENP covers Ukraine, Moldova, Belarus, Armenia, Azerbaijan, Georgia, Algeria, Egypt, Israel, Jordan, Lebanon, Morocco, Palestinian Authority, Syria and Tunisia. Libya has also been included by the Council as a potential ENP partner. See further M Cremona, 'The European Neighbourhood Policy: More than a Partnership?' in Cremona (ed), above n 99.

values'.[115] In June 2003 the Council stated that the overall goal of the new policy would be to create an 'area of shared prosperity and values':

> The EU wishes to define an ambitious new range of policies towards its neighbours based on shared values such as liberty, democracy, respect for human rights and fundamental freedoms, and the rule of law.[116]

Elsewhere, it is made clear that in speaking of shared values the Union has in mind sharing its own values with others, rather than looking for a set of values that are shared. In his December 2002 speech on the Wider Europe, Prodi declared that '[t]he aim is to extend to this neighbouring region a set of principles, values and standards which define the very essence of the European Union'.[117] More concretely, the Lisbon Treaty contains an affirmation that relations with its neighbours are to be based on the Union's own values:

> The Union shall develop a special relationship with neighbouring countries, aiming to establish an area of prosperity and good neighbourliness, founded on the values of the Union and characterised by close and peaceful relations based on cooperation.[118]

The language of shared values, while very much in evidence in the recent policy papers on the new neighbourhood policy, is not an innovation in EU policy towards these regions. The Common Strategies adopted by the European Council in relation to Russia, Ukraine and the Mediterranean (now all expired) made explicit references to a strategic partnership based on shared values and common interests,[119] and 'foundations of shared values enshrined in the common heritage of European civilization'.[120] In the case of the Mediterranean, the promotion of 'core values' embraced by the EU and its Member States was made a key goal of Union policy towards the region.[121] Both the existing Partnership and Cooperation Agreements with the Eastern ENP partners and the Euro-Mediterranean Association Agreements contain in their Preambles a reference to 'the common values that they share'.[122]

[115] Joint Letter on the Wider Europe from Javier Solana and Chris Patten to the Council, 7 August 2002, available on: <http://ec.europa.eu/world/enp/pdf/_0130163334_001_en.pdf>, para 1.

[116] Council Conclusions, 16 June 2003 on Wider Europe—New Neighbourhood, para 2. For a discussion of the development of 'shared values' within the ENP, see G Bosse, 'Values in the EU's Neighbourhood Policy: Political Rhetoric or Reflection of a Coherent Policy?' (2007) 7 *European Political Economy Review* 38.

[117] R Prodi, 'A Wider Europe: A Proximity Policy as the Key to Stability', Brussels, SPEECH/02/619.

[118] Art 8 TEU.

[119] Common Strategy of the EU on Ukraine, adopted by the European Council at Helsinki, 11 December 1999, at para 1.

[120] Common Strategy of the EU on Russia, adopted by the European Council at Cologne, 4 June 1999, Part I.

[121] Common Strategy of the EU on the Mediterranean Region, adopted by the European Council at Feira 19–20 June 2000, at para 7; the core values include 'human rights, democracy, good governance, transparency and the rule of law'.

[122] See, eg, Partnership and Cooperation Agreement between the European Communities and their Member States and Ukraine, [1999] OJ L49/3; Euro-Mediterranean Agreement establishing an association between the European Communities and their Member States, and the Republic of Tunisia, [1998] OJ L97/2.

The shared commitment to specific values is also found in the Joint Declaration of the Prague Summit, which launched the Eastern Partnership, a re-launching of the ENP with the Eastern neighbours:

> [T]he Eastern Partnership will be based on commitments to the principles of international law and to fundamental values, including democracy, the rule of law and the respect for human rights and fundamental freedoms, as well as to, market economy, sustainable development and good governance.[123]

The Commission's policy paper on the Eastern Partnership again links these values to progress in relations with the EU (conditionality):

> The level of ambition of the EU's relationship with the Eastern Partners will take into account the extent to which these values are reflected in national practices and policy implementation.[124]

As well as being based on the claim of existing shared values, a noticeable element of the ENP is the EU's encouragement of the partner countries to embrace international norms and standards, notably by signing up to international agreements. This includes support for accession to the WTO where necessary, but also many other agreements and Codes of Conduct, on corruption,[125] arms control[126] and mine control,[127] for example. So, the references to shared values carry a number of layers of significance: we can see them as a political statement designed to support the idea of a partnership, of joint ownership, the absence of dividing lines. They also provide a touchstone for political conditionality, a justification for that dimension of the ENP: the extent to which the EU's neighbours share its values will determine the extent to which the EU is willing to deepen the level of integration. Thirdly, they reflect the way in which the EU is not only engaged in promoting its own foundational values, but also promotes the values and principles derived from international law.

E. Shared Values as an Essential Element of a Contractual Relationship

Since 1992 the Union's development cooperation, association, trade, and cooperation and partnership agreements have included clauses stating that the respect for human rights and democratic principles is an 'essential element' of the agreement.[128] These clauses have gone through a number of variations, and despite

[123] Joint Declaration of the Prague Eastern Partnership Summit, Prague, 7 May 2009, Doc 8435/09 (Presse 78).

[124] Commission Communication on the Eastern Partnership, 3 December 2008, COM(2008) 823 final.

[125] Eg, the Council of Europe Civil Law and Criminal Law Conventions on Corruption of 1999.

[126] Eg, the EU Code of Conduct of Arms Exports.

[127] The Convention on the Prohibition of the Use, Stockpiling, Production and Transfer of Anti-Personnel Mines and Their Destruction.

[128] Commission Communication on the inclusion of respect for democratic principles and human rights in agreements between the Community and third countries, 23 May 1995, COM(95) 216 final; approved by Council, 29 May 1995.

some standardisation their substantive elements also differ according to the partner country in question.[129] For example, agreements with the central and eastern European countries and the Western Balkans contain references to the principles of the Organisation for Security and Cooperation in Europe (OSCE); agreements with countries outside Europe contain references to the Universal Declaration of Human Rights. The following two examples illustrate this point. The first is Article 2 of the Agreement on Trade, Development and Cooperation between the EC and South Africa:

> Respect for democratic principles and fundamental human rights as laid down in the Universal Declaration on Human Rights, as well as for the principles of the rule of law underpins the internal and international policies of the Community and of South Africa and constitutes an essential element of this Agreement. The Parties also reaffirm their attachment to the principles of good governance.

The second is Article 2 of the Stabilisation and Association Agreement between the EC and Croatia:

> Respect for the democratic principles and human rights as proclaimed in the Universal Declaration of Human Rights and as defined in the Helsinki Final Act and the Charter of Paris for a New Europe, respect for international law principles and the rule of law as well as the principles of market economy as reflected in the Document of the CSCE Bonn Conference on Economic Cooperation, shall form the basis of the domestic and external policies of the Parties and constitute essential elements of this Agreement.

These examples also illustrate that alongside references to human rights, democracy and the rule of law, other values such as respect for international law may appear, as well as principles the status of which as values at all is questionable (the principles of a market economy). As the European Court of Justice pointed out, the stipulation that the clause constitutes an essential element of the agreement is significant in legal terms, as it may justify the suspension or termination of an agreement in case of a serious violation.[130] In most current agreements there is explicit provision for

[129] For a discussion of their evolution, see M Cremona, 'Human Rights and Democracy Clauses in the EC's Trade Agreements' in N Emiliou and D O'Keeffe (eds), *The European Union and World Trade Law after the GATT Uruguay Round* (Chichester, Wiley, 1996); E Reidel and M Will, 'Human Rights Clauses in External Agreements of the EC' in P Alston (ed), *The EU and Human Rights* (Oxford, Oxford University Press, 1999); E Fierro, *The EU's Approach to Human Rights Conditionality in Practice* (The Hague; London, Martinus Nijhoff, 2003); L Bartels, *Human Rights Conditionality in the EU's International Agreements* (Oxford, Oxford University Press, 2005).

[130] Case C-268/94 *Portugal v Council* [1996] ECR I-6177. For a discussion, see M Cremona, 'The EU and the External Dimension of Human Rights Policy' in S Konstadinidis (ed), *A Peoples' Europe, EC—International Law Forum III* (Aldershot, Dartmouth Press, 1998). See also Case C-162/96 *A Racke GmbH & Co v Hauptzollamt Mainz* [1998] ECR I-3655, where the Court of Justice held that suspension by the EC of the Cooperation Agreement with Yugoslavia was in conformity with international law under the principle of *rebus sic stantibus*, in spite of the absence of an 'essential element' clause, on the grounds that 'the maintenance of a situation of peace in Yugoslavia, indispensable for neighbourly relations, and the existence of institutions capable of ensuring implementation of the cooperation envisaged by the Agreement throughout the territory of Yugoslavia constituted an essential condition for initiating and pursuing that cooperation' (at para 55).

cases of breach: typically, a 'material breach' of the Agreement, justifying the taking of 'appropriate measures' without prior consultation, is defined in terms *inter alia* of a violation of an essential element of the Agreement. However, in spite of their legal status and high political profile, the real effectiveness of these clauses may be questioned.[131] They are applied somewhat selectively,[132] and there is no doubt that it is easier for the EU actually to use conditionality in the positive sense, as a condition of deepening relations and of financial assistance.

Although originally the essential element clauses were focused on democracy, human rights and the rule of law, there is a growing tendency to add clauses to Union agreements which go beyond these foundational values, or which instrumentalise them in specific contexts. Thus on 17 November 2003 the Council agreed, as part of its policy to 'mainstream' non-proliferation policy into its wider external relations, to include a non-proliferation (WMD) clause in agreements with third countries.[133] The clause contains two elements.[134] First is the 'essential element': an obligation to comply with and implement *existing* commitments under international disarmament and non-proliferation treaties. Since this part of the clause is an 'essential element' of the agreement, it may lead to consultations and ultimately to suspension of the agreement if there is a serious failure to comply. Secondly, there is a commitment to cooperate in order to promote accession to and implementation of further instruments, and to strengthen export controls.

It was agreed to include a 'non-proliferation clause' in all future mixed agreements with third countries, and to seek to include a clause where existing mixed agreements are renewed or revised, either in the agreement itself or in a separate

[131] K Smith, 'The Use of Political Conditionality in the EU's Relations with Third Countries: How Effective?' (1998) 3 *European Foreign Affairs Review* 253.

[132] A Ward, 'Frameworks for Cooperation between the European Union and Third States: a Viable Matrix for Uniform Human Rights Standards?' (1998) 3 *European Foreign Affairs Review* 505.

[133] Council Doc 14997/03. The Conclusions include a standard form of clause:

Countering proliferation of weapons of mass destruction

The Parties consider that the proliferation of weapons of mass destruction and their means of delivery, both to state and non-state actors, represents one of the most serious threats to international stability and security. The Parties therefore agree to cooperate and to contribute to countering the proliferation of weapons of mass destruction and their means of delivery through full compliance with and national implementation of their existing obligations under international disarmament and non-proliferation treaties and agreements and other relevant international obligations. The parties agree that this provision constitutes an essential element of this agreement.

The parties furthermore agree to cooperate and to contribute to countering the proliferation of weapons of mass destruction and their means of delivery by:

— taking steps to sign, ratify, or accede to, as appropriate, and fully implement all other relevant international instruments;

— the establishment of an effective system of national export controls, controlling the export as well as transit WMD related of goods, including a WMD end-use control on dual use technologies and containing effective sanctions for breaches of export controls.

The Parties agree to establish a regular political dialogue that will accompany and consolidate these elements.

[134] Council General Secretariat Note on the implementation of the WMD Clause, 19 January 2009, Doc 5503/09.

legally-binding instrument between the parties.[135] In addition, the Council stated that the EU and Member States might propose to a third country partner the amendment of an existing mixed agreement to include such a clause outside a normal treaty renewal or revision procedure, 'if specific WMD concerns warranted such action'. A refusal to do so might lead to 'appropriate measures', including possibly denunciation of the agreement. Examples of mixed agreements including the new WMD clause are the Cotonou Convention,[136] the Stabilisation and Association Agreement (SAA) with Serbia[137] and the SAA with Albania.[138] The SAA with Croatia was concluded before the policy was introduced, but on 26 April 2005, on the occasion of the first meeting of the SAA Council, a Joint Declaration was adopted which follows closely the wording of the standard WMD clause, without explicit linkage to the SAA.[139]

Community-only agreements have required a different approach. The Council clearly regarded the WMD clause as falling outside Community competence. Certainly the objective of the WMD clause (countering a threat to international peace and security) fell outside EC objectives.[140] It is not so clear that the actual content of the clause, in particular that aspect relating to export controls of dual-use technologies and materials, fell outside Community competence. One possibility would have been the conclusion of a parallel instrument, presumably via an agreement concluded by the EU under former Article 24 EU. Alternatively, the practice has been rather to adopt Joint Declarations, rather than binding agreements, and this has been done with the US, China and Croatia. On 8 December 2004 the EU and China adopted a Joint Declaration on Non-proliferation and Arms Control,[141] a formal document identifying specific areas for cooperation following the EU's priorities, which is nevertheless neither legally binding nor linked expressly to the EC–China Cooperation Agreement. On 20 June 2005 the EU and the US signed a Declaration on enhancing cooperation in the field of non-proliferation and the fight against terrorism, and established a Joint Programme of Work on the Non-proliferation of Weapons of Mass Destruction.[142]

[135] For an assessment of the clause, see Council Secretariat Note on the implementation of the WMD Clause, Council Doc 5503/09, 19 January 2009.

[136] Partnership (Cotonou) Agreement between the members of the African, Caribbean and Pacific (ACP) States and the European Community and its Member States, [2000] OJ L317/3, Art 11b.

[137] Proposal for a Council and Commission Decision on the conclusion of the Stabilisation and Association Agreement between the European Communities and their Member States, of the one part, and the Republic of Serbia, of the other part, COM/2007/0743 final, Art 3.

[138] Stabilisation and Association Agreement between the European Communities and their Member States, of the one part, and the Republic of Albania, of the other part, [2009] OJ L107/166, Art 8(3).

[139] Council Doc 8484/05.

[140] Joined Cases C-402/05 P and C-415/05 P, above n 27.

[141] Joint Declaration of the People's Republic of China and the European Union on Non-proliferation and Arms Control, signed 8 December 2004, Doc 15854/04.

[142] EU–US Declaration on enhancing cooperation in the field of non-proliferation and the fight against terrorism, Washington, 20 June 2005, Doc 10306/05. Joint Programme of Work, Doc 10312/05. A Declaration on WMD had also been agreed at Dromoland Castle on 26 June 2004, Doc 10761/1/04 REV 1.

A statement on non-proliferation and WMD also appears in the EU–Brazil Joint Action Plan.[143] Similarly, in its conclusions of 8 December 2008, the Council agreed to include a clause on small arms and light weapons (SALW) in all agreements with a CFSP dimension.[144] The Lisbon Treaty offers the possibility of including these clauses not only in mixed agreements but also in Union-only agreements, since international peace and security is clearly an objective of the Union, and the Treaties appear to envisage the possibility of agreements covering both CFSP and non-CFSP matters.[145]

V. BUILDING VALUES

The third dimension to the place of values in EU foreign policy is that of 'building' values by spear-heading or influencing the production of new norms at the regional and international levels, their adoption, interpretation and enforcement through diplomacy and participation in international organisations and agencies, including the UN. It has been suggested that this aspect of the EU's action, in putting its weight behind both multilateralism and a 'rule-based international order', could be regarded as a value or normative principle in its own right.[146] In distinguishing this dimension from the promotion of values discussed in the previous section, I wish to emphasise that here the EU is contributing not only to the spread, implementation or enforcement of norms, but also to the creation of new norms which reflect its values. However, it is in the nature of international law that practice is instrumental in the passage from *lex ferenda* to *lex lata*,[147] and so the promotion and the building of norms may be closely connected. In addition, this third dimension of EU action is harder to assess concretely than the two dimensions we have already discussed: EU action of this kind is necessarily often more informal and harder to document; it is also more difficult to be sure what influence the EU as such has had on the development of an international norm. For these reasons a full account of the EU's contribution to norm-building in a specific field would require a study of its own. Here, I shall map out some of the processes by which the EU acts to build international norms, the substantive examples serving to substantiate the claim that this activity is a conscious ingredient of the EU's foreign policy.

[143] EU–Brazil Joint Action Plan adopted at the Second EU–Brazil Summit in Rio de Janeiro, on 22 December 2008, Doc 5522/09.

[144] Council Doc 15506/08.

[145] See Art 218 TFEU.

[146] See section I above. Cf Manners, who calls this normative principle the supranational rule of law: I Manners, 'The Normative Ethics of the European Union' (2008) 84 *International Affairs* 45.

[147] H Thirlway, 'The Sources of International Law' in MD Evans (ed), *International Law*, 2nd edn (Oxford, Oxford University Press, 2006).

A. Consensus-building

An important aspect of the EU's strategy in norm-building is the building of policy consensus. This starts with the Member States, facilitating the convergence of Member State policies through the formation of Strategies, Common Positions, Council Conclusions and in less formal ways. A CFSP Common Position may seek to build consensus at a number of levels. In addition to the consensus among the Member States themselves, necessary for its adoption, the EU may invite other countries to associate themselves with a particular Common Position; this includes but is not limited to candidate States; it also may include ENP partner States, and as such is an important part of the ENP objective of creating a 'ring of friends' around the EU, States which share at least some of the Union's interests and priorities.[148]

Further, the Common Position may itself have as one of its objectives the creation of a policy consensus. We have already referred to the Common Position on WMD, adopted in November 2003,[149] which commits the EU and its Member States to work towards the universal ratification of and adherence to five key international agreements, including the Chemical Weapons Convention and the Biological and Toxin Weapons Convention. The Common Position is intended to further the Basic Principles for a strategy on WMD adopted in 2003 which—in addition to the commitment to universalisation—states:

> With regard to biological and chemical weapons, we will work towards declaring the bans on these weapons to be universally binding rules of international law.[150]

In this campaign the EU has enlisted the direct support of its neighbours as well as candidate States: an EU Declaration on the 10th Anniversary of the Chemical Weapons Convention, for example, is subscribed to by a group of candidate, potential candidate, EEA and ENP States:

> The Candidate Countries Turkey, Croatia and the former Yugoslav Republic of Macedonia, the Countries of the Stabilisation and Association Process and potential candidates Albania, Bosnia and Herzegovina, Montenegro, Serbia, and the EFTA countries Iceland, Liechtenstein and Norway, members of the European Economic Area, as well as Ukraine and the Republic of Moldova align themselves with this declaration.[151]

Consensus-building is not limited to the EU and its neighbours. In discussing the need to develop strategic partnerships in order to achieve its objectives (including

[148] Commission Communication, Wider Europe—Neighbourhood: A New Framework for Relations with our Eastern and Southern Neighbours, 11 March 2003, COM (2003) 104, p 4. The eastern ENP partners have been invited, on a case-by-case basis, to align themselves with EU declarations, *démarches* and CFSP Common Positions: Ukraine since February 2005, Moldova since June 2005, Armenia, Azerbaijan, and Georgia since June 2007.

[149] Common Position 2003/805/CFSP, above n 102.

[150] See above n 62 at para 5.

[151] Declaration of the Presidency on behalf of the EU on the 10th Anniversary of the Chemical Weapons Convention, 29 April 2007, Council Doc 8797/07 (Presse 91).

among these strengthening the international order through effective multilateralism, and tackling the 'new threats' of terrorism, WMD, failed States and organised crime) the European Security Strategy proclaims the Union's readiness to work 'with any country which shares our goals and values and is prepared to act in their support'.[152] It will subscribe to relevant initiatives launched by others in order to build broader consensus. So for example, in a statement in May 2008 in support of the Global Initiative to Combat Nuclear Terrorism (GICNT), the EU stated that the Initiative corresponds with the objectives of its own WMD Strategy and that 'the European Union and its Member States therefore fully endorse and subscribe' to its principles.

To take another example of a different nature, the EU's campaign for a consensus on the abolition of the death penalty has been well documented, Ian Manners using this as a prime example of what he termed 'normative power Europe.'[153] The Guidelines on the Death Penalty, originally adopted on 29 June 1998 as the EU's first set of Human Rights Guidelines and recently revised and updated,[154] state that the EU objectives are

> To work towards universal abolition of the death penalty as a strongly held policy view agreed by all EU member states … [and] where the death penalty still exists, to call for its use to be progressively restricted and to insist that it be carried out according to minimum standards

The EU's campaign against the death penalty has been carried out at both bilateral and multilateral levels. Initiatives include declarations and *démarches* on the death penalty in international fora, raising it in dialogues with third countries, as well as *démarches* in specific cases where the use of the death penalty violates international commitments or internationally recognised minimum standards; the use of the death penalty is to be included in the EU's human rights reports. The Guidelines thus serve two purposes: they are intended to ensure consistency in EU policy on a specific issue where the EU has clear objectives; they also serve as a public statement of those objectives, in itself a policy tool. The EU's policy has specific practical consequences too, going beyond diplomatic *démarches*: extradition of a suspect to a requesting jurisdiction may be blocked if there is a real risk that he or she may be subject to the death penalty,[155] and the extradition treaty between the USA and the EU contains a clause permitting the requested State to make non-application

[152] J Solana, 'A Secure Europe in a Better World', adopted by the Thessaloniki European Council, June 2003, as the European Union's Security Strategy, at 15.

[153] I Manners , 'Normative Power Europe: A Contradiction in Terms?' (2002) 40 *Journal of Common Market Studies* 235.

[154] 'EU demarches on the issue of the death penalty—Declaration' in Conclusions of the General Affairs Council, 29 June 1998; EU Guidelines on the Death Penalty, 5 June 2008, Council Doc 10015/08.

[155] Art 19(2), Charter of Fundamental Rights. All EU Member States are party to ECHR Protocol 13 which provides for the complete abolition of the death penalty; candidate States are required to abolish the death penalty.

of the death penalty a condition of extradition.[156] The Exchange of Letters between the EU and Kenya establishing the conditions under which persons suspected of piracy and detained by EUNAVFOR, the ESDP operation off the coast of Somalia, may be transferred into custody and tried in Kenya, stipulates among other criminal process guarantees that 'No transferred person will be liable to suffer the death sentence'.[157]

It is at the multilateral level, however, that we can most clearly see the EU seeking to secure universal standards with respect to the death penalty and its eventual universal abolition. Since 1999 the EU has regularly proposed Resolutions in the UN General Assembly calling for a moratorium on the use of the death penalty, Resolution 62/149 eventually being adopted in December 2007.[158] In a Declaration on the World Day Against the Death Penalty in October 2009, the EU stated that in addition to its bilateral initiatives, it will 'contribute to building further support for resumed work on the issue of the death penalty at the UN General Assembly in 2010,' as well as supporting civil society organisations campaigning for the abolition of the death penalty.[159] The Guidelines on the death penalty state that the EU has 'moved beyond' promotion of minimum standards and 'espouses abolition for itself and others'.[160] In addition to general and specific *démarches* towards third countries, the Guidelines envisage action in multilateral fora:

> The EU will raise the issue of the death penalty in relevant multilateral fora and seize all appropriate opportunities to put before them initiatives aimed at introducing a moratorium on the use of the death penalty and, in due course, abolition. Whenever appropriate, the EU will seek to include references to the establishment of a moratorium on executions and the abolition of the death penalty in documents produced under the proceedings of these multilateral fora. The EU will encourage relevant international organisations to take appropriate steps to encourage states to ratify and comply with international treaties and standards relating to the death penalty.[161]

In addition, the Guidelines propose minimum standards for the imposition of the death penalty, including rights to a fair trial, right of appeal, the prohibition

[156] Agreement on extradition between the United States and the EU, [200] 3OJ L181/27, Art 13.

[157] Exchange of Letters between the European Union and the Government of Kenya on the conditions and modalities for the transfer of persons suspected of having committed acts of piracy and detained by the European Union-led naval force (EUNAVFOR), and seized property in the possession of EUNAVFOR, from EUNAVFOR to Kenya and for their treatment after such transfer, [2009] OJ L79/49, para 4.

[158] UNGA Resolution 62/149 on a Moratorium on the use of the death penalty, 18 December 2007, reaffirmed the following year in Resolution 63/168. In its 2008 Guidelines on the Death Penalty (Council Doc 10015/08) the EU says 'The European Union actively participated in the cross-regional alliance which successfully led and guided this initiative through the General Assembly and all EU partners co-sponsored this initiative'.

[159] Declaration by the Presidency on behalf of the EU on the seventh World Day and the third European Day Against the Death Penalty, 9 October 2009, 14235/09 (Presse 286), P 113.

[160] EU Guidelines on the Death Penalty, 5 June 2008, Council Doc 10015/08.

[161] *Ibid*, 6.

of the death penalty on minors and the insane, and the prohibition of public executions.[162] As well as issuing public statements calling for adherence to these minimum standards,[163] the EU filed *amicus curiae* briefs in two US Supreme Court appeals against the death penalty in cases involving juveniles and mentally-retarded offenders.[164]

B. Decision-shaping and Treaty-making

In general terms the EU may participate in the creation of new international norms through the negotiation and conclusion of international agreements either on its own account, or indirectly through its Member States. Although it is not itself yet a party to the ECHR, in its campaign against the death penalty the EU points to the fact that all its Member States have acceded to its Protocol No 13 on the abolition of the death penalty. As a result of the coming into force of the Treaty of Lisbon the EU now has the competence to accede to the ECHR and its Protocols, and in due course will be able to help shape the development of human rights protection in Europe through this means.[165] Indeed EU involvement in the negotiation of human rights conventions, such the Convention on the Rights of Persons with Disabilities, is already taking place.[166]

A striking example of the EU's involvement in shaping the development of new international norms is its campaign for an Arms Trade Treaty (ATT), which finds its impetus in the European Security Strategy, as part of the EU's policy on disarmament and SALW,[167] and its own code of conduct on arms exports.[168] Action was launched by the EU in 2005, with Council Conclusions affirming EU support for an international treaty to be negotiated under the aegis of the UN with a view to establishing common standards for the global trade in conventional arms (the

[162] *Ibid*, 7–8.

[163] For examples in 2009, see Declaration by the Presidency on behalf of the European Union on imminent executions of minors in Iran, 9 October 2009, 14329/1/09 REV 1 (Presse 289), P 115; Declaration by the Presidency on behalf of the European Union regarding the recent executions of nine persons in Xinjiang, 12 November 2009, 15843/09 (Presse 326) P 125/09.

[164] US Supreme Court, *Atkins v Virginia*, 536 US 304 (2002), in relation to a mentally-retarded offender; US Supreme Court, *Roper v Simmons*, 2004 WL 1619203 (US), in relation to juvenile offenders; see further Hoffmeister, above n 99, 115–17.

[165] Art 6(2) TEU.

[166] Council Decision 2010/48/EC concerning the conclusion, by the European Community, of the United Nations Convention on the Rights of Persons with Disabilities [2010] OJ L23/35..

[167] EU Strategy to combat illicit accumulation and trafficking of SALW and their ammunition adopted by the European Council 15—16 December 2005, Council Doc 5319/06; Council Joint Action 2002/589/CFSP on the European Union's contribution to combating the destabilising accumulation and spread of small arms and light weapons, [2002] OJ L191/1.

[168] The 1998 Code of Conduct on Arms Exports was replaced in 2008 by Council Common Position 2008/944/CFSP defining common rules governing control of exports of military technology and equipment, [2008] OJ L335/99. See also Council Joint Action 2008/230/CFSP on support for EU activities in order to promote the control of arms exports and the principles and criteria of the EU Code of Conduct on Arms Exports among third countries, [2008] OJ L75/81.

initiative was the UK's).[169] Since then the Council has regularly reverted to the issue, its Conclusions timed to coincide with developments within the UN,[170] and all Member States have voted in favour of UNGA Resolutions which have made gradual progress towards the start of negotiations.

A number of features of the EU's campaign are worth noting. First, the EU held out its own arms export control mechanisms as an example of

> the feasibility of agreeing on an instrument without depriving States of their national prerogative to license or deny individual exports, and … the effectiveness and efficiency of a multilateral export control mechanism.[171]

Secondly, the EU has included the ATT among its priorities in the UN General Assembly.[172] Thirdly, the EU has used its regular meetings with third countries to reaffirm its support for the ATT process,[173] and has included the ATT in joint action programmes such as the proposed Association Agenda for Ukraine, which is designed to replace the EU–Ukraine ENP Action Plan.[174] Fourthly, the EU adopted, in January 2009, a Council Decision aimed at promoting the ATT process through, *inter alia*, a number of regional seminars.[175] On 30 October 2009, a UNGA Resolution, with support from the EU Member States and the US but with abstentions from Russia and China, set in motion a process of negotiation with

[169] Council Conclusions 3 October 2005, Council Doc 12529/05.

[170] Council Conclusions 11 December 2006, Council Doc 16692/06, welcoming the formal start of the process towards the elaboration of a legally binding international Arms Trade Treaty through the adoption by the UN General Assembly of the resolution 'Towards an arms trade treaty: establishing common international standards for the import, export and transfer of conventional arms' on 6 December 2006; Council Conclusions 17–18 June 2007, Doc 10605/07; Council Conclusions 10 December 2007, Council Doc 15850/07.

[171] Council Conclusions 17–18 June 2007, Doc 10605/07.

[172] See, eg, the EU priorities for the 64th United Nations General Assembly, adopted by the Council 15 June 2009, Council Doc 10809/09.

[173] For example, in the Final Communiqué of the 15th ECOWAS–EU Ministerial Troika Meeting held in Luxembourg, 16 June 2009, 'The EU and ECOWAS reaffirmed their interest for a successful process leading to the adoption of an Arms Trade Treaty (ATT)', Council Doc 11146/09 (Presse 183). See also the European Union's position for the EU–Egypt Association Council's fifth meeting, 27 April 2009, para 68, Council Doc 8725/1/09 REV 1; and the EU–US Summit in Washington, 3 November 2009, Declaration on Non-proliferation and Disarmament, Council Doc 15351/1/09, REV 1.

[174] The proposed Agenda includes 'further cooperate on arms exports in the light of the content and principles of the Council Common Position 2008/944/CFSP defining common rules governing the control of exports of military technology and equipment and also in jointly supporting the process leading to the negotiation of an Arms Trade Treaty'. COM(2009) 381, Appendixes, 23 July 2009, Council Doc 12631/09, ADD 1.

[175] Council Decision 2009/42/CFSP on support for EU activities in order to promote among third countries the process leading towards an Arms Trade Treaty, in the framework of the European Security Strategy, [2009] OJ L17/39. Seminars on arms export controls have also been occasions for explaining the EU position: 'The EU side also provided information its support for the envisaged Arms Trade Treaty, and details of the outreach events planned under Council Decision 2009/42/CFSP; it provided information on discussions and the position of various states during discussions at the ATT Open-ended Working Group in New York. Ukraine confirmed that its government supports the envisaged ATT.' Report on the Seminar on the control of arms exports, Kiev, Ukraine, 23–24 April 2008, Council Doc 9738/09.

the aim of finalising an ATT in 2012.[176] My purpose here is not to assess the actual impact of the EU's support for and sponsorship of the progress towards an ATT, but rather to draw attention to the way in which consciously seeking to further the development of new international norms in multilateral fora such as the UN has become a recognised part of EU foreign policy.

VI. CONCLUSION

The purpose of this chapter has been to explore the processes through which values are both imported into and exported from the EU legal order, and the part played in that process by international legal norms, which may be both a source of, and a means of promoting, values. For the EU, values have a constitutive as well as an instrumental aspect. In fact in the Treaties, including the Treaty of Lisbon, the same concepts (the rule of law, including respect for international law, democracy and human rights, for example) are presented both as foundational Union values and as principles and objectives of Union external action. This chapter has taken three different perspectives on the place of values in EU external policy. First, values as an integral part of the Union's identity and therefore its constitutional order. We have seen that subscribing to core values is a condition of EU membership, but also that the EU presents itself as a model of its core values, including peace, the rule of law, human rights and democracy. An important dimension to this perspective, however, is the incorporation into the EU legal order of internationally-derived norms, including the ECHR, which become part of the fabric of the Union's own value-system, creating obligations for the Member States as well as the Union institutions. The commitment to international law which provides a normative basis for the Union's foreign policy is directed at its own Member States as well as at third countries.

The second perspective is the promotion of its values: the Treaty directs the Union to promote as well as to uphold its values in its external action.[177] We saw the ways in which the Union engages in promoting its values, through Guidelines, dialogue and *démarches*, trade preferences, technical assistance programmes, bilateral agreements, using positive and negative conditionality, and by attempting to build reciprocal partnerships with third countries on the basis of 'shared values' expressed in binding and non-binding instruments. The values promoted include the Union's core values (human rights, democracy, the rule of law), but also include the promotion of the international rule of law, including international treaty norms on fundamental issues such as non-proliferation and core labour standards.

[176] UNGA First Committee, 30 October 2009, available at <http://www.un.org/News/Press/docs/2009/gadis3402.doc.htm>.

[177] Art 3(5) TEU.

The third way in which the Union engages its values in its external policy is through the shaping and creation of international norms which reflect those values. We looked at the campaign for the abolition of the death penalty as an example of EU consensus-building, and at the campaign for an ATT as an example of norm-creation. In both cases a whole range of instruments and initiatives has been used.

The absence of a human rights policy for the Union as a whole[178] is perhaps one reason why the operation of EU values in its external policy has hitherto functioned in a variety of ways and on a somewhat ad hoc basis. More recently we can point to the use of strategy documents and guidelines on specific issues to pull different instruments together. The Lisbon Treaty could assist in this process by generalising the requirement to promote its values to all aspects of EU external policy. Article 21(1) of the TEU states that Union action on the international scene shall be guided by the values set out in Article 2 (although here called principles) 'which it seeks to advance in the wider world'. Thus not only development policy but also trade policy and associations with third countries all have as one of their objectives the promotion of Union values. This change is part of a more general attempt in the Lisbon Treaty reform to unify Union external action under a single set of principles and objectives, which include the safeguarding of the Union's common values (formerly a CFSP objective under Article 11 TEU) and which was a key recommendation of the Constitutional Convention's Working Group on External Action.[179]

The three dimensions to the role of values in EU foreign policy that we have been considering here are closely interconnected. The same values will often appear in each of the stages, but their relationship is not static; it is possible to see the relationship between them as dynamic, even reiterative. Thus, the EU may contribute to the formation of international norms which it sees as reflecting and giving concrete substance to its values; it may then integrate those norms into its own legal order, either directly as a result of adhering to an international treaty or indirectly, including them in policy documents, guidelines and even membership conditionality; it then champions them (as EU norms, or international norms or both) in its relations with third countries. We can see all these stages in, for example, the EU's campaign for the complete abolition of the death penalty, which seeks to extend universally a norm which has been accepted regionally and which is now a condition *sine qua non* of EU membership.[180] We see them also in the EU's policy in relation to non-proliferation and WMD, as the EU seeks to promote adherence to key international agreements, contributes to multilateral enforcement processes and encourages implementation by its own Member States.

[178] P Alston and JHH Weiler, 'An "Ever Closer Union" in Need of a Human Rights Policy: The European Union and Human Rights' in P Alston (ed), *The EU and Human Rights* (Oxford, Oxford University Press, 1999); Williams, above n 4.

[179] Final Report of Working Group VII on External Action, CONV 459/02, 16 December 2002.

[180] Charter of Fundamental Rights of the EU, [2010] OJ C83/389, Art 2.

In a slightly different dynamic, the Union may seek to share its own values with its neighbours and other partners, thus allowing it more effective influence in shaping the development of norms at a multilateral level. Thus the Union's campaign for an ATT has deliberately drawn on the EU's own experience in arms export control, and the EU has sought not only to strengthen its own Member States' practice in this respect but also to promote the EU model of export control to neighbouring countries.[181]

This contribution has argued that the role of values in EU foreign policy is inseparable from its fundamental relationship with international norms, and especially multilateral norms. Respect for international law is, for the EU, part of the rule of law and one of its founding values. At the same time, in the Union's view, the development of a rule-based international order will contribute to the defence and promotion of the Union's values, including democracy and human rights. We can expect to see the Union increasingly involved not only in the familiar process of application and enforcement of international law through its legislation and its courts, but also in the development of new international norms bilaterally, regionally and multilaterally, through which it seeks to advance its own rule-based approach to meeting global challenges and to promote its own normative standards. This is not of course to forget the potential for conflict between international law and the Union's fundamental values; it is rather to point to the fact that the Union is becoming an ever-more active player in the evolution and development of international law, and that its own perception of its fundamental values influences the part it plays in that process.

[181] Council Joint Action 2008/230/CFSP on support for EU activities in order to promote the control of arms exports and the principles and criteria of the EU Code of Conduct on Arms Exports among third countries, [2008] OJ L75/81. For a recent example, see Report on the Workshop on the control of arms exports for the Eastern European and Caucasian partners of the European Neighbourhood Policy Tbilisi, Georgia, 27–28 October 2009, Council Doc 15345/09.

12

Principled Monism and the Normative Conception of Coercion Under International Law

GEORGE PAVLAKOS AND JOOST PAUWELYN*

I. INTRODUCTION

IN THIS CHAPTER, we argue that the existence of a global legal order, where the lines between national and international law are increasingly blurred, must be grounded on a scheme of principles of justice ('Principled Monism'). Rather than neatly structured, based on strict separation, automatic incorporation or formal hierarchy of regimes, sources or norms (eg, 'international law trumps national law'), these principles of justice are in many instances elaborated and further developed, if not constituted, by formally inferior or sub-international law contexts. The global legal order thereby presents itself as a collection of institutionalised norms which develop, expand and promote a scheme of principles of justice which itself does not depend for its *existence* on any act of legal authority, but merely requires for its *activation and implementation* some concrete instances of institutional intervention.

The chapter demonstrates this point by evoking a number of controversial examples in which formally inferior legal orders (ie German law *vis-à-vis* EU law and EU law *vis-à-vis* international law or the UN Charter) have trumped or

* The authors would like to thank the organisers and the participants of the workshop 'Beyond the Established Orders' that was held at Bristol Law School on 5 and 6 March 2009, and in particular Panos Koutrakos for his constant encouragement and advice on how to place the piece amongst the more doctrinal contributions of the other authors. Special thanks go to Jan Klabbers, Patricia Popelier, Achilles Skordas and Nicos Tsagourias, all of whom read the chapter and sent detailed written comments. Some sections of the chapter were presented in June 2009 at the brown-bag seminar of the World Trade Institute, Bern and in October 2009, in improved form, at an inter-disciplinary seminar at the University of Nijmegen. On these occasions the authors benefited considerably from comments by Thomas Cottier, Katja Gehne, Sylvie Loriaux, Thomas Mertens, Ronald Tinnevelt and Julien Chaisse, as well as from the very lively discussion with the audiences. George Pavlakos is indebted to AJ Julius, N Stavropoulos and A Sangiovanni for discussion, as well as for making available their manuscripts very early on. The sections authored by Pavlakos are part of a five-year research project entitled 'The Constitution of Globalisation', which is funded by an Odysseus research grant from the Research Foundation Flanders (FWO).

otherwise disabled formally superior parts of international law on the grounds of sound moral principle ('the inferior controls the superior'). This pattern is generalised by reference to any legal order that guarantees coercive enforcement which can afford better protection of principles of justice. In accounting for this phenomenon, the chapter puts coercion centre-stage and argues that:

a) coercion extends beyond authoritative acts and comprises any form of interference with a person's autonomy/freedom (including interference by international law or institutions even in the absence of a formal *Leviathan* at the global level);
b) for any actual instance of coercion to be permissible, be it at the national or international level, it ought to be justified on the grounds of sound principles of justice[1];
c) justified coercion generates normative obligations which may be legally enforced in a permissible manner.

All three propositions combined lead to what we call the Normative Conception of Coercion (NCC) and Principled Monism.

In advancing our argument, we rely on an understanding of law which we call 'the model of reasons'[2]: in a nutshell, this says that legal obligations are grounded on reasons that are antecedent to authoritative institutional facts. These reasons derive from principles of justice that regulate the interaction between agents, specifying under what conditions an interference counts as permissible or impermissible coercion. Instances of permissible coercion are eligible for legal enforcement, taking into account the shape and form they have acquired on earlier occasions. Granted the priority of reasons over institutions, no particular institutional set-up enjoys special privilege in the determination of legal obligation. Hence, any institutional setting that is suitable to serve sound principles of justice, by enforcing legitimate coercion or by blocking illegitimate coercion, is deemed authoritative. This picture affords significant leeway for constructing a unified account of the various legal orders of international and national law: what determines unity is no longer some authoritative feature of institutions but the capacity of these institutional orders to enforce obligations, the legitimacy of which is an antecedent

[1] A more precise discussion of the nature, form and content of these principles must be postponed for a future occasion. For the purposes of the discussion that follows, it suffices to point to universal principles of corrective justice (such as human rights norms) as well as a general principle of distributive justice. Whether the latter would be of an egalitarian or other nature must be left open at this stage. For an illuminating discussion of the mapping problem, which concerns the mapping of egalitarian principles on concrete contexts of social interaction, see A Sangiovanni, 'Justice and Social Interaction', manuscript on file with authors.

[2] Alternatively, the term 'model of principle' could be employed in the present context. However, this would evoke the impression that we are transcribing parts of Ronald Dworkin's theory of law with an eye to the field of international law, which is not what we intend here. In any case, the concept reason is a general normative concept, which can be readily taken to incorporate principles too.

question of justice.[3] Against this theoretical backdrop the chapter argues that those principles are often better realised in institutionalised legal orders such as domestic Constitutions (*vis-à-vis* EU law) or the EU (*vis-à-vis* the UN Charter), which can guarantee better implementation of those principles. Even if these principles have become explicit in formally inferior legal orders (such as domestic law or an inferior treaty), they ought to control and account for the coercion exercised at the international level (be it through international law or other instances of institutional interaction between agents). Formal hierarchies amongst international norms or between national and international law (instituted on State consent or to promote effective international cooperation on, for example, international peace and security) must, as a result, be complemented and can, at times, be overturned by a substantive competition or hierarchy of principles. When properly balanced, formal hierarchies kept in check through a competition of principles may allow for a system of regulation that is both effective/coherent and just/pluralistic.

II. THE PROBLEM

In 1989, Lea Brilmayer introduced what she called a 'vertical analysis' of international law: why, she asked, do the American people worry little about the CIA wiretapping national party offices in Central America, but wiretapping by the FBI in some small town within the United States would create an outcry? Her answer was that, traditionally, international law is built on a 'horizontal' ethic of the relations between co-equal actors, namely States. Brilmayer's 'vertical approach' advocated instead

> that whenever a state exercises coercive power, in either the domestic or international arena, the issue of political legitimacy arises ... governmental coercion that extends across international borders is governmental coercion nonetheless. As such, it is subject to the same requirement of political justification as the state's coercion of its own citizens.[4]

We want to take this approach one step further. We do so in light of more recent developments where international institutions themselves directly govern or impact individual welfare (think of UN Security Council sanctions or the UN administration of Kosovo). Coercion, whether it emanates from governments *or international institutions*, is coercion nonetheless, and all forms of coercion ought to be subject to the same requirement of legal justification.

[3] We should emphasise that this is primarily a conceptual point, which aims to illustrate that the grounds of obligation are principles of justice. It is a further question to specify under what conditions such obligations become active, or which form they acquire when they do become active. Their importance notwithstanding, such questions appear later in the order of explanation of legal obligation and, what is key, they need to be treated in the light of the antecedent answer about the grounds of legal obligation.

[4] L Brilmayer, *Justifying International Acts* (Ithaca, Cornell University Press, 1989) 2 and 11.

Although so much has already been written about the *Kadi* case before the Luxembourg courts,[5] for our purposes as well it offers a good example. Remember that in *Kadi* the European Court of Justice (ECJ) annulled an EC Regulation freezing the assets of suspected terrorists on the ground that the Regulation violated EC fundamental rights (especially the rights to be heard and to effective judicial review). The ECJ did so even though the Regulation was implementing a UN Security Council Resolution which, pursuant to the UN Charter, is legally binding on all UN members and prevails over all other treaties including, at least under public international law, EC Treaties (Article 103 of the UN Charter). The case confirms, first, that international law and institutions nowadays have a direct impact on individuals and individual freedom: by putting Mr Kadi on a list of suspected terrorists, the UN Security Council froze his assets. The case illustrates, secondly, that these new types of international coercion are contentious and elicit demands for accountability, control and justification: before the Luxembourg courts, Mr Kadi argued that his fundamental rights to property, a fair hearing and effective judicial review were breached, and that, as a result, the Court should annul the EC Regulation implementing the UN sanctions.

The Court of First Instance followed a rather traditional, international law approach.[6] In the pecking order of international law (eg Article 103 of the UN Charter), UN Security Council Resolutions trump EC law. This happens for good reasons, as fulfilment of the UN's central role of ensuring international peace and security requires prompt and effective cooperation and implementation by all UN Members. As a result, Luxembourg is not to exercise judicial review of the Security Council. The Court of First Instance, nonetheless, gave an interesting (but very controversial) twist to its 'monist' approach: to the extent that the Security Council were to violate *jus cogens* (that is, a norm of international law 'accepted and recognized by the international community of States as a whole as a norm from which no derogation is permitted'[7]), the Court can and must exercise an indirect review. Under this review, however, the Court concluded that the Security Council had, in this case, not violated *jus cogens* and therefore upheld the EC implementing regulation.

The monist/internationalist approach of the Court of First Instance in *Kadi* is reminiscent of the European Court of Human Rights' (ECtHR) approach in *Behrami*.[8] The *Behrami* case addressed questions of responsibility of the UN, and countries like France and Norway under UN command, in the context of the UN's administration of Kosovo.[9] The ECtHR refused to review conduct which

[5] See ch 7 in this volume by Tridimas.

[6] Case T-315/01 *Kadi v Council and Commission* [2005] ECR II-3649.

[7] Article 53 of the Vienna Convention on the Law of Treaties.

[8] For a full discussion, see, eg, M Milanovic and T Papic, 'As Bad as it Gets: The European Court of Human Rights' Behrami and Saramati Decision and General International Law' (2009) 58 *ICLQ* 267.

[9] One might question the grounds of the analogy on the premise that in *Kadi*, as opposed to *Behrami*, there existed EU legislation which had been adopted and the legality of which was being contested before the EU courts. Our claim remains unscathed by this objection, for it rests on a more

it considered to be attributable to the UN (and not, for example, France) on the following, essentially functional/political argument:

> Since operations established by the UNSC Resolutions under Chapter VII of the UN Charter are fundamental to the mission of the UN to secure international peace and security and since they rely for their effectiveness on support from member states, the [European] Convention [on Human Rights] cannot be interpreted in a manner which would subject the acts and omissions of Contracting Parties which are covered by UNSC Resolutions and occur prior to or in the course of such missions, to the scrutiny of the Court. To do so would be to interfere with the fulfilment of the UN's key mission in this field including ... with the effective conduct of its operations.[10]

Returning now to the *Kadi* case, on appeal, the ECJ took a radically different approach.[11] Whereas the Court of First Instance followed what Brilmayer would call a 'horizontal approach', underlining the State-to-State political role of the UN Security Council which ought not be subject to judicial review by individual Member States (with the exception of *jus cogens*), the ECJ concluded that even an EC Regulation implementing a Security Council Resolution does remain subject to EC fundamental rights. The ECJ found, moreover, that Mr Kadi's fundamental rights had been violated, and on that ground annulled the EC Regulation.

We applaud this outcome in *Kadi* to the extent that it recognises that all forms of coercion, even that stemming from the UN Security Council, require legal justification. At the same time, the ECJ limited this need for justification to the EC implementing legislation as it operates in the domestic legal sphere of the EU, not the Security Council Resolution itself. In other words, the ECJ took a distinctly 'dualist' turn, stressing that its ruling against the EC Regulation implementing the sanction does 'not entail any challenge to the primacy of that resolution in international law'.[12] In other words, only acts implemented within the sphere of the domestic EC legal regime require legal justification and review; at the international, State-to-State level, the UN resolutions stand, and the EU may continue to be held responsible for non-implementation of a UN Security Council Resolution. Our 'Principled Monism', in contrast, calls for all forms of coercion, whether they

fundamental point. In the account we propose, legal obligation does not arise from institutional sources but from the successful mapping of institutional sources onto a set of moral principles, which remain invariable across institutional arrangements. Relatedly, the jurisdiction of any court to control norms is not a mere function of institutional sources but—more crucially—a function of its responsibility to uphold the principles that generate genuine legal obligations. To that extent, the courts in *Behrami* and in *Kadi* are not engaged in activities that are radically different from one another. Of course, it goes without saying, some factual link must exist between any court and the relevant moral principles; however, any such link needs to meet a threshold that is much lower than formal validity. See section IV. of this chapter. We owe the incentive for this clarification to the editors of the volume, Malcolm Evans and Panos Koutrakos.

[10] *Behrami and Behrami v France, Saramati v France, Germany and Norway* [Judgment by Grand Chamber], nos 71412/01 and 78166/01, 2 May 2007, 45 EHRR 85, para 149.

[11] Joined Cases C-402/05 and C-415/05, *Kadi and Al Barakaat International Foundation v Council and Commission*, judgments of 3 September 2008, [2008] 3 CMLR 41.

[12] *Ibid*, para 288.

emanate from State institutions or international organisations, to be legally justified, even if this requires control under formally inferior legal regimes.

As many people have pointed out before us, the problem in *Kadi*, where formally superior UN sanctions were pitted against, and ultimately had to give way to, EC fundamental rights, is reminiscent of the problem faced by the German constitutional court in the *Solange* cases. In those cases, the tension was not between UN sanctions and EC fundamental rights, but between an EC Regulation and provisions of the German Basic Law. Yet in that dispute as well, the German Constitutional Court, albeit the formally inferior body (at least looked at from the EU perspective), reserved the right to review EC regulations under the German Constitution in case the ECJ were to fail adequately to protect fundamental rights.[13] In 2009, the German Constitutional Court similarly checked the Lisbon Treaty for compliance with the German Basic Law.[14] The Court found no incompatibility, but did rule that for the German bill implementing the Lisbon Treaty to be constitutional, it must provide for more participation by the German Parliament.

An approach similar to that in the *Solange* cases was taken by the ECtHR in *Bosphorus*,[15] where the Court, formally equal to the EU legal order, at least under public international law (where there is no inherent hierarchy between treaties or sources of law), put out a marker (i) deferring to a great extent to EU law, but (ii) telling the EU that, if it were to fail to achieve protection of human rights 'equivalent' or 'comparable' to that under the European Convention on Human Rights (ECHR), the ECtHR would intervene and exercise judicial review.

Admittedly, the role of the courts involved in these cases may be re-stated in the light of a host of alternative descriptions, such as may appear to undermine the analogies drawn at present. Thus, the ECJ in the *Kadi* case was not confronted merely with the issue of the application of human rights and the authority of the UN Security Council, but also with the question of the supremacy of the EU. Similarly, the German Constitutional Court did not regard itself as an inferior court entrusted with the protection of human rights, but as one which was free to define the context within which the German Parliament ceded powers to the Union. Despite their seeming plausibility, these descriptions should not distract from the deeper point we are trying to make. Namely, that questions about boundaries and institutional relations between legal orders are not defining of the content of the legal obligations, which the courts are called to enforce as a matter of duty. Rather, such questions are subject themselves to the substantive normative principles which determine the existence and the content of the relevant legal obligations. On the picture we shall be advancing, the final instance for determining

[13] *Solange I*, BVerfGE 37, 271 (1974), [1974] 2 CMLR 540 and *Solange II*, BVerfGE 73, 339 2 BvR 197/83 (1987), [1987] 3 CMLR 225.

[14] BVerfG, 2 BvE 2/08, 30.6.2009, Absatz-Nr (1-421).

[15] *Bosphorus Hava Yollary Turizm ve Ticaret Anonim Sirketi v Ireland* [Judgment by Grand Chamber], no 45036/98 ECHR, 2005-VI, 42 EHRR 1.

the limits or the formal positioning of any legal order is not any institutional facts but substantive arguments that draw on principles of individual (and collective) morality. Now, on this understanding, the ECJ, the German Constitutional Court and even the ECtHR are doing the same thing when they appear to be demarcating the limits of the legal orders in which they operate, or to be settling matters of supremacy and hierarchy. They are actually determining—with different degrees of success—the conditions under which the related institutional facts become legally obligatory, precisely in the light of those substantive principles capable of grounding legal obligations.[16]

The above cases, in varying degrees, advance a model of law that is markedly different from the received understanding, which takes law's essence to lie on a hierarchical ordering of its sources or norms. Many Constitutions, for example, provide for a formal hierarchy between national and international law. Similarly, Article 27 of the Vienna Convention on the Law of Treaties puts international law above national law when specifying that 'internal law' is no 'justification' for failure to respect international treaties.[17] In turn, Article 30 of the same Convention specifies that a later treaty prevails over an earlier one. This non-conventional model can be regarded as coherent only if two conditions are met: first, that the law's normative authority is grounded on principles of justice (not its formal source), which is to say that the law's force or normativity is of a moral kind, or else it fails to ground genuine obligations; secondly, that the authoritative sources of (international) law cannot be identified independently of sound moral principles. Both parts of the argument are held together by a fresh account of coercion, which provides the basis for linking moral autonomy with legal institutions.

In a nutshell, the argument is that any form of coercion (broadly defined as interference with persons' autonomy) evokes, on moral grounds, the need for legal regulation: in other words, law is deemed to be the appropriate *moral* response to coercion, because only law can *legitimately* interfere with the external behaviour of otherwise autonomous agents. This claim involves a number of steps. To begin with, coercion is particularly apt in demonstrating the link between principles that determine the moral worth of agents and concrete contexts of interaction between agents. Time and again in everyday life we set out, in groups or individually, to pursue ends which involve others' contribution for their realisation. And yet any instance of action-direction, ie of trying to get others to contribute to our ends, is not a morally neutral exercise: it ought to comply with principles that render others' contribution morally acceptable. These principles

[16] We are indebted to the editors, Malcolm Evans and Panos Koutrakos, for pressing us to clarify the issues raised in this paragraph.

[17] Art 3 of the International Law Commission's Articles on State Responsibility imposes the same pecking order between international and internal law when stating: 'The characterization of an act of a State as internationally wrongful is governed by international law. Such characterization is not affected by the characterization of the same act as lawful by internal law.'

assemble the morality of coercion *qua* action-direction.[18] Although there is great controversy over the exact content of the morality of coercion, for the purposes of the present discussion we adopt a sparse account: it may be understood as comprising principles that guarantee the moral worth of agency, by ensuring that others contribute to our plans for reasons they share independently of our prompting them to comply with our plans. Such principles, and the reasons that flow from them, ground obligations which may be legitimately enforced through some appropriate system of institutional enforcement. Any other form of unreasoned cooperation imposed on others counts as illegitimate coercion and ought to be blocked by some appropriate system of institutional enforcement. Such systems of institutionalised enforcement count as paradigmatic instances of law.[19] The upshot of this line of reasoning submits that while law may count as the most appropriate means for regulating coercion, legal regulation is not unconditioned but, granted the moral weight coercion carries, it ought to respect the constraints imposed by the morality of coercion *qua* action-direction. In section III. we explore the details of the argument, relying on the well-established Kantian premise that agents, in their co-existence, have an obligation to exit the state of nature and enter conditions of legality.[20] Owing to its contribution to the moral grounding of law, this account of coercion will be referred to as the Normative Conception of Coercion (NCC). The chapter then moves on to examine some key consequences of NCC in two key areas: (i) law's force (or normative authority); and (ii) law's sources. The main consequence of NCC with regard to law's force is that law's ability to generate obligations derives from its moral justification. Thus, law cannot be conceived of independently of, let alone contrary to, those background moral principles that render it a legitimate form of coercion. This applies to both national and international law, hence our notion of Principled Monism. With respect to consequences of NCC for law's sources, the following aspects will be highlighted: NCC takes legal obligations to be grounded alike on institutional fact and moral principle. However, far from taking principles of morality to flow directly into law, NCC selects as relevant only principles that have materialised in past instances of institutional practice. Here, institutional relevance is not pre-determined conclusively by a hierarchy of sources or norms but through the

[18] For some highly incisive arguments on the morality of action-direction, see AJ Julius, 'Getting People to Do Things', draft paper presented at a workshop on the 'Relevance of Coercion' that was held in April 2009 at the Centre of Law and Cosmopolitan Values, University of Antwerp (MS on file with authors); see also N Stavropoulos, 'The Relevance of Coercion: Some Preliminaries' (2009) 22 *Ratio Juris* 339, where the author explores consequences of the morality of coercion for law. We owe many thanks to both authors for letting us consult their manuscripts early on.

[19] However, law may not be the only means of implementation. Our explanatory framework allows for considerable leeway in determining the institutional form of enforcement: not only legal, but also any alternative institutional set-up which can effectively promote the salient principles, may be deemed appropriate. Given the limitations of space, we shall refrain from exploring this possibility here.

[20] The Kantian premise resolves in favour of the law any uncertainty over which institutional system is more appropriate for enforcing legitimate coercion. For more details on the Kantian premise, see section III.A. below.

strength of normative argument (values) in the light of the (moral) obligation to exercise coercion permissibly. This leads to a non-linear understanding of the sources of law, where the content of the law can be determined or kept in check by reference to distinct legal orders, which may relate to one another even in a hierarchically reverse order. In conclusion, the explanation offered by NCC of the force and the sources of law submits that both legal and non-legal forms of coercion ought (morally) to be permissibly exercised within the purview of the law. When we look for law, we have to find an institutionalised scheme of moral principle: so while at the level of 'force' morality commands that all coercion be justified, at the level of 'source' it is only institutionalised schemes of principle that can discharge the claim to justification.

Proceeding from this, we ask how this model can be applied to the global context. Here we distinguish between two models of international law: the 'authority model', which understands law's normative force as deriving from the formal hierarchy of sources and introduces a stop-clause of State consent for justification at the level of the domestic legal order; and the 'model of reasons', which is grounded on the requirements of NCC and extends law's justificatory function beyond the limits of national sovereignty, while requiring that the sources of law be defined accordingly. In conclusion, the 'model of reasons' leads us full circle to the notion of Principled Monism, or the idea that the multitude of institutional sources of law (both national and international) are held together by a scheme of substantive principles of justice. What follows is that there is room for a pluralistic and non-hierarchical relation between various institutional orders without authorising an incoherent or ineffective system of regulation.

III. LAW'S FORCE

The examples that were discussed in the previous section may come across as counter-intuitive to legal consciousness because they make it difficult to explain how legal orders can communicate standards or values to one another. And yet the problem with allowing communication between distinct legal orders usually has nothing to do with identifying moral values that are worth serving. More often than not, lawyers agree about the values that law ought to be serving; their problem is to explain how values that one may encounter in one legal context may become relevant in another context and, if they do, how one is to balance or weigh competing values in a manner that may curb further the order of hierarchy between legal orders. An answer to this problem requires two things: first, to illustrate that there is a common element which undercuts the use of law in every context; secondly, to argue that, by virtue of this element, law must, in all cases, serve sound principles of justice. To account for both tasks we take on board the concept of coercion. Coercion will explain deviations from the formal hierarchy of sources or norms, on the grounds that it establishes a firm connection between sound principles (of justice) and the law. Painting with a broad brush, the potency of coercion is due to its capacity to invoke the dimension of moral justification in a manner that avails itself of law's institutional framework.

Such an understanding of coercion is not self-evident. Rather, in order to arrive at it, one must dispense with a purely descriptive conception of coercion as grounded on facts of authority, and refer instead to an NCC or concept of coercion that understands coercion as any limitation on a person's autonomy (the first prong of NCC). As a next step, NCC relies on the idea that coercion, because it is an interference with autonomy, ought to be regulated externally by law (the second prong of NCC). It is important to note that the 'ought' in this case is a *moral* 'ought', while the type of regulation postulated remains *legal*. The idea unfolds in more detail as follows.

A. A Kantian Premise

A good starting point is the Kantian idea that autonomous agents in their coexistence have an obligation[21] to exit the state of nature and enter conditions of legality.[22] Kant takes this obligation to be one of justice and to flow from his analysis of the internal autonomy of persons. The obligation to enter conditions of legality entails that all instances of coercive imposition on one's will ought to be taken out of the hands of individuals and be subjected to 'regulation' through an external normative order. Along these lines, law becomes the only *locus* of permissible coercion. Further, following from this, all coercive relations between autonomous/free agents either become instances of permissible coercion—hence it is impermissible to obstruct them—or they are rendered instances of impermissible coercion—and it is permissible to invoke coercion to block them. There is *no third* possibility (*tertium non datur*).[23]

The moral obligation[24] to set up a system of norms (law) that regulates external behaviour has a special significance for the normative force of those norms, for it

[21] This obligation is more of an enabling condition for making effective the obligations, or more generally the normative relations, pertaining between autonomous persons. See more in section V of this chapter.

[22] See I Kant, 'Toward Perpetual Peace: A Philosophical Project' in I Kant, *Practical Philosophy* (ed and trans M Gregor) (Cambridge, Cambridge University Press, 1996), 8:349–8:350 (beginning of section II and footnote); I Kant, 'The Metaphysics of Morals', *ibid*, paras 41, 42, 43 (among others); and section 'Introduction to the doctrine of right', cf 'Division of the doctrine of right—A. General Division of Duties of Right' (6:236–237). We owe many thanks to Sylvie Loriaux for drawing our attention to the relevant passages.

[23] See T Pogge, 'Is Kant's Rechtslehre a Comprehensive Liberalism' in M Timmons (ed), *Kant's Metaphysics of Morals. Interpretive Essays* (Oxford, Clarendon Press, 2002) 133.

[24] Kant's moral postulate to regulate coercion through law needs further elucidation: far from suggesting that for something to count as a genuine obligation it must be grounded on institutional facts of (legal) authority, it purports to show that law can coerce legitimately because only it amongst all other forms of coercion actually enforces sound obligations, ie obligations that are grounded in the morality of action-direction. For a fuller exploration of this rationale, see the discussion of the model of reasons, section V.A.2. below.

puts the conditions of permissibility with respect to the exercise of coercion in a moral light: permissible coercion, as a result, cannot be conceived of as self-standing but needs to be linked sufficiently with the very principles that ground the obligation to set up conditions of external freedom. As hinted at earlier, external freedom comprises the set of conditions that regulate the spatiotemporal coexistence of free and equal agents. To that extent, those conditions must be deemed adequate or justified from the point of view of a free or autonomous agent in order to fulfil the task of reconciling the external freedom of everyone with the freedom of everyone else.[25] Along these lines the moral conditions that guarantee individual autonomy and build the core of universal morality *par excellence* are linked up with the conditions that regulate external behaviour of free agents with an eye to harmonious coexistence.

While it remains the object of great dispute in Kantian scholarship[26] whether and to what degree Kant's moral philosophy is linked to his legal philosophy, we can for present purposes adopt the following modest line of argument: without assuming any direct application of moral principles in the domain of the regulation of external freedom (law), we must assume an overall coherence between universal principles of justice (those that express the agents' moral point of view) and the exercise of permissible coercion through legal institutions. Instead of a long argument, a succinct justification can be adduced: Kant's duties of morality and law are not different in content but only in the manner in which they are brought about (or 'legislated' in some appropriate sense of the term). While, notably, morality defines its duties by asking agents to purge their incentives of anything that cannot become a universal reason for action, law postulates its duties irrespective of the internal incentives of its subjects, and enforces them coercively. To somewhat simplify the picture, while morality cares to ensure that agents are motivated purely by sound duties, law is interested that sound duties are properly institutionalised, even though law's subjects may not be moved purely by duty. It is for that reason, after all, that law does not rely on agents' incentives but equips duties with coercion. That said, neither law nor morality is interested in grounding anything other than duties (and rights).

B. The Sparse Connection Thesis

Even legal obligations must remain worthy of their name if they are to constitute genuine obligations and become the source of permissible coercion. It follows that no genuine legal obligation can be in disarray with duties of morality, for

[25] See I Kant, 'The Metaphysics of Morals', above n 22, section 'Introduction to the doctrine of right'.

[26] For a discussion of the various interpretative stances, see the very illuminating collection: Timmons (ed), above n 23; and the very comprehensive W Kersting, *Wohlgeordnete Freiheit. Immanuel Kants Rechts- und Staatsphilosophie* (Frankfurt am Main, Suhrkamp, 1993).

then it would cease to be a binding duty from the point of view of an autonomous agent since, in Kant, nothing can be a duty if it is not a moral duty.[27] Conversely, anything that would be imposed by an external legal order and would contravene universal duties of justice would cease to be a duty in the most basic sense of the term. Hence the connection between law and morality is obtained on a relatively sparse basis: law and morality are connected to the extent that, first, both are about duties (and rights) and, secondly, 'being any kind of duty' cannot be defined independently of morality (call this the 'sparse connection' thesis).

The sparse connection thesis needs to be qualified adequately before it can lead to any workable conclusions in the present context. Two aspects are of relevance at present. First, all permissible coercion must be linked to sound principles that any autonomous agent could accept (universal principles of justice). To this passive connection there is an active aspect: principles of justice are not merely background conditions for legitimate instances of coercion; rather, any past instance of permissible coercion is also to count for the future as a permissible course of action, ie there is a claim of agents to the coercive enforcement of the same rights and duties that were permissibly enforced in the past. Secondly, universal principles of justice do not flow into law directly but only in the form in which they have been institutionalised in past instances of the practice of coercive enforcement.[28] The topic of the latter condition falls properly under the discussion of law's sources (see section IV. below), thus here we confine ourselves to a few brief remarks.

The condition of past coercion shows that there is no direct flow of moral principles into law but only approximations of moral principles as these have been institutionalised in the past (approximations that may, moreover, be different from society to society). Thus, institutional arrangements that serve (better or worse) valid principles (and in the form they serve them) will point the way to future law. This may also be put as follows: past institutional instantiations are in themselves valuable because they embody permissible instances of coercion. To the extent that, on the view defended earlier as NCC, coercion is a normative concept, such instances of permissible past coercion hold normative sway over future cases.[29]

C. The Relevance of Coercion

Before turning to examine the consequences of the NCC for the sources of (international) law, we need to clarify a key outcome that NCC yields for the

[27] Thus 'being a moral duty' is a necessary but not sufficient condition for 'being a legal duty'. The reverse is, of course, not the case.

[28] Although legal practice should be awarded a prominent role for shaping principles of justice, other practices of joint action are relevant too.

[29] However, it should be cautioned against thinking that instantiations of impermissible coercion can also count as law. Thus, to use an obvious example, an institutional practice of discrimination against a particular portion of the population would be incapable of generating genuine obligation, for it would be falling into a normative void, *viz* there would exist no antecedent normative reasons to underpin it. For an explanation of legal obligation as the impact of institutional events on an antecedent network of reasons, see the discussion of the model of reasons in section V.A.2. of this chapter.

relationship between coercion and justification. On the NCC, coercion becomes relevant for justification because of its intrinsic connection with autonomy: since any form of external coercion may only be permissible or impermissible, justification (and the attendant need for law) becomes relevant in each and every instance of coercion. Along these lines the NCC removes coercion from the vicinity of two requirements that have been traditionally linked to it: that of the State, and that of brute force (or the possibility thereof).

On the one hand, it is not merely *State coercion* that invokes the obligation for justification but any institutional instance of limiting autonomy in ways that infringe on the principles that regulate the legitimate interference with the external behaviour of agents. This entails that no particular feature of State authority is required in order to render coercion relevant for justification. In the past, two such requirements of relevance have been advanced: either that coercion be imposed on the basis of the legal regulation of contract and property (private law) (Blake)[30]; or that coercion be imposed in the name of those subject to State authority (Nagel).[31] Those adhering to either of those conditions have required their presence as a condition for the requirement of justification to kick in. In the NCC, those conditions come too late to ground the need of justification. What actually delivers the link between coercion and justification is principles of justice that delineate a person's autonomy and regulate external behaviour. As a result, the absence of a world government or other form of Leviathan at the global level does not stop international law from being a genuine instance of action-direction in need of justification in the light of the morality of coercion. Similarly, it matters little whether coercion is exercised through hard law (eg UN Security Council resolutions) or soft law (eg non-binding OECD codes of good practice), or via a highly institutionalised international agreement (such as the WTO) or very informal transnational networks (such as the Internet Governance Forum or International Organisation of Securities Commissions). What matters, and triggers the need for justification, under the NCC is the consequential limit on autonomy. The rejection of those particular elements as conditions of justification can *mutatis mutandis* be extended to include every other statist element outside the private law or the authorisation of law's subjects.[32]

[30] M Blake, 'Distributive Justice, State Coercion, and Autonomy' (2001) 30 *Philosophy & Public Affairs* 257.

[31] T Nagel, 'The Problem of Global Justice' (2004) 33 *Philosophy & Public Affairs* 113. It should be pointed out that Nagel and Blake invoke the said conditions with respect to principles of social justice only and not to core human rights, whose validity they take to extend beyond the narrow confines of the state. However, their reasoning is indicative of any strategy that attempts to limit the obligation to justification within the state and it is as such that it is considered here. We thank Sylvie Loriaux for drawing our attention to the limitations of Nagel's and Blake's argument.

[32] If taken to the limit, this line of reasoning can support a deeper rejection of statist elements as conditions for justification: this would suggest that justification pertains not only to acts of States but also to those of non-State actors (be they private actors, NGOs or international organisations). The latter are also subject to the requirement of public justification in so far as they with their actions infringe on the principles that regulate the external behaviour of autonomous agents. Of relevance here is also

On the other hand, the NCC views as coercion in need of justification not only instances of physical force exercised upon agents, but also such cases as reduce the options of an agent to only a number of detrimental ones. These may be described as *Zugzwang* cases, to borrow a graphic term from the practice of chess. An example might help to illustrate the point: an immigration policy that limits the options of a group of immigrants either to starvation or to a degrading way of living (say prostitution) is coercing them. Or again, if a company invests in new agricultural technologies which lead the farmers of the relevant area either to starve or to take up jobs as unqualified workers in other industries, then the investor is coercing them.[33] Lastly, in so far as the earlier remarks on State coercion hold good, *Zugzwang* cases may emanate equally from States as well as from non-State actors.

It follows that, for justification to be drawn into the picture there is no need for instances of coercion to possess some additional feature that makes them relevant. The mere infringement of those principles that condition autonomy is sufficient.

IV. LAW'S SOURCES

So far we have discussed the key consequences of the NCC for the force of law. Two points are worth repeating. First, that law is the only legitimate means of regulating coercion. According to the NCC, coercion raises a moral claim to justification as a result of its interference with persons' autonomy; yet this claim is not discharged by directly importing morality into law but, instead, by setting up legal institutions that are morally sound in a sparse manner. Sparseness in this context—this is the second most important point raised—stands for a one-way relationship between law and morality: while legal duties and rights are also moral duties and rights, not every moral duty and right is also legal.[34] In other words, while law needs to be legitimate as a result of its task to regulate coercion, its legitimacy refers to moral principles only indirectly, through the various institutional forms that moral principles have assumed as legal precepts in the past. This institutional explication of moral legitimacy, yielded by the NCC, is central to the discussion of the sources of (international) law.[35]

the doctrine of the so-called horizontal effect (*Drittwirkung*), which was devised to deal with infringements of autonomy between non-State actors, albeit within national legal orders. Cf with n 50 below.

[33] See for an expansive understanding of coercion the classic account of R Nozick, 'Coercion' in S Morgenbesser, P Suppes, and M White (eds), *Philosophy, Science, and Method: Essays in Honor of Ernest Nagel* (New York, St Martin's Press, 1969) 440; see also the very useful collection of papers in JR Pennock and JW Chapman (eds), *Nomos XIV: Coercion* (Chicago, Aldine-Atherton, Inc, 1972).

[34] On this, see R Dworkin, *Law's Empire* (London, Fontana Press, 1986), ch 6.

[35] No claim to a comprehensive theory of sources of international law is raised here. Our ambition is to highlight some key ideas that might contribute to a fresh account of sources.

A. Institutions, Morality and Law's Sources

The sparse connection thesis leads to an understanding of law's sources that requires reference to past institutional facts of permissible coercion. This should not come as a surprise: while the quest for justification of coercion is a moral claim, the means for regulating coercion permissibly are institutional. To that extent, legal institutions become significant or relevant on grounds of autonomy, which is to say moral grounds. Why does morality make institutional facts indispensable for determining law as the instantiation of permissible coercion?[36]

First, the grounding of law on autonomy places agents in a symmetrical relationship: past institutional facts of permissible coercion create an expectation *in the future* for the enforcement of the same rights and duties *for everyone*. If I have been permissibly coerced as a result of failing to comply with my duty toward X, then I have a legitimate expectation in the future to coerce others permissibly with regard to similar duties owed to me. To give an example: if the European Court of Justice (ECJ) has in the past enforced fundamental rights of due process and judicial protection vested in the subjects of EU Member States, it must do the same when the UN Security Council orders the EU to freeze the bank accounts of any of the EU's subjects.[37] In this instance, EU subjects have a right, which corresponds to a duty of the Court that it activates past institutional facts of coercion in their favour. As the ECJ put it:

> It is ... clear from the case-law that respect for human rights is a condition of the lawfulness of Community acts ... and that measures incompatible with respect for human rights are not acceptable in the Community ... It follows ... that the obligations imposed by an international agreement [*in casu*, UN sanctions] cannot have the effect of prejudicing the constitutional principles of the EC Treaty ...[38]

Secondly, the fact that law is the *locus* of permissible coercion on moral grounds implies that institutional facts are suitable for exercising coercion not merely because they are *de facto* authoritative, but as a matter of normative justification. This internal link between justification and institutional set-up brings about a dialectic of fact and value which is illustrated by a number of consequences. On the one hand, it poses a limitation on the moral principles that can be evoked with a view to grounding past institutional practice. Not any principle of morality or justice is relevant to the project of a reconstruction of a global legal order, but merely those principles that justify in the best way those instances of institutional coercion, which have *already* taken place. This highlights, and finds support in, the incremental expansion of, for example, customary international law which Article 38 of the Statute of the International Court of Justice defines as 'general practice accepted as law'. It also allows for, and partly explains, the increasing,

[36] A similar line of argument is pursued by Stavropoulos, above n 18.
[37] Cf Case T-315/01, Kadi, above n 6.
[38] Joined Cases C-402/05 and C-415/05, *Kadi*, above n 11, paras 284–85.

practical importance of 'precedent' in international dispute settlement. The WTO Appellate Body found, for example, that even if 'Appellate Body reports are not binding, except with respect to resolving the particular dispute between the parties', its reports and rulings 'create legitimate expectations' so that 'absent cogent reasons, an adjudicatory body will resolve the same legal question in the same way in a subsequent case'.[39]

On the other hand, no principle that is evoked to justify past coercion can be one that does not belong to morality or justice, or be one that is unjust or immoral. The special relation coercion bears to autonomy comes out clearly here: all those normative principles that are evoked to justify and extend into the future past coercive practice must be sound principles of justice, for otherwise they would be failing in their justificatory capacity. This has further implications: if there is a rogue practice of coercion then it is not possible to say that it is justified or that there is an expectation to extend it into the future; the practice of exterminating an ethnic group, or the practice of exploiting some members of the community for the benefit of those in power, cannot be justified. These practices do not deserve normative respect in any manner, and no one (including those benefiting from them) can evoke them to justify own entitlements or ground duties of others.[40]

At this point, we may face the following objection: even if the assumption about the normative significance of institutional facts of coercion holds good, it does so in domestic legal contexts, where there is a State apparatus that may enforce the law; however, the global level surely falls short of that condition. The objection is misplaced. Coercion, in the way used in the proposed model, does not rely on the actual possibility of physical force, neither does it concern merely the officials of the State (see section III.C. above). The type of coercion that is relevant to the argument is a normative concept. And, as every normative concept, it needs to be individuated in the light of more fundamental normative considerations. As the analysis of the force of law sought to identify, those considerations include principles of justice that are authorised from the point of view of autonomous persons. Such higher-order principles explain why past institutional facts of coercion, and the rights and duties to which they gave effect, have legal (and moral) authority for the future. What is more, the normative concept of coercion counts as normatively relevant not only institutional acts originating in the will of State officials,

[39] *Appellate Body Report on United States—Final Anti-Dumping Measures on Stainless Steel from Mexico*, WT/DS344/AB/R, adopted 20 May 2008. See also *Saipem SpA v The People's Republic of Bangladesh*, in the context of the International Centre for Settlement of Investment Disputes (ICSID): 'The Tribunal considers that it is not bound by previous decisions. At the same time, it … believes that, subject to compelling contrary grounds, it has a duty to adopt solutions established in a series of consistent cases' (Decision of 21 March 2007 of the Arbitration Tribunal, Case No ARB/05/07, ICSID IIC 280 (2007), p 20, para 67).

[40] This is a point already familiar from Dworkin, above n 34; see also N Stavropoulos, Interpretivist Theories of Law in EN Zalta (ed), *The Stanford Encyclopedia of Philosophy* (Fall 2008 edn), available at <plato.stanford.edu/archives/fall2008/entries/law-interpretivist/>.

but also those acts that originate in the will of private actors of globalisation. Also these instances of coercion generate for the parties concerned claims that they be protected through a coercive enforcement of their rights. Now what is markedly different, of course, from the domestic context is that, at the global level, there is not always an official (say, a judge) who has a duty to enforce the said claim. But the lack of a State (and its officials) may be of secondary significance, normatively speaking, if one has established that there is a norm of obligation. What, instead, is normatively significant is to say that we ought to set up an appropriate institutional context for enforcement. As Kelsen sought to demonstrate, the concept 'State' does not contain anything over and above a collection of legal norms; hence, where the norms exist, so does the 'State'.[41] Its further empirical existence may not be a normative shortcoming but the subject of a normative obligation. Besides, one would not need to set up a global government; usually what is simply needed is the appropriate coordination between existing levels of domestic and international governance, and the delegation to them of the various tasks of enforcement, including appropriate mechanisms of control, transparency and accountability. Bright examples in this context are the German Constitutional Court in its famous *Solange* case, when it enforced the rights of the German Constitution against instances of potential unjustified coercion from the EU; or the ECJ in its recent *Kadi* case, when it enforced EU fundamental rights against an intrusion on liberty by means of a UN Security Council resolution.

V. PRINCIPLED MONISM IN INTERNATIONAL LAW

The analysis of the force and sources of law yielded by the NCC, when transposed into the field of the emerging global legal order (encompassing both national and international law), leads to *Principled Monism*. Principled Monism is the doctrine that the grounds of legal obligation at the level of the global legal order are unified: they are located in the principles of justice which function as justificatory reasons for the permissible exercise of coercion on agents. Although it remains monistic with regard to the grounds or force of the law, Principled Monism is pluralistic as regards law's sources. It seeks to identify as valid law any institutional instances of permissible coercion (be it national or international law, highly formalised law or soft law, a formally superior or formally inferior legal order), ie coercion that is in line with principles of justice that regulate external behaviour amongst autonomous agents. However, this kind of pluralism is well-founded: far from

[41] This should be qualified appropriately, for Kelsen identifies State with law but not vice versa: in other words, there can be law without State. See H Kelsen, *Introduction to the Problems of Legal Theory*, a translation of H Kelsen, *Reine Rechtslehre* (1st edn, 1934) by B Litschewski Paulson and SL Paulson (Oxford, Clarendon Press, 1993), para 48 (at 99). What is more important in our context is that the concept of the State can be analysed in that of the legal norm, meaning that there is nothing in the content of 'State' over and above a sum of legal norms.

being forced upon us as a sociological *factum* or because all conceptions of justice are of relative value, pluralism is grounded on the dialectic between coercion and autonomy.

Lest the impression arise that Principled Monism is an 'imperialistic' theory that aspires to imposing values uncritically, a few remarks are in order. To begin with, Principled Monism can work as an explanatory device for legal obligation, irrespective of what one assumes to be the content of those postulated principles of justice. To that extent, Principled Monism can be combined with a handful of views on justice, if not with every such view. Far from being a thesis about the substantive content of justice, substantive monism merely submits that all legal obligations ought to be derived in line with whatever count as the legitimising grounds of coercion.

Admittedly, Principled Monism is not entirely devoid of content. Given that it evokes only principles such as may ground coercive behaviour, it follows that the content of those principles must count universally, ie for all agents, as a sound reason of justification. However, the condition of universality is only minimal. The universal principles that yield the idea of *Principled Monism* are not true propositions independently of human practices. Rather, they are principles that ensure the possibility of self-legislation for the international community as a collective comprising autonomous persons, who are equal and free. In this sense, the principles supporting the type of monism we propose have a procedural aspect in that they leave open the precise content or configuration of the more particular norms or values, which arise, and may be different, in each and every society.[42] What these principles do not delegate, however, is the set of conditions that guarantees that the legislation of any particular norm or value remains an instance of self-legislation, to wit, it flows out from the persons on whom those norms or values apply. To coin an illustrative distinction, we seek to distinguish between *principles simpliciter* and *principles in a domain*. While the former are universal norms that provide for conditions of self-legislation, the latter are primary norms prescribing a concrete course of action within a particular context.

A. Two Conceptions of International Law

Principled Monism is contrasted with a more traditional understanding of the global legal order ('traditional view'). The traditional view, espoused, for example, by the ECtHR in the *Behrami* case and, to a lesser extent, by the Luxembourg

[42] See similarities with the philosophical programme of discourse theory, which has been advanced through the work of J Habermas and, with respect to law, by R Alexy. See, instead of other places, J Habermas, 'Discourse Ethics: Notes on a Program of Philosophical Justification' in J Habermas, *Moral Consciousness and Communicative Action* (Cambridge, Mass, MIT Press, 1996); R Alexy, *A Theory of Legal Argumentation: The Theory of Rational Discourse as Theory of Legal Argumentation* (Oxford, Clarendon Press, 1989).

Courts in *Kadi* discussed above, fails fully to appreciate the dialectic between coercion and autonomy as this unfolds at the global level: on this view, the State functions as *a stop-clause* with respect to justification. States are supposed to justify coercion *vis-à-vis* their subjects in the vertical relation between a State and its subjects. Yet horizontal arrangements between States are subject to the principle of voluntary agreement (*pacta sunt servanda*) and the rule that international law, once validly entered into, prevails over, and tolerates no scrutiny under, national law (the stop-clause of the State in pursuit of effective, coordinated action at the international level). In contrast, Principled Monism posits that especially modern international law and institutions (notwithstanding the absence of a formal global Leviathan) coerce legal subjects beyond the fixed boundaries of the State (witness both the widening of international law in fields formerly reserved to domestic regulation and the deepening of international law with the proliferation of international courts and tribunals) and, hence, defy the stop-clause traditionally accepted in international relations. On this view, such horizontal arrangements between States (that is, international law) must be subjected to the same principles of justice that national Constitutions usually see to, if their precepts are to be considered genuine norms.

The difference between the two views of international law can be traced back to their adherence to two very different conceptions of law. While the traditional view seeks the point of law in institutional facts of authority (model of authority), Principled Monism takes law to be serving those normative principles in the light of which the social practice of law acquires special moral meaning and becomes valuable (model of reasons).

1. *The model of authority*

On this view, the requirement of normativity is satisfied by the existence of a given structure (the structure of authority), while authority lies in the (brute) fact that someone (the sovereign) issues commands which are treated as authoritative by the addressees.[43] The belief of the subjects about the authority of the sovereign is underpinned by the instrumental imperative that this belief ensures the best coordination possible, one that is advantageous for the realisation of individuals' interests/desires in the maximal possible manner. And this is all it takes to ground legal obligation. This view eschews the dimension of justification: there is no requirement to justify coercion, for authoritative facts (eg the fact that the UN Security Council passed a resolution) are treated themselves as a source of justification.

[43] The model also comprises more subtle variants such as the idea that authority serves right reason by issuing authoritative norms, which purport to replace any reasons that would apply to a particular case in the absence of the relevant authority (this is very roughly the view of J Raz, *Practical Reason and Norms* (Oxford, Oxford University Press, 1999)). For a critical analysis of the model of authority that has inspired the present discussion, see Stavropoulos, above n 18.

Where does the model of authority leave law at the global level? Simply put, it facilitates the move to a stop-clause of justification as regards international law. The reason is that, in reducing legal obligations to facts of authority, it leaves no space for accounting for justification where none of the usual facts of authority are to be found (in the traditional sense of brute force or the existence of some form of Leviathan). As, in international law, there are no facts of authority linking immediately institutions with persons, it follows that there is no need for justification. Hence, on this view, international law passes the buck of normativity to the only one authority which is treated as authoritative by its subjects, that is the State (and even there the notion of justification remains extremely 'thin'). As regards the global level, States may further their interests through agreements into which they enter voluntarily. Yet as the model of authority puts the emphasis on structure rather than justification, it leaves international law in a normative vacuum: it encourages a view of normativity that is grounded on the hierarchy of the sources of law (eg national Constitutions trump statutes; international law trumps national law). However, in trying to discover this hierarchy at the global level, the international lawyer realises there is none: since all sources of international law (mainly treaties and custom) are ultimately grounded on State consent, international law, unlike national law, knows no inherent, value-based hierarchy between its sources or norms (with the possible exception of *jus cogens*) and is structured rather on purely mechanical, value-free hierarchies of timing (*lex posterior* rule) or specificity (*lex specialis* rule). This normative vacuum, in turn, may lead the international lawyer to doubt that there is any unity or system of law on the global level to speak of.

However, if it is possible to afford the conclusions of the model of authority in domestic law, it is untenable to do so at the global level: on the domestic level, the model of authority gains a certain momentum because it is implicitly carried by a deeper level of justification. In any well-ordered Constitution, it is permissible to build a short-cut from justification to a formal understanding of authority precisely because the latter rests on an institutional, hierarchical structure that is already the product of those substantive principles that render it legitimate. That fact, however, should not distract one from the essential point: that it is those principles which actually carry the structure and not vice versa. To put it differently, it is always possible that two authorities are identical in structure but not in normative value, for the relation between substance and form is not a two-way avenue.

2. *The model of reasons*

On this view, the claim to justification, upon which normativity rests, is disconnected from institutional facts of authority. Justification acquires an absolute priority, in that it purports to account for interferences with the rights and duties of autonomous agents. In order to retain the understanding of law as an instance of justified coercion, the model of reasons moves beyond the formal characteristics of authority (its factual existence, or its structural configuration) and reconstructs it in terms of its coercive impact on the entitlements of persons as those are to be found in such principles of justice that no agent could reasonably reject.[44] At the global level, the model of reasons submits that any institutional arrangement that exercises coercion in the normative sense is subject to the obligation of justification by being answerable to the same principles of justice which also inform domestic law. These principles constitute a self-standing (as opposed to derivative) ground for legal obligation at the global level, and can be used as interpretive constraints for the doctrinal understanding and the application of the relevant norms of the system (including instances where formally superior law must be balanced with, and may even have to give way to, formally inferior law).

Some additional remarks are owed with regard to the general rationale of the model of reasons.[45] The fundamental intuition behind that model is that institutional facts, legal or other, cannot be constitutive of normative obligations. For no fact is capable of generating normative reasons on its own; or in more familiar language, no 'Is' is capable of generating an 'Ought' by itself.[46] Does this mean that institutional facts have no impact on obligations? To so claim would be far from true. Institutional facts contribute to the activation and shaping of normative obligations in virtue of their rearranging the normative space that is demarcated by pre-existing, fact-independent reasons (principles) plus any earlier institutional rearrangements thereof.[47] An instructive analogy for illustrating the normative relevance of institutional facts might run as follows: institutional facts develop normative force only as a result of the impact they have on a network of pre-existing reasons, in a manner similar to that of a stone that creates a wave, when thrown into a pond, on its surface. Assume that the pond of liquid stands for the network of reasons that precedes institutional facts. Then the stones would stand for institutional facts and events, while the waves caused by the impact of the stones on the surface of the pond would represent the normative force of those institutional arrangements.

Of course, there exists a lot of controversy over the details of the normative space of reasons; over its location or the possibility of accessing it (epistemically speaking). Postponing a more detailed discussion of such complicated matters for some other occasion, we side with a number of contemporary authors who locate

[44] For the best elucidation of a contractarian view of moral principles, see T Scanlon, *What We Owe to Each Other* (Cambridge, Mass, Harvard University Press, 1999); also Julius, above n 18.

[45] These remarks rely heavily on the work of N Stavropoulos, above n 18.

[46] See M Greenberg, 'How Facts Make Law' (2004) 10 *Legal Theory* 157; also G Pavlakos, 'Practice, Reasons, and the Agent's Point of View' (2009) 22 *Ratio Juris* 74.

[47] Of course, in specifying the elements that demarcate the normative space between persons, one should also count, aside from non-institutional principles, any earlier institutional instantiations thereof. In fact, there is no actual point in time where one can find the normative space between persons free of any institutional instantiations of principles, with the exception perhaps of some idealised starting point, at which principles would exist in some ideal form.

the space of reasons in the relations of persons as bearers of moral worth.[48] This view, although not free of contestation itself, meets with considerable consensus amongst contemporary philosophers and should be deemed adequate for present purposes. That granted, a plausible suggestion with regard to the contribution of institutional facts to the content of legal obligations may run as follows: any context of cooperation where agents undertake joint projects tends to give effect to a rearrangement of the normative building blocks that determine the normative space between them.[49] Think again of our analogy of the pond: each successive drop into the pond will lead to a rearrangement of its surface. Now, if the surface stands for the normative footprint of institutional facts, which in our analogy are represented by stones, then every successive impact of institutional fact will bring about a fresh rearrangement of the normative space within which agents are entitled to move freely. Although this is an over-simplification of the discussion at the normative level, it helps us grasp the main point: namely, that obligations are the result of rearrangements of pre-existing normative relations between agents. Such rearrangements take effect when agents unilaterally or within the purview of a joint project undertake actions that aim at directing the action of other agents. Usually, such moves are invested in some institutional context (of a promise, an agreement or other joint commitment), which may or may not have a legal form. In effect, it can be said that obligations arise from contexts of institutional interaction, which effect the rearrangement of reasons that pertain to agents independently of any fact of rearrangement.

In this explanation we need to account for one further aspect: legal institutions vary from other institutional intervention, only by the fact that they are performed by specially designated agents (officials) and in a more differentiated institutional setting.[50] However, they are not different as regards the requirement of justification that pertains to any institutional rearrangement of the normative space of persons. As much as these, institutional legal interference must also live up to the same normative requirements that govern the validity and existence of any other interference that arises from social interaction. To account for the main difference between the two types of institutional intervention, ie legal and general social, one may say that legal institutional intervention aims at grounding special (legal) obligations with a view to securing the effectiveness of a certain class of normative relations which in most cases would *anyway* amount from social

[48] Starting with Kant, there is a long line of authors who locate the normative force of reasons in the reciprocal relation between autonomous agents; amongst the key contemporary exponents of this idea count: J Habermas, *Between Facts and Norms* (Oxford, Polity Press, 1997); C Korsgaard, *The Sources of Normativity* (Cambridge, Cambridge University Press, 1996); Scanlon, above n 44.

[49] See Stavropoulos, above n 18.

[50] A further feature of law relates to the fact that, usually, it is created in the name of those whose actions it purports to direct. For the moment, we shall bracket off a discussion of the democratic dimension of the law and shall assume that any requirements posed by democratic legitimacy are prima facie met if a legal system achieves action-direction in a manner consistent with the morality of coercion.

interaction. That said, the law, in instituting special legal obligations, is subject to the independent constraint that any interference with persons' autonomy needs to satisfy: to respect the justification conditions imposed by the morality of coercion *qua* action-direction. Thus, legal and non-legal institutional interventions mesh in their ways of impacting on the pre-existing scheme of reasons that demarcates the normative space between agents. Both legal and social interactions are, in effect, capable of giving rise to obligations which are binding on agents, even though usually only legal institutions are equipped with the power to enforce the obligations instituted by them. However, this should not obscure the fact that, crucially, many of the obligations created by non-legal forms of interaction are of the same rank and importance as those created in the purview of legal institutions, hence they deserve the same degree of protection even in the absence of appropriate enforcement mechanisms. In deserving such protection, they invoke the need for regulation through the means of law, wherever this is available, but they may also invoke the further duty to set up appropriate means of institutional enforcement.[51]

The model of reasons underpins a conception of legal obligation that is *in tandem* with the requirements of the NCC and the idea of Principled Monism. Its main advantage over the model of authority lies in its ability to demonstrate the existence of a coherent network of obligations, which, even though they may arise in distinct legal orders, can be traced back to the same normative grounds. Crucially, this picture lends support to an argument for 'recruiting' any available order of international law in the service of enforcing any legitimate obligation at the international level. It follows that, by mapping existing legal orders onto a seamless network of obligations, the model of reasons successfully accounts for the coherence and unity of global law. Conversely, the model of authority, in rendering facts of authority constitutive for the grounding of obligation, fails to represent the various legal orders as forming a unified order, assuming instead that there are as many different types of obligation as there are separate authoritative institutional orders.

VI. CONCLUDING REMARKS AND FUTURE AGENDA

In this chapter we have proposed a way of understanding the various legal orders of international and national law (including EU law) as forming a unique normative order.

[51] Although the relation between obligations arising from general contexts of social interaction and legal obligations is highly incisive, it will not be pursued further here, given that our focus is the parity between legal obligations belonging to distinct legal orders. And yet the fact that no sharp distinction can be defended between legal obligations and those that arise from social interaction in general serves as strong evidence for the unity of legal obligation across the various orders of international law. See also above n 31.

The account was based on the idea that legal obligation requires for its constitution to be grounded on sound principles of justice. In other words, this is the idea that no rule or precept can be authoritative simply by virtue of its institutional pedigree or the acts of authority that generated it, but instead derives its normative power from the impact it has on a scheme of normative reasons that pertain between agents, in their dealings with one another. This explication of legal obligation was labelled the 'model of reasons'.

The model of reasons relies on the NCC. According to the NCC, any act of directing the action of others is normatively significant and may amount to legitimate or illegitimate coercion. What makes such acts normatively significant is the fact that any instance of action-direction triggers off the special morality that underlies the normative relations that pertain between persons. It is, then, the content of that morality that decides whether a particular instance of coercion *qua* action-direction is or is not legitimate. As such paradigmatic instances of coercive acts count all institutional acts of authority that aim to direct in a general manner the action of groups or individuals.

The model of reasons and the NCC yield, at the global level, the doctrine of Principled Monism. Principled Monism proposes to reconstruct the various fragmented orders of international and national law (including EU law) into a unified order. The guiding idea behind the proposed reconstruction is that there exists a unified network of valid obligations, which can be reconstructed against the backdrop of the morality of coercion *qua* action-direction, and which extends across the existing institutional orders of international and national law. These obligations are particular instantiations of the morality of coercion, arising from the impact of legal institutional facts on the scheme of principle that assembles the morality of coercion. Principled Monism requires, in effect, that the *plural* legal orders of international law be directed at the protection of a *unique* network of obligations, grounded on the interplay between coercive fact and the morality of coercion. And this is what brings together the various legal orders of international and national law (including EU law) into a unified global legal order.

The implications of this fresh look at international law are numerous, and deserve far more detailed attention than any that could be offered within the confines of this brief chapter. Some are so important, however, that they are worth addressing, even if in a sparse manner:

a) A major argument against the existence of a global legal order has been about the lack of a central institutional apparatus that would produce, manage and adjudicate the materials of such an order. The doctrine of Principled Monism has shown that this worry is misplaced. Once we have left behind the model of authority, what grounds legal obligation depends on special institutional facts only in a secondary manner. In the model of reasons, which underpins Principled Monism, obligations are grounded on the 'responses' of the morality of coercion to any attempt to direct the action of persons. Hence, any institutional act, stemming from any of the existing orders of international law, that amounts to an instance of legitimate coercion is capable of grounding a legal obligation, even in the absence of a world government or an institutional apparatus similar to the one we find in a domestic legal order.

b) The detachment of obligation from a special category of institutional fact amounts to a widening of the jurisdiction of the existing orders of international law. If an obligation has been deemed valid on the proposed model, it deserves respect and protection (even if, under a more traditional approach, it would be regarded as mere 'soft law' or an informal, transnational network). Given law's appropriateness in guaranteeing the effectiveness and respect of obligations, there is a normative pull to employ any of the existing legal orders with an eye to paying heed to any valid obligation. This was, crucially, the rationale behind the *Kadi* decision of the ECJ, where a regional legal order was appealed to in order to protect human rights obligations that had been infringed as a result of an instance of illegitimate coercion imposed on behalf of the UN. There is a further aspect to the widening of jurisdiction: where separate legal orders deal with the same obligation, there is a normative reason for postulating a coherent solution that would avoid imposing conflicting interpretations and, eventually, answers to the same legal question. This normative postulate from Principled Monism may work in tandem with the existing canons of interpretation with an eye to a normative corroboration of the general requirement of interpretative coherence (set out, for example, in Article 31.3(c) of the Vienna Convention[52]), which otherwise may remain ungrounded.

[52] Vienna Convention on the Law of Treaties, Art 31.3(c), directing interpretation of any particular treaty with reference to 'any relevant rules of international law applicable in the relations between the parties'.

Index